Anne Evans is one of the most accomplished and least known of the many women who have contributed to making Colorado a special place. Her achievements in helping to develop the institutions devoted to the cultural enrichment of life in Denver and Colorado— art museums, public libraries, an art commission to further the ideal of a well-designed civic environment—are an extraordinary tale told well in this book. Barbara Sternberg resembles Anne Evans in that she achieves much because she lets others take or share credit, including the wonderful book, Anne Evans—A Pioneer in Colorado's Cultural History: The Things That Last When Gold Is Gone.

—Tom "Dr. Colorado" Noel
University of Colorado Denver

Anne Evans—A Pioneer in Colorado's Cultural History: The Things That Last When Gold Is Gone *is a delightful account of how the impact of Anne Evans aligns beautifully with the Governor's Residence Preservation Fund's focus on celebrating the bounty of Colorado. It not only highlights our modern day treasures but also reaches back to showcase the real pioneers who shaped our state.*

—Jeanne Ritter
First Lady of Colorado

I have been hearing about Anne Evans since I was a boy. Her selfless generosity, her remarkable cultural leadership and vision, her astute collecting and her ebullient social role have become legendary in the history of Colorado's capital. Now a book comes forward that not only puts a face and personality to those attributes but broadly enhances our understanding of and appreciation for the story of Denver's evolution, in large part to Anne Evans, into a cultural center for all the Rocky Mountain West.

—Peter H. Hassrick
Director Emeritus, Petrie Institute of Western American Art,
Denver Art Museum

Anne Evans—A Pioneer in Colorado's Cultural History

For Jeannie,

Barbara E. Sternberg

Anne Evans—A Pioneer in
Colorado's Cultural History

THE THINGS THAT LAST
WHEN GOLD IS GONE

by
Barbara Edwards Sternberg

with Jennifer Boone and
Evelyn Waldron

Foreword by
Tom Noel, Ph.D.

This project is co-published with the Center
for Colorado and the West Auraria Library

Center for
Colorado & the West
at Auraria Library

Cover Image Credits:
Emma Richardson Cherry, *Anne Evans Portrait,* n.d. Watercolor, 10 x 15
(detail) Courtesy History Colorado
Anne Evans, 1940, Denver Public Library Western History Collection

Please note: Occasionally, a grammatic usage or incorrect spelling will
be found in quoted historical material contained in the text. They have
been left unchanged and faithful to the historical author and/or
publication. Although every precaution has been taken to verify the
accuracy of the information contained herein, the author and publisher
assume no responsibility for any errors or omissions. No liability is
assumed for damages that may result from the use of information
contained within.

Book Shepherd: Judith Briles, TheBookShepherd.com
Cover: Nick Zelinger, NZ Graphics, Inc.
Interior Design: Ronnie Moore, WESType Publishing Services, Inc.
Editor: John Maling, Editing by John

Library of Congress Catalog 2010939156

ISBN 978-0-615-38399-6

1. Colorado History   2. Denver Cultural History   3. Colorado Women's
History   4. Native American Art   5. Central City Opera   6. New
Mexico Mission Church preservation

First Edition Printed in Canada

*With gratitude
for the many years of companionship shared
with my late husband, Eugene, and for the constant
support of the five unique children we raised together.
Elizabeth, Francesca, Patrick, John and Jennifer, and
the families they have created, have widened my horizons
and brought much joy into my life.*

Also by Barbara Sternberg

Towards An Urban Sociology of Denver

Co-authored:

Evergreen, Our Mountain Community with Eugene Sternberg

Community Centers and Student Unions with Eugene Sternberg

If I Die and When I Do: Exploring Death With Young People with Franki Sternberg (Francesca Starr)

Anthologies:

Womanthology: A Collection of Colorado Women Poets

Seasonings for a Colorado Afternoon: Gourmet Poems and Spicy Recipes

Acknowledgments

From his first reading of this manuscript, historian Dr. Thomas Noel, professor of History University of Colorado Denver, has been consistent in his opinion that it was worthy of publication. Dr. Noel and Mary Somerville, Library Director of the Auraria Library, have created the Center for Colorado and the West. I am immensely appreciative of their decision to make this biography of Anne Evans the first book publication sponsored by the Center.

Grateful thanks are due to Frederick (1928-2007) and Jan Mayer, who bought Anne Evans' sadly deteriorated mountain cabin and did a superlative task of restoring it and updating its facilities in an appropriate, unobtrusive and award-winning manner. Jan Mayer generously shared with us documents and information that she had gathered in her own quest to learn more about the life and activities of Anne Evans.

Kevin Gramer, Director of the Byers-Evans House Museum was warmly interested and encouraging from our first meeting.

The often-mentioned "we" who did the research, interviewing, and editing were myself successively paired with; my granddaughter, Megan Boone Witucki, during the time she was a student majoring in history at the University of Colorado Denver; my daughter Francesca Starr, with her well-honed library research skills; my multi-talented daughter Jennifer Boone, whose computer writing savvy and online research capabilities were invaluable in producing the original manuscript; and Evelyn Waldron, an MA candidate in the Department of Western History at the University of Colorado, Denver, and a King Intern with the Center for Colorado and the West. Her intelligence, patience and efficient help with the endless tasks of preparing a manuscript for publication were invaluable. The writing, the ideas expressed in the manuscript, and the responsibility for any errors within it are mine alone.

We delved into the fine resources of the Western History Department of the Denver Public Library and the collections of the Colorado Historical Society's Stephen H. Hart Library. Among the indispensable materials in the Denver Public Library were the archives of the Denver Fortnightly Club which preserved some of the few extant writings by Anne Evans. We searched the archives of The University of Denver's Penrose Library, the Auraria Campus Library and the Norlin Library of the University of Colorado at Boulder. From the records of the City and County of Denver, we obtained copies of some Evans family wills. The Library of the Denver Art Museum yielded valuable data assembled by Marlene Chambers for her chapters in *The First Hundred Years*, the history of the Museum. The Art Museum staff responded promptly to inquiries about the destiny of Anne Evans' many early donations to the Museum. We were given access to the archives of Kent Denver School. The staffs of all these institutions were uniformly competent and helpful.

I want to acknowledge the valuable help and materials provided by Stephanie Cassidy, Archivist of the Art Students' League of New York, the staff of the Central City Opera House Association, and Janet Kerschner, Archivist of the Theosophical Society in America in Wheaton, Illinois.

By their conscientious production of a 2009 exhibit in the Western History Department, on the work of the Denver Artists' Guild, Deborah A. Wadsworth and Cynthia A. Jennings brought to our attention yet another of Anne Evans' cultural affiliations, as well as unearthing one of her few surviving oil paintings.

We were fortunate to have access to two well-researched college papers: *Anne Evans: A Preliminary Biographical Sketch,* by Katharine Davis, a great-great-granddaughter of Governor and Margaret Evans[1] and *The Evans Family and Their Historic Ranch*, a Master's Thesis by Rebecca C. Dorward.[2]

For a book we wrote about the history of Evergreen, my husband and I had already interviewed John Evans Jr. (1915-1993), Peg Hayden (1918-1999) and her wonderful mother, Margaret Evans Davis (1889-1981). For this new venture, we interviewed additional gracious and helpful Evans family descendants. In addition to Mag (Margaret) Hayden, these included Mary Ann Davis, Anne Freyer Sweeney, her daughter, Anne Harrill, and Barbara Moore Rumsey. I also had a phone conversation with William Davis in Alaska.

We were introduced to Ethelind Elbert Austin (1909-2009) and her daughter, Sue Ricketts. When we first met Ethelind, she was a marvelous 90+ Elbert family member who still enjoyed horseback riding on her family property on the Evans/Elbert Ranch. She spent many summers there as a child and had lively stories to tell about Anne Evans.

A detailed picture of Anne Evans' contributions began to emerge. But we were also faced with serious challenges in the research. And almost until the last moment, Anne Evans surprised us as additional activities and affiliations came to light, revealing unexpected dimensions to the character of this remarkable woman.

Finally, I would like to acknowledge the valuable services of Judith Briles, Book Shepherd, her husband John Maling, copyeditor and indexer, layout artist Ronnie Moore of WESType, and cover designer Nick Zelinger, who all helped to get this manuscript into print.

Center for Colorado & the West

Center for
Colorado & the West
at Auraria Library

Founded in 2009 and situated in downtown Denver, the Center for Colorado & the West at Auraria Library (CC&W) advances understanding of Rocky Mountain history through "Preserving History; Creating Knowledge." Signature projects enrich educational experiences for students enrolled at the University of Colorado Denver, Metropolitan State College of Denver, and the Community College of Denver on the Auraria Higher Education Center campus. In the first year, students selected as Kenneth King Foundation Fellows and interns worked with faculty supervisors to build digital image collections, review historical book publications, produce digital video documentaries, write biographical profiles, and create Colorado resource guides. Project activities advance student learning experience, faculty curriculum development, and community outreach activities. Active partnerships with Denver Public Library and the History Colorado/Colorado Historical Society ensure coordinated efforts to further public history scholarship on Colorado and the West.

Now in its second year, CC&W is initiating a new book publication series to advance student learning. In keeping with the organization's mission of preserving history and creating knowledge, students will work closely with experts in the field. Their research activities will deepen their knowledge of local history and their writing activities will catalyze their experience in professional publication. In this initial series publication, King intern Evelyn Waldron worked with local historian Barbara Sternberg to prepare a manuscript on Anne Evans. This community-campus collaboration has produced an original historical interpretation of an important cultural leader from Denver's past. In addition, the project illustrates the promise of extending historical knowledge while enriching student learning.

—Mary M. Somerville, MA, MLS, PhD
University Librarian and Director, Auraria Library
Co-Director, Center for Colorado & the West at Auraria Library
March 20, 2010

Contents

Foreword

A nne Evans is one of the most accomplished and least known of the many women who have contributed to making Colorado a special place. Her achievements in helping to develop the institutions devoted to the cultural enrichment of life in Denver and Colorado— art museum, public libraries, an art commission to further the ideal of a well-designed civic environment—are an extraordinary tale told well in this book. The daughter of devout Methodists, she spent time reverentially taking in Christmas Masses and ancient tribal rituals in Native American Pueblos and became an active member of the Theosophical Society in America. As the sister of a man accused of blatant manipulation of the electoral process, who suffered greatly as the result of personal shortcomings, Anne Evans retained an immaculate reputation for selflessly pursuing the greatest common good. She happily lived by the philosophy that you can get much good work done if you let others take the credit.

Anne Evans herself provided the title of this first ever biography when she wrote about why she was so passionately interested in restoring Central City's crumbling opera house and starting a summer festival there. She hoped that the initiative would help to maintain the other institutions that the miners believed would outlast the gold rush. Barbara Sternberg first learned about Anne Evans while working on a book with her husband, Eugene Sternberg (*Evergreen: Our Mountain Community*, 1987) in which they included a chapter on the history of the vast Evans Ranch, located in the mountains above Evergreen.

Although Eugene David Sternberg died in 2005, Barbara has followed up on many of their collaborative efforts. I hope you will allow my digression on Gene, because his work was also her work. One of Colorado's most influential modern architects, Sternberg started his architectural education in Prague. He was fortunate to leave Czechoslovakia for England right after Hitler's invasion, to take up a scholarship to continue his schooling at the University of London (evacuated to Cambridge) where he earned degrees in architecture and city planning. Gene then worked in the office of Sir Patrick Abercrombie, Britain's most active architect-planner at that time, and also taught at London and Cambridge Universities.

In London, Gene met Barbara Edwards again; he had known her briefly in Cambridge. She had graduated from the London School of Economics with a BA in Sociology and was working as a research assistant in the American Embassy. The two became engaged and decided to emigrate together to the United States. This meant that they each had to secure work there. Barbara got a job working for the British Information Services in New York. Eugene accepted an invitation to teach city planning at Cornell University. He and Barbara were married in Ithaca, New York, the site of Cornell. Barbara was awarded a Teaching Assistantship at Cornell and started working on her MA in Urban Sociology. When Gene found that Cornell had a rule against full-time teachers being involved in a professional architectural practice, he resigned. In the Fall of 1947, the Sternberg family, now including a small daughter, came West so that Gene could take up an appointment as Associate Professor at Denver University's new School of Architecture and Planning. At Denver University, Barbara received a Teaching Assistantship so she could continue her MA studies, which she completed in 1949. Her thesis was published by the University of Denver Press.

Due to under-funding, the School of Architecture and Planning lasted only five years. Meanwhile, Gene had established the firm of Eugene D. Sternberg & Associates. Realizing that architectural commissions in the region's large cities were virtually monopolized by existing architectural practices, Gene set himself the task of meeting the architectural and planning needs of small towns in Colorado, Wyoming and Nebraska. Most of his work is generally considered to be in the category of social architecture: hospitals and clinics, schools and colleges, courthouses, offices for Rural Electric Associations and Credit Unions, and neighborhoods of affordable housing. Of these, the best-known today is Arapahoe Acres in Denver, which is now a National Historic District of Modernist Architecture.

Sternberg opened an office in Littleton where he designed office buildings and several schools, including Heritage High School and Arapahoe Community College. He also won the 1965 competition to design a new Denver General Hospital.

Barbara collaborated with Gene on all of his many writing projects, which included articles in newspapers and professional magazines and two books (*Doctors' Offices and Clinics*, Reinhold, 1971, and *Community Centers & Student Unions*, Van Nostrand Reinhold, 1971), she also wrote a variety of non-fiction articles for *Colorado Woman Magazine*, *The KVOD Magazine*, and other publications. With her daughter, Francesca, she co-authored *"If I Die and When I Do": Exploring Death with Young People* (Englewood Cliffs, NJ, 1980) Some of her poetry was published in magazines and in two anthologies.

For most of her adult life, Barbara Sternberg invested a great deal of time and energy in leadership roles in non-profit organizations; she worked in the fields of educational improvement, race relations, mental health, and civil rights. She had a challenging and rewarding late-life career as a Jungian psychotherapist.

Eugene and Barbara raised their family of two sons and three daughters in Arapahoe County. They lived successively in subdivisions in two homes, designed by Gene, before moving in 1972 to Evergreen. Two of Barbara's daughters—Francesca Starr and Jennifer Boone (yes, she married a man related to Daniel)—and granddaughter, Megan Boone Witucki, helped with the research for her book. Evelyn Waldron, an editor, historian and writer, also contributed immensely to the later stages of the book as an Intern at the *Center for Colorado & The West* at the Auraria Library.

Barbara Sternberg resembles Anne Evans in that she achieves much because she lets others take or share the credit. She is now working on the story of her husband and his architectural adventures along with, let us hope, more insight into her own considerable achievements, including the wonderful book, *Anne Evans—A Pioneer in Colorado's Cultural History: The Things That Last When Gold Is Gone*, now in your hands.

—Tom "Dr. Colorado" Noel
Denver, Colorado

1

Who Was Anne Evans?

There is no need for a monument for Miss Evans. Her
personality is so stamped upon the Denver Art Museum
and the Central City Opera House that one never thinks
of either without the sweet, firm directing features of
Anne Evans with her empire-building strength, rising like
the sun, always at the right time and ever in the right
place to quietly dominate the picture.
—Denver Taxpayers' Review

She was often called the patron saint of Colorado artists.
—New York Times January 7, 1941

To the librarian she was a warm and sympathetic friend,
a wise counselor, constructive in her criticism and
encouraging in her interest and enthusiasm for high
standards in library development.
—Biennial Report of the Denver Public Library
for 1939–1940

One of the fruits of the long, uneven movement towards the recognition of women as full persons, rather than as the property of men and inherently inferior to them, has been a growing interest in the historical achievements of women. Writing about the early development of the West, historians have analyzed women's letters and diaries as virtually the only documentation of their pioneer experiences. In Colorado, from the 1950s on, an increasing number of biographies have been published about the almost-forgotten women who made significant contributions to the development of the state. It is past time to add the story of Anne Evans to that literature.

It is impossible to understand how Anne Evans was able to achieve what she did without knowing something about her background and the springboard this created for her in the Denver of the late nineteenth century. Her father was John Evans, the second Territorial Governor of Colorado, a man of prodigious accomplishments even before he came to Denver from Chicago. An ardent Methodist, he supported the building of the first Methodist churches in the Territory and was the prime mover in the foundation of the University of Denver, originally a Methodist institution. He spearheaded the development of the first railroads in the state, so crucial to its growth. He acquired and developed real estate in the young City of Denver, and participated in the organization of many of its earliest civic organizations.

Anne's highly-educated New England mother, Margaret Patten Gray, was a "founding mother" of many of the first social, philanthropic, and cultural organizations in Colorado. William Gray Evans, Anne's much older brother, in whose household she spent her adult years, developed into a powerful political and business force in Denver, greatly admired or reviled, depending on the political and social mindset of the observer. William inherited the sense of civic responsibility that characterized both of his parents and made major contributions to his native city and state. His son, another John Evans, to whom Anne was something of a second mother, became one of Denver's most important bankers and also carried on the family tradition of civic service. Therefore, it is not surprising that Anne Evans also was motivated by a powerful drive to contribute to the development of Denver and Colorado. Her own interests were in the arts and literature; these were the areas into which her impulse for public service was channeled.

Anne benefited from the emphasis placed on education by both her mother and father. After attending private schools in Denver, she was sent to Evanston, Illinois, to spend a year under the tutelage of an older cousin—with the intent of having her tomboyish character molded into something more acceptably civilized. Like her mother, she then spent her late teens in schools in Paris and Berlin where she focused on art studies. Back in Denver for a few years, she enrolled in classes at the University of Denver's School of Art. In 1893, Margaret Evans and her daughter, Anne, became associate members of the newly created Denver Artists' Club. The following year, to her great joy, Anne was accepted as one of the small number of professional members. She spent the last years of the nineteenth century at the Art Students' League in New York.

From 1900 on, though she traveled quite extensively, Anne Evans' life was firmly anchored in Denver. It followed a satisfying pattern: the fall-through-spring period was spent in Denver; the brief and beautiful summer months were spent on the Evans/Elbert Ranch in the mountains west of the city. In Denver, Anne had quarters in the household of her brother, William. On the Ranch, she built her own mountain home.

Anne Evans died at home in Denver in early 1941. What was it that she did in the years between 1900 and 1941 that merits attention? What were her accomplishments that could justify a biographer spending years in research or entice the public to read about her life?

Anne Evans was one of the most influential founders of the Denver Art Museum. Involved from the start in its evolution out of the Denver Artists' Club, she enthusiastically served in any needed capacity, unpacking art materials, helping to hang exhibits, hosting social occasions in the early days, serving for many years as unpaid executive secretary, and even, at a time of crisis, as interim Director.

One of the early pioneers in working for the recognition of the art of Native Americans *as art*, not just as colorful craftwork with which to decorate dens and recreation rooms, Anne Evans started the Native Arts Collection of the Denver Art Museum with her own gifts. She was also ahead of her time in valuing and collecting the neglected "Santos" sculptures of the Southwest, and enriched the Art Museum's holdings with the bequest of her own collection.

In a quiet but effective manner, she was an important leader in the 1920s effort to preserve the mission churches of New Mexico. At the

Anne Evans, Courtesy History Colorado

time, these were either falling into disrepair or being remodeled in totally inappropriate ways.

On the Evans/Elbert Ranch located above Evergreen, Colorado, Anne Evans built one of the most original mountain homes in Colorado. She furnished it with high quality art from many sources, with a special emphasis on the art of Native Americans of the Southwest.

As a member of the Denver Public Library Commission from 1907 until the year before her death in 1941, when she resigned for reasons of ill health, Anne was a major factor in the Library's evolution. She was honored mainly for her constant insistence that only the very best was good enough for Denver—in the caliber of library staff, the architecture of its buildings and the art integrated into them, and the quality of its collections.

Personally, as well as through the organization, Denver Allied Arts, Anne Evans was a constant and unassuming supporter of artistic talent, especially young talent. She accomplished this sometimes through financial support, sometimes by making crucial introductions, and sometimes by directing commissions for work when her position gave her the ability to accomplish this.

As a member of the Denver Art Commission from its inception in 1904, Anne Evans was an enthusiastic participant in Mayor Robert Speer's plans to transform Denver into a City Beautiful, and especially active in helping to achieve the dream of a Civic Center.

Governor John Evans, Anne Evans' father, is honored as the founder of Denver University. His son, William, and grandson, John, carried on his tradition of support for the University through difficult times, each serving for extended periods as Chairman of the Board of Trustees. Anne Evans too gave generously of her time and energies to the University, especially to its Art and Civic Theater Departments. In turn, she was the recipient of two honorary doctorates from DU for her civic and cultural contributions.

In Central City, Anne Evans invested the final nine years of her life. In cooperation with Ida Kruse McFarlane, another remarkable Colorado woman, Anne Evans raised the funds to preserve Central City's crumbling Opera House, persuaded the University of Denver to accept ownership of the building and initiated the unique—and still vibrant—summer festival there. All this was accomplished in the depths of the Great Depression. Although literally hundreds of people were involved in the fund-raising, hospitality, and work of putting on high quality professional productions, the event was universally acknowledged as "Miss Evans' show."

Different aspects of the character and personality of Anne Evans are discussed in the following pages. In all tributes paid to her, in her life and at her death, one characteristic was stressed: she never acted in the pursuit of honors or material rewards. Thanks to the efforts of her mother, she was assured a modest income for life as a stockholder in the Evans Investment Company. Though sometimes autocratic in her dealings with people, she was singularly lacking in what we might call today "an inflated ego." What she cared about was getting the job done. She was content either to lead or to act behind the scenes, whichever best served the cause she believed in.

Anne never married. She lived out her adult years as a whole-hearted participant in the family life of her brother, William, his wife, Cornelia, and her three nieces and a nephew. Her engagement with the family, in its dark days as well as the busy and happy ones, was an integral part of her life story.

Gov. Ralph Carr invited all of the Governors in the United States to be his guests at the opening of the eighth annual Central City festival. The governor is shown here signing the invitations while Miss Anne Evans, official of the festival and daughter of the second territorial governor of Colorado, looks on. Denver Public Library Western History Collection.

There was an extraordinary summer life in the mountains on the 3,600-acre Evans\Elbert Ranch, where Anne Evans spent her childhood summers and later built her own mountain cabin. There she could indulge her love of horseback riding and her passion for play and pageantry in the fellowship of family and friends from all over the nation, and indeed from many other parts of the world. There also she could savor the natural beauty that nourished her.

My first involvement with the personality and accomplishments of Anne Evans came when my husband and I were gathering materials for a book on our adopted hometown of Evergreen, Colorado.[1] We wanted to include the story of the Evans Ranch because of its connection with Evergreen's development. The nucleus of the ranch was acquired in the late 1860s by Governor John Evans and his son-in-law Samuel Elbert. Successive generations of the Evans and Elbert families enjoyed the ranch, where they built some of the most interesting summer homes in the area.[2]

We interviewed Peg Hayden, a great-granddaughter of Governor Evans, who lived year-round in her home on the Evans Ranch. She told us colorful stories about the ranch, the foremen who had taken care of it over the years, and the family members who had enjoyed summers on it for almost a century and a half. Peg also talked, with great affection and admiration, about her Aunt Anne Evans and the contributions she had made to the cultural development of Denver. As we were finishing the Evergreen book, I told Peg that I had become seriously interested in the life of Anne Evans and believed that more people should know about her achievements. I said that I would like to write her biography.

Peg was a very definite lady: "Oh no!" she said. "*I* am collecting material about my Aunt Anne, and *I* am going to write about her life!" I moved on to other projects.

Some years later, I attended Peg Hayden's funeral in the little Church of the Transfiguration in Evergreen. In the weeks after this, a good friend introduced me to Peg's daughter, Mag Hayden. I had a chance to ask the question that had naturally come to my mind: did Peg leave behind a manuscript about Anne Evans? After looking through her mother's papers, Mag Hayden found that Peg had done a good deal of research about the Evans Ranch and also about the New England family of Governor Evans' wife, Margaret, but apparently very little about Aunt Anne. Mag offered to share with me, from her mother's papers, whatever might be of help in writing a biography of Anne Evans and encouraged me to go ahead with the project.

This started an intriguing treasure hunt. As the "we," gratefully mentioned in the acknowledgements section, began the process of interviewing family members and canvassing library archives, a detailed picture of Anne Evans' contributions began to emerge.

Since there was a great deal of material in the public domain, it took us some time to realize that an important element was missing from the archival record of Anne Evans' life. Her mother and father, John and Margaret Evans, left for posterity a wealth of written materials: letters—to each other, to friends and other family members—as well as much official correspondence. Two brief diaries kept by Margaret Evans in the 1860's are treasures for a biographer. But aside from writings by Anne Evans that were preserved by others, or survived by accident, there was a great dearth of personal materials.

While I was talking on the phone to an Evans family descendant living in Alaska, and bemoaning this lack, I first heard the explanation. "I always understood," said William Davis (a great-grandson of Governor Evans), "that Anne ordered all her personal papers destroyed at her death." Later, a senior member of the library staff at the Western History Department of the Denver Public Library verified his statement. A serious attempt to understand why she made this choice was just one more challenge added to a number of tantalizing questions encountered during our research.

Why, after spending many years training herself as an artist, did Anne Evans give up her own painting entirely, devoting herself instead to supporting the artistic talents of others and to helping to develop the cultural institutions needed by a young city?

As a student in Paris and Berlin in her late teens and at the Art Students' League in New York in her early twenties, Anne Evans must have produced scores—if not hundreds—of drawings, sketches and paintings. We were only able to identify three oil paintings by her in our searches. What happened to all the rest?

Why did she never marry?

Was there any truth to the conjecture that her concern for the well-being of the Indians of New Mexico arose out of guilt for the excesses of the Sand Creek Massacre, which occurred during Governor Evans' term of office?

Why have so many memorials to her contributions disappeared?

Why, as far as our research could discover, did Anne not belong to a church in Denver? Her parents were devoted Methodists. They helped to found the original Methodist church in Denver. Her brother, William, and sister-in-law, Cornelia, in whose household she spent her adult life, were also loyal Methodist church members. Tracing the possible reasons why Anne became an active member of the Theosophical Society in America, revealed another dimension— that of a spiritual seeker—to this intriguing woman.

There was a period when, if we had been superstitious about small omens, the outlook would have seemed far from promising. Karen Jagelle, an intern at the Colorado Historical Society, did extensive research for a brief biography of Anne Evans: the biography survives, but the appendix listing her sources has disappeared. Reached by mail in Philadelphia, she wrote, "I left all of my research papers at my parents' house, and my mother believes she threw them out."[3]

Because of her lifelong friendship with Mary Kent Wallace, one of the founders of Denver's prestigious Kent School and its Head Mistress for many years, Anne Evans took a lively interest in that institution and was involved in many of its activities. School personnel gladly gave us access to their newly created archives area, where files of materials used by a former headmaster for a history of the school were stored. Unfortunately, the files were there but most of their contents were missing.

Marilyn Griggs Riley, author of the spirited book *High Altitude Attitudes: Six Savvy Colorado Women*,[4] listed Anne Evans among the list of significant women in the history of the state whom she considered as subjects but did not include in her final list. When I asked for any references she might have come across in her research, she sent one small comment. "Sorry, this is *all* I have on Anne Evans. She's going to be a real challenge to research. Good Luck!"

However, our efforts also turned up some unexpected nuggets. Especially valuable was a little accordion file, used by Anne Evans in the 1930s to store a variety of current information and penciled notes. These yielded worthwhile insights into her activities and ideas. The file was in the Denver University archives, a little bit of personal material that escaped the destruction order.

Writing this biography has been for me a fascinating journey into the development of Denver from its beginnings in 1858. I was raised in England, a country with a history of continuous settlement going back to the Stone Age. So it was intensely interesting to follow the creation—from scratch—of a large, diversified modern city, complete with all necessary physical, social and governmental structures, in less than 100 years. The odds against success were enormous. But those pioneers, with the blue-print of a city in their minds, forged ahead—in the face of fire, flood, plague, Indian uprisings, economic depression, and serious competition from rival settlements—to bring into being their version of a Capital City Beautiful.

As the beneficiary of training in Jungian psychology, I was not surprised to learn that there were dark sides to this history. The success of Western settlers entailed the complete displacement of the original inhabitants of the land. The process of developing the city and the state involved fierce competition for resources and power among the new immigrants. Those who won out were no saints, and there were losers as well as winners. Indeed, the winners in one round could well be losers in the next. There was no system of corporate welfare to rescue them from financial ruin. Dying silver king H. A. W. Tabor, his fortune gone, and David Moffat, whose resources and life energies were drained away by his long, unsuccessful struggle to built a railroad tunnel through the Continental Divide, are only two of the more dramatic examples of fortunes risked and lost in the building of Colorado.

Entwined in this economic and political narrative of Denver and Colorado's development is another story—about the development of its cultural life and institutions. About its libraries, art museums, concert halls, opera houses and theaters, and the artists, writers, musicians, and actors who brought them to life—all those elements which make the difference between a city that merely survives and one that exuberantly flourishes. It was with this cultural component of Denver's development that Anne Evans was involved.

As I learned about the different facets of Anne Evans' background, life and work, I discussed them with my generally well-informed friends. Despite the efforts of the indefatigable Dr. Tom Noel[5] and other historians of the West to educate us all, I found that most of my friends had as hazy and intermittent understanding of Denver's history as I had. And so I decided to write the life of Anne Evans in its appropriate context—which is that of a powerful family deeply involved in creating Denver and Colorado.

2

Patriarch John Evans:
Doctor, Governor, Methodist,
Capitalist, Philanthropist

*Hers was a distinguished and splendid heritage, which
she administered with wisdom for her own honor and the
common good; her own life but adding to the luster of
her name.*

—Memorial tribute to Anne Evans read
at the Denver Fortnightly Club,
April 15, 1941

*If you look deeply into the palm of your hand, you will see
your parents and all generations of your ancestors. All of
them are alive in this moment. Each is present in your
body. You are the continuation of each of these people.*

—Thich Nhat Hanh

When Anne Evans' name is mentioned in print, she is first identified, not by any accomplishment of her own, but by the fact that she was the daughter of John Evans, the second Territorial Governor of Colorado. There is some merit in this. Anne Evans certainly owed much of what made her so effective in her chosen fields of activity to the example set by her remarkable parents. She also used to advantage the influential position she inherited in the emerging social elite of the young city of Denver. Because she inherited a modest lifetime income, she was able to volunteer her total dedication in time and effort to the causes she espoused.

Anne's father, John Evans, was one of those dynamic, complex, ambitious and visionary men that the vast opportunities of the nineteenth century in the United States produced in abundance. Into his long lifetime he packed enough different careers—doctor, mental health hospital founder and administrator, medical school professor, real estate investor, railroad promoter, politician, ardent Methodist—and enough civic accomplishments—builder of cities, co-founder of two private universities, supporter of churches and champion of public education—to occupy at least three ordinary life spans. He also experienced major setbacks and failures that changed the course of his life at crucial junctures. His early medical practice failed to thrive. His first wife died of tuberculosis and the one surviving child, out of four from that marriage, died as a young woman. One of the four children from his second marriage, a five-year-old daughter, died of scarlet fever. He lost heavily on some of his railroad and land investments. Great damage to his reputation and political opportunities resulted from the infamous Sand Creek Massacre, which occurred on his watch as Governor.

Overall, John Evans is remembered favorably in Denver as a notable contributor to the creation of the city and the state. His memory is honored by the naming of majestic Mount Evans; the town of Evans, near Greeley, Colorado; Evans Avenue; and the old Evans School built in 1904 at 1115 Acoma Street "in an era when school buildings contributed to the beauty of the civic realm."[1]

John Evans, Painting by Waldo Love, Courtesy History Colorado

Early life and education

John Evans was born March 19, 1814, in a log cabin on a farm outside the young Quaker settlement of Waynesville, Ohio. He was one of ten children born to David and Rachel Evans, deeply committed Quakers. Among Waynesville's prosperous businessmen were John's father, David, who ran a general store and had considerable investments in real estate, and his uncles Benjamin, Owen and Jason. John attended log cabin schools for three or four months and worked hard the rest of the year on the farm, in his uncles' augur shop, and in his father's general store. John learned early what he did *not* want to do with his life. Against his father's wishes, he set his mind on getting a better education than his father and aspiring to a professional life. John managed to persuade his father to send him in 1834 to a Quaker school in Richmond, Indiana.

John and his older cousin, Benjamin, had been deeply impressed by the professional dedication of the Doctors Isaac and Elias Fisher, a father and son team who had a successful medical practice in Waynesville. The Evans cousins decided to become doctors. While Benjamin secured the support of his family and entered a leading medical school in 1835, John was only able to get his father's financial support to attend another Quaker boarding school in Pennsylvania. Gwynedd Boarding School was an unhappy experience: enrollment was small and the headmaster was not a highly educated man. John's time at Gwynedd seems to have shaken his faith in the Quaker religion. To Cousin Ben he confessed: "I am almost no Quaker."[2] Benjamin's excited letters from Transylvania Medical School in Kentucky confirmed John's determination to continue his education and have a career in medicine. David Evans was still bitterly opposed to the idea. A compromise was reached: he would lend his son the money for his studies, but it would have to be repaid. John transferred to Clermont Academy, outside Philadelphia, where he finished his college preparatory courses.

Medical Career and First Marriage

The next summer, John and his cousin Benjamin studied medicine in Waynesville under the Doctors Fisher. In October, Benjamin, John and young Dr. Isaac Fisher, who practiced as a doctor but had not attended medical school, enrolled in Lynn Medical College in Cincinnati. Benjamin and Isaac graduated at the end of the college year. John needed one more year of study. Returning to Waynesville for the summer, he courted Hannah Canby, daughter of a prominent physician in Bellefontaine, Ohio. She was connected by marriage to the Evans family in Waynesville. Although not yet fully qualified, John opened a practice in Frederick, Ohio, near Hannah's home. The practice paid poorly.

John Evans returned to Lynn Medical College in Cincinnati in November and devoted himself single-mindedly to his studies. They went so well that he started to imagine himself one day teaching in a medical school.[3] Financially, John's last year in medical school was a strain. He had to resort to asking for financial assistance from his friends, the Fishers. Elias sent him enough money to pay his necessary expenses so he could graduate in March of 1838.

John Evans married Hannah Canby in December 1838. She "was a girl of delicate health and was almost continually ill during their 10 years of married life."[4] Evans set up his medical practice in Attica, Indiana, in partnership with Isaac Fisher. Twenty-five-year-old Dr. Evans rented a two-bedroom house which he remodeled to suit Hannah's tastes and needs. The couple soon had two sons, Joseph Canby Evans in 1839 and David Evans in 1841. The medical practice flourished, but much of the payment Drs. Evans and Fisher received was in the form of corn. To sell it, they decided to take the corn down the Wabash River to the Mississippi to find a suitable market. As they journeyed south, they had their first personal experiences of slavery and were horrified. Evans realized why his Quaker ancestors had left the south for Ohio and wrote that "Slavery can only be maintained by the most inhumane barbarity."[5]

John Evans Becomes a Methodist

John Evans' adherence to Quaker teachings had worn thin. He and Hannah were not active in a Friends' group in Attica[6] and so were understandably open to conversion to the dynamic, emotionally satisfying, Methodist faith as preached by an eloquent young Bishop, Matthew Simpson. Simpson was the first president of Indiana Asbury College, which later became DePauw University. He was exhorting Methodists to get into the field of education, especially higher education. This fit well with Evans' own life-long conviction about the importance of education and helps to explain his passionate interest in the founding and nurturing of Methodist universities. Evans and Simpson became lifelong friends. Bernard J. Knittel, in his thesis, "John Evans, Speaker and Empire Builder," discussed the implications of Evans' conversion from Quakerism to Methodism. He noted,

> His enthusiasm was tempered by a broad tolerance and a kindly regard for all religious expression, which brought him much respect and personal admiration.[7]

We shall remember this observation when we trace Anne Evans' own spiritual journey.

John Evans retained his independence of thinking even while becoming an active and devout Methodist. For example, though there was a strong strain of anti-Masonic feeling in the Methodist community in Indiana in the 1840s, he followed family tradition and joined the Masonic order in Attica. When he later moved to Indianapolis, he rose to the office of Worshipful Master of his Lodge.

While in Attica, Evans developed interests and abilities that were to characterize his active lifetime. He enjoyed the risks and rewards of real estate investment and began to build a reputation as a successful businessman. He was also an enthusiastic participant in civic organizations and affairs and was popular in the community. It was in Attica that "He calmly informed a group of his fellow townsmen that before he died he intended to build a city, found a college, become governor of one of the States of the Union, go to the United States Senate, and make himself rich."[8]

Founding a Mental Hospital

Not long after opening their practice in Attica, Doctors Evans and Fisher realized how dire was the situation of those who were poor and mentally ill. They saw a great need for a state hospital to care for them. Year after year Evans raised the issue before the state governor and legislature, in the face of continuing inaction and disinterest, until the goal was accomplished. This tenacity in pursuit of a visionary goal, until it was either accomplished or decisively defeated and regardless of adverse publicity or the size of obstacles to be overcome, characterized Governor Evans throughout his life. The same tenacity, in pursuit of visionary cultural goals, later distinguished his daughter Anne.

It took five years from the first proposal sent to the State Legislature in 1841, to the legislature's acceptance of a building plan prepared by John Evans. Evans managed to secure the aid of the great philanthropist, Dorothea L. Dix, an American activist on behalf of the indigent insane. In January, 1845, the 30-year-old Evans was appointed as superintendent of The Indiana State Hospital for the Insane. He was given the task of overseeing its construction.

Evans was a forward-looking thinker and an innovator throughout his life. In planning for the new facility for the mentally ill in Indiana, he stressed that no force should be used in treatment except what was necessary for the protection and comfort of the patients. He insisted that the facility be called a hospital rather than a lunatic asylum. It was to be a curative establishment and not a jail or warehouse. He made it clear to the board that when the hospital was completed and the general plan for the treatment of the patients established, he would offer his resignation. In late 1845, while still deeply involved in the foundation of the hospital, Evans had accepted an invitation to give a series of lectures at Rush Medical College in Chicago.[9] For three years, he commuted the 200 miles between Indianapolis and Chicago on horseback, giving lectures in the winter and returning to his post as superintendent of the State Hospital in the summer. In 1848, the construction of the Indiana hospital was completed. At that time, Dr. Evans accepted a teaching appointment as Professor of Obstetrics and Diseases of Women and Children at Rush Medical College and moved with his family to Chicago.

Chicago Years

The Rush appointment, together with the favorable notices associated with the founding of the Indiana State Hospital for the Insane, meant that Evans came to Chicago with a fine reputation. Dr. Evans immediately opened a private practice and participated in the founding of the Illinois Hospital of the Lakes in Chicago, later renamed Mercy Hospital of Chicago. He found time to invent an "obstetrical extractor" which he considered a great improvement over forceps.[10]

In 1849, there was a disastrous outbreak of cholera in Chicago. Evans published an article claiming that cholera, contrary to the prevailing medical view of the time, was a contagious disease. He documented his assertion by careful studies of the spread of the disease following transportation routes and advocated the introduction of federal quarantine laws. An outburst of criticism greeted the article, but Dr. Evans stuck to his conclusions and continued urging that Congress pass legislation on the subject. Finally, a National Quarantine Law was passed.[11]

Evans valued professional publication, constantly encouraging his fellow faculty members to publish their medical findings. He participated enthusiastically in the development of a medical publication which eventually became *The North-Western Medical and Surgical Journal*. He became a part owner, then editor, and finally, in 1850, sole owner of the publication. In spite of difficulties in collecting for delinquent subscriptions, Evans built the journal into a moneymaking enterprise.

Too Many Deaths

In his personal life, Evans was faced with tragic developments. His two young sons died in 1844, the year in which his daughter,

Josephine, was born. She was the only child of this marriage to survive to adulthood. A third baby son died in 1848, just before the family moved to Chicago. The move was not a happy one for Hannah Evans. Chicago was a rough new town with no paved streets and a raw climate. Suffering from tuberculosis, Hannah went back to Indiana for the summer of 1849 to recuperate. She seemed to be recovering well. In the summer of 1850, Evans' improving financial condition enabled them to build a new home just a short distance from his new office. Immediately after they moved in, Hannah became ill again. She died on October 9, 1850.

John Evans was devastated by the deaths and for a time, as his letters reveal, he felt that his professional and financial achievements were worthless. He was at a loss to know what to do with his life or how to take care of Josephine. He considered placing her in a boarding school and taking a long trip to Europe to recuperate. In the end, he decided to rent his new home to friends and have them provide room and board for his daughter and himself. Later, dissatisfied with the care provided for Josephine, he rented the house to his sister, Ann, and her husband, Dr. John Nutt, after they moved to Chicago. In addition to living with his sister, Ann, John Evans' house accommodated other Evans family members for varying periods of time. Close relations with family members was an important element in John Evans' life, as it was later in the life of Anne Evans.

Dr. John Nutt joined Evans' practice in 1852. He was a young physician who got his medical degree from Rush and had worked for Dr. Evans on the staff of the Indiana Hospital. He was appointed to a teaching position at Rush. The medical partnership lasted until 1857.

Renewed Interest in Business and Public Service

Contributing to Evans' decision to stay in Chicago was an unexpected opportunity to profit from the sale of one of his real estate investments on riverfront land. He felt that the sale could make him independent financially: this apparently helped restore his energy for living.[12] He began again to channel his enthusiasm and capacity for hard work into his teaching, his practice and his financial investments.

Chicago was a town of 12,000 when Evans was appointed to the Rush Medical College and was growing rapidly. Building on

John Evans, Courtesy History Colorado

his experience in Attica, he began as early as 1847 to speculate in real estate. Perhaps symbolically, it was in 1852 he traded his ownership in the medical journal for five acres of land on Chicago's west side. "By the mid-fifties his wealth ran to six figures, and in 1862 his income from Chicago real estate alone was $20,608.24."[13]

From the beginning of his association with Chicago, John Evans believed the town was destined to grow rapidly and become a great city. He saw that one of its greatest needs was for improvement in transportation. He invested heavily in road improvements and in a railroad connecting Chicago with Fort Wayne, located on the Wabash and Erie Canal. Though Evans used all his organizational and political skills to help get the railroad established, it failed in the end to sustain itself as an independent enterprise. However, he gained invaluable experience in railroad development that he used to advantage later in Colorado.

In 1852, Evans ran for a seat on the Chicago City Council on a platform of improving public schools in the city. After his election, he was appointed chairman of the Committee on Schools. During his tenure, he won approval for the appointment of a superintendent of public instruction and secured approval for the building of the city's first public high school. To quote him:

> The education both of the heads and hearts of the people is an essential element of the public wealth; the only sure ground of hope for the improvement of our social and political condition; the only guarantee of the perpetuity of our free institutions.[14]

This passage from Evans' final report to the City Council in 1855 is worth noting, for it illustrates something important about both John and Anne Evans. Both of them participated in the founding and nurturing of private schools, but they were also consistent and enthusiastic supporters of public schools.

Founding Northwestern University

Leadership in the founding and sustaining of Northwestern University was perhaps the greatest contribution John Evans made to the enrichment of life in Chicago. Even before he moved to the city, Evans had been in discussions with Bishop Matthew Simpson about the importance of creating a Methodist University in the growing mid-west. In 1850, John Evans was made chairman of a committee to prepare a charter for the proposed "North Western University."[15] Piloting the charter through the state legislature for approval was accomplished fairly easily. Evans was named president of the new Board of Trustees. Securing financing for the new institution proved much more difficult.

The Board of Trustees started a search for a suitable site for their new institution. On the recommendation of board member, Orrington Lunt, they settled on a beautiful 379-acre farm north of Chicago on the shore of Lake Michigan. When Evans ascertained that a new railroad would run near the site, he not only concluded that it was worth the steep price of $25,000 but apparently contributed most of the down payment himself. As the name for the new town, the group selected Evanston as a tribute to their hard-working chairman. To raise money for university buildings, the trustees sold lots around the future campus for $500 each. They also sold tuition certificates "at the extremely low price of one hundred dollars each."[16]

Second Marriage

By 1855, great changes had taken place in the life of John Evans. The most significant of these was his marriage to Margaret Patten Gray,

Margaret Evans, Courtesy History Colorado

the sister of Orrington Lunt's wife, Cornelia. Some have questioned whether this marriage could really have been a love match in view of the seventeen-year difference in their ages. However, the subsequent development of this relationship, enduring through many harsh trials and difficult times with mutual appreciation and affection, tends to confirm that this was a marriage based on genuine love. At the same time, it was a proper Victorian marriage, in the sense that the partners were judged to be suited for each other by reason of their backgrounds and accomplishments. The union was blessed by both families.

In contrast to the scarcity of documents on which to build an accurate picture of the life of Anne Evans, John Evans left behind copious correspondence. This leaves no doubt that he fell deeply in love with Margaret, courted her passionately, and sincerely appreciated her presence in his life throughout their marriage.

Margaret was sensitive, intelligent and self-confident. According to Evans' biographer, Harry E. Kelsey, Jr., she "brought back John's former optimism and enthusiasm."[17] The marriage took place in her family home in Maine on August 18, 1853. Margaret soon made it clear to John that he was going to need to update his "plain Quaker notions of style."[18] The couple planned to live in the house Evans built for himself and Hannah, but the Nutts, his tenants, had difficulty finding another home. The newly-weds lived in either the Tremont House or the Mattison House so that John could retain his seat on the Chicago City Council until his term expired.

A Life in Evanston

By this time, Evans had become quite wealthy from investments in real estate and much of his time was taken up with activities other than medical practice. He decided to give up his practice and move to Evanston, though he maintained his professorship at Rush Medical College until 1857. By the summer of 1855, when Margaret was expecting her first child, construction began on their new home in Evanston. The house was a comfortable two-story building on a half-block lot with a broad lawn, shaded by oak trees, which stretched down to the lake. The grounds were as carefully planned as the house, complete with a barn and storage building, orchards, vegetable garden, formal flowerbeds and gravel walks.[19]

The Evans family quickly became leaders in the developing social life of the new city. One resident, who moved to Evanston in

1862, wrote that John and Margaret were prominent in the social life of Evanston, and that "Mrs. Evans was a woman of superb presence, and the daughter, Josephine, a favorite among young people."[20] The daughter of Orrington and Cornelia Lunt, Cornelia Gray Lunt,[21] who later played a significant role at a crucial turning point in the life of Anne Evans, wrote about the Evans household in Evanston in a delightful memoir of her own early years, *Sketches of Childhood and Girlhood: Chicago, 1847–1864.*[22]

Demon Drink and Methodist Aspirations

John Evans' Quaker mother, Rachel, was a vocal and active advocate of temperance. In his youth in Waynesville John himself saw enough evidence of the disastrous effects of alcoholism to follow in her footsteps. Margaret, as an ardent Methodist, fully concurred with his convictions. Evans' attempts to get statewide prohibition through the state legislature failed, but he did succeed getting an amendment to the charter of Northwestern University adopted, prohibiting the selling of "spirituous, vinous, or other fermented liquors" within four miles of the school. As early as 1834, while still a Quaker, Evans wrote,

> Last second day was our election for State and County officers. There were a vast number of people drunk that day, one who boards at the hills got drunk and run his face against the pavement as if diving: Horribly bruised was his mouth and chin. O! poison to the human family! O thou enticing though baneful fluid![23]

In the Evanston gatherings and later in their roles as leading arbiters of social life in the young city of Denver, Margaret and John Evans never served alcohol. Despite this example, teetotalism was not a practice followed by most of their descendants.

Much of Evans' time between 1855 and 1862 was consumed in political activity as an active and influential member of the Methodist community. He also invested considerable resources and energy in the attempt, which ultimately failed, to establish a new town called Oreapolis. It was to be located in the territory of Nebraska at the junction of the Platte and Missouri rivers. The most lasting legacy from this endeavor was Evans' friendship with Samuel H. Elbert, a member of the Nebraska Legislature whom Evans met while seeking a charter for his new town.

Though Evans was one of the delegates to the 1860 Illinois Republican State Convention in Decatur, Illinois, where Abraham Lincoln became the nominee for president, he was not part of the Illinois delegation to the Republican National Convention in Chicago. Evans did campaign actively for Lincoln, however.

Search for a New Challenge

By the time Lincoln was elected, and in spite of the fact that Margaret was happy with her growing family and life in Evanston, Evans was ready for a new challenge. He was ambitious politically, but the ranks of Chicago Republicans seemed too crowded for Evans to have a chance of successfully running for congressional office from Illinois. His hopes turned to securing an appointment as governor of one of the new western territories.

Samuel Elbert and Bishop Matthew Simpson (whose interest in having Evans appointed to an important federal post was part of his conscious effort to increase the political influence of Methodists in the nation) first tried to secure for Evans the governorship of Nebraska Territory. However, one of Lincoln's Cabinet members obtained the appointment for his son-in-law in the spring of 1861. In October of that year, Lincoln offered to appoint Evans governor of Washington Territory. Deciding that this would be too distant a location for him to continue to attend to his business and other interests in Illinois, Evans declined. Simpson and other Methodists maintained their pressure for more federal appointments of Methodists. When a decision was made in Washington to replace Governor William Gilpin of Colorado Territory, Lincoln was persuaded to nominate Evans. The nomination of Evans was approved by the Senate, and the president signed the commission on March 26, 1862.

Evans left Illinois immediately to travel to Washington and be sworn in to his new office. He also used the occasion to secure the appointment of his Nebraska friend, Samuel Hitt Elbert, as Secretary for Colorado Territory, believing that having someone in this important office, with whom he knew he could work well, would be of great importance to his chances of success. He could not have been under any illusions that this new assignment was going to be easy. He was well aware that he was required, under the act that created Colorado Territory, to be both commander-in-chief of the militia and superintendent of Indian affairs. In addition, Governor

Gilpin's fate made it clear that reconciling these responsibilities, without adequate support from a federal government already pre-occupied with the coming Civil War, might prove difficult. However, Evans was a man who sought challenges and faced them with confidence. He set out for Denver, accompanied by Margaret's brother, William Patrick Gray, planning to return later in the year for his wife and family.

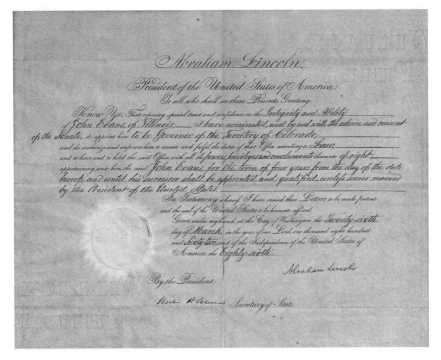

President Abraham Lincoln appointed John Evans to be Governor of the Territory of Colorado on March 26, 1862. Denver Public Library Western History Collection

3

New England Mother: Cultural Pioneer

There is nothing in the universe that I fear, but that I shall not know my duty or shall fail to do it.[1]

—Mary Lyon

In many ways, it would be easier to write the biography of Margaret Patten Gray Evans than that of her daughter, Anne. Margaret came from Bowdoinham, Maine, where her parents united two well-known families, the Pattens and the Grays, each with pedigrees going back to the Mayflower and the American Revolution. The flavor of life in Margaret's Bowdoinham home was lovingly captured, through the perceptive eyes of a child, in a memoir written by one of Margaret's favorite nieces.[2] Margaret herself left two invaluable, though short-lived diaries. Each was undertaken for a different purpose, providing different windows into her aspirations and her life. Governor John Evans and his wife preserved much of their personal correspondence. They wrote regularly to one another when they were apart, the longest periods being those when Margaret and her children were living in Europe for two extended periods. Since the life of Governor Evans was essentially a public life, there are many newspaper references to his wife's life and activities. She too was a public figure in the early days of Denver, especially in its social and cultural development.

A Well-Regulated New England Household

Margaret was born on August 21, 1830, the eighth of eleven children of Samuel and Susan Fulton Gray. Margaret's father was a successful and respected lawyer and shipbuilder and an active Mason. His granddaughter, Cornelia Gray Lunt, described him as "erect, impressive, with fine features, keen eyes and firm mouth."[3]

His manner demanded deference quickly yielded. He brooked neither criticisms nor advice in matters of business, any more than he would endure the least interference in domestic rule. He directed and domineered, but was generous and kind at bottom.[4]

Education was a paramount value in the Gray household. Margaret's own education included schooling in Europe, where she learned to read and speak both French and German fluently and acquired a lifelong enthusiasm for learning. She and her sisters were known as both cultivated and beautiful. The home was also deeply religious. Susan, Margaret's mother, was a native of Bowdoinham and married Samuel Gray when she was just seventeen. After a personal conversion experience, she was baptized as a Methodist in the stream running through the Gray homestead meadow. Prayer was a regular part of her day and "one of the fondest memories she bequeathed to her children was the often overheard words of her private devotions."[5]

A Melding of the Evans and Gray Families

When John Evans was appointed governor of Colorado Territory in 1862, the Evans family was settled in their comfortable home in Evanston. It had grown by the addition of a son, William—known as Willie, born in 1855, and Margaret—"little Maggie"—born in 1857. John Evans' daughter Josephine, almost 17, was also part of the household. A window into the goals and anxieties of Margaret Evans at this time is available from the first of her two diaries.[6]

The lives of several of Margaret's siblings were interwoven with the fortunes of the Evans family. Her oldest brother, Horace, who had been a shipbuilder and sailing ship captain in his early years, came to live in Denver with his wife, Eliza. He was associated with John Evans in a number of financial ventures and was a trusted friend. Horace Gray and Margaret Evans apparently took on the responsibility of raising and educating Sunie Lowell, one of the children of their sister Nancy Gray Lowell Cooke, who had fallen on hard times. Another of Margaret's brothers, William Patrick Gray, also started out life as a sea captain. He moved to Chicago where he got into the harness business. He was associated with John Evans in the founding of Northwestern University. When Evans came to Colorado to take up his appointment as Governor, William Patrick Gray acted as his business agent in Chicago. In 1878, he moved with his wife, Kate, and family to Denver and worked as an assistant to Governor Evans in a number of ventures. His daughter, Cornelia, married her cousin William "Willie" Evans, Anne Evans older brother, in an elaborate wedding ceremony in Denver on December 12, 1883. Other Gray family involvements with the Evans' emerge from time to time as we follow the life of Anne Evans.

Margaret was a gracious hostess, managing a busy and welcoming home. She confessed to certain doubts about her ability to be successful as a stand-in mother for Josephine, taking seriously her responsibilities. In her diary entry for September 30, 1861, she wrote, "Today is Jo's birthday. Seventeen years of age. What a responsibility devolves upon me, I did not consider it sufficiently before I undertook the charge. I deeply feel my incompetency." Since she had also come to be in charge of the upbringing of her niece, Sunie Lowell, she found that caring for both of them, and supervising their education, was difficult to reconcile with giving enough time to the care of her own younger children. Margaret eventually concluded that the best thing she could do for the older girls was to send them to Wesleyan Academy, a well-recommended boarding school in Wilbraham, Massachusetts. While they were there, she wrote to them both regularly and conscientiously monitored their progress.

Mothering her "Little Ones"

To become acquainted with Margaret's written thoughts about how to raise a daughter is important. They are the best clues we have to her attitudes and expectations later in life, when raising her daughter Anne. She was no longer keeping a diary during Anne's childhood, some ten years later. The only direct information we have about her concerns at that time are occasional comments in letters she wrote to her husband.

Margaret worried mightily over how well she was doing as a mother to Willie and Maggie. She had high standards for their moral and religious development as well as for their learning. Her Evanston diary, which lasted from January 1 to October 7, 1861, was quite consciously devoted to a daily monitoring of the success of her efforts in these areas. Only briefly and tangentially did she refer to events in her life, such as the frequent absence of her husband on various business or political trips, or major national developments. At the beginning of the diary, she noted that Willie was five years old and Maggie three years and three months. The first entry is typical of the way she constantly berated herself for her shortcomings, urging herself on to do better. "I am afraid I have done nothing today for the improvement of my children...Oh that I may bring up those committed to my care in the fear and favor of the Lord, cleansing my own heart first."[7]

She had different concerns about the two children. With Willie, she was constantly afraid that he lacked "moral courage," having caught him in some episodes of telling less than the truth about things that he had said or done. Margaret also worried about Willie's fears of the dark and of sleeping alone.

Margaret had less inner conflict about disciplining little Maggie. Maggie was a challenge to her mother, even at the age of three and a half. The diaries are full of regrets about Maggie's disobedience. "Have been obliged to whip Maggie twice for disobedience,"[8] and the next day, "whipped Maggie for disobedience—now I must not relax my authority in exacting obedience."

On many of the days when she found herself impatient and hasty with the children, her husband was away from home. Margaret had help in the household, but occasionally noted that she was taking the place of cook in the kitchen or managing the household while the maid was away. On June 24, she wrote that the maid, Jane, "left tonight for good. I feel somewhat relieved because I think I ought to economize." However, she found managing the household without a maid extremely tiring. The next day she wrote, "Seth and his boy, Frankie, and Robert Nutt have all come upon me tonight and no Jane—well, I must do the best I can—A New Englander must not be beaten." Jane eventually returned to the household.

Two days later, Margaret wrote of sickness, a recurring and anxiety-producing problem at that time. "I have been taking care of Maggie today who is sick with diarrhea. Am sick myself but have to keep up. Willie did not go to Sunday school today or to church. I spent about half an hour reading to him." In the nine months of this diary's coverage, sickness hovered over much of the action. Behind a mother's normal concern was the ever-present fear of the direst consequences. Only once did she put this into writing,

> Dear little Willie is sick. I trust it is but transient—husband is gone—Help me God to be resigned if it is thy pleasure to remove

him—O how much grace I need to train him for a life of usefulness
if he lives, and if bereft of him, to bow in submission.

There was only one mention of her husband being ill, but he was
absent from home for much of the period covered by this diary.

A curiously modern subject that Margaret worried about was
whether the children were coming to expect that she would bring
them a present whenever she went away. On January 14, she wrote,
"Have been absent from home today—contrary to usual custom
would not promise, neither did I bring them home, anything, I hope
it will teach them to value the toys they have and to be careful of
spending money."

Another of her parenting concerns, one that still worries modern
mothers, related to food. On April 8, she recorded, "Have just returned
from a lecture on Physiology in which I was warned (as well as other
mothers) of the injury resulting from allowing children to eat rich
food and pastry—I do try to be careful in that particular, I doubt however if they always have that which is most nutritious and proper."

It is remarkable that Margaret was able to focus so exclusively,
in her diary self-examination, on her duties in relation to her own
two children, at the same time doing her conscientious best to raise
her niece, Sunie Lowell, and her husband's daughter, Josephine.

Margaret's life was not confined to her home. She was out of
the house a great deal, attending parties at the homes of friends
and neighbors, visiting in Chicago where she sometimes stayed
overnight, taking part in many activities connected with the
church. These varied from regular attendance at church on Sunday
and at Sunday School to special "camp" meetings and a "straw-
berry festival." Once she mentioned that she had given a party,
at which 50 people were present. On April 22, she had attended
a meeting "called to give expression to the war feeling. I have no
children old enough [to serve in the army] Am I not glad! Ought I
to be? Ought I not to glory in sending forth children to battle for our
country?"

She also worked hard at household duties. In addition to the
times she substituted for cook in the kitchen or went for a time without a maid to help with the children, she recorded spending an
entire week doing a thorough house cleaning. She also sewed many
of the family's clothes.

No Improvement is Enough

Margaret questioned constantly the allocation of her time. Should she have spent so much of the day in not being with her children? When she was sewing, she worried that she had let Willie play outside, unsupervised, for too long. Even on her birthday, she worried. On August 31, her entry read,

> This is my thirty first birthday—I wish I could have the energy to improve myself and family as I know would be of great importance—when I look back over the last year I can see that I have improved some—but not so much as I might.

Indeed, Margaret Evans often faulted herself for not doing enough and for falling below her almost impossible standards of molding her children into ideal human beings. She constantly mentioned how affectionate Willie was towards her; how he told her that he loved her more than anyone on earth. However, she dwelt upon his lack of courage, his tendency to "tell stories" when that was easier than telling the truth. Maggie, on the other hand, she saw as independent and strong-willed: "a determined little thing."[9] "She is extremely vivacious and has a quick intellect but growing very self-willed."[10] Margaret could not take comfort from Maggie's positive qualities because she was so worried about the little girl's unwillingness to obey her mother's commands. She did not admire herself for whipping Maggie, however, and demanded of herself that she find better ways of reinforcing her discipline. On March 4, she wrote,

> Maggie is difficult to govern. She dislikes exceedingly to obey and I, to speak the truth, do not know how to compel her to obey me, unless I use brute force and that I do not wish often to do—I ought not so often to come in collision with her but when I do, enforce obedience.

Margaret believed strongly that it was her duty to set an example of openness and truthfulness to her children. On one occasion, she wrote, "Have just returned from a war meeting. I left the children asleep, telling them I was going and wished them to go to bed—I take care not to deceive them in the least thing."[11] Perhaps this constant stress she put upon herself to do more, to do it better, and her harsh judgment of her own failings was responsible for an extraordinary entry on October 7, two days before the diary ended,

> I feel tonight the most unhappy of creatures—How little true happiness I experience, more than probably it is my fault but I am not situated as I ought to be—I am rendered unhappy by circumstances, and it sours my disposition so I do not my duty by my children.

There is very little in the diary that reveals anything about the relationship between Margaret Evans and her husband. Apart from noting his many absences, and on one occasion his sickness, the only reference she makes to him is on August 18:

> This is the eighth anniversary of our marriage day—and I sleep tonight under our own roof with everything to make me comfortable and happy, were it not for the infirmities of my natural disposition—[I have] two dear little children whom I must tenderly watch and care for.

Educating Willie

One duty that Margaret Gray Evans took very seriously was that of educating her children. In July of 1861, she started systematically to teach Willie to read.

> Commenced today to teach Willie his letters and at the same time I taught him a verse. I propose every day, directly after dinner to take him alone and teach him—it has a salutary effect, this training in the middle of the day; I hope I shall persist in it—

On September 23, she noted, "Willie commenced school today, an epoch in his life. He was very much interested. I did not care so much about his learning as the discipline he will be under. I must see that he is punctual and regular." Some disappointment set in a couple of days later when she found that "Willie is learning naughty words and things; and I am at a loss how to proceed with him—I hoped by saying nothing he would forget but he does not." In general though, he seemed to have been well prepared for school.

Little Maggie, Courtesy History Colorado

Little Maggie Dies of Scarlet Fever

In the spring of 1862, John Evans set out for Denver, which was then a small frontier town with a population of 2603, according to the 1860 census. He was accompanied by Margaret's brother, William Patrick Gray.

Whenever they were separated, John Evans and Margaret carried on a regular correspondence. One theme of their letters back and forth between Denver and Evanston in the summer of 1862 was the great fear that the children may be exposed to the scarlet fever that was taking a toll in Chicago that year. John wrote to Margaret about the importance of keeping away from families where the fever was present and of being careful "to be thoroughly aired and ventilated and washed" after she had had any suspicious contacts before "going to our own dear little children." He told Margaret, "You know I was always so much afraid of that malignant scarlet fever—by all odds the worst scourge of children and the most fatal."[12] All the precautions were in vain. Little Maggie came down with the fever, and in a few days—before there was any chance her doctor father could get home—she was dead.

4

Life in Colorado Territory

The Colorado Territory of 1861 was the same huge rectangle that the state of Colorado is now—nearly four hundred miles from east to west, three hundred from north to south ... The Pike's Peakers created it, propelled by faith, greed, ambition, and zest for achieving the impossible. Few of them were serious thinkers but some had gifts of leadership and foresight.[1]

—Marshall Sprague

All her life, Anne Evans was aware of the debt that she and her generation owed to the pioneers. When she engaged in her last major cultural endeavor—the restoration of the Central City Opera House and establishment of the annual Central City Festival—she insisted that the entire effort be recognized as a tribute to the pioneers of Colorado. She knew about her father's almost super-human enterprises, both the failures and the successes. She listened with fascination to her mother's stories about Denver's early years. That pioneer era was already legendary by the time Anne Evans took her place as an active adult citizen. However, her character and her aspirations grew out of that matrix.

A Speech from the Tremont Balcony

The new Governor of Colorado Territory arrived in Denver on May 16, 1862. He stayed at one of the few suitable hostelries in the raw little town, another Tremont House. It was fashionable to name hotels in the most unpretentious places after the pioneer Tremont House that opened in Boston in 1829. The Boston Tremont was one of the first buildings in the United States constructed as a hotel with the innovation of private rooms, each with its own key. The Tremont House in Denver, where the Evans family stayed for a period after

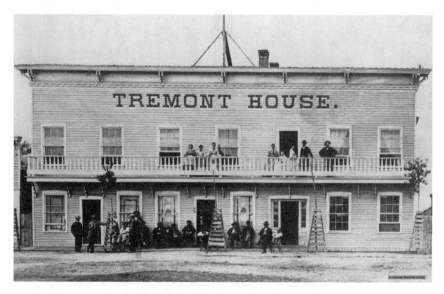

Tremont House, Courtesy History Colorado

Governor Evans made the trip back to Evanston to bring them west, evidently offered the same amenity.

A band serenaded Governor Evans on the evening of his first day in Denver. From the Tremont balcony he addressed a large crowd who "saw a big man—he was nearly six feet tall and weighed 180 pounds."[2] Clearly demonstrating a familiarity with the problems of the new Territory, he noted that people were paying "famine prices" for food. He related that problem to the need for a railroad connection with the east. Pleased that Congress had passed the Pacific Railroad Bill paving the way for a transcontinental railroad, he expressed the hope that the route could come across the mountains and through Denver. Encouraged by the farms already existing in the South Platte Valley, Evans was confident that Colorado would become a fertile and well-populated Territory. Well received by the audience, the speech was particularly welcomed by William Newton Byers, the editor of the *Rocky Mountain News*. Byers had been "a little dazed" by the quixotic pronouncements of Evan's predecessor, Governor Gilpin[3], whom Byers described as "a very peculiar man." The *News* editor, an enthusiastic Colorado booster, looked forward to a more solid gubernatorial presence in John Evans.

William Byers and the Rocky Mountain News

Byers, who would prove an invaluable ally and supporter of Governor Evans' early projects and policies, was himself one of Colorado's influential pioneers. Trained as a surveyor, but having already demonstrated a flair for reportorial writing, Byers came to the Pike's Peak gold region in the spring of 1859. He was armed with a small printing press and a determination to establish the first newspaper in the area. The front page he set in type before leaving home, including the very latest news from "the States" and a statement of the newspaper's aspirations. Mostly laudable, these also illustrated what to our current sensibilities was one of the great moral failures of nineteenth century western expansion—the total discounting of the rights of the Native American population.

William N. Byers, Denver Public Library Western History Collection

> We make our debut in the far west, where the snowy mountains look down upon us in the hottest summer day as well as in the winter's cold; here where a few months ago wild beasts and wilder Indians held undisturbed possession—where now surges the advancing wave of Anglo Saxon enterprise and civilization, where soon we fondly hope will be erected a great and powerful state, another empire in the sisterhood of empires.
>
> Our course is marked out. We will adhere to it with stedfast (sic) and fixed determination to speak, write and publish the truth and nothing but the truth, let it work us weal or woe.[4]

William Byers' wife, Elizabeth, became a good friend of Margaret Evans and worked with her on the promotion of many worthwhile community causes.

William Byers campaigned vigorously for the creation of Colorado Territory, separate from Kansas Territory, which came into being in February of 1861.

In 1862, Denver and Colorado Had Problems

At the time he received the sad news of Maggie's death, Governor Evans was too consumed by his new duties and too far away for there to be any chance of his attending the funeral. Just to get to the Missouri River at that time involved a whole week's journey.

The list of ills plaguing Colorado Territory in 1862, and of the decisions and actions required of the new Governor, would have overwhelmed a man with less self-confidence, less life experience and perhaps less strength of religious conviction than John Evans.

The precarious state of relations with the different Indian tribes inhabiting the Territory was causing great anxiety, both among isolated settlers and in the populations of towns and cities, all of whom felt vulnerable to attack. For their part, the Indians were deeply disturbed by the steady increase in numbers of settlers traveling across the plains—in covered wagons, with handcarts, even on foot—disturbing the buffalo herds and beginning to settle down and farm on more and more of their traditional hunting grounds.

Politically, there was a vast array of legislative and administrative problems to be solved in setting up the framework for effective local, county and state government in a rapidly growing new state-in-the-making. The urgent matter of tying Colorado into the emerging transcontinental system was far from resolved. A myriad of problems with mining claims, rights of corporations, and the creation of a judicial system needed attention. From the beginning, Evans had political enemies.

Tensions in Relationship with the Indian Population

Evans's responsibilities for Indian Affairs came directly from the federal legislation that created Colorado Territory. It specified that the governor was to be both commander-in-chief of the militia and superintendent of Indian Affairs.

As recorded in historian Hubert Bancroft's interviews with Evans, the Governor had a chilling introduction to the Indian problem on his first Sunday in Denver, when he watched a "war dance staged by a victorious Sioux, Arapahoe, and Cheyenne war party."[5] They had attacked a band of Utes and taken a scalp, which was carried on an eight-foot pole by a young squaw—"in gorgeous attire with a big cape—made out of Eagle's feathers, and other feathers that were gaudy and red." Evans, accompanied by some troops, visited the camp of the exultant Indians the next morning and made a speech to them about how their war with the Utes served no meaningful purpose. He later realized that the only result of this speech was to convince the Sioux, Arapahos and Cheyennes present that he was on the side of the Utes.

The following day, a delegation of Utes paid a visit to the new governor, spoiling for a renewal of the fight with their traditional enemies. The Utes advised Evans "the best thing that could be done with an Arapahoe or a Cheyenne was to kill him."[6]

Denver Comes Together and Stakes its Claim to Dominance

The legislature of the new territory had met once in Denver, on September 9, 1861. At this time, it was far from clear that Denver would become the leading city in the new Territory.

Denver was formed on November 22, 1858, while Colorado was still part of Kansas Territory. It was the result of the union of two town

Horse-drawn wagons are parked near building on Blake Street in downtown Denver. (1860) Denver Public Library Western History Collection.

sites, one on each side of Cherry Creek. These had been established by different parties of gold-seekers lured by such headlines as the one in a Kansas City newspaper of August 26, 1858: 'THE NEW ELDORADO!!! GOLD IN KANSAS!! THE PIKE'S PEAK MINES!'[7] The "Auraria Town Company" was formed on November 1, 1858 on the west bank of the creek. Earlier, on September 24, a town named St. Charles had been laid out on the east bank by a small group of men from Lawrence, Kansas. They went home for the winter, leaving just one man to defend their claim.

A party from Kansas, led by General William Larimer, arrived in the area with the intention of making substantial real estate profits from the creation of a new town in this latest gold mecca. The party traveled slowly, "weighted down with the building supplies necessary to create a city, including planed boards and window glass."[8] Larimer had persuaded Kansas Governor, James W. Denver, to name him and his associates as the officers for Arapahoe County—the vast area of Kansas Territory in which the gold diggings were located. It existed in name only, since no officials had ever been appointed for its administration.

The party proceeded to jump the St. Charles claim, and on November 22, 1858 adopted a constitution for the "Denver City Town Company." Unaware that Denver was no longer the Governor of Kansas Territory, they named the town for him. If their claim jumping was challenged by the St. Charles founders, they hoped Denver as governor would support the legality of their claim. In case they should lose their title, Larimer established a second community north of the point at which Cherry Creek ran into the Platte, and named it Highland. Larimer and David Colyer, the civil engineer who was a member of his party, laid out their Denver city grid in alignment with a road created by wagon traffic along the South Platte River.

The communities of Auraria and Denver City overcame their lively rivalry largely out of fear that, in keeping their focus on fighting each other, they would lose sight of the more important struggle, to prevail over emerging rivals—such as Arapahoe City and Golden— for the role of pre-eminent city of the region. In December of 1859, the leading citizens of Denver and Auraria agreed to "charter and consolidate the towns of Denver, Auraria, and Highland."[9] Highland had no government and nobody lived there; it was not settled until years later. The real integration of Denver and Auraria did not take place until the following April 1860, when the completion of a bridge over Cherry Creek was celebrated by members of both communities in a moonlight party at midnight.

Once Colorado Territory was created by Congress in 1861, the city pushed aggressively ahead to stake its claim as the logical capital. As early as May of 1859, General Larimer had managed to arrange for stagecoach service from Kansas to Denver. This assured that mail and passengers arriving from the east came first to Denver. As a result of this, freight companies also located their offices in Denver, enabling it to become the pre-eminent trading center between "the States" and the emerging mining communities in the mountains, as well as between other cities on the plains.

The other communities in the Territory did not give up their own claims easily. At the close of their first meeting in the fall of 1861, the legislators had decided to move the capital to Colorado City, a location that is now part of Colorado Springs. They scheduled their next meeting there in the summer of 1862. (The capital was later moved to Golden in 1862 and to Denver in 1867.)

Evans hoped to postpone the meeting of the legislature until 1863, to allow him to become better acquainted with the needs of the Territory. He did not travel to Colorado City, however, convinced that they would bring the meeting back to Denver when they saw actual conditions there. He described the "city" in a letter to Margaret as being like "a deserted Nebraska village at or near the mouth of the Platte River." The delegates did indeed adjourn the session to Denver.

On July 18, 1862, Governor Evans put forth his hopes and plans for Colorado to a joint session of the Territorial Legislature. The delegates were enthusiastic in their response to his proposals, and passed most of them into law. However, on two of the most pressing issues—adequately financing a militia, and recommending that treaties be negotiated with the different Indian tribes in the Territory for the extinction of their title to such parts of the Territory as may not be permanently reserved to them—the actions of the Legislature failed to produce decisive action from a Federal government already embroiled in the terrible carnage of Civil War.

Evans Heads Back to the States

After the close of the legislative session, Evans left for the east. When Congress had passed the Pacific Railroad bill, authorizing the construction of a transcontinental railroad, Evans was appointed as one of 158 commissioners to advise on its construction. At his request, a survey had been made of the possible Berthoud Pass route, involving a tunnel through the mountains, which would bring the railroad through Denver. The preliminary surveyor's report was negative. Evans went to a meeting of the railroad board in Chicago, where he tried without success to argue the case for a route through the mountains. It is a commentary on the far seeing vision of John Evans that this railroad route was not completed in his lifetime, though he worked hard for it, nor even in the lifetime of his son William, who, along with David Moffat, virtually bankrupted himself pursuing this dream. William died in 1924, after the construction of the Moffat Tunnel was assured but four years before its completion in 1928.

From Chicago, Evans went to Washington to see what progress he could make on the defense of Colorado Territory against Indian raids, and on the negotiation of new treaties with some Indian bands.

The Indian Dilemma

The question of Evans' attitude towards the Indian tribes in Colorado Territory, and how their future was to be determined, has been extensively discussed by historians of the West. The subject becomes especially acute whenever the matter of the 1864 Sand Creek Massacre is raised.

Almost from the beginnings of European settlement in America, there were two vastly different views of how to deal with the native population. Some advocated making treaties with the different tribes, allocating to them vast areas of land in the seemingly limitless new continent. Others insisted that Indians should be dealt with as individuals, the same as European settlers, and allocated parcels of land and supplies if they would agree to settle down and farm. Evans inherited an uneasy mix of the two solutions in the Treaty of Fort Wise, which had been signed in 1861 between the U.S. Government and some bands of Cheyenne and Arapahoe, but never enforced.

The Fort Wise Treaty replaced the 1851 Treaty of Fort Laramie, which had recognized the claim of the Cheyenne and Arapahoe tribes to a vast territory lying between the North Platte and Arkansas Rivers, and eastward from the mountains to western Kansas. The gold discoveries, in what later became Colorado, stimulated a flood of white emigration. Territorial officials petitioned the federal government to reduce the amount of land granted to the Indian tribes. The Fort Wise Treaty was signed by six Southern Cheyenne chiefs and four

Arapaho chiefs. It established a reservation for the Cheyenne and Arapaho Indians on the Arkansas River. This reservation was less than one-thirteenth the size of the Fort Laramie Treaty lands and was virtually empty of buffalo. There the tribes were to be confined, issued supplies to compensate for the losses of buffalo hunts, and encouraged to take up farming.

By the time Evans visited Washington in the summer of 1862, he knew that many bands of Cheyenne and Arapaho had not signed the Fort Wise Treaties and wanted nothing to do with confinement to a reservation. He urged the Commissioner of Indian Affairs to negotiate further with these groups and expressed his fears that these particular tribes would not settle down to farming, although they might be persuaded to start raising sheep and cattle. Evans also brought an urgent request for more troops to guard the Territory from Indian raids, stressing that infantry would be useless in combat with mounted Indians. Evans received no satisfaction from the Indian Commissioner but did secure from Secretary of War Edwin M. Stanton promises that the First Colorado Regiment would become a cavalry unit, and that the Platte route into the Territory would be secured.

Margaret Evans Comes to Denver

Having done what he could on the railroad issue, and on getting what he could from Washington to solve Colorado Territory's pressing problems, Evans took the train from Washington to Chicago to be reunited with his family and make arrangements to bring them to Denver. The family was considerably smaller than the one he had left: little Maggie was dead and Jo and Sunie had left for school in Massachusetts.[10]

Governor and Mrs. Evans set out on the long journey to Denver with son Willie, Margaret Evans' brother, William Gray, and Mrs. O. A. Willard. Mrs. Willard's husband, Rev. O. A. Willard, had traveled to Colorado in October to become minister of the first Methodist church in Denver. John Evans knew Reverend Willard in Chicago—where his sister, Frances E. Willard, was already a famous women's temperance reformer[11]—and was instrumental in bringing the young minister to Denver. The Willards became close friends of the Evans during their early years in Colorado Territory.

The Evans party traveled first by train to Atchison, Kansas, and made the journey from there by a stagecoach specially chartered by

Governor Evans. He arranged that the coach, which left Atchison on November 6, should be driven straight through to Denver, stopping only for the passengers to eat at stations along the way. The journey took almost a week. Space for sleeping was created by flooring over the space between the coach seats to make a bed. The coach arrived in Denver on November 12, 1862. Governor Evans had bought land for the family's future house before leaving in August but their first home in the rough and tumble town was at the Tremont House.[12]

Life at the Tremont House

The Tremont House, "on Front Street at the head of Blake" in Auraria had its first, short-lived, existence as Mrs. Maggart's Temperance Hotel.[13] With the prudent addition of a bar and new ownership, the Tremont Hotel enjoyed a 20-year career among the best that Denver had to offer, along with the Elephant Corral, originally the Denver House, and Pacific Planter's House, first named Broadwell House. These early hostelries were later displaced by the arrival of such truly elegant hotels as the Windsor (1880), the Markham (1882), the Metropole (1889) and the Grande Dame of them all, the Brown Palace (1890–92).

Margaret settled in at the Tremont House and began her second diary. It is not easy to figure out the actual dates covered by this journal: it started on the January 1 space in 1863, but at one point in the entries (January 11), she placed a notation "March 26." The diary generally covered the first months of 1863. This was the time before the family moved into its new home and before the birth of Margaret's third child, Evan Elbert, in June. It is a much more revealing and interesting chronicle than the 1861 diary, Margaret did not limit its subject matter to the upbringing of her children and her own development in Christian piety, but recounted her activities on a daily basis. She also indulged, usually with an immediate expression of self-criticism, in pungent evaluations of the many people on whom she called or who called on her.

The diary opened with a heart-breaking lament at the still unbearable loss of her little daughter. She thought back to the previous summer, when

> ... my *dear* little Maggie, who is now an angel above, was playing around me—the eight [sic] of last July she died, her breath went

out in suffering and anguish, but a kind Father sustained and strengthened me and I was enabled to administer to her through all the nine days of her sickness—Sweet little one!

Margaret's expression of grief continued:

Though experiencing a sense of relief that she was released from her suffering, still her death filled the house with sadness—for days it seemed as if I was wandering around in a dream, that it could not be real but alas, her sweet voice and footsteps were no more heard and the house seemed silent and sad—the light of the place seemed to have died out with my sweet little daughter's life—I could not feel any interest in or for anything, and added to painful bereavement were feelings of disappointment that friends could have been so completely frightened as to loose (sic) all thought or care for my feelings, panic stricken, as if the plague was with us— they could not have behaved worse—but I will not think or write, I must try to forget, but my heart turns away from Evanston though my pleasantest days were spent there and the house seems almost sacred to me ...

She went on to note that two dear friends, Mrs. Ludlam and Mrs. Bragdon, as well as Dr. and Mrs. Nutt and her sister, Cornelia, "stood fast by me, through it all and by their sympathy and love have bound my heart to theirs more closely than before."[14]

The end of this passage helps to explain why Margaret felt ready to leave the cultivated and settled environment of Evanston and take up life in Denver, accepting her responsibilities as the Governor's wife. She was sensitive to the obligations imposed on her as an educated New England and Christian woman in a rough and uncivilized outpost.

Her location in rooms at the Tremont House plunged Margaret immediately into the midst of whatever social life Denver had to offer. It was centrally located and had a "parlor" where visitors could be entertained. Margaret's life quickly organized itself into an agreeable routine. This afforded her time for herself and her family responsibilities as well as ample contact with other ladies in the small community.

During the entire period covered by the second diary, Margaret was pregnant. Frequently she wrote that she was feeling unwell and tired. She constantly upbraided herself for lying too long in bed in the mornings, breakfasting too late in the dining room downstairs, and spending time in the "forenoon" lying on the "lounge." However, any objective evaluation of her expenditure of time would indicate that she met her responsibilities admirably.

The Daily Round

Each morning, after breakfast, she "arranged her rooms." Next, she heard Willie's lessons in reading, writing and counting, noting approvingly his rapid progress in reading with good comprehension and his increasing skill in "mental arithmetic." Typically, Margaret then went out, with or without Willie, to make calls upon ladies in the community, unless she herself was called upon. The midday meal was dinner which she took either at the Tremont or with various friends. In the afternoons, she rested, wrote letters faithfully to Jo, Sunie, her friends in Evanston, and her Mother and family in New England and alternately either sewed or read. There were usually then more calls, and frequently the evening meal, tea, was taken with friends. Very soon, a good part of her time was taken up with church or civic responsibilities, which she undertook in a confident and matter-of-fact manner, only agonizing over her limitations in one area—her performance as a Sunday School teacher.

Her attitude towards child raising seems to have softened by Maggie's death. This is only an inference, since the second diary primarily chronicled her own activities. It was not focused, as the first one was, upon her successes and failures in the daily task of bringing up her "little ones." She was responsible for Willie's education and took this duty seriously. Otherwise, she often lamented that she had allowed Willie to "run about" too much. Once, she discovered that he had run away to a lynching on the Cherry Creek bridge. There was no more commentary about his lack of truthfulness or other moral weaknesses. She seemed to be more able simply to enjoy his company.

Though Margaret was no longer keeping a diary in 1871 when her daughter Anne was born, there seems to be evidence from family interviews and recollections that her attitude towards her second daughter was more similar to this loving acceptance than to her daily, quite judgmental, evaluation of little Maggie.

A Trip to the Mountains

On her first trip to Black Hawk and Central City with Governor Evans, she wrote, "We were all as merry and blithe on the ride as could be—Willie particularly manifested an exuberance of spirits."[15] The journey to the mountains in their "nice, comfortable ambulance"—the term Margaret Evans used to describe their carriage—was of great interest to her. They set out around three in the afternoon and spent the first night in Golden City with the Lovelands, who tried to convince them that they should move from Denver and take up residence in Golden. ("Bah!" wrote Margaret.) The next morning they were joined by Secretary Elbert. The party entered "what is called the Golden Gate" and wound their way to Black Hawk, catching glimpses of "most magnificent views of mountains, the snowy range far in the distance" and stopping for midday dinner at the Michigan House. They reached Black Hawk at dusk, staying with a Mr. and Mrs. Kinney. The next day, they

Central City, Colorado (1860) Denver Public Library Western History Collection, D.C. Kemp

visited some quartz mills, which used a new desulphurizing process, which Margaret confessed she did not fully understand. In the evening, they attended services in the Presbyterian Church with the Kinney family. After his sermon, the Rev. Warner "called upon Bro. Evans to lead in prayer, which he did."[16]

The next day, the Governor and Mr. Elbert addressed a "war meeting" at Central City. "They had been on an expedition to Gold Dirt [a mining camp, now a ghost town] and were very tired, but I pressed them to do it because there would be disappointment, and they were glad they decided to do so." On Sunday, being pregnant, she was tired, and only attended two church services, at the Presbyterian and Episcopalian churches. She heard one good address and one, "a very poor attempt at sermonizing." However, she reproached herself that she did not make the effort to get to the Methodist Church also, afraid they "may feel slighted though the Governor ... attended."[17]

Health Fears

Margaret Evans rejoiced in Willie's educational development and worried only, and understandably, when he was not well.

In March 1863, there was an outbreak of smallpox in Denver. Margaret reported that "Doctor vaccinated the Willards, Willie, and myself and himself."[18]

The Evans family moved from the Tremont House on April 27, before their new home was completed. They occupied two small but comfortable rooms in the home of Mr. and Mrs. Veasey, both of whom she described as "very kind." Margaret found the new quarters much quieter and more home-like than the hotel, and she also felt that the Veasey home provided a more wholesome environment for Willie. In successive entries in her diary, shortly after the family moved she noted,

> Willie has not seemed well all day, flushed face—About six came in with bad headache and burning fever I administered his father's remedy Salts and he still seems very restless and sick—I do wish his Father was at home—if he grows much worse I will send for Dr. McLellan though I am afraid he will dose him too much.

On May 3, the following day, she reported,

Willie was very restless and sick through the night till two o'clock when he began to rest and sleep—his brain seemed to be affected and I was fearful of this epidemic which is raging, 'Miningetis' (sic) as the physicians call it.

Methodism in Early Denver

Very soon after her arrival in Denver, Margaret Evans took on the responsibilities that she perceived as falling to her in her capacity as the Governor's wife and a prominent Methodist woman. The Methodists were the first to establish an organized religious presence in Denver as well as in many other new towns and mining camps. The structure of the Methodist Episcopal Church in America was remarkably appropriate for this pioneering outreach. As Linda Kirby explains in *Heritage of Heroes: Trinity United Methodist Church 1859– 1988*, "The primary elements in the Methodist church's success were the 'democratic gospel' and the peculiar mixture of lay leadership, brotherly democracy, and Episcopal authority in the structure of the church."[19] The policy of itinerancy of Methodist ministers was ideally suited to areas like Colorado Territory, where population was fluid and scattered among a number of small communities.

> The young church in Denver was supported by missionary money raised from the established churches in the east for several years before it became financially self-supporting. This was true of every church founded in Colorado, as well as throughout the entire frontier.[20]

The spring of 1859 saw a flood of gold-seekers, astonishingly estimated by some at as many as 100,000, pouring out of towns along the Missouri River and heading for the Pike's Peak Region, as the area was called at the time. Ever watchful for opportunities to expand Methodist evangelism, the Bishop of the Kansas-Nebraska Methodist Conference dispatched "William H. Goode, an experienced frontier minister, and Jacob Adriance, a 23-year-old probationary member ... to establish a mission to the miners and settlers."[21] At the end of June 1859, after thirty days of travel across 600 miles of prairie, the two arrived at the Auraria/Denver settlement, which had 31 saloons and no churches, schools, hospitals, libraries, or banks.

The first Sunday after they arrived, they held a church service at the Pollack House Hotel. The ministers next traveled to the diggings which became Central City, then to the small communities which later came together to form Golden, and established Methodist Episcopal Churches in both places. George Fisher was left in charge of the Central City Church. On their return to Denver, Goode and Adriance proceeded to organize the Auraria and Denver City Methodist Episcopal Mission, the settlement's first religious organization.

Goode returned home after six weeks, leaving Brother Adriance in charge of the three new churches for the first year. Adriance founded a church in Boulder and "regularly rode the circuit between Denver-Auraria, Golden, and Boulder, preaching wherever and whenever he could."[22] In February 1860, Adriance left Colorado to attend the annual Methodist Conference at Leavenworth. He was not reassigned to the Denver church, which was now sufficiently large to have its own minister, but returned to Colorado to serve the churches in Golden and Boulder.

By this time, a new figure in the development of Methodism in Colorado had arrived in Denver. This was John Chivington, a larger-than-life-figure who "served as Presiding Elder during two years of growth for all the Methodist churches of the area. His commanding presence and imposing personality, coupled with a blustering hawkishness, fit the needs of the raw frontier territory."[23]

Reverend Willard's Contributions

The years from 1860–1862 were unstable years for both Denver and the Methodist church. A succession of ministers had to leave because of ill health, and it was fortunate that Chivington was available to serve when there was no regular minister. The Denver church was in urgent need of some stability in its ministry. This arrived in October of 1862, when O.A. Willard came from Chicago. According to church historian Kirby,

> Willard was a well-known, talented minister and, though young, had many connections in the Methodist church nationally. Two men were primarily responsible for securing Willard's unlikely appointment to the frontier church: the Presiding Elder who succeeded John Chivington, Baxter C. Dennis, and Governor John Evans ... an active and influential Methodist layman from Chicago, who was appointed

Colorado's Second Territorial Governor ... Along with his duties as governor and his crucial leadership in the business community, he took an active role in the small Methodist church he found here. It was largely through the efforts of this layman that the Denver Methodist church became the religious leader in the community and in Rocky Mountain Methodism in the 1860s.[24]

The new minister rented a portion of Henry C. Brown's one-story frame building. The other half was used as a carpenter's shop.

A new and commodious Methodist Church was opened for services on Sunday, March 1, 1863, and attended by a remarkably large and respectable congregation. It was the largest church in the country [region] and a source of gratification to the members of this denomination. The building was situated on the west bank of Cherry Creek, at the upper side of Larimer Street Crossing.[25]

Margaret Evans described the great excitement in the congregation when they attended church in their new place of worship. She noted that "it is ... a vast improvement on the old place—Mr. Willard had a great many out to hear him, he is very much liked and I think is doing a great deal of good."[26]

The church's road to financial independence was greatly helped by the support of the Evans' family. Margaret described her role in raising funds to pay the minister's salary, going out with a Mrs. Burton or other Methodist Church members to collect money for Mr. Willard's salary—"by two o'clock we had collected one hundred and three dollars." The next day, February 28, she was "not feeling very well I did not go out with the subscription book." She comments that asking for money is not a very pleasant undertaking, but "as the stewards neglected it on account of their own business, we thought it our duty to do it."

Membership in the Methodist Church consumed a great deal of time. There were two Sunday services, morning and evening, in addition to Sunday School for both children and adults. Sometimes, Margaret noted that she sent "Doctor and Willie" off to church in the morning while she tried to prepare herself to teach her Sunday School class. Not once does she report feeling satisfied with her performance.

On February 8, she wrote, "I am afraid I fail to interest them—they are unusually trifling and stupid—I must try harder to do my duty and plead for God's assistance." During the week, there were additional services, including a teachers' meeting and a Friday afternoon gathering of ladies interested in developing their spiritual lives. Occasionally there was the excitement of a revival meeting, and also quarterly meetings of the congregation, including a traditional Methodist "Love Feast."[27]

The Governor's Finances

It is generally accepted that by the time he arrived in Colorado, Governor Evans had acquired a considerable fortune. However, Margaret's diary indicates that the family finances were quite strained at the time they came to Colorado Territory. Perhaps this was a result of the failure of John Evans' attempt to build the town of Oreapolis in Nebraska. Margaret mentioned in her January 12 entry, when she was having one of her recurrent spells of homesickness,

> I am sure it is better for us to be here for a great variety of reasons, first the salary which the Doctor receives is a great help to him in his straitened circumstances—it gives us a living and allows him to apply all his income to the extinguishment of debts, thereby lightening his mind of a load and thereby affecting his general health.

On February 11, Margaret Evans received a letter from her mother expressing great concern about the fate of Margaret's sister, Nancy Lowell, who was impoverished and suffering at the hands of a brutal husband. Margaret lamented that she could not help Nancy financially: "If only we were out of debt, I would like to take care of her myself."

Whatever the actual state of the Governor's finances, he was more than generous in his donations to the Methodist Church. He also gave $100 to any new church starting up in Denver—and Evans devoted considerable resources to another ambitious Methodist enterprise, the Colorado Seminary. Though incorporated at the same time as the start of construction of the Lawrence Street Church, the first Methodist building in Denver, the Seminary had an intermittent existence. It was many years before it finally became a stable element of the city's life as the University of Denver.

Helping the "poor, sick soldiers"— Birth of the Ladies' Aid Society

On February 19, Margaret Evans was drawn into the first of a number of civic enterprises she headed up during her active life-time in Denver. A Mrs. Hamilton came to ask if she would go with her to the Camp Weld hospital.[28] That same afternoon, Margaret and three other ladies visited the facility and "found about twenty-five poor soldiers sick and surrounded with discomforts which a little energy might obviate—We decided to call a meeting of all the ladies in town to aid in forming a Soldiers' Aid Society."[29] Two days later, the meeting was held at the Broadwell, the Society formed, and "all the officers elected harmoniously and pleasantly—[they] elected me president, I hope I shall fill the office properly." In another couple of days, she realized that it was up to her to appoint people to purchase the supplies necessary for the Society members to get to work. The work was preparing sanitary supplies for the hospital and sewing shirts for the soldiers. Margaret worked long days with the other ladies to complete their tasks.

> I cannot say I *admire* the ladies of Denver ... she wrote ... many of them are rude coarse but there are good qualities in them all and I think I will *profit myself* if tomorrow I *especially* look for them—*I will try.*

Funding for a Methodist Church Building

When Methodist Bishop Edward Ames came to Denver in July of 1863 to preside over the meetings of the newly formed Rocky Mountain Conference of the Methodist Church, there were 14 churches or circuits and 15 preachers, "241 white members and 14 colored."[30] Bishop Ames promised to provide $1,000 to the Denver church if it would meet his challenge of building a substantial brick church eligibly located in the city of Denver, and have it completed without debt by January of 1865. On July 22, the Denver church became independent and self-supporting. Rev. Willard and John Evans were two of the five incorporators. Evans immediately pledged $1,000, and the congregation quickly purchased a lot at the northeast corner of Lawrence Street and what is now 14th Street.

Trial by Fire, Flood and a Plague of Grasshoppers

A spectacular saga of woes afflicted Denver and its small Methodist congregation between that hopeful beginning in 1863 and the congregation's first meeting in the new church in 1865. In the April before the 1863 Conference meeting, a major fire had destroyed most of the buildings on the Denver side of Cherry Creek. In May of 1864, just as construction of the church was getting under way, a combination of spring rains and snow melt turned meek little Cherry Creek into a raging torrent, sweeping away the 'neat and commodious' quarters of the Methodist Church in Brown's carpenter shop, as well the *Rocky Mountain News* building and all the structures that had been injudiciously erected in the creek bed. Their builders had arrogantly ignored warnings by Indians and scouts who had seen floods in the past. Other buildings destroyed included the city hall, the jail, and law offices.

Poor William Byers not only lost his newspaper offices and all of his printing equipment but also his summer home on the Platte River. Intensely interested in promoting agriculture in Colorado, Byers enjoyed experimenting to find out what crops might be successfully grown in the state and which trees could be induced to flourish in Denver with adequate irrigation. He bought acreage south of Denver on the Platte River—around the area of today's West Byers Place and South Bannock Street—and lived there in the summer with his family. He planted the first fruit trees and grapevines. The raging waters moved the river channel from one side of the house to the other and stranded the Byers family on the roof. They were rescued by the redoubtable Colonel Chivington and some of his militia, who constructed a raft out of a wagon bed. The family found shelter in the Evans home.

This setback in no way discouraged William Byers from his life-long interest in, and promotion of, agriculture in Colorado.

The 1864 flood drowned thousands of animals, which led to serious health and sanitation problems. To add to the misery, a grasshopper plague of biblical proportions decimated the crops that summer in the surrounding countryside. Some immigrants lost faith in the new city and became part of the intermittent stream of "go-backers" returning to the States. Most of the resilient citizens of Denver, as they had after the fire and as they have done many times since in the boom and bust history of the city, took their losses and started to rebuild—this time a little further out of the flood plain and in brick instead of wood.

The Lawrence Street Church and its Successors

Many members of the Methodist church suffered financially from the flood. The construction of their new Lawrence Street Church almost ground to a halt for lack of funding. However, members of the Building Committee took over contracting responsibilities, dug into their own pockets, and managed to complete the building, debt-free, for a total cost of just under $23,000. Evans contributed at least $3,500, as well as paying completely for the site and construction of a parsonage across the street from the church. The new red brick Gothic Revival church, seating 500, was far and away the tallest and most impressive building in town. The first services in the new church were held on February 12, 1865.

Lawrence St. Methodist Church at 14th and Lawrence Streets, (c.1870) Denver Public Library Western History Collection

The Lawrence Street Church served the congregation until July 31, 1887. By that time, the city's growth (the population of Denver increased from less than 4,759 in the 1870 census to 35,629 in 1880) had greatly reduced the number of families living in the area around the church. The city was growing and homeowners were selling their increasingly valuable land for commercial use. New houses were built either along Lincoln, Grant and Sherman Streets, or in the Evans Addition. This was the first platted residential addition to Denver, west of Broadway and south of Colfax, which John Evans filed on June 29, 1868.[31]

Four new Methodist churches were built or under construction by 1880, including the one to which the John Evans family and

Samuel Elbert transferred their membership in 1879. Both men continued their interest in the Lawrence Street Church but the loss of their membership, along with that of most of the Church's original leaders, precipitated a crisis for the congregation.

Under the leadership of a dynamic new pastor, Henry A. Buchtel, whose achievements are described more fully in the chapter on Denver University, the crisis was resolved by the building of a magnificent new church at 18th and Broadway. This was Trinity Methodist Church, designed by Robert S. Roeschlaub, one of Denver's preeminent architects of the time.

The final cost of Trinity Church was about $220,000, which included $18,000 for the land, $30,000 for the organ and $21,000 for the parsonage.[32]

> The beautiful sanctuary and the Roosevelt organ were highly acclaimed and reestablished the congregation's place in Denver and Methodism. Throughout the 1890's, Trinity Church led the community in cultural and educational programs, engaged in extensive local charity work, and supported the rapid expansion of Methodism throughout Denver, earning the title "Mother Church."[33]

Robert S. Roeschlaub

Robert Roeschlaub was born in Germany in 1843. Like so many other ambitious young men of the time, he came west and opened a practice—architectural—in Denver in 1873. The Central City Opera House was his first big success. His later buildings included the Chamberlin Observatory at Denver University, the Hall of Chemistry at the Colorado School of Mines, and the Corona—now Dora Moore—School, as well as many of Denver's most important commercial buildings. In 1909, when Colorado passed the first licensing law for architects, Roeschlaub was given License Number One.

Judging Denver and its People

Margaret's forthright evaluations of the many people with whom she came into contact, in her new role as the Governor's wife, must have made her an entertaining companion for John Evans, and later in life for her grown children. There is no evidence that Margaret ever let her sometimes-acerbic judgments be known in public, though in her diary she occasionally castigates herself for having shared her opinions with a friend.

In her diary, Margaret freely expressed her changing impressions of Mrs. Willard, the wife of the Methodist minister. She went to Mrs. Willard's home several times a week while living at the Tremont. On February 2, she commented,

> Mrs. Willard is not a happy disposition—she seems unhappy and dejected all day from some cause—I think she is tired of the duties of housekeeping and besides does not like the responsibilities of a preacher's wife—but I am trying to cure myself of the habit of looking for people's faults and dwell more on their good qualities ...

However, by March 4, she wrote that in addition to washing and ironing all her handkerchiefs, she enjoyed

> ... talking very confidentially with Mr. and Mrs. Willard. I think they are good friends of ours—Mrs. Willard succeeds nicely in her housekeeping arrangements and I think is perfectly contented— I am pretty well contented the most of the time but occasionally a pang of homesickness comes over me though I say nothing to anyone. I do not feel like going back to Evanston to live, yet.

On February 7, a Mrs. Sargent came and spent some time with Mrs. Evans. Of her, Margaret reported: "Poor woman she has her troubles, possesses some good qualities which I would do well to emulate; she is more discreet in talking of people than I am." The next day she noted that "George Brown called at noon to see Doctor—he is a well-meaning young man but something of a bore." On March 30, a Mrs. Corbin came over and spent the rest of the forenoon with her; "found her stay somewhat tedious, I am afraid I am somewhat selfish but it is with great effort that I can make myself passably agreeable when I am not interested in the person; for that reason I do not make friends as fast as some others."

On March 15, Margaret "met Judge Armour for the first time, he was our guest at tea—a very pompous, conceited person from Baltimore."

A devout Methodist, Margaret Evans had her heart firmly set against demon drink. On April 3, she said she had just laid down for a nap when she was disturbed by a call from a Mrs. Steck, "so

I smoothed my hair and descended to the parlor—she is a very pleasant, lady-like lady and were it not for the fact that I once saw her drink whiskey I should like her." It did not seem to her at all inconsistent that she occasionally revived herself with "a little brandy"—but this of course was taken for medicinal reasons. On February 22, she lamented, "so much drunkenness in town today."

The Governor continued to spend many days away from home, visiting various parts of the state, and she missed his presence keenly. On May 8, she wrote that she was so glad that he had returned from a trip to Black Hawk in the company of Mr. and Mrs. Willard, and expressed the hope "that our separations be few and far between."

By this time, Margaret's pregnancy with her third child was quite advanced. On May 10, she dispatched her family to church without her. "I do not expect to go again until after my confinement." She paid a moving tribute to her "kind, loving husband—his affection for me is so pure and constant." On May 17, she again stayed home from church, writing that "the closer a lady keeps at home at such times, the better it speaks for her modesty ... I have grown very uncomfortable to myself." The last entry in this second diary was made on May 19, when she noted that the day had been very warm "but we can endure them—the morning and evenings are so cool."

New Baby and New Home at 14th and Arapahoe

Margaret's second son, Evan Elbert, was born on June 26, 1868. Margaret returned to Evanston for the birth. There is no evidence to support biographer Harry E. Kelsey's typically masculine comment, "with a new baby to care for, Margaret soon forgot her sorrow over the death of 'precious, little Maggie'."[34] By the fall of 1863, the family was in their new home at 14th and Arapahoe, the place they called home until the Governor's death in 1897. The original house was quite modest, but, as noted by Edith Eudora Kohl in her book about Denver's historic mansions, it was much more gracious and sturdy than others' houses built at this time. It stood out "with its iron fence and grounds of grass and shrubs reaching clear down to Cherry Creek."[35] It was built of "red brick, trimmed in white and a story and a half, whereas the regulation house in that district was the low-roofed cabin of log and rough lumber. It even had a library ..."[36]

Indeed, one of the features that attracted people's attention was the library, which housed not only Governor Evans' books but also those belonging to Margaret Evans. Both collections were brought to Denver by prairie schooner. Margaret was a constant reader and "a great lover of books."[37] Her brief 1863 diary gives a glimpse into her reading habits. Early in January, she was reading Mrs. Browning's poetry. At the end of the month, a great deal of her time was spent on *Ecclesiastical History, Ancient and Modern* by Dr. Laurence Mosheim. From time to time, she reported on reading in it the history of the Quakers, of the American church, and of the Lutherans: "I do not like them; in my opinion they are not very far removed from Romanism—have degenerated since Luther's time."[38]

Gov. Evans house at 14th and Arapahoe Streets (c. 1865) Denver Public Library Western History Collection

She drew great inspiration from a biography of Mary Lyon, portions of which she read to her husband when he was feeling unwell. Lyon, a religiously motivated pioneer of higher education for women and the founder, in 1837, of what became Mount Holyoke College, served as an inspiration to Margaret Evans. At the end of March 1863, Mrs. Evans was studying the geography of England. Margaret Evans felt obligated to devote her reading hours to serious subjects: in one entry, she scolded herself for wasting precious time on two frivolous articles in *Harper's Magazine*.

Margaret Evans' stories of pioneer life in Denver were of great interest to her grandchildren and great grandchildren. They summed up their memories in the citation prepared in 1938, when a chair at the Central City Opera House was dedicated to her:

> All the gist of that pioneer life was pressed into the stories she used to tell of the early days; old Chief Colorow calmly climbing through the window to smoke a pipe in the Governor's armchair ... an Indian raid, when, cramming a loaf of bread into each pocket of her "duster," she carried baskets of food to the women herded for safety in Mr. Kountze's bank; and her innumerable tales of odd characters and visiting celebrities.[39]

Josephine Evans Comes Home to Denver

Josephine Evans Elbert, Courtesy History Colorado

Twenty-year old Josephine, having graduated from Wesleyan Academy in Massachusetts, came to live in the new Evans home in Denver in January 1864. "The Academy's records show that Miss Evans graduated in the class of 1864—one of eight ladies, (and) that she was a diligent student of literature and the classics."[40] On January 30, 1864, "the *Daily Commonwealth* reported that Governor Evans had returned by stagecoach from a trip East accompanied by his invalid daughter, whose health was much improved by the trip out."[41]

At this time, Governor Evans was working hard in the attempt to achieve statehood for Colorado. Lincoln, facing a bitter re-election campaign, believed that the votes of Colorado, Nebraska and Nevada, if they could secure statehood, might prove crucial. All three were believed to be strongly pro-Union.

The effort failed as far as Colorado was concerned, but Governor Evans traveled to Washington to attend President Lincoln's second inauguration. He was accompanied by his wife, Margaret, daughter Josephine, and Margaret's niece, Cornelia Gray Lunt (Cousin Nina).

Josephine Becomes Mrs. Samuel Elbert

Samuel Elbert had visited Josephine in Wilbraham and had fallen in love. He obtained permission from Margaret Evans to enter into a correspondence with her. Now that she was back in Denver, Elbert was able to move from the romance-by-mail to an ardent courtship. There are only a few surviving descriptions of Josephine. According to one author,

> It has been said that Secretary and Mrs. Elbert made one of the handsomest bridal couples ever seen in Denver. "Sweet little Josie," as she was affectionately called, was very fair and petite while he was large (tall) and very dark. Amiable and a brilliant conversationalist, though retiring in manner, she was a social favorite.[42]

Cornelia Gray Lunt of Evanston wrote quite vividly in her memoirs about the cousin she obviously loved. They became acquainted when John Evans used to bring his daughter with him to visit Cornelia and Orrington Lunt. Jo and Cornelia considered themselves cousins after John and Margaret (Cornelia's Aunt) were married. In the period when the Lunts remained in Chicago and the Evans family had already moved out to Evanston, young Cornelia and Jo Evans, who were the same age, visited each other often. Cornelia describes her early impressions of Evanston,

Samuel Elbert, Courtesy History Colorado

> ... there were a few nice houses, and the Evans had a great big square for grounds and a lot of Lake shore, and had built a cottage

that was brown-painted and had little gables and wandered over a good deal of ground. It looked pretty so near the Lake and all surrounded by tall beautiful trees ... we exchanged visits—frequently—I going to Evanston, she coming to Chicago. And Jo was always a sort of Star in the little plays, dances, and tableaux we got up.[43]

Cornelia and Jo kept up their friendship by correspondence after the Evans family moved to Denver and Josephine went to school at the Wesleyan Academy in Massachusetts. Cornelia described how, as she neared graduation, Josephine's letters

... were full of the development of a romance. She had met the man of men and the swift recognition of his supremacy had glorified her days. He had deigned to woo the Governor's daughter, and she felt he had stooped from a height of unapproachable manhood to crown her wondering self with the royal signet of choice. I laughed at (her) undue humility ... I longed to look upon that paragon of his sex.[44]

After Josephine returned home to Denver and Samuel Elbert had proposed to her, Cornelia was delighted to learn that the wedding was to take place in Evanston.

It was one of the greatest pleasures I had experienced for long, to hear that Joe was coming to stay awhile with me before her contemplated marriage, in the Evanston home, when summer bloom was at its freshest. She wanted me for "maid of honour," and said General Custer was to stand with me.

Joe was very fragile, delicate in build and with a certain luminousness that surrounded her like an aura. The death-marked sometimes have a peculiar look long before they leave us, that seems to ask, to plead, to grieve as if indeed they saw the cloud that was so soon to shroud all nature from their eyes. And yet, God be thanked! She had her year.[45]

Samuel Elbert was thirty-two and Josephine twenty-one, when they were married in the summer of 1865 in the lovely garden of the Evans home in Evanston. Officiating was John Evans' long-

time friend, Bishop Matthew Simpson. Cornelia Lunt described
the scene:

> The sun flashed its last rays of splendour over the Lake, and, as it
> slipped out of view in the west, light still lingered in hovering films
> of colorful clouds deepening to orange and rose, and tones of ever
> changing loveliness till they died into the night, as music dies into
> silence.
>
> The sky and the lake were vying with each other, the waves
> breaking on the shore ... There was a sort of unearthly beauty in
> that hour and place ...[46]

The marriage was all too brief. The couple moved into Elbert's
"quaint little red brick cottage surrounded by a white picket fence
located on E (Fourteenth) Street between Arapahoe and Lawrence
Streets,"[47] near the Evans' home. Josephine had suffered intermittently all her life from the tuberculosis that took her mother's life.
She had a baby boy named Johnnie in March of 1868, but he was
weak and lived only a few months.

Evans and Elbert Buy a Mountain Ranch

In the summer of 1868, more than two years before Anne Evans
was born, her father and Samuel Elbert purchased the nucleus of
the Evans Ranch which played such a vital role in shaping her
character and the seasonal structure of her entire life.

The Elbert and Evans families took an excursion up the Bear
Creek Valley for a camping trip, while Josephine was still alive. The
party drove in spring wagons to the mouth of Mount Vernon
Canyon, and followed this to Bergen's Ranch (present-day Bergen
Park). From there they turned southwest towards Bear Creek, reaching the stream at a place now known as Bendemeer where they
camped for several weeks."[48] Evans and his son-in-law bought an
attractive 320-acre piece of land further up the Bear Creek Valley.
They called it Kuhlborne Ranch, although it was also known for
many years as the Evans/Elbert Ranch. According to Governor Evans'
first biographer, Edgar McMechen, "Luxuriant grass in the wide creek
bottom stood as high as timothy hay, and this feature, with the
width of the valley, impressed both as excellent cattle range." The
first attempt at year-round cattle raising was less than successful,

according to McMechen, due to a particularly harsh winter. Nevertheless, Governor Evans decided to hold on to the property primarily because it was such a delight to his wife, Margaret.

Before the advent of air conditioning, and before Denver had developed its carefully cultivated canopy of trees to mitigate the ruthless heat of the summer sun, it became fashionable for families who had the means to do so, to escape in summer to the relative cool of the mountains. A summer home was soon built on the new property, which was steadily expanded by the purchase of additional land. It became a favorite summer holiday locale for the Evans and Elbert families and their many relatives and friends.

Death of Josephine

Josephine's consumption returned, and she died in the cottage on October 22 of the same year, 1868.

While studying in the East, Josephine had been a frequent visitor to the home of Bishop Simpson and had become a good friend of his daughters. Like her father, she had been deeply moved by Simpson's eloquent and persuasive Methodist teachings. He awakened in her "the strong, calm religious faith which marked her personality and made Methodism one of the dominant interests of her short life."[49]

Evans Chapel and Grace Methodist Church at 13th and Bannock Streets, Courtesy History Colorado

Not long before her death, as she was talking to her father about the fact that she was dying, it is reported that "she smiled and said: 'I have no pain and no fear.'"[50]

And so, the Evans family was left without daughters. Anne, born less than three years later, would occupy a unique position in the family.

Josephine's death was a heavy blow for both her husband and her father. Governor Evans built a little Gothic chapel of Colorado sandstone in her memory at West 13th and Bannock, which was completed in 1878. Evans and his wife and Samuel Elbert transferred their membership in 1879 to this new Evans Memorial Chapel. Later a larger building, Grace Church, was erected next to it. It was completed in 1889 and served until its membership was transferred to a new Grace Church in University Hills.[51] In 1960, after the closing of Grace Church, the Memorial chapel was carefully moved, stone by stone, to the Denver University campus.

> One of the chief features of the chapel is the Memorial Window that occupies much of the east wall. The wainscoting, the arches, the side light fixtures, bearing the state seal, and one of the chancel benches and the windows are from the original Chapel. The Bible on the pulpit is the original pulpit Bible of Grace Methodist Church.[52]

In its new location, the 1878 building, constructed in memory of Josephine Evans, is still the site of many weddings, memorial services and other functions.

Samuel Elbert Carries On

Samuel Elbert never remarried, though it seems he had a strange, brief engagement in Evanston to Cornelia Gray Lunt.[53] For his remaining years, much of both his business and social life was bound up with the Evans family.

Often, when he was not traveling, he lived with the family. Part of the summer, he would spend with the Evans' in the "Cottage"—sometimes called the "Cottage Yard"—on the Evans/Elbert Ranch. Sometimes he stayed in the Evans' home at Fourteenth and Arapahoe, which was much more gracious and spacious after extensive remodeling and additions in the early 1870s. The simple two-story brick cottage became

a three-story dwelling with a mansard roof and a basement.
A four-story addition was also added at the rear of the house; a
formal staircase was placed in the entry hall; and a conservatory
was built off one side. Within a few years, the gardens became the
envy of Denver.[54]

Elbert had a brief term as Territorial Governor, at which time the
Evans' home became once more the Colorado executive mansion.
Elbert had been elected to the Territorial Legislature in 1868. His
appointment as Governor came from President Ulysses Grant in
April of 1873. Less than a year later, Grant was persuaded by
political enemies of Elbert and Evans to remove Elbert from the
Governorship—an act for which Grant later apologized.

> At the time of his removal, he had the entire confidence and respect
> of the people. No charge was ever made or established against him.
> His removal resulted in great dissatisfaction in the Republican
> Party, and at the next general election the territory for the first and
> only time in its history, went Democratic.[55]

While Governor, Elbert had two major achievements to his
credit. Certain that without irrigation there would be no permanent
prosperity in Colorado, he initiated the Western Irrigation Conference
in 1873.

He met with Ute leaders and laid the groundwork for a September 1873 treaty "that opened more than 3 million acres of the
Indian reservation to mining and railroad activity."[56] This was as an
important achievement for the forces pushing for the development
of Colorado's natural resources, and a major defeat for the last
substantial Indian presence in the Territory.

For a time after he lost the Governorship, Elbert "was at loose
ends ... and spent most of his time at the Evans home, reading and
brooding."[57] He then took an extended European tour "where he
studied the political economy of Europe's prominent cities."[58] When
Colorado was admitted to statehood in 1876, Elbert was elected to
the new Colorado Supreme Court. Serving with distinction for six
years, he spent the last four as Chief Justice. Declining renomination
in 1882, he was persuaded to run again in 1885, and was re-elected
in 1886 by an overwhelming majority. He resigned after two years,

citing failing health and the need to attend to his own financial investments.

Samuel Elbert died in Galveston, Texas, in 1899, leaving a generous legacy to the family he had embraced as his own for so many years.

5

Sand Creek and After

In virtually every case, the story of how the war got started and how it proceeded is a long, detailed and tangled business ... These are tales from hell ... because they are stories that drive their tellers and readers to a confrontation with the darkest and grimmest dimensions of human nature. Torture, maiming, rape, mutilation, murder—all of the worst injuries that human beings inflict on each other serve as the capstones to these stories ... Of course, one can never lose sight of who started the whole business ... And it is also perfectly clear who, when the dust had settled, had maneuvered whom into surrendering land, food, and the weapons of aggression and self-defense. But in between those two points of clarity lies a great stretch of historical turf in which people of all ethnicities and backgrounds embraced brutality and committed atrocities.[1]
—Patricia Nelson Limerick

Evans' predecessor, Governor Gilpin, was dismissed from office because of his inventive solution to Washington's impossible directive: raise troops to defend the Territory, but expect no funds with which to pay them. Gilpin did succeed in forming the First Regiment of the Colorado Volunteer Infantry, which played a crucial role in foiling Texan plans to march up from New Mexico, defeat whatever troops Colorado Territory could muster, and take over the gold fields as a way of providing desperately needed funds to finance the Confederacy.

Chivington and Glorieta Pass

Derisively nicknamed "Gilpin's Pet Lambs" by the Texans, the Colorado Volunteers marched south to confront the invaders. While the main forces were fighting several inconclusive battles between Las

Vegas and Santa Fe, New Mexico, at the end of March 1862, a small detachment of the Volunteers climbed over high ground and descended upon the Texan rear supply train at Glorieta Pass. The Volunteers destroyed the train's provisions and killed almost all their horses and mules. The Texans were forced to withdraw.

The detachment was under the command of Major John Chivington. A former prizefighter, Chivington was a huge, belligerent man (about six foot three and 260 pounds). After the Glorieta Pass victory, he was promoted to Colonel and returned to Denver and a hero's welcome. He was now in command of all Colorado troops and became a natural ally and confidant of Governor Evans in the struggle to deal with the Territory's Indian problems.

John Chivington, Denver Public Library Western History Collection

Unrestricted Immigration, Broken Treaties, Indian Reprisals

Governor Evans inherited the Fort Wise Treaty, which had been signed by some, but not all, groups of the Territory's Cheyenne and Arapahos. It was one of the depressingly long list of instances where the federal government reneged on an earlier treaty—in this case the Fort Laramie Treaty—in order to give white prospectors and settlers access to land reserved to Indians. Under the terms of the Fort Wise Treaty, the Cheyenne and Arapaho were to be allocated a reservation on the Upper Arkansas River. Since there were few buffalo left in the area, the tribes would have to be supplied with food and other goods until, it was hoped, they would settle down to farming. Evans thought that these tribes would do better raising cattle and sheep and so recommended to Indian Commissioner William Dole. Dole's response was to ignore this recommendation and instruct Evans to try to persuade the tribes to accept the terms of the Fort Wise Treaty. But with all federal resources being poured into the Civil War, he indicated there would be no money to supply the Indians with food or agricultural supplies.

Evans sent out messengers to summon the Cheyenne and Arapaho to a meeting on the Republican River, on the eastern plains of Colorado, but not a single one came. Kelsey reports in his biography of Evans that one of the chiefs asked the messenger exactly what the Governor wanted the Indians to do. On being told that he wanted the Indians to settle down and live like white men, the chief responded, "You can just go back to the governor and tell him we are not reduced quite that low yet."[2]

Governor Evans was a man of his time, in terms of the way he perceived the possible future of Colorado Territory's Native American tribes. During his interviews with historian Hubert Bancroft, a quarter of a century after Sand Creek, Evans summarized his perception of the situation at that time of rising immigration to the Territory from the United States. It was, he said "ridiculous" to think that "a country a thousand miles long and five hundred miles wide, one of the most fertile in the world, should belong to a few bands of roving Indians." He believed that "they had a right to hunt on the land, but that right must be subject to the higher occupation of the land, for a larger population and for civilization."[3]

It is relevant here to note that Evans' views were the prevailing views of Colorado Methodists at the time. "Because they saw themselves as the vanguard of a progressive American civilization, these pioneers and settlers could not comprehend criticism over their treatment of Indians."[4] Bishop Kingsley, for example, wrote in 1865,

> There is no reason why an ignorant pagan should be allowed land enough for hunting grounds to sustain a thousand civilized and Christianized persons living in accordance with the precepts of the Gospel ... I have no fellowship with that sentimentalism which is ready to die of grief because the red man is not allowed to hold back civilization and Christianity just for the sake of being a savage.[5]

The situation in Colorado Territory began to spiral out of control. Immigrants continued to pour in. The Indians became more desperate, suffering from the ravages of unfamiliar diseases and from hunger, as once plentiful game became scarce and corrupt Indian agents failed to deliver food and other promised supplies. There were increasing attacks on wagon trains. Telegraph wires—the lifeline of the Territory's communications with the States—were cut and isolated ranches were raided.

Denver's sense of fear and vulnerability was sharply increased by a horrifying event: the peculiarly grisly murder on June 11, 1864, of the Hungates, a settler family living about 30 miles east of Denver. The mutilated bodies were put on public display. Governor Evans on June 27 sent out an urgent message to "the friendly Indians of the Plains" urging them to surrender themselves to the military authorities and separate themselves from hostile elements. He promised those who obeyed this order that they would be safe. Cheyenne and Arapaho bands were instructed, in the proclamation, to go to the former Fort Wise, now renamed Fort Lyon. The edict was largely ineffective.

The "Thirdsters" and the Prelude to Sand Creek

Governor Evans received permission from the War Department on August 11, 1864, to form a Third Colorado Regiment for a period of 100 days to fight the Indian threat.[6] On that same day, Evans issued the proclamation that is often quoted to prove that his underlying desire all along was to rid the Territory of Indians. Evans proclaimed that all the evidence pointed to the fact that most of the Indian tribes on the plains were already at war with the whites. He called upon all citizens of the Territory, either individually or in groups, to "go in pursuit of all hostile Indians on the plains" and to "kill and destroy, as enemies of the country, wherever they may be found, all such hostile Indians." He did urge that citizens should scrupulously avoid "those who have responded to the said call to rendezvous at the points indicated."[7]

The "Thirdsters," as the new Regiment came to be named, numbered over 1150 men. For most of their hundred-day enlistment, they were camped at a site along the Platte north of Denver. Pressure mounted on Chivington and Evans from all sides, inflated by the local newspapers, to put the soldiers to use to deal with the feared Indian menace.

The Indians were divided in their response to Evans' proclamation. Major Edward Wynkoop, the young commander in charge of Fort Lyon, developed an unexpected sympathy for their plight. He saw that they were hungry and poorly armed, and so he failed to obey the orders from Chivington to shoot all Indians on sight. Instead, he earned the trust of a significant group of their leaders,

*Camp Weld Council, Denver, Colorado. Standing (back row) l. to rt.:
1. unidentified, 2. unidentified, 3. John Simpson Smith, interpreter,
4. White Wolf, 5. Bosse (Cheyenne), 6. Dexter Dole Culley, 7.
unidentified. Seated (middle row) l. to rt.: 1. Neva (Arapaho),
2. Bull Bear (Cheyenne), 3. Black Kettle (Cheyenne), 4. One Eye
(Cheyenne), %. unidentified. Kneeling (front row) l. to rt.: 1. Maj.
Edward W. Wynkoop 2. Maj. Silas Soule. (September 28, 1864) Denver
Public Library Western History Collection*

including Chief Black Kettle, and brought them to Denver to discuss
peace possibilities with the Governor. This placed Evans in an uncomfortable position, and no one reading the written account of
the ensuing meeting at Camp Weld, at which Chivington was also
present, can miss the stiff and suspicious character of the Governor's
reaction to the Cheyenne and Arapaho leaders. He maintained
that he could do nothing about the situation between the Indians
and the whites, which was now in the hands of the military and if
they wanted to make peace, it would have to be with the soldiers.
Chief Black Kettle and others returned to Fort Lyon, where Wynkoop
continued to promise that those Indians who placed themselves
under the protection of the Fort would be safe.

But Major General Samuel R. Curtis, in charge of the Military
Department of Kansas, which included the Territory of Colorado,
recalled Wynkoop and replaced him with Major Scott Anthony,

who told the mixed group of Arapaho and Cheyenne gathered there that he could no longer supply them with food rations. He suggested that they move to a camp on Sand Creek, about forty miles from the Fort, where they might be able to hunt buffalo.

Evans Heads for Washington

Governor Evans, having taken the position that the solution of problems with the Indians was now in the hands of the army and also convinced, according to Kelsey's account, that no real action would take place until spring, set out for Washington with his family on November 16, 1864.[8] He went to pursue goals related to his incompatible twin positions as Indian Commissioner and as Governor of a young Territory. Evans hoped to convince the War Department to halt the transfer of soldiers out of the Territory, which desperately needed them for its own defense.

There were many other unsettled issues relating to the future of Colorado, including the question of Colorado access to the proposed transcontinental railroad and needed changes in mining law, which required federal action.

There was also the continuing controversy over the question of statehood for Colorado Territory. In a frankly political effort to line up additional congressional votes for his policies, Lincoln advocated the admission of Colorado, Nebraska and Nevada to the Union, signing the act enabling Colorado Territory to apply for statehood on March 21, 1864. Evans called immediately for a convention to draw up a constitution.

At first, success seemed assured. But opposition soon appeared, coming from a number of different quarters. The Spanish-speaking people of the southern part of the Territory felt their rights as a minority would be better protected by the federal rather than state government. Many other residents felt the population of the Territory was too small to afford the costs of state government. Some opponents were motivated by the fear that statehood would bring with it the military draft law. The looming threat of war with Indians caused others to fear the loss of federal assistance in the Territory's defense. Then there were the twin disasters in successive springs, with fire practically destroying the heart of Denver in 1863, and the flooding of Cherry Creek in 1864, sweeping away some of the young city's important buildings and inundating many others.

Such events exposed Denver's vulnerability and its continuing dependence on federal assistance.

Evans, having been appointed by Lincoln, was a natural target for much of the opposition to statehood, fueled in part by hostility to Lincoln's policies. Unfavorable and sometimes vitriolic articles about the Governor appeared in some of the Territory's newspapers. The opposition gathered momentum through the summer of 1864. A referendum on statehood was soundly defeated in September.

Evans was still firmly committed to pursuing the goal of statehood, and hopeful that in the process he could realize a cherished ambition for his own future—to become one of the new state's senators. He knew that an influential group of Territorial officials, opposed to the drive for statehood, were agitating in Washington for his removal from office. Countering this effort was another reason for his trip to the capital.

Sand Creek

Soon after Evans' arrival in Washington, news began to arrive about "A Foul and Dastardly Massacre"[9] that had occurred in Colorado Territory.

Colonel Chivington, faced with the imminent expiration of the enlistment term of his hundred day volunteers, had led the Regiment out of Denver to Fort Lyon. With the addition of soldiers commandeered from the Fort, he made for the peaceful camp of Arapaho and Cheyenne at Sand Creek. The United States flag and a white flag of surrender were flying conspicuously, but the soldiers attacked the camp's occupants, most of whom were women and children, with extraordinary violence. They killed indiscriminately old men, women and children, and afterwards scalped and otherwise mutilated the bodies for souvenir trophies. Chivington initially claimed to have killed 400–500 Indian warriors but in reality, the casualties were 160–165 Cheyenne and Arapaho, two thirds of them women and children.

Chivington and his Third Regiment were at first welcomed in Denver as heroes. But as a few of the participants in the "battle" began to tell their stories, public opinion was split. Congressional hearings on the event, which quickly became known as the Sand Creek Massacre, were held in Washington in March of 1865. A military enquiry took evidence in Denver. The political enemies of

The battle at Sand Creek, Colorado, between U.S. troops and Cheyenne. Women and children panic behind trees in the foreground, warriors and soldiers fight among tepees in the background. Photo copy by Dow Helmers, 1969 of oil painting by O. Y. Rookstool, Denver Public Library Western History Collection

Evans in Washington immediately seized upon the issue, seeking successfully to pin blame for the massacre on him and making every effort to turn the Congressional hearings against him. The weak and unconvincing testimony he gave only bolstered their arguments. Lacking first-hand knowledge of what happened at Sand Creek, he attempted to justify his own actions as Indian Commissioner and those of the soldiers as being totally in line with all the military directives given to him. He believed that he would later have an opportunity to testify in greater depth. But events moved quickly and that opportunity never came.

After-Effects of Sand Creek: Indian Wars and Evans' Resignation

In April of 1865, Lee surrendered to Grant at Appomattox, thus ending the long and immensely costly Civil War. President Lincoln, Evans' sponsor and supporter, was assassinated shortly thereafter. The Congressional Committee report on Sand Creek was issued in the summer of 1865.[10] It was devastating, highly critical of Evans and others involved in Sand Creek, and recommended Evans' dismissal as Governor. Evans prepared a detailed report challenging the findings, but as there was no official channel through which it could be released, he had to pay for a private printing.[11] President Johnson, mired in the contentious aftermath of the war, was in no mood to entertain Evans' request for a new hearing. He instructed Secretary of State Seward to ask for the Governor's resignation, which Evans tendered on August 1, 1865.

The immediate effects of the Sand Creek Massacre on relations between whites and Indians of Colorado Territory were exactly the opposite of what its perpetrators promised. Far from quelling Indian attacks, it destroyed almost all trust in peace overtures and resulted in a "massive Indian insurrection" in eastern Colorado.[12] In the longer run, the process of displacing the plains Indians from all their former hunting grounds in the Territory proceeded inexorably. The last large engagement, in which the Indians were decisively defeated, was the Battle of Summit Springs in the summer of 1869. Most of the remnants of the southern branches of the Cheyenne and Arapaho Indians were settled on a reservation in Oklahoma. Members of the Northern Cheyenne were moved in the 1880s to a Montana reservation, and the Northern Arapaho were sent to a reservation in Wyoming.

Chivington's Fate

After a triumphant return to Denver with his "Thirdster" troops, trumpeting his great victory at Sand Creek and being lionized by the relieved population and fulsomely praised in the city newspapers, Chivington's fortunes began to decline. Some of the soldiers and officers involved in the Massacre denounced his monstrous conduct at Sand Creek in the military inquiry hearings in Denver in February 1865. Captain Silas Soule, the chief witness against him, was murdered outside his home in Denver, giving rise to widespread suspicion that Chivington was responsible.[13]

Chivington was never charged with any crimes because of Sand Creek. He resigned from the military in December, 1864, and, after a brief final involvement in Denver politics, left the city a year later. His subsequent career was full of financial shady dealings, fraud, and rapid changes of residence to escape prosecution. Near the end of his life, he returned to Colorado, where in some quarters he was again greeted as a hero. In September 1883, he addressed the newly formed Colorado Pioneer Society on the topic, "I stand by Sand Creek." He served as a deputy sheriff in Arapahoe County[14] and in 1891 was elected County Coroner. Dying of cancer in 1894, he was given an elaborate Masonic funeral and burial in Fairmount

Cemetery. As the years have gone by and the disgrace of Sand Creek is more universally acknowledged, the consensus of opinion is that Chivington was indeed a hero in defense of the Union at Glorieta Pass, and also a genocidal murderer of Indians at Sand Creek.

The events of November 29, 1864, indelibly characterized as the Sand Creek Massacre, ended John Evans' tenure as Governor.[15]

Ongoing Drive for Statehood

Evans and his allies continued to press for statehood, even after he was removed as Governor. They carried the effort through several votes in Colorado Territory and in Congress, resulting in two vetoes by President Johnson. Evans spent much time in Washington as one of two senators-elect, along with Jerome Chaffee, between 1865 and 1868. In the spring of that year, the forces arrayed against statehood, led by Henry M. Teller of Central City—a one-time political ally of Evans—succeeded in defeating a final attempt to pass the statehood for Colorado bill in Congress. Nevada was admitted to the Union in 1864 and Nebraska achieved statehood in 1867, but Colorado had to wait until 1876. When that day came, it was Henry Teller and not John Evans who became U. S. Senator from Colorado.

Henry M. Teller

Teller had joined the movement west soon after the Pike's Peak gold rush, opening his law office in Central City in 1861. Like so many of his able contemporaries, he diversified his activities, engaging in railroad building, mining, politics and other interests in addition to law. Teller, who became known as "Colorado's Grand Old Man,"[16] served as the state's Senator from 1876 to 1909—with the exception of the years from 1881 to 1885 when he served as President Arthur's Secretary of the Interior. Teller left the Republican Party over the issue of withdrawing federal support for silver, and in 1901 joined the Democratic Party. When he retired from the Senate in 1909, he was widely regarded as an effective representative of Colorado and a legislator of integrity.

Evans Leads Efforts to Connect Denver to the Transcontinental Railroad

The issues for which John Evans was advocating in Washington in the winter of 1864 were not confined to statehood matters. He was also still pursuing his conviction that Denver must have a connection to the transcontinental railroad. He had extensive experience with the development of railroads in Chicago and was well aware of their vital importance in the commercial future of frontier communities. Evans' first public speech as Governor from the balcony of Tremont House had stressed the importance of this link for Denver's future, and he lobbied hard for the newly authorized railroad to be brought through Colorado over the route surveyed in 1861 by Captain E. L. Berthoud. Work on the proposed railroad was postponed for the duration of the Civil War. When it was resumed, the decision was made to bypass Colorado and take the easier route through Cheyenne, Wyoming.

This decision came at a low point in Denver's fortunes. The city had lost population during the war years, falling from more than 5,000 to less than 4,000.[17] Mining had stagnated, as gold miners had to follow veins deeper and deeper into the ground. At the surface, the rock enclosing the mineral had been softened by erosion and gold was easy to recover by water processes, but as the miners went deeper, these processes were inadequate. The technology was lacking to separate out gold from the ore.

Some of the city's businessmen were persuaded by the leaders of the Union Pacific railroad that the future development of the region lay with Cheyenne. Thomas Durant, vice president of Union Pacific, pronounced, "Denver was too dead to bury."[18] But when a representative of the Union Pacific came to Denver later, in 1867, to suggest that the businessmen of Denver should form a railroad company and build a line to Cheyenne with help from the Union Pacific, there was an immediate response from men like David Moffat, John Evans and William Byers.

In the autumn of 1867, these three spearheaded the formation of a Board of Trade, which in turn sponsored the creation of the Denver Pacific Railroad Company. Capitalized at two million dollars, the Company secured a favorable vote from citizens of Arapahoe County to buy one quarter of the stock for half a million dollars. The new Company faced a rocky road: the first president resigned and the second died shortly after taking office. Evans was elected president early in March, 1868, and soon discovered that no one was interested in buying the railroad's bonds. Getting the railroad line built involved an overwhelming series of financial organizations and reorganizations, contracts with construction companies, and congressional lobbying to secure land grants. At one point, with no prospects and construction at a complete standstill, Evans resigned as president of the board of directors and signed a contract to build the railroad and pay off its debts. At the beginning of 1870, Evans again became president of the Denver Pacific board, and was on hand at the Denver depot when the tracks finally reached the city on June 23, 1870.

"With the completion of the Denver Pacific, Colorado railroad construction developed at an astounding pace."[19] And John Evans was right in the thick of it. Kelsey, with faithful attention to detail, tells the story of the spreading network of rails to major communities and the mining areas in Colorado. He also documents the bitter play of rivalries, as well as the opportunistic alliances, between the major figures in this vigorous and rapid expansion: John Evans, David Moffat, Walter Cheesman, General William Palmer of Colorado Springs, W. A. H. Loveland of Golden and eastern financier, Jay Gould. Evans continued to be deeply involved in founding, building and securing financing for railroads to serve Denver's commercial interests—chiefly the Denver, South Park and Pacific and the Denver and New Orleans Railroad Company—until his health began to fail around the age of 80. In no other area of investment could the old aphorism, "You win some, you lose some" have been truer: Evans made a handsome profit on some of his railroad ventures; others drained his resources and went into bankruptcy.

Nathaniel Hill's Smelter

In addition to the vigorous railroad building activity, there was another major factor in the recovery of Colorado's economy: the importation to Black Hawk of a smelting process from Swansea, Wales, that was capable of successfully dealing with Colorado's complex ores. The man who brought this much-needed development to Colorado was a young Brown University chemistry teacher named Nathaniel P. Hill. His smelter went to work in December 1867. According to historian, Marshall Sprague, "the plant was a success almost from the start. An immediate effect was to stop the stampede of Denver businessmen north to the coming rail metropolis of Cheyenne."[20] The hard rock mining skills needed to get at the ores brought hundreds of Cornish miners to the region. "These 'Cousin Jacks' with their picturesque dress and language and colorful singing and dancing brought a much-needed touch of gaiety to the drab mining camps."[21] This legacy echoed down through the years and was honored by Anne Evans in her 1930s' efforts to revive the prosperity of Central City and Black Hawk.

Adverse Publicity Hard on Margaret Evans

Conflicts over railroad ownerships and rights-of-way were bound up with media coverage and political stands. From the early days of his governorship, Evans had to deal with adverse publicity, some of it justified and some of it patently unfair. Evans himself was able to make choices in dealing with press attacks—sometimes ignoring them, sometimes answering them in writing, sometimes taking political action behind the scenes to out-maneuver his detractors—while continuing to pursue his goals. However, from references in the voluminous correspondence between the Governor and his wife during two long sojourns she made in Europe, it is clear that the newspaper attacks were hard on her. One example of such attacks, out of many that could be cited, comes from *The Denver Gazette* of September 16, 1865, under the headline, *Removal of Governor Evans*:

> We do not really know whether he was relieved or whether he resigned but we do know that ... if the advice of his best friends had been taken he would have resigned long ago ... With all due deference to Gov. Evans—who after all said and done, makes a pretty fine old woman, if he had come out here with scarce a cent as Governor of Colorado, he might have stood a much better chance for the Senate than now ... He has been ruined by those that have pimped for him—fawned on him—puppy licked him—soft sawdered him—and in the dark—stabbed him. He was never made for politics or office hunting. We would advise him to go back to Chicago and Evanston, lay his politics on the shelf, endow a Methodist Church with his large fortune, and leave Sam (Elbert) his cast of clothing, and good name.

The barrage of unfavorable and unbridled hostility towards Evans was accelerated after the emergence of the real story of what happened at Sand Creek. Many historians believe that it was in reaction to this hateful, and in her eyes undeserved, criticism that Margaret Evans decided to get away from Denver, and even from the United States, to spend some months in London.

From several passages in their correspondence, it is obvious that Evans made a commitment to his wife to avoid any further attempts to win political office after the failure of the statehood efforts. On March 8, 1876, in a letter from London, Margaret reminded her husband, "Do not on any account swerve for an instant in your determination to have nothing to do with politics—you must not be classed among that class."

In seeking to understand why Anne Evans, at the end of a long life filled with contributions to the cultural life of Denver and Colorado, chose to order the destruction of all her personal papers, it may be relevant to remember her mother's hurtful experience of adverse media publicity as well as the many bitter newspaper attacks on her brother William, in whose household Anne spent her adult life.

6

A Birth in London and an Uncommon Childhood

I don't believe I can stand this absence from you much longer. Since I got home I have a constant feeling that I must go to you or have you come to me—I am sure it is not the way for us to live happily; for even should you improve to perfection, and I make piles of money, if it takes all of our lives to do so and we are apart during the time, when and where would come our enjoyment?
—Letter from Governor John Evans to his wife Margaret,
July 2, 1876

Margaret Leaves Denver for Europe

Margaret Evans developed a yearning to get far away from Denver and Colorado. Partly, this was a result of the constant stream of problems preoccupying her husband and the virulent criticism of him in some of the local newspapers. Perhaps also she was tired of the very limited cultural opportunities in Denver and missed intensely the varied offerings and welcome anonymity she found in European cities. Whatever the source of her restless desire to travel, it evoked a sympathetic and supportive response from her husband. By May of 1870, the Denver and Pacific Railroad project to link Denver with Cheyenne—the connection to the transcontinental route—was almost finished. Governor Evans' finances were in good shape. He escorted Margaret, Willie and Evan to New York and saw them safely onto a ship bound for London. Margaret suffered acutely from seasickness. John Evans worried constantly in his letters about her health, always fearing that she may be concealing problems from him. It seems that she was in the very early stages of a new pregnancy when she embarked, and this likely contributed to a difficult passage. On the return journey, Evans applied his always-inventive mind to Margaret's problems of travel sickness.

Evans returned to Denver to oversee the completion of the Denver Pacific railroad. Since he was a leader in developing many of the new lines that followed this watershed event, he frequently needed to travel to secure funding from eastern and international financiers based in New York, and even in London and Amsterdam. Depending on the economic interests of their owners, his ventures were supported in some of the Territory's newspapers and vilified to a point of libel in others. It is a safe bet that Margaret Evans was glad to be far away when she received selected Colorado news items from her husband about his challenges, and the continuing and heated public discussion of his organizational abilities and trust-worthiness of character.

Anne is born in London

In November of 1870, Governor Evans sailed to England to visit the family. He stayed in London for the birth of their daughter, Anne, on January 23, 1871. By this time, Willie was enrolled in an English boarding school. While the Governor felt obligated to return to the States to take care of his business interests, Margaret did not feel ready to face another seasick voyage, and perhaps decided that it was too soon for her baby daughter to travel so far.

Evans came back to Denver in March and returned to London in the late summer. After doing some traveling in Europe with the family, they would all make the return journey across the Atlantic in the fall. It is unclear whether Margaret, seven-year-old Evan, and baby Anne actually did any traveling on the Continent with the Governor when he returned in August, or whether they stayed on in London while John Evans and 16-year-old Willie took a rapid trip about the Continent.

News of the terrible Chicago Fire of October 8 and 9 reached the Governor in Switzerland. The fire demolished the spacious home of the Orrington Lunts but did not destroy enough of Evans' properties to make him feel it necessary to return home immediately. His major investment in the center of Chicago—the Evans Block—had been sold just before he left for England.[1] The Governor and his son went on to visit a number of cities in Italy before returning to London.

Return to Denver

The whole family boarded ship in November, 1871, with an invention of John's installed on Margaret's berth. This was an arrangement whereby the bed remained level whatever the motion of the ship. Kelsey observes that the invention must have been successful, because Margaret felt comfortable some years later in taking another major trip abroad. The family arrived back in Denver on December 9, 1871.

"Annie's" World

For the first 25 years of her life, Anne Evans was known as Annie, in newspaper references as well as at home. From December 1871 to the spring of 1875, the years of Annie's young childhood, fall and winter were spent in Denver, and most of the summer months in the lovely, cool world of the Evans/Elbert (Kuhlborne) ranch in the foothills, above the small resort community of Evergreen. Edgar McMechen, in his biography of John Evans[2], makes it quite clear that Evans himself was not a fan of spending time in the great outdoors, just for the sake of breathing in the clean air or enjoying the magnificent mountain views.

John Evans came from a farming background. Though he early resolved to leave that way of life behind and make his living in a more challenging urban setting, his view of land was that of a farmer. It was to be used for human purposes: to be logged, to serve as pasture for cattle, cultivated for crops, or built on. The Governor once tried trout fishing on the ranch, "attacking the sport with his always admirable patience and persistence. With an old gray shawl wrapped about his shoulders, to prevent a drenching from the wet willows, he cast, hour after hour, 'from morn to noon to dewy eve,' and at sundown, he had as many fish as at the break of day. He decided that he had exhausted all the possibilities of the art, and thereafter confined his interest to trout that appeared, brown and crisp, upon his plate."[3] The rest of the Evans' family, however, appreciated the beauty of the land and the children loved the freedom to explore and play in the wild environment.

Anne's two brothers were too old to be playmates for her. She and Willie, 16 years older, were almost a generation apart. The eight-year gap between Annie and Evan was still too great for him to be interested in the same activities as his much younger sister.

Therefore, she grew up relying on her own resources and was quick to make friends with children her own age.

Willie's first school in Denver was the Colorado Seminary, a small boys' preparatory school that was the forerunner of the University of Denver. Classes there started in November of 1864. The school was housed in a new building on Arapahoe Street, across the road from the Evans home. The institution was founded in an expansive and optimistic spirit by Governor Evans and a number of other leading citizens who were interested in promoting education in the new settlement. Their eventual goal was to found a Methodist Seminary and University along the lines of Northwestern, but they started with a preparatory school because there was no high school in the Territory to prepare students for university studies. The economy became quite depressed in the later 1860s, and the school had to be closed in 1867. Will apparently attended one or two other short-lived schools in Denver as well as an English boarding school while the family was in England. In the fall of 1873, he entered Northwestern University as a freshman. His father took advantage of the lifetime certificate he had purchased many years earlier.

Following the family's return from Europe, Governor Evans' time and energies continued to be invested in a variety of business enterprises, primarily railroads, and efforts aimed at community improvement. Anne Evans is quoted as saying that her memory of home in her childhood was

> ... a feeling of continuous and subdued excitement. If children were too boisterous at play, they were reminded that their father was deep in concentration and must not be disturbed. He received visits from friendly Ute Indians, became interested in mining and smelting and worked hard on his various railroad ventures.[4]

Margaret Evans resumed her involvement in Denver's rather minimal literary and artistic activities, and undertook more entertaining in her newly expanded home and gardens. All accounts of her style of entertaining note that it was "sober," in the sense that alcohol was never involved, yet the hospitality was said to have been gracious and enjoyable.

A Second Stay in Europe for Margaret, Evan and Annie

However, a worrying health problem developed. Margaret began to have violent headaches. Exactly when a New York physician was consulted about this problem is not clear, but a diagnosis of a possible "tumor or abscess in or under the dura mater" was made.[5]

The hope that this problem might be relieved by a change in climate was one of the considerations in Margaret's decision to make another extended trip to Europe. Probably more important was her continued sensitivity to the intermittent harsh criticism of her husband's business and civic activities in some of the contentious local newspapers, and ongoing dissatisfaction with the shortage of congenial friends in the Territory. One *Rocky Mountain News* article later observed that Margaret did not make friends easily.[6] We have seen that she could be quite judgmental in her evaluations of new acquaintances. Compared with the activities available to her in London and on the Continent, the opportunities in Denver for participation in stimulating social, cultural and educational experiences were severely limited. Margaret Evans made plans to travel again to Europe with her children. Eleven-year-old Evan left for a European visit with Samuel Elbert in October of 1874, with arrangements to meet the rest of the family in England in the spring.

John Evans, Margaret and 4-year-old Anne embarked on a Cunard liner for England in May of 1875. They spent part of the summer traveling in Britain and on the Continent. Evans was also attempting to secure financing for his latest railroad venture. He arranged to rent a London townhouse for his family at 39 Arundel Gardens in Notting Hill. Evans and Samuel Elbert then returned to Denver where they had business investments, many of them joint enterprises that needed their attention.

Faithful Correspondence

John Evans and his wife wrote to each other every week during this extended separation. Their correspondence sheds light on their relationship, views on parenting, and activities while living apart. During much of Margaret's second stay in Europe, John wrote to her about his serious worries over money. He was involved in a complex of business interests and problems including investments in the Town of Morrison and its stone quarries, responsibility for the frequently washed-out Bear Creek Wagon Road from Morrison to Evergreen, and the Denver, South Park and Pacific Railroad. This South Park venture was probably the most draining and problem-filled project in Evans' long and varied business career. "In the South Park firm, as in the Denver Pacific, John Evans was the driving force."[7] Its history was dogged by competition from other powerful railroad interests, lack of capital, and the depressed economy resulting from the Panic of 1873.

The Long Depression

What became known as the Long Depression started with a series of bank failures resulting from a vast over-expansion of the nation's railroad network after the Civil War, fueled by years of unregulated, speculative credit. The New York Stock Exchange was closed for 10 days, one quarter of the nation's railroads went bankrupt, and unemployment rose to 14 percent by 1876. At one point, having secured a good manager, Evans told Margaret he was contemplating getting out of the South Park enterprise altogether.[8] However, he realized, not modestly but probably accurately, that "they could not get on without me." The Morrison Stone, Lime, and Townsite Company had been so mismanaged during Evans' earlier absence in Europe that it became impossible to avoid bankruptcy. "Mr. Bailey has been selling the Stone Company (products) for half its true cost, sending it hopelessly into debt."[9] Evans felt keenly the responsibility of the failure and wrote to Margaret "my honor is at stake in many of the debts and I must raise the money to put them right."

From time to time in their correspondence, the issues that had made Margaret so happy to leave Denver came to the fore. On March 8, 1876, after reading some articles in Denver newspapers which her husband had sent to her, she unleashed her anger at their contents. She was especially disturbed by an editorial in the *Rocky Mountain News*, which she hoped had not been written by Mr. Byers.

> I could not keep the tears back when I reflected what you had endured of insult and ingratitude ... it does seem that invective treachery has been everywhere the order—one consolation, it has not changed in the least your character; you seem so unaffected as though you wore an armor that perfidy and meanness *could never* penetrate.[10]

Margaret noted and freely confessed, "What a different testimony must I give; I know it is wicked and degrading to my soul but I would grind them every one to powder if I had the power."[11] A little later, she lamented,

—if you could only arrange business so that we *need never* look upon their *hateful, hateful* faces again, *I should be glad*—but I suppose you could never be happy unless you are doing something to promote the prosperity of Denver and I must be content.[12]

In one poignant passage, John wrote to Margaret that her recent letter to him had "made me feel so sad that I cannot get over it. I have read it over and over and each time it brought my heart into my mouth and the tears to my eyes."

> … The clause in your letter that affected me the most deeply was in winding up your horrible account of our Colorado experience. You say 'but our married life and home has been happy in spite of it all. If we never see each other again you will bear to the grave my deepest thanks for your tender love and care.' I shall never be able to read that without weeping—and even the writing now has baptized this letter with a tear.

Governor Evans tried hard to bring Margaret's attention to developments that might soften her unpleasant memories of life in Denver and encourage her to look forward to returning. On November 28, 1875, he assured her that, in spite of encouragement from influential friends, he was holding firm in his opposition to standing for election to the Senate.

One day in June of the following year, he told her, "You are the most popular lady in Colorado by all odds … Governor Elbert said that Mr. Marsh of Black Hawk, Speaker of the House when he was Governor, who attended your parties, spoke in the highest terms of compliment to your elegant taste and refinement. Everybody I meet nearly who knows you asks to be remembered."[13] A week later, he wrote very sweetly to Margaret, telling her how much he missed her charming, old-fashioned, cordial and kind welcome home, "which in days of yore so often made me happy."[14] "I never see a beautiful thing but I think of you," he told her. In July when he was facing the possibility of selling their Denver home in order to pay his South Park Rail Road assessments, he reminded her that their house "is the nicest place in Denver and you have no idea how beautiful Denver has become by the growth of trees and the elegant grass yards and nice houses."[15]

After Margaret made a move from London to Belgium, he addressed directly her dislike for Denver.

> You seem so averse to Denver that perhaps we would better buy a house in Brussels or some nice place over there and you live in it—I'll visit you as often as I can! But joking aside, how would you like me to be Minister to Brussels ... if Hayes is elected I guess I could get an appointment by a systematic effort. But I have such a supreme contempt for all political life that I should be sorry to take even that and more especially if I had to ask for it.[16]

Evans also kept his wife informed about developments in Denver and Colorado. In March, Evans told his wife cheerfully that he thought he had the whole city on his side in the railroad business. "The *Mirror* has flung dirt but it is so low that nobody minds it anymore." In June he noted that Margaret's brother, Horace, was with Sunie, to "get her off" to London as soon as possible.

> He will look in at the Centennial Great Show in Philadelphia. They say it has a fine display of art from abroad with some of home production that are respectable. I doubt if you would enjoy it though ... You would not have so good a time as among the cathedrals of Europe.

Evans later mentioned that he himself visited the Show on his way to New York to sail for London, and pronounced it "a great show but very crowded."[17] In July, he reported that people "are suffering terribly from the heat—in fact our whole county is very oppressively hot—except up in the mountains where it is always Kuhl." On August 9, he did not conceal from her news "that horrible pest for Colorado, the grasshoppers, have come in myriads again and taken all our late crops in many parts of Colorado. We drove them off of our vineyard and garden and saved them." He noted that the pests had come for three years in succession and feared many farmers would leave.

John Evans' account of the country's excitement over the Presidential election sounded a familiar note to those of us who remember the Bush-Gore election. "Hayes may be elected by one electoral vote and Democrats are talking of civil war if Hayes is counted in." Hayes' Democratic opponent, Samuel Tilden, in fact won the popular vote but finally lost the Electoral College vote after Hayes agreed to terms set forth by Southern Democrats about ending the Reconstruction era and including at least one Southerner in his cabinet. Evans told Margaret he believed that all the excitement would die down after the election was finally decided.

London's Cultural and Social Offerings

Margaret developed an active social and cultural life in London. Her husband wrote, perhaps a little ironically, "I am glad you keep good company and visit Lord Darby's and Countess Cowper's, etc.—it sounds a little aristocratic but I have no doubt is very entertaining." In another letter, he commented,

> So you are off attending concerts with the Queen. After all the fun we poke at the Queen she is really the best and most stable government in all Europe … And I am sometimes led to the question if it is not even better than a republican government—the tendency to corruption and the danger of popular tumults and popular errors in our own country are fearful to contemplate.[18]

Later, he responded to a letter of hers in which she wrote of actually seeing the Queen, "and so your grand vision of royalty has been realized—I am glad you had a good sight of her—it must have been more satisfactory than mine—seeing but for a moment as she passed in her coach while I stood on the platform at the Station."

From her comfortable sitting room in Notting Hill, Margaret wrote that she only had time for a few lines as she was going to a concert where Mrs. Schumann was playing.

> She is a great pianist—her husband's compositions were not appreciated until she interpreted them to the public and now nothing so popular with educated musicians. Her husband died of delirium tremens and in a mad house.[19]

News of the Children

John and Margaret also wrote to each other about the activities of their children. He had a period of anxiety when Willie was home in November of 1875. He was dismayed that his son was enchanted with the prospect of becoming a rancher and "contemplating leaving college before his course is finished." He urged Margaret to "get him cooled off if you can on his 'Kuhlborne' fever."[20] On March 13, 1876, John informed his wife,

> Will sent me his account current with an apology for so much use-less expenditure and a promise to be more careful. He said the making up of his accounts brought to his attention many items that might have been dispensed with. Don't forget to have Evan make up *full* and truthful accounts. Let's try to bring them up to be honest whatever else they may be. 'It is the jewel, is honesty' as the English would say it. Kiss Annie and give her love from Papa. Love to my brave boy Evan and kind regards to the rest of your household.[21]

On June 16, he told Margaret that, while he was attending commencement exercises at Northwestern, he had found out that their son was slacking on his studies and spending too much time and energy on the baseball team. John wrote on August 8 that he had just returned with Governor Elbert from Kuhlborne. "The place looks beautiful—more lovely than ever before and only wants you and the two children and Sunie to make it perfectly charming. It is by all pronounced the prettiest place in Colorado." He went on to tell her,

> A party go up to the top of Mt. Evans tomorrow—the trail has been prepared and all things promise a nice trip. They go up to timberline after dinner (a midday meal) and camp overnight then ascend early and get the grandest view in all Colorado ...

After the trip, Will apparently came down with a sore throat. Evans wrote that they "went up to Dr. Bancroft and got a prescription for him."

Dr. Frederick J. Bancroft had a life and accomplishments that were similar to those of John Evans in energy and diversity. The Bancrofts were good friends of John and Margaret Evans in Denver and both had summer homes on ranches in the Evergreen area.

About Will, John wrote, "He is a very nice boy. Indeed, we have great reason to be thankful for and proud of our children. May they be preserved to lives of usefulness in the world and to an eternity of bliss thereafter." Evans reported in his letter of September 3, Will had come down from Kuhlborne and shown his father Margaret's latest letter as well as a photograph she had sent him of Annie. John commented to Margaret, "How she has grown. She is quite pretty and I judge will make a very handsome young lady if she meets with no mishap to mar the prospect."

Margaret in turn wrote to her husband about Annie and Evan. "We have a new arrival in the shape of a kitten. Annie is delighted but I am not so pleased although the mice are getting troublesome in the kitchen." In the same letter in which she wrote about Mrs. Schumann's concert, she noted that Evan would be home from boarding school when she returned, and "I shall see his dear face."[22] A little later, she wrote that Annie was well and expecting her two little neighbors this afternoon to tea. "Great orders for tea are being impressed upon Cook which I must modify somewhat." On July 16, John let Margaret know that her letter of June 28 was read with great interest. "... The little description you gave of your surroundings—Sunie in the drawing room—Annie bidding good morning and off to play etc. brought all vividly to view in imagination." On August 4, John reacted to Margaret's news that the proprietor of the school that Evan was attending—the same one that Will attended during their first English sojourn—was planning to close it. "Well I am really sorry Mr. Shaw gave up his school, on Evan's account. It was such a nice place and the moral and religious atmosphere around it was so good ... we must make the best of it and be thankful for the good our boys have derived already."

It is clear from the letters that they missed each other greatly. Governor Evans wrote more frequently about his feelings on this score. December 6, 1875, he wrote, "I am left the sole occupant of our mansion, oh! That you could just step in and be with me in person, as you are in my warm love and vivid imagination tonight." On January 16, 1876, he told her,

How I do wish I were there with you and could remain there for a number of years until all the turmoils and annoyances of my position here were over. I have wanted to see and be with you worse during the past week than ever since we left you. Once in a while it comes over me that I must come to see you. But Lord knows when I can leave. There is more business on my hands than four men ought to do, and every part of it so dependent upon my management that I can't leave it a day.

On March 6, 1876, Evans responded to the latest letter from his wife, "And dear little Annie has lost her appetite. Oh! How I do want to see her and Evan and you. I'm very much annoyed with the rail road and sometimes feel like leaving it all to its fate and hie me away to Maggie." On March 8, she wished, "I could get a letter from you letting me know that you are coming and when, but I must possess my soul in patience. I know that you will come as soon as you can, in justice to all."

On July 16, he proposed,

> I guess when I get you by my side again I will keep you there—a long time ago I reasoned not to let you leave me again and now it is going on a year since I left you in a foreign land to shift for yourself. But circumstances alter plans and I suppose as you say we would better resolve to be happy and go on with our work regardless of others—I learn every day and I know you do—But how different our schools.

Health Anxieties

Part of John Evans' concern at being separated from Margaret was his constant worry over her health and that of the children. They reported regularly to one another about health problems. Margaret told John, "My cold has all but disappeared and it is the same with Annie. Nurse's is more obstinate and her coughing paroxysms are fearful and not exactly appetizing when they seize her at about mealtime."[23] John wrote that he had been sick with what Dr. Bancroft had called influenza.[24] There was quite a correspondence later on in 1876 when Margaret refused to send him a photograph she had taken, on the grounds that she looked too cadaverous to let him see her face. She assured him that she was well, and sent him a card giving her weight at 161 lbs. as proof, for which he was grateful. In late September, Margaret wrote from Belgium that her headaches had returned, and that a doctor she had consulted had rather dismissed her symptoms as trivial. Her husband responded with sympathy and practical recommendations,

> I got the letter in which you say your head troubles you now. I fear the troubles you had in moving and your anxiety on account of money, and your concern for me, have given you a setback that may not be so easily recovered from, and I fear you neglected your

pills which are so essential, and am a little afraid of wine and stimulants ... don't fatigue yourself again under any circumstances whatever so as to make your neck feel thick nor allow your bowels to become so costive as to require straining in the least—I think the daily use of a cathartic the best possible treatment for your head. I am so very afraid you have been saving money at the expense of your precious health.

Financial Concerns

The impact of the Governor's increasing financial difficulties on Margaret was that he started to include in his weekly letters to her a plea that she economize on expenses. Tensions between them rose when Margaret wrote to both her brother Horace Gray and Samuel Elbert telling them of her anxiety over her husband's financial troubles and asking them if it would be wise for her to come home. "I am mortified," wrote John to her, "I fear they think I am mean to you ... and that this is the cause of your extraordinary proposition about breaking up and coming home."[25] Margaret was quite upset about this scolding,

> Everybody wrote so dismally and it seemed as though you were keeping back worse troubles ... You ought not to have said that I was acting under resentment, and I do not like it, but I forgive you and feel sorry for all the trouble I have caused you.[26]

John made his own apologies to his wife, "I am very sorry you got so much disturbed that I should have said anything to wound your feelings in my letter. But I am forgiven and so may express my mind freely again."[27] John's financial troubles were not over, however. He was still trying to raise capital for the South Park Rail Road project and hoping to pay off the debts of the ill-fated Morrison investments. And so the requests to Margaret to economize wherever possible continued. "It will be a great relief if you can get the expenses down. Remember they have been very heavy for the past year for only you and Annie—and it will not be by any means necessary to keep them up to that standard."[28] After Margaret's brother Horace proposed, and Evans agreed, that Sunie Lowell should be sent to England to join Margaret, John wrote to ask if she might then consider doing without the services of the nurse (nanny) who helped with the care of the children.[29] Evan was enrolled in an

English boarding school, but was home for the holidays, and Annie was only four and home all the time. This suggestion did not go down well. Later in July, John wrote,

> I have written a suggestion that you give up the nurse. But I did not fully realize the terrible trial it would be to you to do so or my heart would have failed me on your account. Annie is little and could soon get over it but for you it would be too hard—and for the nurse it would be horrible.[30]

Still requests for financial restraint continued. He tried to clarify for his wife the reasons for his concern about family finances, "Now you entirely mistake my admonitions to economy." He explained that it was not any censure over the past, the cost of the house, Evan's school, etc., which were mostly his arrangements anyhow,

> ... we are not now so well off as then. Nor do I see exactly how I am going to get through. But I have at divers times in my life had close work and hard pinches and always got through so far. And I propose to come through now honorably and squarely if I have to sacrifice half I am worth to do so. It is to save all we can consistently I ask for Economy in the future so I may be spared the necessity of making heavy sacrifices to get the money.

Margaret decided not to renew the lease on the Notting Hill house, but to move to Antwerp where there would be new stimulation and cheaper living in a pension. The thought of her coping alone with the breaking up of the London household and the move to another country worried John greatly. He mentioned again in this letter that he has considered selling their house for $30,000, but that this probably would not be possible in the current economic climate, "Since we were struggling to build the Union Pacific Railroad, we have not had such dull times in Denver as at the present time." He ends the letter with a plea for her to consider the totality of their possible future life in Denver and not to dwell on the dark side of their past experiences:

> Now my precious wife do not fret so much about the evil side of human nature we see in Colorado—it is true we have been assailed—or at least I have—but who that is of any account has

not—and then we have always had warm and earnest friends here and have yet. And you are esteemed and admired by almost everybody—I am sure you could be very happy in Denver if I was clean free from political alliances and aspirations as I most assuredly am—There are many very nice people here—more than formerly and we could select our friends and greatly enjoy life ... if we can only get the railroad built it will be a good thing to take attention and give me a salary and some of my friends places—if we can only get free from the present entanglement I will promise not to ask you to Economize again and in fact will be but too proud to give you every enjoyment I can find.[31]

Plans for Return to Denver

It was arranged that Evan, on his return from Europe, would attend Northwestern University along with Will. They would both live in the Evans' home in Evanston, where "Evan is to sleep with Will and study in their chamber while Will studies in the front parlor."[32] In this last letter written before sailing for Europe, John wrote that he "will pass Evan and Sunie on the open sea returning for the United States." John had visited Evanston on his way to New York, where he found that "Orrington and Cornelia were glad to see me." He then traveled to see many relatives in Cincinnati, and went up and stayed "with my good old mother—she of course was glad to see me. Is in quite good health and has just had a host of yearly meeting friends to stop with her."[33]

John asked Margaret to meet him with the family in London because he thought that his business there—trying to sell some of the South Park bonds—would take about a month. They then traveled through Belgium and France and spent the winter in Italy.[34]

They returned to Denver in April of 1877. Annie was 6 years old and the only young child now in the household. Her older brother Will was to graduate from Northwestern at its 19th Annual Commencement on June 21, 1877. He returned as a young man to work in Denver and live in the family home at 14th and Arapahoe.

7

Denver School Days, "Wild, Free" Mountain Summers

*Anne and I were boon companions. Anne always called
me Bobby and I called her Bill, to the great amusement
of the younger generation. One of them was heard to say
(years later), 'As long as it's Cousin Anne and Cousin
Louise everything was all right, but when it's Bobby and
Billy, it's goodbye sense. We had a wild, free life which is
a very real treasure in memory.'*
                —Memoir of Louise Elbert Everett
                Collection of Ethelind Elbert Austin

Miss Street's School

One of Margaret's early friends in Denver was Miss Mary J. Street,
who had come to Denver with her mother not long after the arrival
of Governor Evans and his wife. Mary Street and Margaret Evans
enjoyed getting together to practice their French and talk about
literature and art. According to historian Allen Breck, it was Margaret
Evans who persuaded Miss Street to "open a school and take Anne
as her first pupil."[1] Miss Street's School, located at Fifteenth Avenue
and Court Place, made its debut in September of 1878 when Anne
was seven and a half years old. She was developing into a lively,
outgoing tomboy who cared little for the niceties of grooming and
pretty dresses but loved playing outdoors.

A Gracious Home

Anne's mother and father continued their pattern of frequent social
entertaining. One newspaper noted that "Denver society was born in
the winter of 1864, when the Executive Mansion was opened for the
first time to members of the Legislature of the Territory." On these
occasions "lively conversations, singing, most elegant performances
upon the piano, delightful promenades to the music of the military

band and the discussion of more than bountiful repasts, occupied the time until after the witching hour of midnight."[2]

There is a little vignette of a long-gone Victorian social ritual, in which Margaret Evans participated, in the *Rocky Mountain News* for January 1, 1882. Headlined CALLS AND CARDS, with subheadings "A Complete List of Those Who Will Receive, By Whom They Will Be Assisted, And the Proper Hours Set for Calls Tomorrow, The New Year to be Properly Installed, By the Beauty, Fashion and Wealth of Denver," the article notes:

> The long list of ladies who will receive callers tomorrow speaks for itself as to how the day will be kept in Denver. The social growth of the city and State during the past year has been very rapid, and nothing gives stronger proof of this than the fact that over three hundred ladies will, in the most approved style, wish their gentlemen friends a Happy New Year.

Among the three hundred was listed "Evans, Mrs. Governor, at her residence, corner of Fourteenth and Arapahoe, assisted by Mrs. Howard Evans[3] and Mrs. Captain Gray."

Mountain Ranch Summers

Anne Evans especially loved the summers spent up on the Kuhlborne (Evans/Elbert) Ranch. In those early days, the Evans family, Samuel Elbert, and their many guests and relatives stayed in one main log house, known as the Cottage or the Cottage Yard, built around 1869.

Anne's best summer friend was Louise Elbert, a niece of Samuel Elbert, one of the six children of his brother Benjamin. Louise spent many summers as a girl and young woman on the Ranch. According to her nephew, "Louise and Anne Evans were bosom friends. They called each other Bob and Bill and they both smoked. And that was considered very daring. And I don't know whether they enjoyed it, but they did do it."[4] Louise herself expanded on this impression in an unpublished manuscript about her own life, from which the quotation at the beginning of this chapter is taken.

Many years later, Louise and her husband, Leonard Everett, built their own summer home on a portion of the Evans/Elbert Ranch.[5] Louise was a generous woman who had no children of her own, but helped to put eight nieces and nephews through college, including Ethelind Elbert and her brother, Sam. These two, as children, spent many summers on the ranch. At 90 years old, Ethelind Austin was still enjoying riding horseback and spending summers in the 1909 home built for her Aunt Louise Elbert Everett.

In an interview Ethelind said that her father, Ben, Louise's brother, never came to the ranch because he found Louise 'too bossy.' Ethelind too, found Aunt Louise something of an autocrat—for example, she insisted that the children, no matter what games they were engaged in or how much fun they were having, must be home and cleaned up for tea at four o'clock in the afternoon. But her father, she said, was just as bad as Louise, because he too liked on all occasions to be the boss. Her mother would come sometimes, but not until late in the summer because the family were farmers and summers were their busiest time. When very young, Ethelind and her brother would travel with a nurse on the train overnight from Iowa to Denver, getting into Union Station around 8 in the morning. There they were met by one Leslie Mason, whose mother kept a boarding house in Brookvale, a once thriving little summer resort on Upper Bear Creek. Ethelind remembers that the old road up Bear Creek Canyon from Morrison to Evergreen used to criss-cross the creek many times (it therefore was frequently flooded out) and Mason used to get out of the car every time they crossed the creek with a can, which he filled with water to put in the radiator. So the drive took a long time. Once safely installed at the ranch, the children spent the entire summer there, rarely going even into Evergreen, and to Denver only on very special occasions.

Ethelind Austin's Reminiscences of "Aunt Anne"

Two stories about Anne as a child came from Ethelind Austin.[6] Ethelind dearly loved "Aunt Anne," as Anne Evans was called by all the summer colony's children, and enjoyed hearing about her childish exploits. The "red petticoat" story was a favorite. When Anne was a child of around seven or eight, it was the custom for girls to wear long skirts and, if the weather was chilly, they added a bright red petticoat underneath. One day, Anne was in a large meadow on the ranch, which for some reason was known as the Silver Trumpet,[7] when the thought struck her that this was a great place to turn somersaults. "I will turn a mile of somersaults," she said to herself and started out vigorously. At that time cattle, including one or two bulls, were pastured on the ranch every summer. When one bull saw the whirling red petticoat, he came roaring after Anne.

Only her quick thinking, in running to the nearest tree and climbing it, saved her from what could have been a really unpleasant encounter. She had to wait in the tree until someone came along and rescued her.

Another story, when Anne was a little older, involved "Dutch John," whom Ethelind understood to have been an immigrant from Holland. (Another source, which would rather spoil the details of this story, says that his surname was Walsh and he came from Wales.) He had built himself a little cabin on land adjacent to the Evans Ranch. A tireless prospector, he had dug a long tunnel into a nearby mountain, hoping to strike gold. But, like most prospectors who tried their luck in the Evergreen area, he struck out.[8] So Dutch John used to do odd jobs for his wealthier neighbors. Anne loved to ride for hours in the wilderness area around the ranch, on the slopes of the 14,000 foot Mount Evans. Because it truly was wilderness in those early days, the family did not want their little girl venturing out alone. They hired Dutch John to go riding with her. According to Ethelind's version of the story, Dutch John started almost every sentence with "Mein Gott" (My God).

One day they were riding quite far from the ranch, when Dutch John suddenly said, "Mein Gott, Miss Annie, but there is a corpse." He got off his horse, and sure enough there was a dead man lying face down. Dutch John searched his pockets and found a wallet with over a hundred dollars in it. This was a lot of money in those days. Dutch John was very excited, "Mein Gott, Miss Annie, we tell nobody nuttings about this!"

But Miss Annie had other ideas. "Dutch John, we will go straight home and tell my father, the Governor." Although she was young, she remembered hearing that two men had come through the ranch in the fall, saying they were looking for work and asking about the way on beyond the ranch, but that only one of them had returned. Back in Idaho Springs, the man who returned had been tackled by the wife of the other man: "Where is my husband. What have you done with him? You went off together." He answered, "I don't know where he is. We just separated." The sheriff put the poor fellow in jail and the good citizens were getting ready to lynch him. As soon as Annie told her father what she and Dutch John had found, the Governor sent a letter to the Sheriff by a messenger on horseback, telling him, "Release this man you have in jail. He obviously did not kill his companion. The man died just a day or two ago of exposure. His wallet was not stolen." So they released the prisoner and gave the widow the wallet with the hundred dollars. According to Ethelind, the widow was much happier with the money than she would have been to have the husband back.

Horace Fletcher Lunt's Memories

Another account of the ranch and of Anne's presence there as a teenager in the 1880s is contained in a long letter written by Horace Fletcher Lunt to his nephew, Phelps Dodge. Horace Fletcher and his sister, Regina, Phelps' mother, were children of Judge Horace Gray Lunt. Judge Lunt was the son of Margaret Evans' sister, Cornelia, and Orrington Lunt. He grew up in Evanston, graduated from Harvard, and eventually settled in Colorado Springs. His son, Horace Fletcher Lunt, spent many summers as a child on the Evans Ranch. In July of 1935, Horace wrote to Phelps, "I have been pondering the matter of reminiscences of the ranch, ever since I came home from the Fourth of July celebration."[9] In his account he has a useful five pages about the Evans, Lunt and Elbert families.

Anne Evans and Horace F. Lunt, Summer of 1880 (or 1881), Courtesy Margaret E. Hayden

> I first saw the ranch when I was taken from Evanston on a visit to Denver by Grandfather and Grandmother (Orrington and Cornelia Lunt). I was five years old at the time, 1880, and had a new kilt suit to wear on the trip ... At that time, the Evanses lived in a fairly large house on the corner of Fourteenth and Arapahoe Streets, where the Tramway Building now stands. They had a big yard, which went down to, or nearly to, Cherry Creek. It contained various stables, sheds, and gardens and was a wonderful place to play ... During the course of our visit we spent some time at the ranch. My recollections of that visit are pretty vague and fragmentary. I remember

there was an expedition to the top of Mount Evans, I think under the guidance of Cousin Will. Anne and Grandfather went, representing the extreme age limits. It was Anne's first ascent of the peak.[10]

The Cottage Yard, Evans Ranch, Courtesy Margaret E. Hayden

After his family moved to Colorado Springs in 1887, Horace was up at the ranch "for more or less extended visits every summer." He noted that it was much more remote before the automobile came along and so, "Naturally, when we went up, we stayed for a considerable time." The quickest way to get to the ranch at that time "was to take the train to Idaho Springs and drive over the hill. As nearly as I can remember, it took about two hours on the train and then three hours or more over Squaw Pass. That was some road, up 2500 feet from Idaho Springs and then down 1700 feet to the ranch in eight miles!" An alternate route was to take a train to Morrison and a stage from there to Evergreen.

The stage was a three-seated spring wagon with two horses, driven by an old man with a long beard, at a rather slow pace ... Occasionally the road in lower Bear Creek would get washed out, and we would have to go up Turkey Creek and across through what is now Indian Hills. In any case, it was a fairly long day's drive.

That is a far cry from today's drive time when some year-round residents of the Evans Ranch commute daily to Denver. With the coming of Interstate-70, the ride from the ranch to the center of the city takes only about one and a quarter hours.

Horace Lunt described life in the Cottage:

> It had ... a good many rooms without being very large and was entirely without 'modern conveniences.' Running water was provided by a little ditch from Metz Creek. Just outside the house it ran through a wooden trough with a drop under which a pail or a pitcher could be filled. There was a laundry shack with a stove to heat water and on Sunday mornings all the kids had to take baths. While one bathed, the water was heating for the next one. There was a porch on three sides of the house and sometimes we used to have the dining table out and eat on one of them. The pillars that supported the porch roof had ledges a foot or so above the floor. Judge Elbert used to keep a corncob pipe on each of the front pillars so he would always have one handy. (I remember borrowing one surreptitiously and trying it out with the most unpleasant results.)[11]

The Cottage was a large, two-story, timber building with gambrel roofs and dormer windows.[12] Everyone who stayed there was expected to make "their early morning ablutions"[13] at a rock waterfall by a big pine tree. "A big bench held a basin and pitcher while towels and washcloths hung on antlers."

The stable summer population consisted mainly of women and children, with the men visiting for a few days as they were able. In the early days this meant Margaret Evans with Willie, Evan and Anne, Cousin Horace Gray Lunt and Louise Elbert. After the marriage of William (Willie) Evans and Cornelia Lunt Gray in 1883, Cornelia brought their children, John, Margaret, Katharine and Josephine. Samuel Elbert (co-owner of the property) apparently was at the ranch quite often, as was William Evans, even after his marriage and increasing business responsibilities. But Governor Evans was there less frequently. This core of residents was supplemented by visiting Evans, Gray and Lunt relatives, as well as invited friends, so that, "the 'good many rooms' were often filled to capacity."[14]

Horace Lunt recorded that "Anne was my most constant companion and was practically always there when I was." The children spent their days in the outdoors, riding, fishing, hiking, exploring, and "made an occasional expedition to Idaho Springs or Ever-green."[15] Anne continued to be physically adventurous. "At times when there weren't a lot of other people around who had to be looked after, Anne and I, with Louise if she were there, used to go on exploring expeditions, frequently where there weren't any trails … When Aunt Margaret was there we had to be sure to get home before supper time because she worried a lot if we did not show up." However, when Cornelia, William Evans' wife, was in charge, things were more relaxed. "I remember once when we drifted in about nine o'clock and asked her if she hadn't been worried, she said, 'Oh, no. I knew you would get back sometime."[16]

The Cottage Yard, Evans Ranch, pictured left to right: Fletcher Lunt, Anne Evans, Katharine Evans, Louise Elbert Everett, Leonard Everett, Margaret Evans, Courtesy Margaret E. Hayden

Occasionally, something happened that could have been dis-astrous. "There always seemed to be plenty of ponies for everyone to ride," Horace remembered.

There was a bay named Stella that was rather excitable and once threw Anne onto her head and knocked her unconscious, which scared Louise and me almost to death as there were no older members of the family around at the time. However, by the time we had gotten a doctor over from Idaho Springs she had come around all right.[17]

In the evenings, a tradition developed which lasted until the outbreak of World War II (after which everything changed). Margaret Evans started it—reading classic books from beginning to end— evening after quiet evening. Sometimes reading continued in the daytime too, if it was raining too hard for the children to be outside. Horace Lunt mentioned *Ivanhoe*, *War and Peace*, "and such like books."[18] Louise Elbert Everett remembered that "Anne's mother, Mrs. Evans, used to read to us at night from John Fiske's works.[19] We lay on the floor by the fire while she read. She had a way of suddenly saying, 'You girls are asleep!' So Anne used to stay awake while I slept and I stayed awake while she slept."[20]

Louise recalled how she and Anne continued the tradition with a new generation of children. "In the evenings after a hearty and pleasant dinner Anne and I read aloud to the younger children the Kipling stories and Dumas' *The Three Musketeers*." After the children went to bed, she recalled that the adults sat up quite late, reading aloud books by Walter Painter, Galsworthy, Conrad, H. G. Wells, Edith Wharton, Yeats, and Ibsen.[21]

Winters and Schooling in Denver

After the summer ended, it was goodbye to the ranch until the following year. Successive ranch foremen took care of the livestock, looked after the Cottage and planted crops in the spring, in the years when this was still feasible. For the children it was time once again for school. Just how long Anne attended Miss Mary Street's School is not known. The school itself thrived. William's son, Anne's beloved nephew, John Evans Sr., started there at age nine in 1893.[22] By that time the school had moved to a house on Pennsylvania Street and was accepting students from first through tenth grade.

In some biographies of Anne Evans, including the valuable and well-documented paper written as a college independent study project by Katharine Davis, a young Evans descendant,[23] it is claimed that Anne next attended Wolfe Hall, the first substantial girls' private school in Denver. Davis's information about Anne's childhood came from interviews with Katharine Evans, daughter of Anne's older brother William. Katharine Evans knew her Aunt Anne intimately, since they lived in the same household, at 1310 Bannock Street, from 1900 until Anne's death in 1941. Wolfe Hall was an early project of the Episcopal Church in Colorado.

Wolfe Hall and the Episcopalian Presence in Denver

Bishop George Maxwell Randell was consecrated on January 9, 1866, in Trinity Church, Boston, as "Missionary Bishop of Colorado and parts adjacent" and his church in Denver was named St. John's in the Wilderness. Over the years, this became St. John's Cathedral.[24] In addition to sending out missions and establishing new churches, the Bishop felt it important to establish church schools. In Denver, he decided first to establish a boarding school for young ladies. In September of 1868, Wolfe Hall was opened at Champa and Seventeenth Streets. It was housed in a "new and substantial brick edifice, fifty feet square, centrally and pleasantly located;" it was a three-story building with a mansard roof complete with cupola on top, and a picket fence surrounding it. A plaque on the Boston Building marks the site. Original financing for the school came from John D. Wolfe, a wealthy Episcopalian in New York, and his daughter.[25]

Bishop Randell was succeeded by Bishop John Franklin Spalding. The Spalding family became an integral part of the Evans family's circle of close friends. Their daughter, Elisabeth Spalding, developed into an accomplished painter, a lifelong friend of Anne Evans, and an associate in many endeavors on behalf of the arts in Denver.

Old Wolfe Hall at 17th and Champa Streets (1867), Denver Public Library Western History Collection

It was Bishop Spalding who first enlarged the Champa building and then, as mining and ranching magnates began building mansions in Capitol Hill, relocated the school to an immense and impressive—and very expensive—building on a site bordered by Thirteenth and Fourteenth Avenues and Clarkson and Emerson (formerly Venice) Streets. The new school building was finished in February, 1889, and its subsequent lineage did involve Anne Evans. In a sometimes painful fashion, described in a later chapter, Wolfe Hall became the ancestor of Kent School.

Apparently Anne's love of getting out of the house and into physically challenging games with neighborhood children continued into her teens.

> Anne … enjoyed not so much the schoolroom, but rather, the playground where she soon became the epitome of a 'tomboy.' Disregard for 'girlish' behavior came quite naturally to her. Stories of her youth are full of tickling accounts of how Anne constantly exhibited unruly tendencies, often with behavior embarrassing to her brothers and also quite unsuitable for 'the governor's daughter.'[26]

The Cottage Porch, Anne sitting between her mother Margaret and Cousin Nina, Courtesy History Colorado

A Civilizing Year

When Anne was fifteen the situation apparently became intolerable for her mother and father. They arranged for her to have a year in the more civilized environment of Evanston, entrusting her to the loving care of her much older cousin, Cornelia Gray Lunt, affectionately known as Cousin Nina (sometimes Neana, Neanie, Nina, or Nini.) Katharine Davis wrote, "One can only speculate on the reasons for her having been "shipped off." One account holds that Anne had become such a tomboy, especially influenced by Johnny Cavanaugh, the son of her father's coachman, that her parents thought it was time for her to be "straightened out."[27]

8

Life Lessons from Cousin Nina

*Oh it has been good to live—I love it. And very early
certain longings beset me not to be merely a passenger
but one of the Crew of the Great Ship we call the World*[1]
—Cornelia Gray Lunt (Nina)

The civilizing year, aimed at turning Anne into a more acceptable version of the ideal "young lady" of the day, seems to have been a success in the eyes of her parents. Some of their expectations, both minor and somewhat grandiose, are contained in a letter written to "My dear Neana" by Governor Evans on November 1, 1886, when Anne was already living in Evanston:

> I wrote Annie in reply to her letter to me, quite a long letter, which as she is under your care and should make you her confidant I hope she will show you, notwithstanding it does hope she will take pains in her writing to form a full and well formed letter of everyone in every word she writes—of course this is a slight criticism of the writing of such as think so much faster than they can possibly put on paper. Annie's mother told me one of the objects of your care was to teach her a better handwriting and I just threw in this gentle hint in my letter to her.[2] I hope Annie will be all you hope for and to do so it will be important that she make a confidant of you such as Burns called 'a bosom cronie.'

The Governor concludes his letter,

> We all have great confidence in the influence of your care and the surroundings of your home upon our child and shall pray that she may be guided into that path of rectitude and noble womanhood to which you so hopefully look forward for her ... Love to Annie and to your mother and father, Affectionately, Your uncle, John Evans.

According to what Katharine Evans had gathered in family conversations, Anne "returned to Denver seemingly a different person. She is supposed to have said that it was one of the best things her parents could have done for her, for it exposed her to a new part of life, where her education and outlook had been substantially broadened." Cornelia Gray Lunt was a remarkable woman. Annie's development under her tutelage was not merely a superficial tutoring in manners, but genuine learning from a sensitive, accomplished and culturally active mentor.

The lives of Anne's mother and father were intertwined with those of Nina's parents, Orrington and Cornelia Lunt, from the moment John met Margaret in the Lunt's Chicago home—in 1852 or 1853. John Evans and Orrington Lunt were the two major forces behind the establishment and ongoing support of Northwestern University. Both families were early boosters and residents of the town of Evanston. Information about the Lunt's daughter, Cornelia, comes from two main sources: her papers, which are in the archives of Northwestern University, and her appealingly frank account of her childhood.[3]

Cousin Nina's Memoirs

Cornelia Lunt, Courtesy
Northwestern University Archives

Cornelia Gray Lunt was born in Chicago on March 19, 1843, just a year after her parents moved from Bowdoinham, Maine, to that up and coming Illinois city. All her life Cornelia loved and admired her successful, energetic father and her capable, beautiful mother. In turn, as their only daughter, she was prized by them. She had two younger brothers: Horace Gray Lunt, who followed his Uncle John and Aunt Margaret Evans west and became a judge in Colorado Springs, and George, who remained in Chicago. After the family's spacious home in Chicago was destroyed in the Great Fire of 1871, the Lunts moved to Evanston. Orrington Lunt was a Trustee, and virtual acting Board president, of Northwestern University after President John Evans relocated to Colorado. Lunt was also the Secretary and Treasurer of the Garrett Biblical Institute on the Northwestern campus. His daughter, Cornelia, never married. She remained in the Evanston home, which she named Anchorfast, for the rest of her life. So when fifteen-year-old Annie went to Evanston to spend her year with forty three-year-old Cousin Nina, she was living in the household of Cornelia and Orrington Lunt.

Judge Horace Lunt's daughter, Regina Lunt Dodge, and her husband, Clarence Phelps Dodge, lived in Colorado Springs. They spent summers on their mountain land, which was adjacent to the Evans/Elbert Ranch. Even after the Dodges moved east, they continued to summer in the Colorado mountains. In her privately published memoirs, Nina reproduced the letter that her niece, Regina, wrote to her in 1923. The letter was accompanied by "an attractive Blank-Book, blue covered and gold lettered." In it, Regina requested that Cornelia write down "memories of your yesterdays ... Thus all who love you may benefit ... we shall, as the case may be—enjoy, delight—be inspired to noble deeds—or perhaps, reach for the Stars!"[4] In her Prologue, Cornelia described the frame of mind in which she wrote her memories:

> ... *here,* in my lovely backwater cove, my Anchorfast ... I look out now as I did in babyhood across blue waters under blue skies to the far horizon, and think what a wonderful world it is and that I couldn't have lived but for its beauty. One has to have fellowship with the trees that give shelter and the flowers that scent the air, and all living things that are a part of our world—and of all living things human beings are the strongest and the most interesting for with them lies responsibility ... I was never in the van of the battle as conqueror or leader ... Mine were not gifts that made for struggle and sacrificial labours and royal victories. Life never became spectacular or severe but sheltered, joyous, confident with a message of *love* I wish I could pass on.

Reading Cornelia's account of the childhood experiences that shaped her character, the values that were transmitted to her by loving and highly principled parents, and the events that broke her heart, it becomes clear why she was the perfect role model for Anne at a time when Anne was contemplating what kind of woman she wished to become.

The two were alike in many ways. Cornelia remembered her first big transgression, when she invited lots of neighborhood children to her birthday party without telling her mother. For this she got her first spanking. This may have reminded Anne of having given Cook, in London, grandiose orders for tea for two of her little friends, orders that her mother had to modify.

Anne Evans age 15, courtesy Margaret E. Hayden

Both women had a huge zest for life, a primal fountain of joy and goodwill, which it gave them pleasure to exercise. Cornelia described this in the aftermath to a rather traumatic episode following on her first remembered lie. She had disobeyed her mother's instructions about looking after her little brother George, and then lied about it. There followed a sobering session with her father, who came armed with a Bible and a large "switch" (which he did not use); when he read to her "All liars shall have their part in the Lake which burneth with fire and brimstone, which is the second death." Cornelia was curiously fascinated with the burning fiery Lake, and kept imagining it as her father prayed "his lovely prayer to his God of Love to forgive his child who would try never to lie again." Drenched in tears, the little Cornelia knew that her father "was teaching me that humiliation and shame attached to falsehood. The crime of telling a lie had been impressed on a mind that worked quickly." But soon "Joy and gaiety—the native quality—expressed itself, as, afraid no longer that memorable night, father and child descended the stairs together. 'I like to be lively, Father,' the young Nina confided. 'You know I like to be lively.'"

The grown-up Anne had a passion for books that fueled her lifelong service to the Denver Public Library. This interest, already fired by her mother's lifelong devotion to reading, was undoubtedly amplified by Cornelia's own love of literature. In her memoirs,

Nina wrote about how her reading was not an escape, because she was always happy, "but a growing mind reached out from my unchanging world for other things than the simple days afforded, and I found them ... in my books." She described how she loved words, even though an early effort to compose poetry, "An Ode to Lake Michigan," was greeted by her family "with amusement that I sensed and resented. A child learns early to keep her thoughts to herself."

She described how her family would visit her Grandfather Gray every year in Maine, and how, after talking to him one day about a rather embarrassing subject, he led her upstairs to his library. There he took down a whole shelf of old leather bound books, and told her, "Begin your library, child, since your hobby is reading; you can have all my books to look at, and those you like best to carry away with you." Cornelia remarked how, as the years went by, she was "slowly succumbing without knowledge or clear recognition to the magic of beauty and the love of truth."

"Am I Not Some Pretty?"

Nina did, however, write poignantly about one personal and painful issue in her childhood. This issue may very well have been a common bond between her and Anne, though for this, in Anne's case, we have only a few hints in written accounts. Their mothers, Cornelia and Margaret, were two of four sisters widely described as the beautiful Gray sisters. While she was visiting the Gray household in Bowdoinham as a child, young Cornelia overheard her aunts and Grandmother discussing her appearance. They said that they did not see any Gray in her, that she was "all Sumner" (a family branch on her father's side), and most resembled a relative, Aria Sumner. Cornelia managed to blurt out her concern to her sympathetic Grandfather, "They say ... if I am only smart like Aria, it won't matter how I look and that I don't look like any of you at all ... Grandfather, *don't you think I am some pretty?*" Grandfather temporarily restored her customary gladness by telling her, "You are not half bad looking ... Forget the things you hear about your looks, I like them."

But her "spirit exuberant and gay" was shattered some time later. Coming in to a large family gathering, she heard her Grandmother say to a woman sitting with her back to Cornelia, "This, Aria, is the little girl we think looks so much like you." That, in fact,

Aria was really a "good and clever woman" with a kindly expression was completely lost on Cornelia at the time. What she saw was "a face, to my inflamed imagination, fairly hideous." She saw "… the coarse grey skin; the big features, brow retreating, teeth projecting, and eyes with a cast that made them queerly repellent. The straight hair was drawn back from a countenance which seemed of grotesque ugliness." Cornelia was shattered. She rushed upstairs to an attic and sobbed out, "I want to die—I want to die—I am so homely—I am so homely—I look like Aria Sumner!" until she was utterly exhausted. She was finally found by her mother, who bathed her eyes, listened to her railing against her tragic fate, and told her that God made her face, that her eyes and curly hair were just like her handsome father's.

> To Mother your face is dear and when you smile, everyone likes it …
> God has been very good to you and to us all. I think my little girl
> can love and be loved a lot if she tries, and nobody will mind her
> looks; pretty people are not always nice, we won't talk any more
> about it.

But for the young Cornelia, it was many years before the wound healed. She lived with the hurt caused by her Grandmother's frequent references to her looks, and the adverse comparisons with the "Beautiful Gray Sisters."

Anne undoubtedly heard the story of this traumatic event in young Cornelia's life and at the time when Anne was developing her own attitude as to what importance feminine good looks, fashionable clothing and grooming should play in her own life. From the comments made[5] by Anne's father on receiving a photograph of her from Margaret in Europe, it seems that Annie's looks were a matter of some concern. As an adult, Anne Evans cared little for feminine perfection or grooming, or for dressing in the latest fashion. One author, many years later, described her as "Plain Anne, who wore tweeds and ground-grippers, [and] never seemed … to care much how she looked."[6] Her favorite outfit while staying in her beloved mountain cabin was a pair of old riding britches. Freddie (Frederica) Lincoln, who spent her summers as a child in Evergreen and whose mother was a good friend of the Evans family, said of Anne Evans, "She was not a beautiful woman, but because of her energy, she was attractive. She was a dynamic personality and appeared to me to be an intellectual."[7] However, a *Denver Post* article of January 6, 1941, following Anne's death, noted, "Altho she never married and seemingly disdained accepting modern styles and fashions, there were times when Anne Evans, dressed in pale rose silk and point lace, was the most beautiful woman present and always she was a most womanly woman."

The Legacy of Remarkable Parents

One aspect of Anne's future life that may have been influenced by her cousin Nina's example was a deep appreciation of having remarkable parents and an ability to live harmoniously with them as an adult. In her memoirs, Cornelia Lunt recounts vividly two childhood events that reinforced for her the immense love she had for her home and for her mother and father. She was sent in 1853, at the age of ten, to boarding school in Newburyport, Massachusetts (accompanied by a cousin, Etta Lunt, and by Governor Evans' daughter, Josephine.) There she suffered such extreme homesickness that she was brought home. A little later she was sent on a trip across the Atlantic with an uncle who was a sea captain. Though she was treated kindly by family friends and relatives, Cornelia again suffered greatly from being away from home, and was terrified by the stormy crossing on the way home. Her father met her on landing, and took her to a hotel where her mother was waiting.

Nina went on to describe her mother Cornelia's character and influence.

> Nothing could ever rob her—my Mother—or lessen her unique distinction, in appearance, in bearing, in dress. Her individualism of style was as artistic as distinctive. Her features and colouring were beautifully delicate, and her feminine charm obvious to all … She demonstrated ability and firmness, and surrounded herself with unassailable dignity. Hers was a gift of reticence. It was a Gray characteristic, an inheritance, and yet, in her case, softened by gentleness and generosity of soul … She made us feel we were trusted to the full.

Cornelia also loved and admired her handsome father and fully appreciated his many accomplishments, but made a clear distinction between his large visions and her own contributions, based on her individual temperament.

I was sometimes serious, but I think at the very beginning my mind was bent in the way it has grown; not for any fine or valuable work in life, but for much enjoyment, and an overflowing fund of sympathy; a capacity to see the other side ... Mine apparently was not the soil from which springs great enterprises ... or wonderful sacrificial labours. It was far-reaching philanthropies, splendid self-effacement, devotion to the highest standards, love of Church and State that made my Father's life so worthy and wonderful. To him it was always Causes that appealed—To me it was, and ever has been, the individual.[8]

Cousin Nina on "Uncle John Evans"

Anne knew that she too had unusually accomplished parents: a mother very like Cornelia's in her beauty, dignity, and concern for civic and cultural affairs, and a father renowned for his contributions to the development of both Chicago and Denver. Nina was well-acquainted with Anne's family, since the Evans and the Lunts had close ties for many years even before Anne was born. During the year Anne and Nina spent together, Nina undoubtedly relayed to Anne her great admiration for the role that John Evans played in the history of Denver, although it would not, in 1886, have been as complete a picture as the one she painted in her 1923 memoir. Nina related a charming little anecdote, when the Evans lived in Evanston,

> It's funny to see Uncle John Evans take his breakfast as if he had a whole month to do it in—every minute the train time getting nearer and nobody can ever hurry him. I've laughed inside seeing them all try, with that Buggy always waiting at the door and Aunt Margaret saying, 'Now Pa, you know it's getting late, and he slowly swallowing the last of his coffee ... which he'll relish to the last drop and it seems the whole of Evanston couldn't make him hasten over it ... then up without one evidence of hurry, getting leisurely into his coat and hat, and giving some last directions or farewell words with undisturbed composure. Then—with one jump he's inside, grabs the reins and dashes off like mad. I suppose the train waits if he's not there—They say he comes up steaming every morning, and every morning just the same he alights from his buggy. The boy is always waiting to take it back—and he throws

down the reins and calmly gets into the waiting Cars. He will never hurry beforehand and he was never known to miss that train."[9]

When asked about her memories of Anne Evans, the first thing Freddie Lincoln described was Anne's voice. Her voice, said Freddie, "was low and musical and full of vitality."[10] Nina described other family voices in her memoirs. "Indeed in all our connection I have never heard a voice among the Lunts or Grays, Sumners or Pattens, Evans or Cornells that fell unpleasantly on the ear. They are usually low-pitched and agreeable and some are fortunately sonorous rich and musical."[11]

The Subject of Marriage

One question that inevitably comes up when discussing the life of Anne Evans is "Why did she never marry?" Aspects of this question are discussed in other parts of the book. Here it may be helpful to review Cornelia's experience of courtship and possible marriage, and to consider what messages on the subject Anne may have received from the older cousin she admired and respected. Nina was settled into the role of a spinster daughter, seemingly content with her life of frequent travel, involvement in local cultural and university affairs, and enjoyment of the family home.

One summer when Nina was about eight years old she was staying in the New England Gray household. Reading in a curtained nook off the living room, she was suddenly aware that her "pretty Aunt Helen" and a neighbor, "the tall, thin Father of the two little Davidson's who lived round the corner" had entered the room. To the great fascination of young Nina, Mr. Davidson started to propose. "I implore you Miss Gray—You *must* listen, we could be so happy—They say love is blind—Mine isn't—I know it,—Oh believe me ... Come with me—We will spend our summers in some quiet watering place, and our winters in the Orange Groves of the Sunny South." Nina opened the curtains a little wider so she could hear better. "Do you object to my children?" he asked. "No, I object to you"—Aunt Helen replied in very clear accents, "and I wish you would never again"—The sentence remained unfinished for certain movements of the curtains caught her eye. Nina, to her great embarrassment, was discovered. If she recounted this story to Annie, the lessons seem clear. First, that some marriage proposals are ridiculous and can be properly treated as such in the privacy of the family. (Nina wrote that poor Mr. Davidson's words "have been quoted from that day to this in some hilarious merriment.") Second, that the confident young women in that New England setting were perfectly free to accept or reject marriage proposals.

Marriage and Samuel Elbert

The second story was more complex and concealed far more than it explained. It concerned Nina's involvement with Samuel Elbert. She described how, about three years before Josephine—her good friend and cousin—married Elbert in Evanston, her Father had brought home to supper a dark-eyed young stranger who was on his way to Colorado to "act as Secretary or in some way assist my Uncle." She saw him as "a man of mature years, large, square built and dark as an Oriental. His personality was striking, and he seemed somehow conspicuous." Her mother was not home that evening, so Nina poured the tea as they engaged in unremarkable conversation. But when she looked up at him, she

> felt a gaze so deeply penetrating, so strangely speaking, so keen and flashing in those dark eyes, that it called to me, and made an unforgettable impression although it was only a passing illusion— but it was his moment—and it would never come again. I was vaguely relieved when he left after a long evening.

She forgot about the meeting, and did not even remember his name, and so was quite startled when he came into her life again as Josephine's husband-to-be. She had no doubt that Elbert was deeply in love with Josephine, and entirely devoted to her during her short life. But he apparently came to Nina after Jo's death and courted her. During what she describes as their "ten months' engagement" he told her how he had been affected by that first evening with her.

> ... he told me what a flicker of life and sudden emotion he felt at our table—he said I had intrigued his imagination for those hours; that a dream rose before him that had been long desired, and that seemed to wait and to beckon. Always it was in such a home, it was such a daughter, such youth and gaiety, that he wanted to make his own heart's altar—But the hour was not ripe.[12]

It is the end of the story that is baffling, because the incident she went on to describe as having disillusioned her about Elbert's character seemed to have occurred only after their "engagement" had ended—and she gave no clue as to why that happened. Cornelia had moved on and was apparently receiving the attentions of another beau, a Mr. Emery. The relationship between these two did not develop into anything serious, as was the case with a number of other potential husbands.

> I felt sometimes in life with a few, who thought they cared deeply, something possessive and strangely urgent for a little; but ending always with futile gestures. It was merely an inner urge for complete companionship that went no further and that in several instances left me uneasy dissatisfaction.

Mr. Emery made a brief farewell call to Cornelia, and she introduced him to Samuel Elbert, who happened to be visiting. After the door closed behind the unfortunate suitor, Elbert asked her, in a sharp, curt tone,

> 'Are you going to marry that man?'

The question amused her.

> 'I don't see how it's to be brought about as he's never asked me.'
> 'He'd ask you quick enough if you'd give him a chance—Don't do it—He's not half good enough for you.'

This remark infuriated her.

> The colossal conceit of the brilliant being who was warning me; who undoubtedly thought himself good enough for any woman on earth; who certainly thought himself good enough for me … I was permanently poorer for promises unfulfilled.

The lesson Nina learned was in her own words, "The light had come to me from within instead of without, the light which his own character and conduct quenched in a moment; that, in its illumination, released me from lifelong misery, since it meant escape and gave me back my freedom."[13] It appears that, although Nina admired her own parents' marriage and found no flaws in it, she perceived the potential marriages proposed to her as less enticing than the boundless opportunities open to her as a single woman. She rejected the whole concept of being dominated by a male partner.

An Overflowing Love of Life

One gift which Nina had to offer to her young protégée was akin to the modern concept of networking. This was based on a naturally over-flowing love of life, which apparently both women had in common. On Nina's part, this was expressed often throughout her memoirs, for example, when she described the kind of books she enjoyed as a child, "... I could never explain unhappy endings; to be joyous I considered essential and part of the Divine Plot. Solemnity was not for me, nor denials or restraints ..."[14] Anne, later on in her life in Denver, was quoted as saying, "I never went into anything in my life on a pass ... I like work. I like people, I love Colorado."[15] This joyful, open-minded attitude on Nina's part involved a willingness to meet new people, listen to their opinions, and especially to seek to meet people of accomplishment who might have important ideas to communicate.

In her memoirs, Nina described how she and a school classmate decided to write to Ralph Waldo Emerson, then visiting their town, and ask for a chance to meet him. She realized, later on, the "superb arrogance" of the request. Yet he met them graciously, sat down with them, and asked them questions about what schools and churches they attended. Nina told him, "You know, Mr. Emerson, we've been very anxious to meet you—we are reading your books, and we haven't skipped a single page." He asked them what they had read lately, and she answered "The Oversoul."

"With an unmistakable twinkle" he asked, "And do you under-stand it?"

Having, as she noted, "no instinct for prevarication," she an-swered, "With a remarkable impressive, inconsiderate and emphatic negative, 'No, I do not. I don't *quite*. I'm sorry.'"

The great Transcendentalist ... said, in a tone full of laughter, "*Neither do I.*"

It is reported in Cornelia Gray Lunt's Northwestern University biography that on one of her visits to New England she had the chance to meet the actor Edwin Booth. He "introduced her to what became a lifelong patronage of, and participation in, drama and music." This was undoubtedly one of the areas in which Anne felt that her year with Nina "had substantially broadened her education and outlook."[16] Since Nina traveled frequently to the east coast and to Europe, she undoubtedly took Anne with her on some of her trips and introduced her to the world of theater and opera. The fruits of this new interest, and her consequent connections with people in these fields, were eventually seen in the creation of the Central City Festival.

Spiritual Values

Nina also must have discussed with Anne her lively interest in religious and philosophical ideas. In the course of describing a much enjoyed visit with the family of Bishop Matthew Simpson in Philadelphia, Nina incidentally gave another humorous vignette about Anne's father.

> The Bishop had been several times at our house and was a very close friend of Uncle John Evans. It was almost a family joke, whenever the great Orator was to preach, and the latter had his coveted chance to be among the hearers, that he always deliberately provided himself with two extra pocket handkerchiefs. Very cool and indifferent to the amusement it aroused, for he declared 'it was necessary, as he would pretty certainly be moved to tears by transcendent eloquence and must be prepared.'

Nina had visited the Simpson household at a momentous time in American history—when Lincoln was temporizing in issuing the Emancipation Proclamation. Bishop Simpson was preparing to make a well-publicized address to his followers condemning Lincoln's delay but felt he must make one last private appeal to Lincoln before doing so. When he returned from Washington, Simpson described "that memorable interview" to his family and assembled guests, including Nina. He had told the President that he believed the country would suffer immensely unless the Proclamation went out promptly, that he had come to tell the President first of his convictions, and that "now I go to tell the people." The President was perceptibly aging, Simpson felt, and sat silently through his remarks, "hands loosely clasped and head bent low, the pathetic figure of a burdened man." He did not at first make any response to Simpson's appeal, but called out to him as he was leaving,

"Bishop, the Master whom you serve was very patient and long suffering with the sinner—even until seventy times seven He forgave. Could you not be patient with me a little longer?"

To Nina, Bishop Simpson was, like Emerson, a lifetime influence and spiritual hero. She described him as

> grave, imposing, impressive and commanding in pulpit of an rostrum. Always dignified, a stately figure, conspicuous in the foremost ranks in that stirring eventful period in our History. There was about him an imperishable distinction—his simplest statements affirmed a proof more trenchant, more convincing, than any oath sworn by bell, book and candle. His was a heart of oak—that spirit of daring which marks the hero ...

But Nina was no simple adherent of her parents' Methodism. One of a number of people she characterized as mentors was a man whom she described as "revered Guide, Philosopher and Friend!" He introduced her to what he said was the source of all religions and taught her "something worthwhile about the Saints and Sages of the Far East."

Like her mentor, Cousin Nina, Anne Evans did indeed broaden her religious horizons to include a familiarity with Eastern spiritual disciplines. Anne was often heard to say, "all the world's religions, I want to know about all of them."[17] One way in which she pursued this quest for universal spiritual and philosophical values was through membership in the Theosophical Society.

Cornelia Gray Lunt went on to become, in the words of Northwestern University President Walter Dill Scott, "the First Lady of Evanston." She was one of the founders of the University Guild, a town and gown organization dedicated to promoting the arts, and also of both the local Chapter of the Daughters of the American Revolution and the Chicago branch of the Society of Colonial Dames. In addition, she was a charter member of the women's Fortnightly Club of Chicago and founder of the Evanston Amateur Concert Club. Cornelia Lunt became a member of the Board of Trustees of Northwestern University in 1896, a position she held until her resignation in 1920.

Nina visited the Evans family in Denver from time to time. There is a picture of her up on the Evans Ranch in the summer of 1886. Perhaps this was the year that she took Anne back with her to Evanston.[18] At some point, probably after Anne became a member in 1919, Cousin Nina must have been a guest at the Denver Fortnightly Club. She appears in their Year Books for a number of years as a rare Honorary Member.

Anne Evans' lifetime accomplishments eventually surpassed those of her cousin, probably because the cultural opportunities and needs in the young city of Denver were so much greater than in the relatively mature environment of Evanston and Chicago. Without doubt, the year under the tutelage of Cousin Nina broadened Anne Evans' horizons, especially in the cultural, spiritual and philosophical realms. The year confirmed many of the values practiced by her energetic father and mother, and prepared her well for the next two phases of her education: schooling in France and Germany followed by college-level studies at the Art Students' League in New York.

9

Paris, Berlin, Denver, New York: the Artist Years

Paris offered women opportunity to hone their professional identities by detaching from their families ... In setting their own hours, meeting new colleagues and immersing themselves without distraction in art, women had the opportunity to direct their own lives in ways unavailable to them at home, where they were often entangled in household and familial duties ... their months and years abroad created a detachment and self-assurance that broke down deference to familial wishes and fostered an autonomy invaluable for professional development.[1]

—Kirsten Swinth

It was in seeking sources to understand the critical twelve years of Anne Evans' life from 1887 to 1899 that the lack of any personal account of her experiences was most keenly felt in writing this biography. From 1886–1887, immediately prior to the years abroad, Annie Evans was listed as a student in the College Preparatory Section of Denver University.[2] Thereafter, until 1890, she was in Paris at the Misses Ferris School, and in Berlin at the Willard School. In 1891–1892, Annie Evans was enrolled in art classes at the University of Denver. From 1895 to 1899 she was engaged in intermittent studies at the Art Students' League in New York.

Art Studies in Paris and Berlin

By studying in Paris and Berlin, Anne was following in the footsteps of her mother, who also studied in Europe in her youth. Margaret Evans valued this experience highly, and from it gained not only an easy proficiency in both French and German but also a strong sense of what constituted a civilized society and a mature, livable city.

Evidently these schools for young American women offered students the opportunity to concentrate on subjects that particularly interested them, as well as a general immersion in the culture. Anne's mother appears to have focused especially on European literature. Anne's energies were directed into art classes. The family tradition of having daughters spend some years in study in Europe was later continued by William and Cornelia Evans, Anne's older brother and sister-in-law, with whom Anne lived out her life as a family member after the deaths of her father and mother. William and Cornelia's daughter Margaret, who later became Mrs. Roblin Davis, was passionately interested in music, the subject of her studies in Paris. She became an accomplished pianist and had a fine singing voice. Their oldest daughter Josephine's chosen area of overseas study, like her Aunt Anne's, was art, though she tended to focus more on the crafts side. Some fine examples of her work in leather tooling can be seen in the Byers-Evans House Museum.

The Ferris and Willard Schools were probably in the category of "finishing schools." The American Heritage Dictionary defines a finishing school as "a private school for girls that emphasizes training in cultural subjects and social activities." Given the ferment of debate in these years about the changing position of women, especially women in the higher social classes, there was undoubtedly lively discussion within these schools about the possible futures of the young women being educated there. Particularly in the area of art, Anne Evans' chosen field, these years were a period of great progress for women artists, both in Europe and in the United States.

Women Artists in the Late Nineteenth Century

In her study of women artists, and their role in the development of modern American art, author Kirsten Swinth identified the forces that were at work loosening restraints on women's "urgent desire to become artists." She noted that great changes took place in the American art scene after the Civil War.

> The relatively small, intimate world of antebellum artists and patrons dissolved as the cultural nationalism that had fostered close patronage and dedicated purchase of American landscape

paintings lost favor to a cosmopolitan taste for contemporary
European figure and Old Master paintings.[3]

This new preference fed into the movement for professionalization
of an artist's training.

Before the Civil War, art education in the United States was limited to a few art academies, and was conducted on the lines of
apprenticeship rather than systematic training. Students and recognized artists painted and sketched together with little formal
instruction. Where life or figure drawing classes were offered, they
were strictly limited to men. As opportunities for artists to earn a
living for their work expanded, and as the preference of collectors
for paintings of the human figure rather than landscapes grew,
there became an increasing demand for serious training, along
European lines, in figure drawing and painting. In the European
tradition, beginners drew first from flat objects, and then progressed
to plaster casts of ancient classical sculpture. Drawings were evaluated, and only after students had proven proficiency, through
time-consuming and repetitive practice, could they pass to the next
level. The final stage was drawing a nude model.

Even when such classes were made available to women students,
they were for a long time segregated by sex. But the last quarter
of the nineteenth century saw the development of a serious curriculum, open to women, leading to their recognition as professional
artists. This made possible great progress for women in pursuing
the right to be accepted, on a par with men, as artists. Artists, and
those who supported them, came to believe that it was lengthy,
rigorous study more than inherent talent that made someone an
artist. Impatient with the pace at which traditional art academies
in the United States were updating their curricula, a group of men
and women artists founded the Art Students' League in New York
in 1875. On its founding board, women had equal representation
with men.

Another factor in the changing art scene was the rise of huge
new industrial fortunes, some portion of which was spent on ambitious art collections and on supporting major art museums in cities
like New York, Chicago and Boston. The resulting infusion of money
into the pockets of recognized artists helped to change the image of
artists as necessarily starving, thereby reducing the reluctance of

families to allow children to enter the art profession. The cumulative result of these forces, according to Swinth,[4] was that women entered the art world in unprecedented numbers after the Civil War, "flooding art schools, hanging their pictures alongside men's, pressing for critical recognition, and competing for sales in an unpredictable market."[5] Swinth noted that in the 1870 census, only 414 women artists were listed as practicing their profession compared to nearly 11,000 in the 1890 count.

It was still true that, to be well prepared to launch an art career and to be recognized as a knowledgeable connoisseur of the contemporary art scene, a period of study in Europe, and especially in Paris, was virtually obligatory. Anne Evans had this advantage.

Art Appreciation in the Gilded Age—
A New Role for Middle-class Women

An interesting feature of the late nineteenth century in the U.S. was that an appreciation of art, and its promotion in society at large, was seen as an important part of the role of middle-class women. This was Mark Twain's Gilded Age, inaugurated by that popular Centennial Exhibition of 1876, visited by both Governor Evans, on his way to join his family in Europe, and by Margaret's brother Horace, when he was traveling to put Sunie Lowell on a boat to England. Swinth wrote that this Exhibition "sparked the wildly popular aesthetic movement."[6] It fostered the extension of art education to the public schools, in the belief that training in art encouraged both individual development and social harmony. "Gilded Age Americans, particularly the middle class, placed extraordinary faith in the power of art (and high culture generally) to instill values and unify society."[7] Swinth saw this Gilded Age period as a time when "women began to include the protection of art and culture among their duties."

One vehicle of implementing this responsibility was through the explosive club movement that started at the end of the nineteenth century. Both Margaret Gray Evans and her daughter, Anne, were involved in this movement. Among many other social and cultural endeavors, Margaret was a founder of the Denver Fortnightly Club, and its first president. Anne's initial involvement with cultural development in Denver was being accepted in 1894 as a professional member of the Denver Artists' Club, a forerunner of the Denver Art Museum.

One of her many honors was being named by the Denver Chapter of the National Federation of Business and Professional Women's Clubs as the outstanding Denver woman of 1933. In the Gilded Age, common interests and goals united those American women who were making a career of art with other women "who followed well-established routes for middle class women into charitable activity and civic reform. Gilded age women entered the public sphere through this work, where their endeavors included what might be called 'cultural housekeeping.' "[8]

Anne Evans, for reasons now known only to herself, decided later in her life, to give up her own activity as an artist and focus on encouraging the artistic talent of others and on the development of cultural institutions in Denver. Her decision appears to have been a reasonable one, consistent with the general artistic climate and ideals of the times in which she was educated.

Art vs. Marriage—Women's Dilemma

One topic of lively debate among American women art students, both in Europe and at home, was the question of marriage. Should those who wanted to devote their lives to a career in art, to become accepted as professionals on an equal footing with men, remain single? Did traditional obligations of a woman's role in supporting the husband's career and raising children preclude a married woman from focusing on her own artistic development? These questions still have no clear and satisfying solution—even after one hundred intervening years of feminist advocacy, advancement of women in all the professions, and extensive public debate. They were as real and urgent a concern in the last quarter of the nineteenth century as they are to women today.

Laura Prieto, in her 2001 study of women artists in the United States,[9] considered how this perceived incompatibility of marriage and career operated in the lives of women artists in the last thirty years of the nineteenth century. She argued that it helped to elevate the status of single women who were consecrated to art. The presence of spinsters—unmarried women who usually lived quietly in family households all their lives—was a familiar feature of Victorian society. But the presence of large numbers of women who were single by choice, and who played a significant role in civic and cultural affairs, was something new. Prieto also noted that this conscious rejection of marriage by ambitious women in the arts made the cohabitation of women artists, and even intimate relationships with each other, acceptable at a time when, in general, there was a decreasing tolerance of homosexuality.

Karen Swinth also discussed the dilemma that marriage presented for women artists at the end of the nineteenth century. She commented on the message transmitted by an influential magazine of the time, *The Art Interchange*: "running through its pages was an ideal woman who was assertive, independent, and dedicated to her own spiritual evolution through art."[10] According to one editorial in the magazine, marriage in the future "will be a something to be carefully weighed and to be declined if it offers less of happiness or less congenial life work than her profession or her trade."[11] Swinth quoted the comment of a dedicated woman artist, who married a supportive husband much older than herself. When their daughter started going out to dances and dating, she wrote, "all she seems to want to do is to get married and have children. It isn't *serious!*"[12]

That Anne Evans was not presented with opportunities to marry, given her prominent social position in Denver as the only daughter of an affluent and successful father and a gracious, active, and well-educated mother, seems highly unlikely. Despite the fact that she was not considered conventionally attractive, there is every indication that Anne related well and easily to men, both within her large family, and in the community at large. She lived amicably with her older brother, William, and affectionately described her admiration for the tenacity that brought him success in so many endeavors, "When he had become interested in a project he studied all around it, up and down and crossways. One couldn't dent his attention with an ax when he was thinking. But the moment his attention was diverted, it was a gate wide open to suggestion or experience or thought."[13]

She admired the financial acumen of her banker nephew, John Evans, welcomed his involvement on boards of civic organizations, and made him the Executor of her will. She worked comfortably with Mayor Speer, after he appointed her to the city's first Art Commission, to help develop the city they both loved into a City Beautiful.

Perhaps the truth was that Anne Evans did not so much reject marriage as that she embraced the freedom of being an independent woman.

One insight on this question of Anne Evans and marriage was given by a member of the Denver Fortnightly Club in a paper read in 1973. The minutes of the meeting of March 3 read, "Mrs. Arndt's remarks broadened our picture of Miss Anne Evans. Among other things, she told us that Miss Evans *decided not to marry*, preferring to devote herself to the enrichment of Denver."[14] (Emphasis added.)

Women in the Art World of Early Denver

In the artistic world, the fine expansion of women's opportunities did not last. As in so many areas of women's progress towards equality, there was a backlash. In the artistic sphere, this started in the 1890s when women were perceived as becoming too successful too quickly. The backlash did not develop out of any conscious plan but was the result of what Swinth called a fundamental reorientation of the art world. Essentially, the locus of major art sales shifted from juried art shows and exhibitions open to all artists, to much smaller and more exclusive venues in a gallery/dealer system.

At the same time, a critical rebellion developed against elaborately polished academic art work. Such work required arduous professional training, access to which women had fought for so long and so successfully. At the heart of the rebellion was a new enthusiasm for a freer, bolder style of painting. Bolstered by a mishmash of rationalizations, based on social Darwinism and revived notions of creativity as essentially masculine, the value of professionalism in art was downgraded, and women's role as artists was reduced to what the mostly male art critics came to define as "the essentially feminine."

These changes started in the 1890s, but perhaps fortunately did not reach provincial Denver until much later. Women artists like Emma Richardson Cherry, Elisabeth Spalding, and Anne Evans were prominent in the small art world of this city. They worked diligently with male colleagues towards establishing the rudiments of a civilized arts community; art schools, an art museum, a Civic Center, venues for local artists to exhibit and sell their work, and ways to showcase the work of nationally-known artists.

One advantage that Swinth believed women art students derived from their sojourns in Paris may well have benefited Anne Evans. As described in this chapter's opening quote, this was the experience of women detaching from their families and managing their own time, money and professional interests. From descriptions of Anne Evans, as she worked for the cultural causes she espoused so totally and so vigorously, it is obvious that she developed a healthy sense of autonomy and an ability to maintain her chosen goals in the face of determined opposition, whether from family members or other powerful interests in the community.

Boom Times in Denver

By the academic year of 1891–1892, when Anne Evans returned to Denver from her European studies, the city had grown and changed considerably. The city's population, 35,629 in 1880, had swelled to 106,713 by 1890. The 1880s had seen new silver discoveries, which, as one author observed, "rained riches on Denver."[15] First came the lodes discovered in Leadville starting in 1878; soon thereafter one of its new "Silver Kings", H. A. W. Tabor, gave it a 5,000-seat opera house and theater. Like many other mining millionaires, Tabor later brought his fortune to Denver where he built the imposing Tabor office block at 16th and Larimer, an expensive mansion for his wife, Augusta, and the Tabor Grand Opera House, which opened its doors in September 1881.

Other major silver discoveries followed in Aspen, Ouray, Telluride, Silverton, Durango, Georgetown, Silver Plume, Nederland and Caribou. "Silver was King in Colorado in the 1880's. Men were

Tabor Grand Opera House, (c. 1890) Denver Public Library Western History Collection

making fortunes in mining, railroading and banking industries. Over-extended investments and sometimes sheer extravagance ruled the day."[16] In Denver, "... the Midas-men and their ladies set the pace, and they turned a town into a city."[17] Colorado production of silver was greater than ever: in the years from 1890–1893, it averaged more than $20,000,000 per year. Colorado was producing almost 60% of the country's silver.

Though the state's economy was still heavily dependent on mining, a number of pioneering manufacturing concerns were started in Denver in the early 1890s. Agriculture too was prospering, since the sad saga of removing the original inhabitants from the land had been virtually completed. Most of the Utes were moved out of Colorado, following the Meeker massacre,[18] the majority being settled on the barren Uintah Reservation in Utah. Their former lands were thrown open to white settlement. The towns of Grand Junction, Montrose and Delta came into being, followed shortly by Glenwood Springs, Meeker, Durango and Cortez.

In the early 1890s, Denver was experiencing a short-lived building boom. The Brown Palace Hotel was under construction, opening its doors in 1892 to those who could afford its astronomical rates of $3 to $5 a night. The building boom ended with panic of 1893. Almost nothing was built in 1893–1894.

In 1890, the cornerstone was laid for the State Capitol with appropriate pomp and circumstance. The building was far enough along for offices in it to be occupied by the governor in 1894 but was not completed until 1900.

The Brown Palace Hotel 17th Street and Broadway, Courtesy History Colorado

Denver University

The University of Denver saw significant improvement in 1890, the result of a long and arduous effort by Governor Evans, which is described in a later chapter.

Margaret Evans was a strong supporter of Denver University, especially of its art and literature departments. She, therefore, was in a position to help daughter, Anne, choose which art classes to enter at the University while she was deciding what the next stage of her life would be. The classes were held in the original building, just across the street from the Evans home. Even after the first University Park buildings were completed and occupied, the downtown building was still used for the art and music departments.

From 1891 to the end of 1894, Anne Evans was in Denver, taking art classes, conscientiously pursuing her own painting career, and becoming involved in the art scene in the city.

The Depression of 1893

In 1893, and for a number of years thereafter, the economy of the United States suffered from a depression which has been described as "one of the worst in American history, with the unemployment rate exceeding 10 percent for half a decade."[19] The entire country was hit hard by this economic setback, but Colorado suffered more than most states. The Evans family fortunes were dealt an almost fatal economic blow.

The causes of the painful depression were complex. One author cites an earlier economic downturn in Europe and major changes in the United States economy as contributing factors. It became apparent, for example, that railroads—one of the foundations of economic growth for the previous 25 years—had been overbuilt. Farmers, especially in the West and Midwest, had heavily mortgaged their land in order to expand production beyond what the markets would support. A fundamental economic shift was taking place in the economy, from major dependence on farm products as the staple products and exports of the U.S. to an increasing reliance on the manufactured goods being produced by new industrial plants. The outbreak of violent labor disputes, the rash of foreclosures and the resultant misery for farm families, and the chaos—especially in silver mining states like Colorado—that resulted from the repeal of the Sherman Silver Purchase Act, all contributed to the widespread panic.

Since the early days of the Republic, the U. S. had based its monetary system on "bimetallism"—the legal coinage of both gold and silver. The ratio of gold to silver was held pretty steady at 16 to 1, i.e. sixteen times more silver in a silver dollar than gold in a gold dollar. The huge increase in the amount of gold available from the 1849 California Gold Rush disturbed this balance, so in 1873, Congress ended the manufacture of silver coins and placed the nation on a gold standard. Under pressure from silver mining interests, the Sherman Silver Purchase Act was passed in 1890, with President Benjamin Harrison undertaking to buy $4.5 million ounces of silver per month. Eastern businessmen and European investors began to fear that the gold dollar would be replaced by the less valuable silver dollar, and that the value of the U. S. currency would therefore be undermined. But in reality this was only one element in bursting an unsustainable economic bubble. Panic set in. Stores and banks went out of business.   '

In an attempt to quell the panic, Congress in 1893 repealed the Sherman Silver Purchase Act. The effects were felt almost immediately in Colorado. Silver prices dropped precipitately. Mines and smelters shut down. Thousands of unemployed miners swarmed into Denver, overwhelming the city's ability to take care of them. Railroads began offering free tickets to encourage them to leave town. Banks and stores in the city closed. The large 1891 gold strike at Cripple Creek did little immediately to mitigate the general suffering. The population of Denver declined from 106,713 in 1890 to around 90,000 in 1895 (although by 1900 it had resumed its upward climb to 133,859). Then as now, the public's ability to understand complex causes for widespread suffering and social unrest was lacking. One cause, the withdrawal of government support for silver prices, was seized upon. Its reversal was touted as an economic cure-all by a charismatic political leader, William Jennings Bryan.

Bryan, nominated three times for the Presidency by the Democratic Party, was joined in some of the campaigns by the "Free Silver Republicans." He lost each time, though he remained one of the most popular speakers ever on the lecture circuit. The nation went firmly on to the gold standard and by the end of the century was making the inevitable adjustments to new conditions. For, as David Whitten observes, "The economy that emerged from the depression differed profoundly from that of 1893."[20]

Depression's Effect on Evans Family's Fortunes

Because Governor Evans was in poor health, and also failing mentally, the panic of 1893 had a disastrous impact on the Evans' family finances. In biographer Kelsey's words, "Nearly eighty years old in

1893, he was no longer able to bounce back from such severe financial blows."[21] He lost much of his downtown real estate through foreclosure, including the 1888 Railroad Building in which he had taken so much pride. The only downtown building that was saved was the Evans Block at the corner of 15th and Lawrence, and even this was heavily mortgaged. It became clear by 1895, the year in which Anne Evans first enrolled in the Arts Students League in New York, that "old John could no longer manage his own financial affairs."[22]

Evan, the son long ago admonished by his father to keep careful accounts of all his financial transactions,[23] was summoned home to help salvage as much as possible from the wreckage. When he and older brother, Will, examined the books, they found that for years entries had been haphazard. It was extremely difficult to determine the exact status of his investments. Meantime, "the old gentleman began to retreat further from reality."[24] On November 18, 1896, Margaret Evans was appointed by the Arapahoe County Court (Denver was still a part of Arapahoe County until 1902) as conservatrix of the estate.

The Art Students' League

Anne Evans enrolled in classes at the Art Students' League in New York almost twenty years after its foundation. This was a serious art facility, established by men and women students determined to get the kind of rigorous training they needed to become successful professional artists. Such a democratic facility, initiated by students, could probably only have come into existence in America at this time. In the spring of 1875, students who were enrolled in art classes at the National Academy of Design in New York learned that the Academy had closed classes for the season and would not reopen them until December.

They further learned that the professor in charge, Lemuel Wilmarth, had not been hired for the coming year. They heard rumors that the Academy was in financial difficulties. Having many other reasons to be less than satisfied with the offerings of the Academy, they arranged a meeting with Professor Wilmarth. At this meeting, the Arts Students' League was founded. A board of directors was named and premises rented in which to hold their first classes the following September. An invitation was issued to "both Ladies and Gentlemen who intend making Art a profession"[25] to become members. It was the first comprehensive independent art school in the country, and the only one offering life classes every day of the week. Admission to classes depended on the school's acceptance of a drawing, either from a plaster cast of antique sculpture or from life.

The school was an immediate success and had to expand its premises in the first year. The Art Students' League was incorporated three years later, allowing it to hold property and to receive gifts and bequests. It continued to grow and in 1882 moved into newer and larger quarters. The faculty expanded to six members. By 1887, even these quarters were no longer sufficient. The school moved to a large but inelegant building on East Twenty Third Street. Enrollment had increased to 652 students, drawn from almost every state in the union as well as many of the U. S. Territories and Canada. By 1891, enroll-ment had grown to 900 and the faculty to ten. This was essentially the same faculty as when Anne Evans enrolled three years later: John Twachtman conducted the preparatory class; Kenyon Cox, J. Carroll Beckwith and William Metcalf the antique classes: four life classes, two for men and two for women, were taught by Metcalf, H. Siddons Mowbray, Cox and B. R. Fitz. There were also four portrait classes daily, under the guidance of William Merritt Chase, Fitz, and J. Alden Weir, and two still life classes a day taught by Augustus St. Gaudens. Thomas Eakins gave lectures on anatomy. There were also three sketch classes three times a week and a costume class with six sessions per week. The school was flourishing in such a healthy fashion that its Board began to think in terms of moving into its own building.

Joining together with the Architectural League and the Society of American Artists, the Art Students League agreed to work on a building plan that would provide space for the three organizations to occupy jointly, in addition to providing space for the New York Art Guild and the Society of Painters in Pastel. The five organizations together incorporated the American Fine Arts Society in mid-1889 and proceeded to buy land, hire an architect, and erect a French Renaissance building on W. 57th Street between Broadway and Seventh Avenue. The Art Students' League moved proudly into its new quarters in October of 1892, occupying more than 11,000 square feet on the three upper floors. "Its studios were considered the most completely appointed, the best ventilated and lighted, devoted to art instruction in the entire world."[26] Besides the studios, the new premises included "a handsomely furnished members' room, a students' clubroom, an instructors' or board room, and the office of the director ... In addition there was a room fitted up as a refectory with stove and other appurtenances for preparing lunches and a store for the sale of art materials at cost to the students."

Anne Evans: New York Years

Into these impressive quarters of the Art Students' League came 24-year-old Anne Evans in January of 1895, at a time when the School was dynamic and growing and full of confidence about the future of men and women artists in America. The Art Students' League was concerned to offer rigorous training in technique along classical lines. There was, therefore, a sense in which it could be called conservative: it was not primarily concerned with encouraging originality but with equipping its students with the skills necessary to develop along their own artistic paths. Anne must have enrolled with the intention of becoming a practicing artist because this was not a school that encouraged amateurs, neither did it offer courses in art appreciation. The League has taken care to preserve its own archives and was able to supply brief transcripts of Anne's studies. Of course, these offer only the bare outlines of Anne's life and training there:

The Art Students' League provided what aspiring students of the time thought essential—a classical training. Where the human

---

In the academic year 1894–1895, she took the following classes:

1/15/95 to 5/3/95: Morning Life class from George Barse Jr.
5/13/95 to 5/27/95: Morning Painting class from William Merritt Chase

For 1897–1898:
11/8/97 to 4/8/98: Morning Antique class from J. H. Twachtman
4/12/98 to 4/29/98: Afternoon Life class from Kenyon Cox

For 1898–1899:
10/17/98 to 12/1/98: Morning Life class from George Barse Jr.
10/20/98 to 4/10/99: Morning Life from Kenyon Cox
11/12/98 to 4/18/99: Costume Evening class from Clifford Carlton
12/27/98 to 4/6/99: Morning Life from Kenyon Cox
1/18/99 to 2/7/99: Art class with Kenyon Cox

figure was concerned, it was an orderly process—in drawing, painting and sculpture—that progressed in stages from plaster casts to
live models.

During her years at the Art Students' League, Anne only furnished
one New York address, 24 W. 59th. Street. At other times, she gave
her Denver address. In these years of living in New York, Anne
Evans formed many friendships which she kept up after returning to
Denver. One of these apparently was with the Walker family. The four
children in this family later spent a number of summers as Anne's
guests in her summer home on the Evans Ranch. "The Walker girls"
became accepted members of the summer colony there, and to one of
them, who kept a diary for two summers, we are indebted for a vivid
picture of those enchanted times.[27]

Anne Evans left no record of her own experience of life as a
student at the League. But a fellow member of the Denver Fortnightly
Club, one who studied at the Art Students' League a few years after
Anne Evans, recorded her impressions of what it was like to be part
of the lively classes and social affairs of the League in those days. For
a 1973 meeting of the Club, Miriam Washburn Adams wrote one of
four introductions to a re-reading of a paper Anne Evans wrote in
1927, "A Christmas Pilgrimage to the South West."

Miriam titled her essay "Artless, Mostly Less" and made it clear
that, though she had enjoyed her art studies as a young woman,
she never believed she had real talent: "I don't think I have brought
out how frustrating my drawing was to me—I could never make
my hand do what I saw or felt—never."[28] After graduating from
high school in Brooklyn, Miriam described how she walked over
the Brooklyn Bridge, "crept over to the Art League" and, apparently
on a trial basis, paid the tuition for a month. She decided to start
in Antiques—the drawing of plaster casts. She soon moved on to a
Life class under a Mr. Dumond, who made the model hold the same
pose for five mornings a week from 9 to 12, with 10 minutes off
every half hour to rest.

Miriam formed close friendships in these early classes and was
part of a group who decided to become serious about their studies
and apply for membership in the League. This meant submitting
drawings to be judged for eligibility. Besides classes, she and her
fellow students attended the Art Students' Ball, joined impromptu
dances in the studios, and took part in a cabaret show. They also
lunched nearly every day at the League "in a big room on the second

floor" where a wonderful cook named Carrie arrived around 10 a.m. and produced the most delicious meals "for never more than forty cents; and even for a quarter you got enough to quietly burst."

At least once a week after lunch, Miriam and a friend would take the 5th Avenue bus and go see an exhibit they had heard of, and then stop off for a delicious soda before going home on the subway. "Such was the Art League—how I loved it."

Miriam Washburn described some summer painting lessons from John Carlson in Woodstock, New York, which very likely paralleled experiences enjoyed by Anne Evans. Miriam traveled with a friend: they sailed up the calm and beautiful Hudson River only to find themselves assigned to a room that was "musty and dreadful." They rushed out and secured a big, clean room with twin beds—at the local undertaker's. When they got to the place they were to eat, they were overjoyed to find old friends from Denver—Maisie (Marion) Hendrie and Elisabeth Spalding—among the large crowd of students. They sketched all day and took trips in the evenings to visit different studios. Maisie and Miriam were

> wild with fury when Carlson, looking at some of Elisabeth Spalding's pictures of Colorado, said she didn't have the proper perspective in her weight of color. (Note: when he was painting here in Colorado a few years later, he admitted he was wrong.)[29]

Some accounts indicate that, at least for a part of her time studying art in New York, Anne Evans had the companionship of Marion Hendrie, a fellow student from Denver who became a long-time ally in efforts to establish the Denver Art Museum and to support artists in Colorado.

For Anne Evans, the 1890s were years of alternating residence at home in Denver, partaking of the city's art offerings, with periods in the heady, challenging world of New York and the Art Students' League.

10

Entering Denver's Art World

There was always an art department in Wolfe Hall during its fifty years of usefulness. This city had some earnest art teachers. Among them was Miss Ida De Steiguer at the Denver University, who had good training and built up strong classes ...

I had the privilege of working for five months (under J. Alder Weir) ... at Cooper Union ... I remember saying sadly to him that there was no art in Denver and nothing to paint—mountains were too big, plains too limitless— and he smiled and said, 'You will find something at your own back yard, for you are looking now in the right direction.' He was right. When I got back I painted our own alley![1]

—Elisabeth Spalding

The Colorado and Denver of 1890 did have an art scene. In fact, artists had been part of the population of the new territory almost from the beginning. Some of them had a touch of the charlatan, like "Professor" H. A. Streight, who arrived in Denver from California in 1870. A self-proclaimed landscape artist, he held spiritualist séances in the dark in his studio, where he claimed to paint landscapes under the influence of spirits. When the lights went on, the blank canvas that had been on his easel was transformed into a still-wet landscape painting.[2] Other artists were more tragic figures, like Alexis Comparet. The journey west to Colorado's famous healing climate failed to cure his tuberculosis.

From Denver's earliest days, there were enthusiastic supporters of the arts who, like *Rocky Mountain News* founder William Byers and John and Margaret Evans, had a vision of Denver's future; they were anxious to encourage the development of every aspect of a civilized, cultured city. As the rough mining camp was transformed into a permanent settlement, there were sporadic efforts to establish the three elements essential for a flourishing of art:

> a reliable venue for exhibitions of the work of local and nationally-known artists, supported by the community; a lively, ongoing organization of artists; and an art school, where potential artists could be encouraged and educated.

Some of the efforts towards these ends were abortive, some succeeded for a while and then faded, but there was rising pressure to achieve the goals. By the middle of the 1890s, the ground work for a permanent artistic dimension to the life of Denver had been laid.

The Art of Early Colorado

After the opening of vast new lands through the Louisiana Purchase of 1803, the first artists on the scene came with official government expeditions to make a careful, factual, pictorial record of these unknown regions. But in the 1830s, according to Patricia Trenton and Peter Hassrick in their fascinating book, *The Rocky Mountains: A Vision for Artists in the Nineteenth Century*,[3] artist Alfred Jacob Miller dared to make form and mood more important in his paintings than accuracy of topographical detail. The splendid, romantic vision of the West presented by landscape painters in the nineteenth century was a major factor in the westward expansion of a new nation. Miller paved the way for the epic statements of Albert Bierstadt and his followers. People suddenly saw the Rockies in a new way.

Following the enormous public interest shown in Bierstadt's western paintings, many other artists came to paint and sketch in the Rockies and to contribute their perceptions to the rising "cult of the wilderness." Thomas Worthington Whittredge, Bierstadt's roommate when they studied together in Dusseldorf, made trips to Colorado in 1866, 1870 and 1871. The 1870 visit included the company of John F. Kensett and Sandford R. Gifford. All were landscape painters, members of what came to be known as the Hudson River School.

But the combined lure of gold and silver, new land and the wilderness—dramatized by painters, journalists and poets—were populating the West by the end of the nineteenth century. Fashions in painting were changing; monumental canvases with inspirational themes were going out of favor. The western states were developing flourishing art colonies of their own.

Emergence of Denver's Resident Art Colony

The first artist to make his home in Denver was John Dare Howland. Of the early pioneers, he was to live in Denver the longest. Born in Zanesville, Ohio, in 1843, he left home at fourteen to join the American Fur Company traveling up the Missouri River. He arrived in Denver in 1859, and became especially known for his depictions of buffalo, which he saw frequently in great numbers on the Plains, until the railroad came to the West. Denver was his home for the rest of his life: he died in 1914.

Another significant artist to make Denver his home was the pioneer photographer, William Henry Jackson, also a talented painter. Born in Keeseville, New York in 1843, he spent his boyhood in Troy, New York and Rutland, Vermont. His mother was a trained and capable watercolor artist. Jackson developed a passion for painting from an early age. When the Civil War broke out, he joined a Vermont infantry regiment, fought right through the war, including the Battle of Gettysburg, and then returned to Vermont. He succumbed, like so many other young eastern men of his day, to the lure of the opening American West. He settled first in Omaha, Nebraska, where he went into the photographic business with one of his brothers. Around Omaha he made his famous photos of American Indians. In 1871 he was invited by Ferdinand Hayden to join the U. S. Government survey of Yellowstone and the Rocky Mountains. The painter, Thomas Moran, was also part of the staff of the expedition, and the two artists worked together to document the Yellowstone region.

Jackson opened a studio in Denver in 1879 at 413 Larimer Street where he produced a vast inventory of national and international photographs. Mary Marturano, in her 1962 Denver University Master's Thesis, *Artists and Art Organizations in Colorado*, says that Jackson was probably the most prosperous artist in the city; however, he was not exempt from the dire effects of the 1893 Depression. To salvage his fortunes, he accepted a commission from Marshall Field to travel the world, taking photographs and gathering specimens for a huge new museum in Chicago. When he returned to Denver, he tried his hand at publishing. In 1897, he sold his entire stock of negatives and his own services to a Detroit photographic company which produced postcards of his work as well as more massive reproductions.

The major legacy of Jackson's years spent in Denver were the thousands of negatives of his pioneering photographs of the early

American West—which finally ended up in the possession of the Colorado Historical Society. After the death of the owner of the failed Detroit photographic company, Edsel Ford bought the entire collection of 40,000 Jackson negatives from the estate. These eventually were divided between the Colorado Historical Society, which received the photographs of the scenes west of the Mississippi, and the Library of Congress, which received the rest.

The first engraver to work in Denver[4] was New Englander J. N. Bagley. Before the Civil War, he worked as an artist for the magazine *Leslie's Weekly*. He served in the Union Army, and after the war ended, like so many others, he headed west, opening a studio in Denver in 1872.

A book will be written one day on *The Disease That Built Denver*, so numerous were the important pioneers who originally came here in hopes that the climate would save their lives by curing their consumption, as tuberculosis was called in those days. One of the more prominent of Denver's early artists came to Colorado seeking a cure for his wife's illness. This was John Harrison Mills, who studied art in Buffalo, New York. He already had some landscape paintings and portraits to his credit before he and his wife came west in 1869. They lived first in Grand County where his wife was a school teacher. Moving to Denver in 1875, he worked on wood engraving and book illustration.

Early Art Organizations in Denver

John Harrison Mills made the first attempt to organize an art school in Denver. He located his studio in the Tabor Building, but apparently there was little interest. He had more success setting up a club in which prominent professionals in the city got together to study and discuss the fine arts.[5] This was the Denver Sketch Club, organized in 1880, which changed its name a year later to the Colorado Art Association. It had about twenty members, half men and half women, and was popularly known as the Kit Kat Club. Its membership grew, and in 1882, it was incorporated as the Academy of Fine Arts Association, with Mills as President.[6] In 1883, the group moved into the fifth floor of the Tabor Grand Opera House, which became known as the Studio Flat, and according to Marturano was the first Bohemian gathering place in Denver. After four in the afternoon it was open to the public, and receptions were held each week. The club functioned as an art school with modeling and drawing

Helen Henderson Chain painting en plein air, Denver Public Library Western History Collection

done from plaster casts "as drawing from life was not socially acceptable in Denver at that time."[7] Mills was the major instructor, Jack Howland his assistant. Like other efforts at organizations of artists in the city, however, the Kit Kat Club dwindled and died. In 1886, Howland tried on his own to create an artists' organization. This was called the Denver Artists' Club, but it only survived for one year. "Violent disagreements among the members caused its break-up."[8] Around 1900, Mills returned to live in Buffalo where he produced engravings for *Scribner's Magazine.*

The first successful art school in Denver was set up by a woman

Marion Hendrie, Denver Public Library Western History Collection

artist, Helen Chain (Mrs. A. J. Chain). She had studied with the well-known Hudson River School landscape artist, George Innes (1825–1894), before coming to Denver. Mrs. Chain started her painting classes in 1877.

Three Artist-Contemporaries of Anne Evans

One of Chain's students was a young man who worked for her husband's bookstore. Charles Partridge Adams came from New England in 1876, another of those drawn to Colorado for health reasons: he moved west with his mother and two sisters in hopes of curing the two girls' tuberculosis. Adams taught art for a short time and also tried studying wood engraving under Bagley, Denver's first engraver, but had to give that up for health reasons. He then took up working on landscapes and portraits in crayon, and made quite a name for himself. Elisabeth Spalding, herself a dedicated and successful Colorado artist, wrote a frank and intelligent appraisal of the early art scene in Denver which included an evaluation of the work of Adams. Her paper, written for the Denver Fortnightly Society, was presented in December of 1924, and titled *Something of Art in Denver As I Think of it*. She said of Adams,

> He painted what everyone liked and never questioned. In those days (the 1870s), he was not well known and coming as he did … for his health and with a family to support, everyone wanted to help him. Mrs. Irene Jerome Hood got up studio receptions for him in his rooms up in the Kittredge Building. He was always able to supply an oil or a watercolor for a needed wedding gift and tourists have always found his work acceptable for souvenir or gift.

Adams eventually attracted quite a wealthy clientele and opened a studio in 1893 on Larimer Street. There he began working in watercolor, a medium in which he was so successful that he soon had paintings for sale in stores in Colorado Springs, Pueblo, Kansas City and Chicago. He married in 1890 and honeymooned in Estes Park where he and his wife began to cherish the dream of building a summer home and studio. The dream was fulfilled in 1905.

Although Adams is best known for his landscapes of Colorado, he also painted subjects in Yellowstone, the Grand Tetons, Canadian Rockies and New Mexico. Spalding notes that "when we art students began to feel he was copying himself and making potboilers, how glad we were to have him go south and come back with fresh subjects and new interest." During the many years he lived in Denver, Adams was one of the most active participants in all the efforts to create community support for the arts. In 1917, he suffered from an almost fatal illness. Probably seeking a gentler climate, he moved in 1920 with his wife to California where he opened a studio first in Pasadena and then in Laguna Beach. At the age of 62, he began working with marine subjects, a totally new field for him. The move was obviously a beneficial one for he lived until 1942, reaching the age of 84.

Elisabeth Spalding (sometimes misspelled as Elizabeth Spaulding) was born in 1868 or 1869 and came to Colorado as a child when her father, John Franklin Spalding, was appointed Bishop of the Colorado Diocese. Her father and mother, Lavinia, were both active in many different areas of life in their new community, including education, the arts and social welfare. They were responsible for the founding of St. Luke's Hospital. Elisabeth's younger sister, Sarah, later wrote a history of the hospital's founding and its early years. Elisabeth developed an interest in art, which was encouraged and financially supported by her parents. She studied art at the Cooper Union in New York under J. Alden Weir, and later at the Art Students' League with Weir and J. H. Twachtman.

Spalding also attended the Academy of Fine Arts in Philadelphia, learning more about her craft from Henry McCarter. She developed a lifetime friendship with McCarter. He made many visits to Denver where Elisabeth introduced him to her friends, Marion Hendrie and Anne Evans. Together they enjoyed what he remembered as "handsome days" up on the Evans Ranch.

> One morning at her wonderful place in the country we talked. I found that I liked Anne Evans and I wanted to know her better. Presently we went to the old ranch house to see her horse ... the one she rode, her favorite, was in an enclosure with the others. When Anne Evans put out her hand and called, the horse wheeled and licked her finger ... so many pleasant little memories, the tiny rill of clean, cold water lined with crystal agate and white flint—thinned trees and Mount Evans beyond the beacon. You know I went up ... and painted Mt. Evans and the pink evening cloud—we were to have stayed the night—the man with me and myself—when I had finished paint(ing) and the pink cloud was no more—I heard the silence and it was too profound ... and so we went back to the house.[9]

Spalding developed into a superb water colorist. Her work was widely exhibited—at the Chicago Art Institute, Corcoran Gallery and at Watercolor Club Exhibits in New York and Washington. As energetic in the promotion of art in Denver as she was in its production, she was one of the key figures, along with Anne Evans and Marion Hendrie, in the long effort to create an Art Museum in Denver. Spalding later served as Chairman for the Church Art Commission of the Diocese of Colorado. Her paintings graced the walls of a number of Denver Public Schools as well as St. Luke's and Children's Hospitals.

Barbara Rumsey, a great-great-granddaughter of John and Margaret Evans who has inherited the family's keen interest in Denver's art heritage, wrote a detailed and well-documented paper on Elisabeth Spalding and her artistic achievements. Rumsey described the trio of able women—Anne Evans, Marion Hendrie and Elisabeth Spalding—who pursued for twenty years the goal of establishing an Art Museum in Denver until it was accomplished. Of the trio, she wrote that, only Elisabeth Spalding "stepped into the professional arena with a full commitment to her artistic nature" and became a fully-fledged artist. The other two—Anne Evans and Marion Hendrie—though both trained as artists—continued in the more traditional woman's role of acting "as sponsors and patrons of the art community."[10] Rumsey pointed out that the sheer volume of Spalding's work—estimated at 5,000 pieces—was astonishing. The works are "scattered now in library and museum archives, home basements, a hospital, a private school and galleries and private homes throughout the country."[11] Elisabeth Spalding outlived Anne Evans, dying in 1954.

Spalding described her first encounter with the young artist, Alex Comparet, who had worked in France. She met him while she was camping in a cabin on Upper Bear Creek with her family. He was staying up on the Evans Ranch at the invitation of Margaret Evans who wanted to give him a chance to paint in the mountains. Spalding was a little taken aback when she saw him at work under a huge pine tree, and realized that he was only painting its roots.

> I did think it would have made a prettier picture if he had chosen the whole tree and the sky. He talked of the character ... of the roots which held his interest ... His work was expressive of the

mood and character of his subject, and often very poetic in feeling and rendering.[12]

Comparet was born to French parents in Indiana in 1856 and ran away from home at the age of twelve, "looking for adventure."[13] He landed somehow in Colorado Springs, where he survived by painting murals in some of the town's bars. But he did not begin painting seriously until he came to Denver, and "found a benefactor" who arranged for him to study in New York.[14] In 1874, he went to France to study under Benjamin Constant. Comparet's paintings were "romantic and idealized landscapes. His coloring was subdued and misty, giving his compositions a very poetic and romantic tone." Marturano characterizes him as the epitome of the poor and consumptive romantic artist. He married, but his wife left him. He was often too ill to paint. But he had many friends in Denver, including John and Mary Elitch, and the press was more than kind to him. In 1904, when he was nearing the end of his life, his Denver friends raised enough money for him to give one last exhibition at the Art Institute in Chicago. He left Denver soon after this for California, hoping the move would restore his health. He died in San Diego in 1906.

1882 Mining and Industrial Exposition Showcases Art— A Showcase for Art

A milestone in the development of art in Denver was the 1882 Mining and Industrial Exposition which opened on Colorado Day, August 1. This was organized by H. A. W. Tabor, at that time riding high as the Silver King of the state. The main purpose of the event was to publicize economic opportunities in Colorado in agriculture, mining and industry. But the Exposition also included an art exhibit, the first major art show in the state's history. It featured landscape paintings, china paintings and some portraits. Works of Denver artists Mrs. Chain, John Harrison Mills, Charles Partridge Adams and J. M. Bagley were included. Adams was awarded a Gold Medal in the Exposition.

Denver University Art Classes

Because of a rising demand for more art education in Denver, the University of Denver began to offer art courses in 1880. They were taught by Ida de Steiguer who, according to Spalding, "had good training and built up strong classes." Spalding notes, "The generosity of Governor and Mrs. Evans equipped the art school for the University. They and Mrs. Bancroft were true patrons of art, always encouraging artists by purchase and with real interest in their work." Anne Evans is listed in the Denver University catalogue for 1886–1887 as a student in the College Preparatory section of the school. In the 1891–1892 catalogue she is listed as an "irregular" student. This is the year when in some biographies she is said to have studied under sculptor Preston Powers, who did teach for at least one year at Denver University.

More Efforts to form a Lasting Art Organization

Early in the 1890s, Mrs. Harriet Hayden organized the Le Brun Club which was both an art school and a club for women in Denver. The membership included professional and amateur artists and part of its success was the social prominence of many of these women. Vice-President was Mrs. Emma Richardson Cherry, a first-rate artist and teacher and a life-long supporter, and creator, of art organizations. She was born in Illinois in 1859 and educated at the Art Institute in Chicago. Lacking funds at that point to further her training, she taught art at the University of Nebraska for three years to finance studies at the Art Students' League in New York. She returned to Nebraska in 1887 and married Dillon Brooke Cherry, who proved to be a remarkably supportive husband. By agreement between the two, Emma left immediately after the wedding to study in Paris. Spalding wrote,

> then and ever since he has so believed in her talent, and so understood the necessity to her of her art work, that he has in a remarkable way furthered her leaving home for travel and study ... True art appreciation came to Denver with Emma Richardson Cherry.

Spalding also observed that among the earlier artists as a group there had been a certain smallness of outlook whereas Mrs. Cherry was altruistic and public spirited. She "was interested in everything and everybody connected in any way with art and art instruction ... Mrs. Cherry always seemed to love to have us come and paint with her, always so generous. "Just come and paint; no, you must not take lessons of me, we'll paint together." Because her own life was so rich and fulfilling, Emma Cherry was convinced that painting could make a great contribution to anyone's health and happiness. She continued to travel and study throughout her life.

The existence of the Le Brun Club for women inspired a group of prominent business and professional men in Denver to form a men's group, the Denver Art League.[15] The president was a successful Leadville mine owner, William Shaw Ward. Judge Moses Hallett was vice-president and among the members were David Moffat, W. S. Cheesman and Senator N. P. Hill. The Club had ambitious purposes including the establishment of a school of design and an art museum in the city. In 1892, the League opened the Denver Art Academy in rooms on the top floor of the California Building.

The Academy was headed up by yet another newcomer drawn to Denver by the hope of a cure for his tuberculosis. This was Samuel Richards, born in Indiana in 1853. Along with three other artists from Indiana and their families, he had sailed from New York in 1880 to study art at the famed Royal Academy in Munich. The enterprising group had raised their own funds to pay for their studies, mostly by committing to sponsors to produce paintings for them—portraits from photographs, or copies of, old masters—while they were studying in Munich or on their return. After Richards came back to the United States, he spent some time in Boston and was offered the Directorship of the School of Fine Arts there. However, he was already suffering from tuberculosis and chose Denver instead.[16] The Academy offered Life Classes taught by Richards and Mrs. Cherry. The Art League sponsored two well-attended exhibitions: the first, of paintings by Walter McEwen, a well-known artist whose work had been exhibited at the Chicago World's Fair, and the second, of works by Thomas Moran. Then, like so many previous organizational efforts, it all fell apart. Samuel Richards died the next year, in 1893, and it became clear that "the finances of the undertaking were so badly managed as to rouse charges of dishonesty and the school came to an end."[17]

Emma Richardson Cherry and the Denver Artists' Club

At this point, Emma Richardson Cherry managed to form a group that endured. It started as the Artists' Club of Denver, evolved into the Denver Art Association and finally into the Denver Art Museum. According to Elisabeth Spalding, Mrs. Cherry called together a few friends one evening, and quite simply and quietly, an art club was formed. At first, it was to be limited to professional artists, primarily to organize exhibitions to showcase their work and to bring to Denver works of nationally-known artists. Those in attendance that evening, as Spalding remembers, were Mrs. Cherry; Harvey Young and Charles Partridge Adams, landscape painters; Charles M. Carter, Superintendent of Art in the Denver Public Schools and a member of the Boston Art Club; Mrs. Egbert Johnson and Miss Ida Failing, china painters; John Henderson, public school teacher and wood carver; and Elisabeth Spalding. Very soon it was decided to add associate members—those who were interested in art as patrons. Mrs. Margaret Evans and Miss Annie Evans were listed among the earliest group of associate members. The original constitution of the Club was officially adopted on December 16, 1893.

The second exhibition of the Denver Artists Club in the University of Denver Seminary building 1330 Arapaho Street, Denver Public Library Western History Collection

The first executive committee consisted of Harvey Young, Charles Partridge Adams, Charles Carter, Emma Cherry, president and Henrietta Bromwell, secretary. The constitution stated as the purpose of the Club "... the advancement of the Art interests of Denver." Dues were minimal, $1.00 a year for professional members, $2.00

for associates. Spalding recalls that "The list of active members was immediately enlarged to include "the English artist of Kensington training, Henry Read ... whom the Colorado climate had brought here from Davos, Switzerland, in search of health, and whose conservative paintings won favor here. Mr. Read's interest in the development of Denver on art lines has been shown in continuous disinterested service. He was for years the President of our Artists' Club." Anne Evans was to work with him in many areas of mutual interest. They had in common this quality of "disinterested service," the pursuit of goals in artistic matters for civic benefit rather than personal glorification.

The members of the new Club immediately set to work to put on their first art exhibition. It was held in the Fine Arts Building of the University of Denver at 1330 Arapahoe, thanks to the efforts of Margaret Evans, who was president of the Art Department's Board of Control. Having very little money at their disposal, the members and associate members did all the work themselves, unpacking the art works submitted, hanging them, preparing and serving refreshments for the opening and other associated occasions, and repacking the works after the show was over. Spalding recalled, "This was great for us; the excitement of opening the boxes; the fun of discovery; the enjoyment that came from handling and learning pictures; the knowledge we gained in the hanging and arrangement."

Anne Evans Becomes a Professional Member

In 1895, Elisabeth Spalding proposed Anne Evans for professional membership in the Club. In recounting the event some twenty years later, Spalding remembered that Anne had already been a student at the Art Students' League. "I knew of her interesting work at the Art Students' League, New York, and the charm that Mr. Twachtman praised in it. I delighted in proposing her."[18] Twachtman was a major figure on the New York art scene of the time and one of Anne Evans' teachers at the League. However, in the transcripts provided by the Arts Students' League, Anne did not register there until January of 1895 and did not have a class with Twachtman until 1897. Spalding recalled "Anne had just painted a portrait of her father, Governor Evans, which I was enthusiastic over." Spalding thought that Anne Evans would be immediately and unanimously elected. "I had an anxious moment when Mr. Read peered through his glasses, examining every detail of her painting, and Mr. Carter said it was not finished enough." Spalding went on to note how fortunate it was for the Club and for Denver that Anne Evans was in fact elected to Active Membership of the Denver Artists' Club at that meeting. "We always had a safe feeling that she was helping and guiding Mr. Read and Mayor Speer through all civic art problems."

The Artists Club of Denver, Denver Public Library Western History Collection

Anne Evans' reaction to her election was one of great joy. She was quoted as saying, "This is the proudest moment of my life."[19] She was one of a small company. A photograph of the time is titled *The Artists Club of Denver, Active Members*. There are ten: Anne Evans, Cherry, Carter, Read, Adams, Spalding, Bromwell, Elsie Ward, Mrs. W. E. Hayden and Frank P. Sauerwen.

Other Artists' Club Members

Elsie Ward was born in Missouri but came to Denver when she was quite young. The first part of her art education took place under the instruction of Ida de Steiguer and Emma Richardson Cherry. According to Spalding, she was one of the most gifted of Denver's art students who "achieved honor."[20] She studied at the Art Students' League where she was "Mr. St. Gaudens' best pupil. He was keen about her work; he used to take friends to see it, and he would say—'Isn't it bully, bully, BULLY!'" She was awarded many honors at the League, and went from there to Paris, where she continued to learn from St. Gaudens. Back in the States, she won many awards and a number of competitive sculpture commissions, including one for a fountain design for the St. Louis World's Fair in 1903. This was sponsored by the Women's Christian Temperance Union, and for it, Ward was paid the then substantial sum of $2,500. She was a member of the National Society of Sculptors and married a sculptor, Henry Hering. Elisabeth Spalding wrote about Elsie Ward. "Her very expressive bas reliefs of Mrs. Margaret Evans and of young John Evans are well known to us here."[21] These still hang in the Byers-Evans House Museum. Elsie Ward died quite young, in 1923.

Frank Sauerwein, who signed his pictures Sauerwen, was yet another talented artist who came to Denver for health reasons. He was born in 1871 in New York or New Jersey but raised in Philadelphia. His father was an artist, so the young Frank studied painting with his father as well as at the Pennsylvania Academy of Fine Arts and the Philadelphia School of Industrial Art. He first came to Denver in 1891 with his older sister, Amelia, who suffered from tuberculosis. He made his first of many trips to Indian lands in 1893 with Charles Craig, a well-known Colorado Springs artist. Sauerwein became famous for his paintings of Indian life and southwestern scenery. As a member of the Denver Artist's Club, he had his first exhibition in 1897. Opening a studio in the Tabor Opera House building in 1898, he became one of the most active and well-known members of Denver's art colony.

In 1899, he left Denver for a time to live in Taos and paint scenes of the pueblos, landscapes and old Spanish missions of New Mexico. He came back to Denver in 1901 to teach at Wolfe Hall and continue his painting. He played an active role in the Denver Artists' Club, for which he served a term as President. However, the Colorado climate was proving too severe for his sister, Amelia; they left for California in 1900. There, Sauerwein painted mission scenes. All of his life he apparently suffered from some unnamed bronchial infection, but in Los Angeles he developed active tuberculosis. He returned to Taos in 1905, hoping for a cure and resuming his paintings of southwestern life and scenery. His condition worsened. He was persuaded to travel to Stamford, Connecticut to try a new "cure", but died there in 1910 at the age of thirty-nine. It is said that, if he had lived, he would have become famous as the seventh founding member of the Taos Society of Artists.[22]

The Evans Family as Art Patrons

That the many members of the Evans family were indeed art patrons is evidenced not only by their many gifts and by activities on behalf of art and artists in Denver, but also by their art commissions and purchases, some of which are still hanging in various rooms at 1310 Bannock. In Anne Evans' sitting room is a portrait of Anne by Emma Cherry, a portrait of Anne's mother, Margaret Evans, and a rather stiff and formal one of Anne by E. Wood Perry, dated 1882. Also in that room is the reclining chair in which Governor Evans spent the last months of his life in his home at 14th and Arapahoe. This is the chair in which he sat for two portraits, which are hanging in the room, one by Emma Cherry and the other by Anne Evans. In the downstairs living room are the two delightful bas reliefs by Elsie Ward, one in bronze and one in white plaster. In the hallway is a Moorish scene by Frank Sauerwein.

In the Byers-Evans house are two of only three known paintings by Anne Evans: a portrait of William's daughter, Margaret, as a young child, and the portrait of Anne's father which gave her admittance as a professional member into the Denver Artists' Club.

There was indeed a lively, developing art scene in Denver in 1895 when Anne Evans went to New York to study at the Art Students' League. She was already a part of it, a promising young artist, a professional member of the active Artists' Club, and the daughter of prominent parents well-known for their interest in, and patronage of, the arts. From her education in Europe, she had an extensive background in the practice and appreciation of the arts. Many of her friends had studied or lived in New York, and she also had access to the extensive network of her parents' friends and acquaintances. There is no evidence that she was ever tempted to consider moving from Denver to New York or anywhere else, though she enjoyed travel. She brought all her new insights and experiences back to enrich the city and the state she loved.

11

John Evans Dies, William Evans' Star Rises

My father (William Evans) was in many ways a remarkable man, beloved by his family and those of his contemporaries who knew him best ... He made money at times like many of his Western contemporaries, but found a multitude of ways to spend it quickly in furtherance of his interests. Money as such was only a means to another end, and this end he shared with my grandfather (Governor Evans). Both were men of vision, dreamers, whose motto 'develop the country' indicated a desire and a willingness to spend time, talent and treasure in the building of a better material and educational base for the society in which they lived. Both succeeded and in their success were the seeds of other ventures as yet undreamed-of.[1]

—John Evans Sr.

Whenever the life of Anne Evans was evaluated—in newspaper and magazine articles and in citations for the many awards and honors conferred upon her—her contributions to the development of cultural life and institutions in Colorado were described in glowing terms. For clarity, her contributions—to the Denver Art Museum, the Denver Public Library, the University of Denver, the Central City Opera House restoration, the recognition of the artistic merit of the work of Native Americans in New Mexico, and the preservation of Mission Churches—will be described in separate chapters. But there are two crucial truths to remember. First, that though these activities will be described separately, most of them were going on simultaneously, often feeding into each other. Secondly, and this aspect is the subject of the next three chapters—that Anne Evans was throughout all these years deeply and intimately involved in family life. Her time-consuming and creative public efforts were not substitutes for playing an active part in the unfolding saga of a remarkable family. There were times of triumph and joy, but there were also failures and dark periods. And Anne Evans was fully present in all of these phases.

The Evans Household in 1890

When she returned from her studies in France and Germany around 1890, Anne Evans found both of her parents still enmeshed in their many commitments to the economic and cultural development of Denver and Colorado. Governor Evans was trying to rescue his last railroad venture, a long-running attempt to build a direct connection from Denver to the Gulf of Mexico so as to secure lower freight rates on imports for Denver. This started as the Denver and New Orleans Railroad and was later renamed the Denver, Texas and Gulf Road. Facing opposition from the four major transcontinental railroads, and going through many legal and financial organizations and reorganizations, this venture eventually passed out of Evans' hands, "taking with it a large part of Evans' personal fortune which he had put into the struggle to save it."[2]

By this time, another transportation venture was progressing rapidly, one which involved both John Evans and his son, William: the development of the Denver Tramway Company.

William Gray Evans Grows in Stature

After Anne's older brother, William, graduated from Northwestern University in 1877 and came home to live with his parents at 14th and Arapahoe, he worked for two years as bookkeeper for a number of his father's businesses, including the Denver and New Orleans Railroad. While still helping with his father's ventures, he participated in a number of small business operations on his own. In 1883, he teamed up with his cousin, Howard Evans, to form a real estate company.

Howard was the son of Governor Evans' older brother, Seth. He had a checkered career. A civil engineering graduate of the Massachusetts Institute of Technology, he came to Denver in 1879. William and Howard were listed in business directories as "W. G. and H. Evans, Real Estate, Loan and Collection Agents, room 21, Evans Block." Later, Howard worked as a bookkeeper for two Denver banks and as cashier for the American National Bank. On December

12, 1881, he married Sunie Lowell, the niece whom Margaret Evans had cared for and educated, in a ceremony at the Evans' home.

Howard suffered heavy financial losses in the 1893 crash. For some years the couple lived in various mining camps in the mountains while Howard tried unsuccessfully to improve his fortunes. They had two children: both died early in life. Later, Howard and Sunie built a home in Idaho Springs where Evans family members used to visit them on their way to and from the Evans Ranch.

In addition to his business activities, William Evans began to follow in his parents' footsteps and serve on boards of public interest and charitable organizations. He was a director of the Academy of Fine Arts in 1882, a member of the Orphan's Home Association and a rising power in the Republican Party.

Marriage of William Evans and Cornelia Lunt Gray

William Gray Evans, Courtesy History Colorado

Cornelia Gray Evans, Courtesy History Colorado

In 1883, Will Evans married his cousin, Cornelia Lunt Gray. She was the daughter of Margaret Evans' brother, William Patrick Gray, an important business aide to Governor Evans, first in Chicago and later in Denver. The wedding took place in the little Evans Chapel at 13th and Bannock which, according to a *Rocky Mountain News* article of December 12, 1883, was fragrant with the odors of rare blossoms. The altar was hand-somely trimmed with roses, hyacinths, and lilies. Pillars of bright tinted blossoms were at either side … The guests at the church included very many of the society people of the city … Rev. David H. Moore, Chancellor of the University of Denver … performed the solemn ceremony …

Allen Breck, William Evans' biographer, wrote that this marriage "was to prove an abiding source of help and inspiration."[3] Cornelia certainly supported William through some dark times and proved a most generous family caretaker. Both her uncle Horace Gray and her father, William Patrick Gray, spent their last years in her hospitable home, where she cared for them until their deaths.

A later chapter deals mainly with the difficult and sometimes harsh aspects of William Evans' public and private life, so it is important to remember that, in his family life, he was regarded with great affection. Late in life, his daughter, Katharine Evans, remembered him as

a warm and happy man who'd say funny things to make us laugh and write amusing notes. He loved vaudeville and baseball games. He'd go to the Orpheum Theatre every week with mother, until once she saw a performer in pink tights and was so shocked she never went to the theatre again. After that he'd take me along, if it was a 'fit' show.[4]

The Denver Tramway Company

For twenty years after the city's founding, the only public trans-portation available in Denver was a limited "Horse Car Railroad Company," granted an exclusive franchise in 1867 by the Territorial Legislature to operate horse drawn vehicles on rails in Denver and Arapahoe County. In early 1885, a group of thirteen businessmen established the Denver Electric and Cable Railway Company, with Rodney Curtis as president, William Byers vice-president and William G. Evans as secretary. Major financing came from John Evans and David Moffat. In 1886, this became the Denver Tramway Company. It proceeded to experiment with a number of technologies using electricity, finally settling on the trolley car, all the while out-maneuvering its many rivals to emerge in a dominant position in the metro area.

Governor Evans' Last Dream for Denver

Though it was clear that Anne's father was aging, (he was 80 in 1894), he was still active in fighting for the fulfillment of his dreams for Denver's future. Indeed, 1894 saw his last major battle in this cause. Evans proposed that the city should begin acquiring land in every section for parks, and that these should be approached by attractive, broad boulevards. William strongly supported his father in this proposal. *The Rocky Mountain News,* which in 1878 had passed out of the hands of Governor Evans' friend, William Byers, mounted a major campaign against the proposal. Their arguments were that watering the parks would be too costly for the taxpayers and that the major beneficiaries of the development would be John and Will Evans. They were the biggest stockholders in the Denver Tramway Company, and therefore, stood to make money from extending lines to all the new parks, and catering to picnic excursions. The opposition defeated the proposal, but the vision was out in the public arena and was eventually fulfilled by another visionary, Mayor Robert Speer.

By 1895, John Evans' health was beginning to fail and the family's financial situation, as has been noted previously, was precarious. There seems, however, to have been no desire on the family's part to save money by denying Anne the opportunity to further her art training, and expand her life experience, by enrolling in classes at the Art Students' league.

During the years she was studying intermittently in New York, Anne was still actively engaged with family, with summer life on the Evans Ranch, and with art affairs in Denver. During the period of her father's decline and death, from the end of May, 1895, until November of 1897, she was not enrolled in classes.

Death of Governor Evans

Apparently feeling a need to express some appreciation for all the services rendered to the State of Colorado by John Evans, while he was still able to enjoy the honor, the state legislature passed a Joint Resolution on March 5, 1895, naming a 14,000+ foot peak, Mount Evans, in his honor. This was a mountain very prominent on the Rocky Mountain skyline as viewed from Denver, and was also the guardian mountain of the Evans/Elbert Ranch.

By the first of July, 1897, it became clear that the end was near for John Evans.

Ropes were strung across the intersection of Fourteenth and Arapahoe to keep traffic away from the house. Streetcars were rerouted along other lines, and policemen were stationed near the house to ward off casual visitors ... Death came to John Evans at 4:30 p.m. on July 3, 1897, with his wife and children at his bedside.[5]

Evans' casket lay in state in the Capitol building on the morning of July 6, then taken to the Masonic Lodge for memorial ceremonies and from there to the Evans home for a short funeral service. Large crowds then joined the procession to Riverside Cemetery to listen to the Masonic burial ritual.

The city's newspapers were filled with obituary tributes. Some contemporary evaluations of Governor Evans' life and contributions had been far from positive. The historian Hubert Howe Bancroft wrote,

About ex-Governor Evans and his son-in-law Judge Elbert ... there is much humbug. They are cold-blooded, mercenary men, ready to praise themselves and each other profusely, but who have in reality little patriotism. I have never met a railroad man who was not the quintessence of meanness ...[6]

This evaluation is somewhat surprising in view of the fact that Bancroft conducted interviews with both Governor Evans and Margaret Evans in Denver in 1889. Margaret was interviewed together with her friend Mary Lowe Dickinson, a professor at Denver University.[7] Both of them describe in some detail John Evans' support, in time and money, of universities and churches, as well as his almost superhuman persistence in opening up Denver's opportunities to grow as a regional center by the building of railroads. Mrs. Dickinson said, "I do not know of anyone who has done so much for the whole country." Perhaps there is a clue to Bancroft's harsh evaluation in a note in Kelsey's biography of Evans. Apparently the Governor consistently refused to pay to be included in Bancroft's subscription biographies.[8]

At the time of his death, there were bitter criticisms of his attitude to the Indian tribes who populated the Territory when he came to it as Governor and condemnation of his role in the Sand Creek Massacre.

Most evaluations of John Evans have been more balanced. Harry Kelsey wrote a meticulously researched biography of Evans, an expansion of his 1960 Denver University term paper on the subject. In his original paper, he made some quite disparaging comments, describing Evans as a "garrulous, determined, optimistic, and somewhat self-righteous person." He observed that "the rather cold-blooded business ethics of this unusually religious man seem to be typical of a businessman of his time."[9] However, after an intensive study of Evans' life, he came to a more positive view of his subject.

> Many historians still cling with a death grip to the classic stereotype of the nineteenth century American capitalist—a ruthless, hardbitten entrepreneur, manipulating church and state, men and money to advance his schemes for wealth. John Evans has frequently been interpreted in this light, for his activities have usually been recounted from the point of view of those on the opposite side of the fence in business and politics. A careful examination of the record seems to justify a more favorable view of his endeavors and accomplishments.[10]

Perhaps evaluations of Evans' life are best summed up by two articles in the *Rocky Mountain News*, quoted by Kelsey at the end of his biography. Kelsey concluded that the most appropriate characterization of John Evans was "Frontier Capitalist." On the death of John Evans, the *News* applauded him as "a valuable citizen for any community" and "a man of brains, of culture and of irreproachable personal character." The article maintained that his lasting monument would not be cast in stone but would be the increasingly "Magnificent Metropolis" of Denver, for which he had worked so ceaselessly. But Kelsey thought that the *News* had caught the essence of John Evans better in an article written seven years earlier. After the *News* was sold in 1878 by William Byers, its editorial policy was no longer particularly friendly to Evans and indeed was often harshly critical, so this was a carefully weighed tribute:

> While he has been very careful to look after the personal interests of John Evans there are few ... that have done so much towards building up and making Colorado great. Governor Evans has been a really useful man.[11]

A New Home at 1310 Bannock

To house his own growing family, William Evans had in 1889 bought a house at 1310 Bannock built in 1883–4 by William N. Byers, founder of the *Rocky Mountain News*. William and Cornelia already had two children: John, born in 1884, and Josephine born in 1887. With another baby on the way, they needed more space. Margaret was born in the Bannock Street home in 1889. Their last child, daughter Katharine, arrived in 1894. After John Evans' death, the house at 1310 Bannock was considerably enlarged to create comfortable quarters for Margaret Evans and daughter, Anne. The addition consisted of bedrooms and a small sitting room on the second floor and a large library/living room on the main floor. The new section of the house had its own entrance but flowed into the rest of the home. There were no kitchen or dining facilities. The plan was obviously that Margaret and Anne would take meals with the family. They moved into their new quarters in 1900. The 14th and Arapahoe house was due to be demolished and replaced with a new headquarters building for the Denver Tramway Company. It was completed in 1910.

1310 Bannock St., Denver Public Library Western History Collection, Jennings & Russell

It was William, and not Margaret or Anne, who bore the cost of the construction of the new wing at 1310 Bannock, for he is quoted as saying that he was still paying that debt off at the time of his death. His decision to take on this expense was understandable, as not only filial duty but because the old home was being torn down to make room for the headquarters of the Denver Tramway Company of which William was in process of becoming the head. The house at 1310 Bannock still stands. Variously referred to as "an attractive Victorian mansion" and "a gloomy old pile," the Byers-Evans house is now an intriguing house museum owned and operated by the Colorado Historical Society.

After her father's death, Anne Evans returned to her studies at the Art Students' League in November of 1897. She was registered continuously to the end of April the following year, took the summer off, and was in classes again from October, 1898, to April, 1899. This marked the end of her years as an art student. She was twenty-eight years old, self-confident and, by all appearances, comfortably single. She was poised at the beginning of her long and fruitful career as what one columnist termed "An Empire Builder in the Arts."[12]

Josephine Evans knitting at home, Courtesy Margaret E. Hayden

12

The Legacy of Margaret Evans

Margaret Evans brought to all her commitments purposeful ambition, a vigorous mind, a Puritan conscience which forbade her to waste time and a personal philosophy that 'a New Englander must never be beaten.'[1]

—Allen duPont Breck

From her father, Anne Evans inherited much: incurably positive expectations about the future of Denver and Colorado, an ability to visualize large goals and the energy to pursue them in the face of setbacks, and the advantage of a respected family name. However, the legacies from her mother were even more influential. It was Margaret Evans who worked to assure Anne's financial future, and it was Margaret's major interests—art, literature, the nurturing of cultural institutions—which Anne Evans pursued as her life goals.

As we have seen, Anne Evans accorded little importance to one aspect of her mother's example: Margaret was a beauty in her day and retained all her life an air of gracious social status and careful attention to her clothes and appearance. Giving little time and attention to how she looked, Anne would twist her hair into a sometimes untidy bun[2] and put on whatever clothes happened to be at hand that were suitable for the weather. Contemporary sources did note that, when she thought it important, Anne could dress as attractively as anyone, with striking results. Anne's great-niece and namesake, Anne Evans Freyer Sweeney, (one of the daughters of Governor Evans grandson, John Evans), remembered, "Aunt Anne dressed 'informally', and loved riding britches, but for the gala events at Central City she could dress very elegantly."[3]

A Great Love of Literature and the Arts

Anne did value highly another part of her heritage from her mother—Margaret's great love of literature and of the arts. This was not just a matter of personal enjoyment, but a willingness to step in where opportunities appeared for expanding Denver's offerings in these areas.

> The library of her [Margaret Evans'] home quickly became a gathering place, for the tall cases of books, many of them water-stained from an upset while fording the Platte, supplied a real need of the town. The initial impulse of many plans since come to fruition could well be traced to that pleasant fire lit room, and to her keen interest in the up building of the community. From the day she stepped off the old Concord coach to the last years of her long life she was an acknowledged leader, a much beloved presence full of gracious dignity, of generous sympathy and of tireless devotion to any cause which she made her own.[4]

Margaret Evans, as we have seen, was a patron of the arts: she bought paintings, commissioned portraits of the family, sponsored the opening of Denver University's first art classes, offered prizes in its art exhibitions and, in company with Anne, was an early Associate Member of the Denver Artists' Club.

Especially after the end of her second sojourn in Europe in 1877, Margaret Evans appears to have made a decision to accept Denver as her permanent home.[5] She assumed leadership of many social organizations in the community and wholeheartedly embraced John Evans' vision of a great future for Denver. According to Helen Cannon, who wrote about Margaret Evans' life in one of her series of articles on *The First Ladies of Colorado*, Margaret often functioned as Governor Evans' "co-partner in civic and educational projects as well as being the initiator of her own projects."[6]

The Denver Fortnightly Club

The Fortnightly Club was of the many organizations of which Margaret Evans was a founder, and of which Anne Evans in her turn became an active member. It has provided for posterity some of the best documentation of Anne Evans' thoughts and experiences.

The Denver Fortnightly Club had its first meeting in 1881. A history of the Club, hand-written for its 10th anniversary in 1891, sheds light on the conditions in Denver at the time of its founding.

> The year 1881 in Denver was a forward looking time. The business and professional men of the city were confident of the future. But

what about their wives? They tried to be optimistic despite the pioneer aspects of their present surroundings. They were ladies ... They had come from shade, security and sanded tree-lined lanes. The homes they had left were gracious mansions containing libraries and music rooms in cities of England and the Eastern United States. They were accustomed to cultural activities ... The Denver these ladies encountered was reached after a thousand miles of prairies covered with waving, waist high buffalo grasses ... Pictures of early Denver show dust, mud, and small houses which were isolated and separated by vacant lots. There were very few trees and the population of about 35,000 was raucous and mostly adult. The books these ladies had brought with them were limited: cook books, Bibles, some history, some poetry ... There is no wonder, then, that these ladies pooled their library resources and gathered supportively around each other like a besieged wagon train. After some months of reading together, six women decided to form a permanent organization. What a coincidence that a recent visit of Mrs. Henry Strong of Chicago to her daughter, Mrs. Charles Denison, came at this opportune time! Mrs. Strong's description of the Chicago Fortnightly Club, of which she was a member, appealed greatly to the sisters-to-be in Denver ... So—on April 13, 1881, the Denver Fortnightly Club came into being ... In the fall of 1881, when the first officers of the Club were elected, Mrs. John Evans was elected Fortnightly's first President.

The purpose of forming the organization was "for the union of congenial minds for study and discussion, and for the furtherance of good in practical ways as may from time to time be approved."[7] Among the officers elected was the Second Vice President, Mrs. Spalding, described as "the English born wife of the Episcopal Bishop."[8] The Club had an interesting mode of functioning built into its constitution, which was formulated in 1881 and substantially revised in 1883. Each year, the membership was divided into four committees, Art, Current Topics, History, and Literature. Every member had a place on one of the committees each year, and was obligated, in her turn, to write an original paper. The chairman of each committee was compelled by the rules to be prepared to lead the discussion on the occasion of the presentation of a paper by a member of her committee.

The Club was founded on friendship. "For two hours twice a month, from October to April, members meet to take part in a free discussion on a topic of the day, and however they may differ, no feeling of opposition is to be carried away."[9] That there was an ability to discuss controversial topics with good humor is indicated by the following account "During 1888–89 Mrs. Hanna wrote 'A Study of Evolution.' A long discussion followed and the hostess, Mrs. Spalding, not being a full believer in evolution, was discovered quietly passing tea and cakes that certainly were not *evolved* but bore the unmistakable marks of a new, delicious *creation*."[10]

Margaret Evans served as President from 1881 to 1885, and read at least two papers during that time. In her impeccable handwriting, they are preserved in the Fortnightly Collection. The first was "Prose Fiction in Europe Prior to the Renaissance," and the second, "Michel (sic) Angelo as an Architect."

Anne Evans Becomes a Member

Anne Evans did not join the Fortnightly Club until 1919, but immediately took on all the obligations of membership. She moved each year from one interest committee to another, taking her turn as chairman from time to time. She served as first Vice-President of the Club in 1928–9, President in 1929–30, and third Vice President in 1930–31, no doubt following the Club's rule that "A member becomes president in the chronological order of her election to membership, assuring that each member eventually assumes that responsibility." But the most important product of her Fortnightly Club membership, from a biographer's point of view, is that she wrote six papers to be presented to the Club, of which two were subsequently widely read and distributed. Both were on topics related to her intense interest in the art and rituals of Southwestern Pueblo Indians.[11] These papers are among the most important of the few writings left to posterity by Anne Evans.

Art Interests: 1893–1900

Through the last years of the old century, Anne divided her time between studying at the Art Students' League in New York and being with her family in Denver. She helped her mother through the death of her father and all the responsibilities that fell to Mrs. Evans afterwards, all the while keeping up with developments on the art scene in Denver.

The Denver Artists' Club was growing. In its original constitution of December 16, 1893, and in the amended version adopted on

October 31, 1896, the stated purpose of the Club was "... the advancement of the art interests of Denver ..." On November 22, 1897, the
organization was officially incorporated and significant additions
to its mission were made.

> The objects for which our said incorporation is formed are to
> cultivate and to promote a general interest in art; to establish and
> maintain a permanent art collection; to acquire real estate and
> to erect thereon a building or buildings for use as an art gallery,
> with all of the appurtenances, belongings, matters and things
> usual or desirable in connection therewith.

If the incorporating members could have foreseen how long it
would take for their enthusiastic plans to come to fruition, their
courage might have failed. For it was not until 1909 that they
purchased their first painting for a permanent collection, and 1910
before they hung their first exhibition in quarters they could, in
any sense, call their own.

Emma Richardson Cherry, who founded the Club, was president
only briefly. Towards the end of the century, her husband's business
interests prompted a move to Texas. There, this remarkable woman
and artist is credited with the founding of art groups, one of which
eventually became the Houston Fine Arts Center and another the
art museum in San Antonio. The leadership role in the Denver
Artists' Club was taken over by Henry Read, who served as president
from 1894 to 1899.

The Club had to move its second annual exhibition from the
University of Denver Fine Arts building because a long-term tenant
had been granted a lease there. The 1896 show was held in rooms
at the Gettysburg Building Annex. A building committee was
appointed to start work on securing permanent quarters for an art
gallery for the Club. At an open meeting in January 1897, the
building committee announced that it had found several suitable
locations for a gallery and exhibited a variety of possible plans
drawn up by architect members of the Club. The eventual opening
of the Club's first real home, in the new Carnegie Library building
on the evolving Civic Center, took place in February of 1910, after
thirteen long and often frustrating years had elapsed. In those years,
Anne Evans moved from the status of being her famous parents'
only daughter, art student and aspiring artist, to the appointments

that would make her a power player in many areas of Denver's cultural evolution.

At the close of the century, however, Anne Evans was apparently still thinking of herself as an artist, though we have little evidence of exactly what she was painting at this time. There appeared a newspaper article in the *Denver Times* on October 31, 1899, head-lined "Pleasant Studio Tea Which Gives a Look at the Work of a Quartet of Denver Women." It noted,

> From an artistic as well as social standpoint, the studio tea given by four ladies at their studio in the Kittredge building was a brilliant success. Masses of gracefully curved palms, snowy white statuary, cool, restful scenes of painted art or glorious splashes of sunset beauty, caught by the quick eye of the artist and transferred to canvas, formed a part of the background for the beautiful costumes worn by pretty maidens and matrons. Miss Elsie Ward, Mrs. Emma Richardson Cherry, Miss Annie Evans and Miss Spaulding were the hostesses for this delightful afternoon.

The reporter reserved the highest praise for the work of Elsie Ward, described as the "young sculptress who but recently returned from Paris" and who "is far above the ordinary women artists, and in the front ranks of the profession. Her masterpiece formed the center of a constantly admiring throng ..." About Elisabeth Spalding, the article said that "her work consisted principally of landscapes, executed both in oil and water color. She won a prize on a larger copy of a painting exhibited yesterday, *The Erie Docks,* some time ago, which was donated by the artist to the public library at Erie." About Mrs. Cherry's work, the writer became quite poetic:

> [Her] pictures were most of mountain scenery and showed a pas-sionate love for the warm-hued tints of mountain scenery. She seems to have dipped her brush into the crimson and gold of mountain sunsets, and used the colors for the background of her Colorado scenery.

Anne Evans apparently had only one painting in the show—the same portrait of her father that had won her admission to the Denver Artists Club in 1894. "Miss Evans is the daughter of former

Governor Evans of Colorado, of whom she exhibited a fine, somber-hued portrait, which is said to be a wonderfully true likeness."

Margaret Evans Provides for the Women of Her Family

Governor Evans died without a will. On August 5, 1897, Margaret Evans reported to the court the assets which had come to her by inheritance. These included the Evans Block at 15th and Lawrence, with a mortgage of $80,000 on it, and seven other parcels of Denver real estate, 450 acres of undeveloped land in Arapahoe County, and a half interest in the Elbert and Evans Ranch, valued at $12,500 and carrying a mortgage of almost $5,000. (When Samuel Elbert died in Galveston, Texas, in 1899, he left his half interest in the ranch equally to William's wife, Cornelia, and Anne Evans.) Stock holdings included 4706 shares of Denver City Tramway stock, a large block of stock in Macon Mining Company—almost one and a half million shares—whose value depended on whether the mines were ever developed, and small amounts of stock in a variety of other companies.

By 1903, thanks to careful management by Anne's older brother, Evan, some measure of stability and future growth in the family portfolio had been restored. The family followed Evan's recommendation to place the remaining assets in the newly-organized Evans Investment Company. This was incorporated on February 4, 1903 by Margaret Evans and her three children, William, Evan, and Anne. According to Allen Breck,[12] "It was incorporated for twenty years ... as a private company to manage and conserve the remnants of the estate by buying and selling property, stocks, bonds, and borrowing and lending money. A capital stock of $600,000 par value was issued, to be divided into 6,000 shares at $100 per share. At the first meeting of the Board of Directors, Mrs. Margaret P. Evans was elected president, W. G. Evans, vice-president, and Evan Evans secretary-treasurer. The fourth director was Anne Evans."

By this time, perhaps in accordance with the inheritance laws of the time for those who died intestate, or perhaps by action of Margaret Evans, the inherited properties were owned one-half by Margaret and one-sixth each by the three children. Mrs. Evans received 3,000 shares of stock for her holdings, and each of the children 1,000 shares each. Evan Evans became the company manager, charged with managing its real estate, collecting rents and other money due to the company, and dealing with its other assets. The Board at first held monthly meetings at 1310 Bannock Street.

At a Board meeting in December of 1903, Anne Evans became one of two Vice-Presidents and Cornelia began attending meetings. For the first few years the Company had little profit to report, most of the income being eaten up by property taxes, interest payments and necessary improvements to buildings. But there were already signs that, with the frugal and attentive management of Evan, who served as manager until his death in 1921, the Company would yield a reasonable return for its shareholders.

Anne's modest income seemed assured. But Margaret Evans had reason to be concerned about the financial future of William's wife, Cornelia, and her four children. Margaret had experienced the huge gains and losses in her husband's fortunes resulting from his railroad and other investments. After great effort and many twists and turns of fortune, he had made money on the Denver South Park and Pacific venture, but had sustained great losses on the Denver and New Orleans project. She could see that her son, William, was on the same path as his father, willing to risk all his fortune on developments that he believed would both be profitable and make a contribution to the economic development of Colorado. She proposed that, when she died, she would leave William's share of her holdings in the Evans Investment Company to Cornelia, provided that he would give his own shares in the company to his wife.

Death of Margaret Evans

Margaret Evans died at home on September 7, 1903, at the age of 74. She was buried in Riverside Cemetery beside her husband. After the death of Governor Evans in 1897, she had given up most of her community responsibilities and virtually retired from social life in Denver, devoting herself more and more to family affairs and to her religious exercises. A little altar was built into her quarters, where she could quietly pray and conduct her daily devotions. The newspapers carried favorable obituaries, praising her "noble character and generous and tender heart."s

> She was one of the most notable women of her time. Tall, dignified and stately, highly educated, polished and refined, Mrs. Evans held a lofty position in the society of the National Capital during the

frequent visits she paid in Washington. Here, in Denver, where she entertained quite frequently at the family mansion on Fourteenth Street, she was the delight of all her guests through her gracious cordiality and earnest solicitation for their welfare. She united heartily, and often with powerful influence, with the Governor in all the great measures he initiated for the up building of the city, the territory and the state.[13]

Mrs. Evans loss leaves a void in the ranks of the early settlers of Colorado ... Mrs. Evans founded the Denver Orphans' home, was one of the chief friends of the Young Woman's Christian Association, and was widely loved because of her charitable works. She was a strong personal friend of Mrs. Elizabeth M. Byers, and the two ... carried on many charitable works together.[14]

Evans Investment Company Shares Redistributed

Shortly after her death, a meeting of the Evans Investment Company shareholders was called in their new office quarters in the Evans Block at 1624 Tremont Place. Evan Evans was elected president and Anne Evans secretary. In March of the following year, the shares of Margaret Evans were allocated to her three children, with the share of William Evans going, as promised, to his wife, Cornelia. William retained just 100 shares, Cornelia having the remaining 900 of his original portion plus the 1000 from Margaret. Evan and Anne had 2000 shares each.

Evan Evans, Courtesy History Colorado

The Investment Company began to yield a modest income for the major shareholders. Margaret died believing that she had assured Cornelia of an independent income, at least enough to maintain her home and meet the daily expenses of her family. Unfortunately, William's business interests consumed him as his mother had feared, and he later persuaded his wife to give him her shares to use as collateral for one of his many business dealings. Cornelia's shares were only restored to her by the generosity of her son John, his wife, Gladys Cheesman, and Evan Evans.

Exactly what expenses Anne Evans had to cover with her income is not clear, nor is information available on just what financial arrangements were made to enable her to build her home on the Evans Ranch. They were obviously adequate for the task, however.

Choosing a Life Style

After her mother's death, Anne Evans chose to remain in her comfortable quarters at 1310 Bannock Street. Her choice of what we today would call a life style seems perfect for the activities she undertook. She could have had a home of her own in Denver. After all, she joyfully elected to build a mountain house for herself on land on the Evans Ranch. Or she could have chosen, like her artist friend, Josephine Hurlburt, to live with a compatible woman companion. In that case, it would most likely have been Mary Kent Wallace, the first headmistress of Kent School. Kentie, as Anne called Mary Kent Wallace, was Anne's best and most constant friend for all her adult years in Denver. Anne left her friend a small monthly stipend in her will.

Anne Evans' quarters at 1310 Bannock reflect her interest in Native American and Southwest arts, Courtesy History Colorado

Anne, however, chose to continue to live in the wintertime in her own separate quarters at 1310 Bannock. There she could work on projects, hold meetings, and come and go freely. In addition to her cultural activities, Anne Evans was an active business woman. She played a serious role both in the Evans Investment Company and the Kuhlborne Ranch Company, which she founded after the death of her mother.[15] At the same time, Anne remained an integral part of the William Evans family. She took meals with them and enjoyed participating in the developing lives of a nephew and three nieces, to whom she remained close all her life. She loved children and had a natural rapport with them.

In the summers, she spent as much time as possible in her beloved mountain home, where the Williams Evans family and other members of the Evans, Elbert, and Lunt families also gathered. There they entertained visitors and participated in a stimulating round of wonderfully varied activities. They organized riding expeditions in the Mount Evans area, took turns hosting parties, and collaborated in staging elaborate pageants and cherished rituals.

Before taking up the story of Anne Evans' adult life, and detailing her contributions to the cultural institutions of Denver, it seems necessary to look at the darker side of her close involvement with family—because of the insight it gives into the depth of her commitment, and the demands it made on her time and energies.

13

Tribulations and Resurgence of William Evans

O the mind, mind has mountains; cliffs of fall
Frightful, sheer, no-man-fathomed. Hold them cheap
May who ne'er hung there.
                                        —Gerard Manley Hopkins

Money-making, social achievement, family and posterity
are nothing but plain nature, not culture. Culture lies
outside the purpose of nature. Could by any chance
culture be the meaning and purpose of the second half
of life?[1]
                                        —C. G. Jung

The Tall, Lanky Streetcar Sultan

"W. G. Evans had a personality strong enough to bring him into prominence even while his father was still alive." So wrote a Denver Post columnist.[2] She went on to say that, after his marriage to his cousin, Cornelia, William "worked *with* his father instead of *for* him." Both William and his father were investors in the Denver Electric and Cable Railway Co., which in 1885 secured a franchise to operate electrically-powered street cars in the city. Renamed the Denver Tramway Company, the organization was a

William Gray Evans, Courtesy History Colorado

success almost from the start. Other transport companies (and there were many) failed, partly as a result of the 1893 depression, so that by 1900, the Company "owned every street railroad in Denver and was worth $10 million."[3]

William Evans became vice-president of the Tramway Company in 1902, succeeding William N. Byers. Later in that same year he became president, on the resignation of Rodney Curtis.

During the first part of the new century, there were bitter political battles over the duration and cost of the franchise to operate a monopoly public transportation system. These produced a lot of lively mud-slinging by the newspapers of the day. William Evans had become the effective head of the Republican Party, though he preferred to remain in the background in this capacity. He became the butt of Denver's cartoonists as "Napoleon Bill" and the symbol of all that was wrong with an economic system that was portrayed as one of corporate domination and greed, corrupting both the political process and the legal system.

> A commanding, six-foot, three-inches tall, Evans was the authoritative utility figure and political manipulator in Denver during the 1890's and early twentieth century ... He developed outstanding ties with political operatives, Republicans and Democrats alike, as he dictated policy to city hall and the legislature ... at least until Evans stepped down as the head of Tramway in 1913, wherever anyone looked in Colorado, the observer was sure to see the shadow of the tall, lanky streetcar sultan." [4]

"Tall, lanky streetcar sultan" is a great phrase, but seems to represent a confusion between William Evans, who was usually described as "stocky" and was of average height, and his son, most often characterized as "banker John Evans," who stood tall and straight at "6 foot 3."

According to Evans' biographer, Allen Breck, it was the hurtful experiences of "the excesses of irresponsible journalism" which prompted William Evans to "shun the public eye as much as possible" and decide to promote his interests through the medium of personal persuasion. The unremitting opposition from the press as well as from business rivals developed in William a steely persistence and an ability to engage in quiet, long-term planning in pursuing objectives he believed in.[5]

Denver Tramway Building at 14th and Arapahoe Streets, Denver Public Library Western History Collection

Before the coming of the automobile, public transportation was essential to the fabric of life in Denver.

> Even the rich usually depended on streetcars to get them to and from their jobs. Hopping on the trolley was the prime means of visiting a park, going to church, or attending a play ... During the last 30 years of the 19th century, entrepreneurs offered a wide variety of transit services, including early efforts at streetcars and cable cars. In 1899, after the trolley, powered by an overhead wire, had shown its superiority, Tramway got hold of virtually all public transportation services. Residents essentially had the choice between walking and paying Tramway's fares.[6]

The Denver Tramway company operated under a franchise dating back to 1885. One of the results of William Evans' preeminence in the political sphere was his effectiveness in averting the levying of additional taxes on the Tramway's virtual monopoly on public transportation in the city.

The Cheesman-Evans Connections

In the efforts to minimize taxes on utilities, William Evans joined with Walter Cheesman, long-time friend and business associate of William's father, Governor Evans. Just as William had emerged from the struggles of the 1890s as the virtually unchallenged head of the Denver Tramway Company, so Walter Cheesman proved to be the most far-sighted developer of water resources adequate for the continuing growth of Denver. The still-indispensable Cheesman Dam and Reservoir are testimony to his enterprise and his vision. He also invested in, and developed, real estate in the expanding downtown area of the city. Cheesman enjoyed sharing his dreams and plans with Gladys, his only daughter.

In 1902, Cheesman decided to build a larger and more gracious home for his family than the three-story brick house at 1540 Lincoln where they had lived for more than fifteen years. The architectural firm of Marean and Norton was selected to design the building. It was to be located at Eighth and Logan, on "a half-block of twenty-two lots, later to be numbered 400 East Eighth Avenue."[7] However, Cheesman became ill with influenza at this time and put aside the plans. He never fully recovered, and died in May of 1907.

Completing Cheesman's Dreams—
Cheesman Park and the Cheesman Mansion

As a memorial to Walter Cheesman, his wife and daughter completed a project which was just barely under way, with Cheesman funding, at the time of his death. This effort had been undertaken upon the urging of Mayor Robert Speer, who told a group of prominent businessmen that "something impressive could be done with the old Congress Park ... on Denver's east side"[8] At the time, this was 84 acres of weeds and rambling paths, but its history went all the way back to the founding of Denver City by General Larimer, when the area that is now Cheesman Park was designated as the city's cemetery. It gradually ceased to be used, however, with the founding of Riverside in 1876 and other cemeteries thereafter. At the urging of one of Colorado's senators, Congress passed legislation allowing it to be converted to a park.

The mishandled transfer of bodies from the old cemetery is one of the more macabre aspects of Denver history. After a 90-day deadline for families to remove the relics of relatives privately had expired, a contract to remove the bodies that were left, for $1.90 each, was awarded in 1893 to a less than honorable undertaker. He was caught separating remains and putting them in more than one container in order to get more money. His contract was canceled and the city simply leveled the land, leaving some 1,000 bodies still buried there.

An interesting diagrammatic map[9] shows the rough locations of grave sites for different population groups. In what is now Cheesman Park—which was previously known as the Mount Prospect or City Cemetery from 1858–1890 and then as Congress Park, were the following provisions: GAR (Grand Army of the Republic) Graves, Odd Fellows' Graves, Society Graves, Masonic Graves, Chinese Graves and a Potter's Field. The present Botanic Gardens site was a Catholic Cemetery and east of that, the parking lot on York was a Hebrew Cemetery. Today's Congress Park was once a Denver City Nursery.

Mrs. Cheesman and her daughter contributed $100,000 "for the permanent improvement and decoration of the park." The Mayor and civic authorities renamed the ground the Walter S. Cheesman Memorial Park, and at its highest point the Cheesmans commissioned a memorial colonnade of Colorado marble, with balustrades and marble reflecting pools. The park and its impressive pavilion became the pride of the city, celebrated in glowing terms in *Denver Municipal Facts*:

> Cheesman Park has one grand natural characteristic that puts it in a class by itself, and that is—the clear unobstructed view which it commands of the city, the valleys beyond and the mountain range in the distance, a view which adjectives are incapable of describing and an inspiring spectacle which no other city on the American continent can boast.[10]

Aside from the fact that the expansion of the city has redefined the park's location, as it is now almost in the city center, this description is still valid today.

Mrs. Cheesman and daughter, Gladys, also decided to reactivate the plans for a new Cheesman home. The building was substantially completed early in 1908. The Colonial mansion, of dark red brick with stone trim and ivy-covered walls, was three stories high, contained 27 rooms and gracious formal gardens, and was surrounded by a wrought iron fence six feet high. In November of that year, although the interior decor was not completed, the house was arrayed in green and white decorations for the marriage of John Evans Sr. and Gladys Cheesman. They were described as "childhood sweethearts" in the press coverage of the time.[11] The couple was married in a ceremony conducted by Henry Martyn Hart, Dean of St. John's Cathedral. Thereafter, they took off for a honeymoon tour of California. The first leg of the trip was in David Moffat's private railroad car. At La Junta, they were met by the chauffeur and maid who accompanied them on the rest of the journey.[12] When they returned, the couple lived for several years with Mrs. Cheesman in the new home at 8th and Logan. Their first child, Alice, was born there in 1906.[13]

Not long after the birth of their first child in the Cheesman mansion, John and Gladys Cheesman Evans moved to their new home at 2001 E. Alameda Avenue, designed by architects Fisher and Fisher. They lived for fifty years in the home they called Hill-top. There two other children were born, John in 1915 and Anne in 1917.

Defending the Utility Franchises: Rough Political Times in Denver

In addition to Walter Cheesman and his water supply monopoly, Will Evans cooperated with the operators of the Denver Gas and Electric Company and the developing telephone system to defend their franchises. At the same time, Evans became associated with David Moffat's long struggle to build a railroad through the Colorado mountains.

In 1902 the Home Rule Amendment, Article XX of the Colorado Constitution, created the City and County of Denver, separating Denver from Arapahoe County. In 1904, Denver residents voted to approve a bitterly contested home rule charter, which established a mayor-council form of municipal government. Democrat Robert Speer was elected the first mayor of the new City and County of Denver. The relationship of Evans, the undisputed leader of the Republican Party, with Democratic Mayor Speer was caricatured as one of puppeteer to puppet: Napoleon Bill was said to be "the Boss of the boss." The entire political and economic system was under attack in the early years of the new century by Denver's native "muckrakers."

Chief among these were Thomas Patterson, then editor of the *Rocky Mountain News*, Edward P. Costigan, a young crusading lawyer who subsequently became a U. S. Senator from Colorado, and Judge Ben Lindsey, an ardent advocate for the rights of the poor and of children. He established in Denver the first juvenile court in the United States. Ben Lindsey's book, *The Beast*,[14] is the passionate story of Lindsey's life in Denver, fighting against "The Beast" which he defined as the

Courtesy History Colorado

over-riding coalition of the wealthy and powerful interests which controlled the lives of everyone living in the cities of America.

The book was a scathing indictment of Boss Evans, whom Lindsey accused of ballot-stuffing and so securing "voters good for 500 votes each while the people had only voters of one vote apiece." He wrote that the election of 1906 was "rigged ... by the tramway-telephone-water-gas corporation powers, manipulated by such men as Field and Evans ... to secure franchises at prices far below what they should have paid."

Lindsey had no great regard for Walter Cheesman either. He described his attempt to get support from Cheesman at a time when Lindsey's work with the juvenile court was being undermined because he was insisting on forging ahead with prosecutions for voting fraud. Cheesman was "seated at his mahogany writing desk ... bald, elderly, with a round and kindly face but shrewd, cold eyes." Lindsey was getting nowhere with his appeal for help. "Well," he protested, "What about the *people*?" Cheesman replied, "You have been long enough in politics to know that the people have nothing to do with these things."[15]

Courtesy History Colorado

Streetcars overturned on Colfax Avenue during the Tramway strike, Courtesy History Colorado

In many ways, William Evans was a stereotypical corporate boss of the early twentieth century, particularly in his absolute and unreasoning opposition to labor unions. In 1910 almost one thousand Tramway employees signed a petition for a raise in wages. The Company fired the most prominent pro-union workers and proclaimed that it would not "tolerate agitators or recognize union labor."[16] Public opinion turned against the Tramway Company. There was already widespread dissatisfaction with what was perceived as its callous indifference to accidents and injuries to passengers. In 1910–1911, the anger erupted into open demonstrations. Rocks were thrown through streetcar windows, and there were fist fights between passengers and conductors. It became obvious that the underlying grievance was the power of the Tramway Company and its leader, William Evans, in protecting its monopoly and paying far less than was felt to be fair in exchange for its franchise. A Denver newspaper fulminated that "Evans was the most conscienceless boss that ever bestrode a suffering people."[17]

Officials of Denver gave in to public opinion and announced that the Tramway's taxes would be raised. Tramway retorted that it would have to raise fares, whereupon the Denver Grand Jury decided that it would undertake a full investigation of the Tramway's franchise. At this point, the Tramway Company reorganized and Evans resigned as president.

Breakdown and Recovery: The Dark Years of 1912–1914

By 1913 William Evans, drained by the struggle, the constant adverse publicity, law suits and counter suits, and an ill-advised venture into newspaper ownership in an attempt to counter the attacks, suffered what was described as a "nervous breakdown." By this time, Evans had also suffered the loss of virtually his whole personal fortune, about a quarter of a million dollars, in the attempt to carry forward the dream of his friend, David Moffat, the dream of carrying a railroad west to Salt Lake City by drilling a tunnel through the Rocky Mountains. Moffat himself had died in 1911, after failing to secure the needed additional financing.

Evans resigned from all his offices in the Denver Tramway Company and also in the railroad and other companies in which he was involved. The sole position he kept was the presidency of the board of trustees of Denver University. Ironically, by this time the revenues of the Tramway Company were already threatened by the burgeoning popularity of that newest innovation in transportation, the automobile. William Evans, a man of uncommon vision in so many areas,

> failed accurately to assay the increasingly disastrous impact of the automobile upon the patronage and earnings of the Tramway Company. He never altered his basic concept that the perpetual right to occupy the streets of a growing city at a service fare of five cents would overcome the extravagance of private automobiles cluttering the streets.[18]

In fact, Evans' shares in the Denver Tramway Company, which once had been worth over a million dollars, had already fallen drastically in value by 1913.

Biographer Breck was content to accept the label of "nervous breakdown" for the catastrophic 1913 development in William's life. This characterization was given to his condition by the Evans family at the time and was commonly used in contemporary newspaper articles. Breck went on to cover the next two years in William's life in a few light-hearted sentences, "He headed for a long vacation in Florida, Cuba, and, later, in California to regain his health and strength."[19] The press, Breck wrote, discovered him in due time displaying remarkable achievements in fishing. In an article head-lined "Bill Evans is Found and He's Going Some," the *Denver Post* commented,

> And right when we had been led to believe that one W. G. (Bill) Evans was an ailing, paling, failing man, along comes *Field and Stream* to tell how the former Denver Tramway Boss pulled a 340-pound swordfish out of the ocean's depths and landed it kerplop on the pier at Catalina Island ...[20]

The truth about this breakdown, another one that preceded it a year earlier, and the two years that followed it, is much darker and more poignant. The only reason to bring this part of the story to light is because it illuminates the role of Anne Evans in the Evans family and the extent of the responsibilities which she shared with her brother, Evan, her sister-in-law, Cornelia, and nephew, John. What actually happened in 1913 is documented in several letters in one of the Evans collections of the Colorado Historical Society Library.

In mid-September William Evans, accompanied by his auditor and stenographer, traveled to New York to consummate arrangements with his company's bankers there to finance $750,000 worth of bonds that were due to mature in Chicago on October 1. Evans was convinced in his own mind that arrangements for this financing had already been made, but it was soon discovered that this was not the case. Two of his Denver Tramway Company business associates were rushed out to New York. They found Evans "confused and helpless ... resorting to stimulants from time to time, which rendered him more confused and helpless, and absolutely forgetful of previous happenings."[21] The necessary financing was hastily arranged by the business associates only thirty minutes before the deadline. They immediately secured William's letter of resignation as president of the Tramway Company, and left New York with him. Anne Evans and William's wife, Cornelia, were dispatched to Chicago to meet William, with instructions to keep him there until decisions could be made about his other business responsibilities and about treatment for his condition. The family came together in a concerted effort to help William regain his mental and physical health and to repair the financial damage caused by his actions.

It seems possible that William suffered from what today is termed Bipolar Disorder and that the episode which ended his financial and political career was the culmination of a long manic episode. Evan Evans wrote:

> ... his acts; especially for the past year; which were those of an unbalanced mind; thousands of dollars used without consulting his associates in wild schemes; numerous and apparently worthless persons drawing salaries at an exorbitant rate; promises to do things that the normal mind would know to be impossible.[22]

William's resort to alcohol and questionable non-prescription drugs was likely what today would be termed self-medication—an attempt to cope with the distressing symptoms of an undiagnosed condition. Whatever the cause, the situation facing the family was dire.

Evan Evans immediately consulted with William's physician, Dr. Pershing, who had treated him a year earlier for a similar condition: "a complete breakdown, sort of mental paralysis ... for several weeks (he) was *helpless*, mentally and physically, at his residence."[23] After a period of "complete segregation from business and an uncompromising withdrawal of all alcoholic stimulants,"[24] William believed he had totally recovered and went right back to the stresses of work and the palliative of alcohol. Evan wrote to Anne that Dr. Pershing's opinion was that "no person on earth, after being in the condition that Will was in last fall, could use alcohol without unbalancing his mind."[25] If he did not stop using alcohol "the end is likely to be pretty rapid ... it is apt to result fatally at any time and it will not be very far off."[26] Dr. Pershing's recommendation was for immediate legal commitment for not less than six to twelve months. "There are institutions in every state where he can have excellent care,"[27] he suggested.

It appears that, after a visit from Dr. Pershing to Chicago, William fully consented to treatment. One week after their arrival in Chicago, Cornelia accompanied her husband to a Sanitarium in Wawatosa, a suburb of Milwaukee, while Anne Evans returned to Denver, bringing to the family direct and encouraging news about William's "present condition and attitude, which is lovable and amenable in all respects."[28]

There was never the slightest suspicion that William's irrational financial commitments were undertaken for personal gain, as Evan

Evans is at pains to emphasize in his letter to a family friend in Chicago. "Serious as the situation was, and is, there was ... nothing of a *fraudulent* nature, or even a *suggestion* of fraudulent intent. From the very beginning of the Tramway Co, until his resignation last Monday, his course has been one of *absolute self-sacrifice*, and it is so regarded ... by all ..."[29] However, settling up for William's actions cost the family dearly.

Responsibility Falls on William's Son, John Evans Sr.

The breakdown was particularly hard on William's son, John. After his graduation from M. I. T. in electrical engineering, John had joined the Tramway Company as assistant electrical engineer at the power plant. According to biographer Breck, he demonstrated from his earliest years there the qualities of "meticulous attention to detail coupled with imagination and daring" that propelled him into a position of leadership among the civic-minded business men of Denver for more than 60 years. He rose quickly to become chief engineer and assistant general manager of the Company. In 1912, he resigned his positions with the Tramway Company, though remaining a stock holder and member of the board of directors.

Through his marriage to Gladys Cheesman, he had inherited two major responsibilities. The first was the ongoing management of large real estate holdings. The second was the task to obtain a fair price for the sale of Cheesman's Denver Union Water Company, a private corporation, and related companies, to the City of Denver. Denver had decided to operate its own municipal water system. His successful work for the water company so impressed one of Denver's major banking figures that he offered the 31-year-old Evans the presidency of, and an interest in, the International Trust Co. There, in turn, Evans established such "a reputation for energy and hard work"[19] that he was offered the presidency of one of Denver's pre-eminent banks, the First National, where he served for 31 years.

In a painfully honest letter written to his father, John Evans listed all the recompenses he made, along with Evan Evans, to settle the loans and financial commitments made by William when he was not in a rational frame of mind.

> It is not easy to write about some of the things that have hurt so much and caused so much anxiety but you must know about them and I must write them to you ... You were wound to the point

of nervous and mental exhaustion over many things during the past year or two which were going wrong, either with loss of money or of power, and these worries you would not admit to anyone, not even to those whose friendship should have been made to share the burdens ... looking back upon the stimulants and drugs like Antikamnia that you have poisoned yourself with, I cannot but thank heaven that things are no worse than this.[30]

He went on to give an additional incentive to his father to take his commitment to treatment seriously: "if you will build yourself up ... you will build Mother's health to where it has not been in years." This allusion gives some clue to how much of a strain William's condition had put upon his long-suffering wife, Cornelia.

A Time of Exile

The years away from Denver while William was at the Sanitarium, and then on a prolonged vacation spent mainly at various prime fishing venues, were hard on Cornelia. The couple had traveled frequently in the first decade of the new century, often to visit their daughters, Margaret and Josephine, while they were at school in the east or, later, in Europe, but this period was different. It was one of exile. William at least had his passion for fishing to occupy him, but Cornelia was essentially just filling in time until they could return home. "How can Christmas be very much to us without you?" she wrote to her daughter, Katharine, from Pensacola, Florida, at the end of 1913, "I miss you terribly all the time but I try not to think about anything too long and so get through the days ... Today Father is off in the Gulf after red snapper. I think he is about ready to move on somewhere else—he seems to have caught every kind of fish around here. We will all be glad to go to some place warmer than this."[31]

Nineteen-year-old daughter, Katharine, who unlike her sisters was educated in Denver, took charge of the household with the help of her Aunt Anne. Anne visited William and Cornelia in their various locations, as is clear from an occasional photograph or letter that has been preserved. Daughter Margaret, in an undated letter to her sister, Katharine, from Key West, wrote,

Mother and I are sitting on the balcony, Mother sewing and I writing. Father and Anne have gone fishing in a motor boat. I hope they'll have good sport. Father wanted to get a shark like the one I've photographed here. Mother and I happened to drive along the beach just after this one had been landed ... It was 11 feet 1 inch and still alive.[32]

She went on to say that she thought they would go on to Havana and find more comfortable quarters.

Father is rather planning to leave us there and go off on a two or three weeks fishing trip ... Havana ought to be more interesting than Key West which consists wholly of saloons and cigar factories.[33]

It did not help that Cornelia, though treasuring the correspondence she received from the family, had great difficulty in writing. In the same letter quoted above, Margaret told Katharine that Mother had started a letter to her. "Writing is fearfully hard for her ... that's one thing we ought all to understand and be patient with."

Letters that have been preserved make it clear that Anne Evans kept up a constant and lively correspondence with family members. She wrote to her nieces when they were away at school in the east or in Europe, and to them at home in Denver when she was visiting or traveling with their parents.

Return to Denver

The exile ended for William and Cornelia in late 1914. For the remaining ten years of his life, William Evans was not involved with money-making. He had few assets left and presumably the family income came from the Evans Investment Company. This was flourishing, thanks to the energy and financial expertise invested by Evan Evans. Of the 6,000 shares in the Company, Evan and Anne held 2,000 each, Cornelia 1900 and William 100. As mentioned previously, Cornelia's 1900 shares, with which Margaret Evans believed she had secured Cornelia's future, had been pledged away by William during his period of mental aberration, but were redeemed by Evan and John and Gladys Cheesman Evans. Evan was Secretary and Treasurer of the Company, William Vice-President and Anne Evans, Secretary.

Evan Evans died of heart failure on June 16, 1921, at the age of 58. He passed away at his Denver home at 1325 Race Street, having come home after visiting his daughter, Madelyne, in Washington, D.C.[34] Evan was buried in Riverside Cemetery.

After Evan's death, his widow, Kathryn, was elected as a director of the company. William became President and his son, John, vice-president and treasurer. Later in the year, Anne Evans resigned as secretary and was succeeded by Howard Evans.

Completing Moffat's Dream of a Tunnel

William Evans no longer had anything to gain personally from the completion of David Moffat's dream of a railroad tunnel through the mountains, but he continued to expend himself tirelessly on the project. In his effort to secure for Denver a rail route west to Salt Lake City, Moffat had constructed part of the Denver, Northwestern and Pacific railroad by 1902, with the tracks climbing Rollins Pass in a series of steep grades and switchback loops. However, the excessive costs of snow removal made this venture unprofitable. Evans managed to get a bond issue passed by Denver voters in 1914 to finance two-thirds of the cost of constructing a tunnel through a shoulder of James Peak. The issue was defeated on the legal grounds that the city did not have a constitutional right to enter into a joint venture with a private corporation to build the tunnel. The only hope then lay with State funding, which seemed impossible given the hostility of so many legislators to Denver. A devastating flood in Pueblo in the spring of 1922 gave Denver legislators an unexpected bargaining chip. They voted for emergency funding for Pueblo in exchange for legislative authorization for the issuance of bonds for the Moffat Tunnel Improvement District.

Construction of the tunnel was more difficult than anticipated. A pioneer tunnel had to be bored parallel to the main one to facilitate the work. This eventually became the water tunnel carrying Western Slope water through to the thirsty residents of the eastern side of the mountains. Construction took 5 years, 28 lives, and $24 million—almost four times the original estimate. The first train went through the tunnel in February of 1928.

The headline of the *Denver Post* article, written when the railroad tunnel was finally "holed through" in 1927, after William Evans' death, proclaimed, "Big Tunnel Should Bear Evans' Name; should share Honors with D. H. Moffat." The article stated, "This recognition is due the late W. G. Evans, whose perseverance and steadfast adherance [sic] to the idea of a railroad bore through the Continental Divide finally brought the project to consummation."

The Man Most Responsible for the Moffat Tunnel

Courtesy History Colorado

Years of Civic Service

William Evans also contributed greatly in his last years to many civic and philanthropic organizations. He was back in town to chair the meeting of the Denver University Board of Trustees on November 27, 1914. The story of his contributions to the University is told in a later chapter. Here, it is enough to cite a tribute from Chancellor Henry Buchtel in recognition of the devoted service Evans had given to the University ever since he became a Board member in 1900.

> Eighteen years ago when I came into service as Chancellor, the University was considered by many to be hopelessly embarrassed. The situation was most depressing as our deficit was large and our income small. The University debt had grown larger and larger year after year. In 1905 you were elected ... President of the Board of Trustees of the University of Denver. But for your timely assistance again and again we could not have kept the University alive and in a state of high efficiency. During these eighteen years we have collected in cash around a million dollars. Fully eleven percent of that gigantic sum has been given by you without any solicitation from anyone. Your knowledge of our distressing needs has always moved you to make great personal sacrifices.

The War Years

The Evans family all volunteered for service in the war effort. Anne Evans was appointed by the Governor of Colorado as a member of the State's Women's Defense Council. Her niece, Josephine, went to France to nurse with the Red Cross. There she apparently suffered severe psychological effects from the war, as life-changing as if she had been physically injured. Josephine became rather reclusive but she continued her art projects, especially tooled leather work and weaving; she worked in an upstairs studio remodeled for her use out of former servant's quarters. In a quiet way, it seems she also continued her relationship with the family's children. For example, she produced from her typewriter, editions of *The Mousetrap News* for her nephew and nieces.[35]

Katharine served at local hospitals. She became the heart of the household at 1310 Bannock. As "Aunt Kay," she seems to have been the one that nieces and nephews talked to most freely. So diminutive in stature that only her head could be seen as she drove her green Buick around Denver, she willingly chauffeured friends and relatives who needed a ride. Katharine remained a faithful volunteer at St. Joseph's Hospital long after the war was over. A brief newspaper clipping told of her efforts to feed hungry children during the Depression years. This came from a gentleman who was, from 1930 to 1944,

KATHERINE EVANS
Sect'y Needle Work Guild

Katherine Evans, Courtesy History Colorado

the minister of Grace Community Church which stood for many years next to the Evans Chapel, across 13th Avenue from the Byers-Evans House. He remembered that one of the many community uses of the Evans Chapel was as the site for the "Children's Luncheon, which was supervised by Katharine Evans. Her brother, John Evans, provided the money for the meals."[36]

John Evans was appointed in April, 1917, to the almost impossible (unpaid) task of organizing, within a ten-day period, the basic machinery for a military draft of eligible Colorado men. After he had this operation up and running, he was commissioned as a captain in the U. S. Army. He was asked successively to head up the Colorado War Savings Committee, to be chairman of the new Denver Branch of the Federal Reserve Bank of Kansas City, and in 1918, to report to Washington, to work with the national Selective Service program.

John Evans and John Jr. , Courtesy History Colorado

Meantime, William Evans was appointed to head up a regional office of the American Red Cross, organized as a supply station and distribution point for an eleven state area. For his effective services, he received a number of prestigious awards from the Red Cross. While volunteering in this capacity, Evans conceived the idea of suggesting to the federal government that they should locate a hospital for wounded soldiers in a quiet and healthy environment on the outskirts of Denver. Evans gathered support in Denver, and traveled with other representatives to Washington to lobby for the idea. In February of 1919, Evans' committee was authorized to announce that, provided certain conditions were met, Denver would have a 1,000 bed hospital for wounded soldiers. Denver would have to supply the land. Guthell Park in Aurora, which was "sufficiently quiet and remote for hospital care," was selected. Denver citizens voted money for the land purchase, on which was built the "William Fitzsimmons General Hospital."

William Evans had continued to pursue his visions for the future of Denver and Colorado even though he no longer had any financial stake in their outcome. He persuaded the Evans Investment Company to lease seventy

Margaret Evans, fishing at the ranch, Courtesy Margaret E. Hayden

acres of land to the City of Denver for use as a flying field. Evans foresaw Denver developing as a transcontinental air traffic center. In addition to his services on behalf of Denver University, he sat on the Board of Colorado Historical and Natural History Society, was an active Mason and member of the Society of Colorado Pioneers, and was quietly helpful as an advisor to the Salvation Army.

Anne Evans and Denver's Political Structure

We have no direct insight into how the public attacks on the character and motivations of William Evans affected Anne Evans. The little tangible evidence remaining indicates that she admired her brother and saw him as having the same combination of hard-headed business acumen and visionary goals for the future of Denver and Colorado as her father had. She had traveled with Will and seen his mind at work. "... in the summer of 1896 he traveled by wagon through the northwestern part of Colorado with his sister Anne. His imagination was set afire by the endless opportunities there ... the idea of a railroad into western Colorado and Utah was thereby born."[37] Daily she saw how hard he worked.

Courtesy History Colorado

An intelligent woman, Anne Evans must have seen that most of the charges of political corruption, particularly of voter fraud and intimidation, were true. It was clear that her brother, the real power in the Denver Republican party, cooperated effectively with Democratic Mayor Robert Speer and his strong-armed *Big Mitt* political machine, when necessary, to secure the franchises and other legislative arrangements needed to operate the Denver Tramway Company and allied enterprises profitably.

It appears that Anne Evans was a quintessential pragmatist in the political arena. Women had secured the right to vote in Colorado in 1893, and there arose a lively feminist movement in the state. Indeed, historian Tom Noel wrote that "Denver was the first large city in the world to give women full suffrage."[38] But Anne Evans was not publicly identified with this movement. She worked within the existing power structure to achieve the cultural goals she believed important. She was undoubtedly helped in her efforts by her close and abiding relationship with the three powerful and prestigious Evans males whose influence in Denver spanned her lifetime: her father the Governor, her older brother William, and her nephew John. John became one of Denver's important bankers; he was a political leader like his father, and a supporter of civic programs.

John Evans, the banker, Courtesy History Colorado

Anne Evans did not care who headed up the organizations and committees that she helped to bring into existence as long as the people were committed to the task. She did not feel the need to be president or chairman of any board and was quite willing just to do the hard work behind the scenes. She cared that the goal, whether it was creating an art museum or restoring a mission church or bringing new life to an old mining town, be done and done well. She had a gift for attracting willing helpers and for ensuring that people working with her as volunteers had a good time. There were only a few occasions, which will be discussed later, when the actions or stands of specific individuals were unacceptable to her, and in those few instances she proved capable of sticking publicly to her convictions, regardless of the consequences.

14

Anne Evans and
the Denver Art Museum

*Trustee Anne Evans, who was always prepared to serve
the best interests of the museum, agreed to act as
interim director ... Certainly, she was the obvious choice
given her intimate knowledge of the institution and her
commitment to its future ... she was described as having
'nurtured the Denver Art Museum as some housewife
would care for a hothouse plant,' and an(other) article
announcing her appointment noted that she had been
'a moving spirit in artistic affairs in Denver and a
supporter of the art museum' for more than twenty-five
years.[1] Her affiliation had by then actually spanned more
than thirty-five years.[2]*

—Lewis Wingfield Story

Before embarking on a study of Anne Evans' contributions in
specific areas, it is important to recognize some fundamental
truths about Anne Evans and her approach to her life's work. She did
not work for recognition or honors, though plenty came to her in her
lifetime. A typical example of this reticence is contained in a brief
1940 correspondence about a forthcoming article on the Denver
Art Museum in a Chicago Art magazine. At the time, Anne Evans
was functioning as the DAM's Executive Secretary. The magazine
editor requested a photograph of Miss Evans and some information
about her, because "Every story ought to have a hero, and from the
moment I met her I realized she must have counted for a great deal
in the Museum history." Anne Evans' assistant wrote, "I have just
talked to Miss Evans and she feels quite strongly that the article
should not contain too much personality, but she is willing and
anxious to see the article go ahead and to do what she can."[3]

The important question for a biographer at this juncture of Anne Evans' life is—how did she do it? How did she make the transition from being a capable student, with a lively interest in the arts and literature, into a mover and shaker in the cultural life of Denver?

The answer, in brief, is that in the years between 1900 and 1910 she was appointed to a number of influential commissions and boards and worked diligently in these positions to accomplish worthwhile goals. No doubt, her family background and connections were influential in suggesting the initial appointments. However, it was her own intelligence, her persistence in the face of obstacles, her confidence in her own judgment, and her cheerful ability to cooperate with dedicated colleagues that enabled her to be so successful. As we shall see, she also used to great effect the potential for fruitful connections between the organizations to which she was appointed.

For the sake of clarity, an attempt will be made to tell the story of each of Anne Evans' major contributions in separate chapters. The truth is that these activities, along with many other involvements as well as her spiritual and philosophical convictions, were all woven together into one rich, full, enthusiastic life.

A Crucial Year for the Denver Artists' Club

The year of 1896–1897 was a crucial one in the development of the Artists' Club. Its growth was so dramatic that two bulletins were issued in the same year. The first, written both as a yearbook and as a membership-recruiting tool, noted, "The Artists' Club of Denver is entering on the fourth year of its existence." It listed its objectives as:

> The encouragement and assistance of every form of art enterprise, whether educational, industrial, or municipal. The maintenance and extension of its annual exhibition, which has already gained recognition beyond the borders of this State, and the holding of frequent exhibitions of work from other cities. The provision of a gallery suitable for exhibition and other purposes.

The bulletin noted that a Building Committee has been appointed "to consider this matter." The appeal for membership is contained in the paragraph stating,

> The Club feels that a wholesome interest in artistic matters and an intelligent appreciation of art products are worth cultivating,

and is sure that a simple statement of its plans will be sufficient to assure your membership and aid.

Under a recently adopted amended constitution, the Club is now governed by a council composed of active and associate members and elected by the entire Club. Every member now has a voice in the management of Club affairs. Active members are defined as those who are engaged in the practice of art, Associate members are those who are not, but are heartily in sympathy with its aims and wish to further its interests.

Annual dues were two dollars for active and associate members, ten dollars for sustaining members. Henry Read was President, Henrietta Bromwell, Secretary and Treasurer. Anne Evans was on the elected governing Council, along with John Cotton Dana, head of the Denver Public Library at that time; Charles Partridge Adams, Edward Ring, Elizabeth Spalding, Charles M. Carter and architect Willis A. Marean. There were twenty-one active members, including Anne Evans, and twenty-two Associate members, including Mrs. John Evans, Mrs. J. F. Spalding, and Samuel Elbert, who by this time had become a Colorado Supreme Court Judge.

In the second bulletin, issued in 1897, Anne Evans was listed as one of three members of the "Membership and Invitation Committee," with the note that, "The Club has made so remarkable a response to the appeal of the membership committee that another bulletin is issued by way of celebration." The Committee had made an appeal to the existing membership to enlist new recruits, and the result was that "The Club now numbers three hundred and fifty." Clearly, one of the reasons for the expansion of the Club's membership was that the cream of Denver society was drawn into its activities. Elisabeth Spalding describes how the opening receptions for its exhibitions became "notable" social affairs."[4] For years the social committee of the Artists' Club gave prestige to all functions … it would be difficult to name any well known Denver family of culture who was not interested in helping at one time or other."[5]

The Impossible Dream—A Building of Their Own

A free building site miraculously appeared. The Denver Parks Commissioners offered the Artists' Club a location on one of the triangular pieces of land being created by the new diagonal Park Avenue.

> There will be no rent to pay and no taxes. No event in the Club's history is of more importance than this proposition ... With its building completed and paid for, the Club will have upwards of $2,000 to spend for pictures. A few years will see Denver in possession of a free art gallery that would be a credit to any American city.

But the celebration was premature. The site offer was eventually rejected as being too far away from the city center. By 1900, the *Denver Republican* articulated a much less ambitious plan:

> Granted that it is given a certain amount of moral support and financial assistance, the Artists' Club of Denver will provide the city with an art gallery. It will not be an ostentatious building, and not necessarily one of which the city will be proud, but it will be an art gallery, and Denver will be relieved of the disgrace it has long been under in having no place, not even a good sized room, in which pictures can be hung and seen in a respectable light.[6]

The article went on to say that the Club had started an active campaign to raise a building fund.

The next possibility for the Club to have permanent gallery space came with the proposed building of the Colorado Museum of Natural History in City Park. Incorporation papers for the museum were signed in 1900, immediately followed by the signing of a contract with the City of Denver which promised to supply a suitable site and a contribution towards the construction cost. Negotiations between the Artists' Club and the Museum were started enthusiastically, but broke down somewhere along the way. The Club raised $3,000 to contribute towards the cost of a gallery. However, when the Museum finally opened its doors in July of 1908, and there was indeed an art gallery on the third floor, neither its contents nor its operation had anything to do with the Artists' Club. Art works were loaned by private collectors in Denver. "Among these works on loan to the museum, not one belonged to the Artists' Club—for the obvious reason that it had nothing to lend."[7] However, the Club did finally move into action on its long-held goal of accumulating a permanent collection. Starting in 1909, the paintings it acquired—mainly between 1909 and 1919—were displayed in the Colorado Natural History Museum Gallery until 1925.

Starting to Acquire a Permanent Art Collection

The choice of these first paintings was strongly influenced by the educational experiences of two women who were active members of the Artists' Club, Elisabeth Spalding and Anne Evans, and a third woman, Marion Hendrie, a good friend, student, and connoisseur of art herself. For years, Hendrie was a vigorous associate member of the Club, elected to active membership in 1916. All three women had studied in the East, as indeed had many other Club artists, either at the Art Students' League or in other settings under individual artists. The strong ties thus formed were largely responsible for the willingness of many eastern artists to send their works to be exhibited in Denver. A reviewer of the 1901 annual exhibit said, "Most of the pictures brought here are sent by their painters as personal favors to the Denver artists."[8] In their travels to New York and other art centers in the east, during the years when the Club was actively collecting paintings by contemporary artists, the three women were constantly on the lookout for likely acquisitions. Anne Evans made a trip to Paris in February of 1910. She was in the eastern United States in January, 1915, in February, 1916, (when she was said by the *Rocky Mountain News* to be arranging for "an exhibit of interest"), and again in March, 1918.[9]

The Club's first acquisitions included works by eastern artists Frank Vincent DuMond, a respected teacher at the Art Students' League; Leonard Ochtman, William Merritt Chase, and Louise Cox. Marion Hendrie and her two sisters presented a painting by J. Alden Weir in memory of their father. The collection also included works by Denver artists Charles Partridge Adams, George E. Burr, Henry Read, and Elisabeth Spalding.

Marion Hendrie—Artist and Collector

Marion Hendrie became an important influence in the art world of Denver. She was born in Central City, one of three daughters of Charles Francis Hendrie. He had opened a foundry in Central City in 1864, and later co-founded the Hendrie and Bolthoff Co., a significant manufacturing and mining supply firm in the Rocky Mountain region. A capable artist, Marion also became an imaginative collector of contemporary art and was responsible for bringing early exhibitions of Cezanne and Matisse to Denver. Marion and Elisabeth Spalding were active members of St. John's Cathedral.

They persuaded the Colorado Diocese to appoint a commission on Church Architecture and Allied Arts to guide parishes and missions "in obtaining the best possible design in buildings and furnishings,"[10] a model adopted by many other dioceses. When the Cathedral decided to build St. Martin's Chapel in 1926, the responsibility for its design was given to Marion Hendrie and the Commission. "She coordinated and supervised the work of architects and artists and achieved in St. Martin's a unity and harmony of design which has stood the test of time and made this small chapel famous."[11]

One of Marion's sisters married librarian Chalmers Hadley. The couple moved to Cincinnati in 1924, when Hadley was appointed City Librarian. In later life, the two unmarried sisters moved into the Hadley household in Cincinnati. When Marion Hendrie died in that city in 1968, she left her valuable collection of contemporary art to the Denver Art Museum. Transcriptions of interviews with Otto Bach, Director of the Denver Art Museum from 1944 to 1974, and Prue Grant, a longtime friend of the Hendrie sisters, are in the archives of the Denver Art Museum. They describe efforts to safe-guard Marion Hendrie's precious collection from damage due to neglect, and to preserve the written materials related to its provenance.

Brinton Terrace—Building an Art Community

Perhaps this is the place to ask a question: where, besides at the relatively rare exhibits of the Artists' Club, did Denverites interested in the arts have occasion to meet each other? One answer is at Brinton Terrace, which according to historian Edgar McMechen was often called "Denver's Greenwich Village."[12] McMechen (1894–1953) played many roles in Denver's early cultural life though he was primarily a historian and author. In addition to his 1924 biography of Governor Evans, he wrote many books and articles, including one on Brinton Terrace. McMechen served as Denver's Director of Publicity during Speer's second term, editing the city's publication, *Municipal Facts,* from 1918 to 1925. His closest association with Anne Evans was probably when he became the first part-time curator for the Native Arts Collection of the Denver Art Museum,[13] a position he left to become the Director of the Colorado Historical Society.

Brinton Terrace was built in 1882 and, with its Queen Anne façade, was regarded as one of the city's early architectural landmarks. Oscar Wilde, on his one trip to Colorado, is said to have remarked that "Brinton Terrace is the only artistic building in Denver."[14] As originally designed by architects E. P. Varian and Frederick J. Sterner, and built by property owner William Shaw Ward, the Terrace contained six apartments of ten rooms each, with dining rooms and kitchens on the first floors, living and drawing rooms on the second, bedrooms on the third, and servants' quarters in the attics. The building occupied 18th Street between the alley behind Trinity Church and the corner of E. 18th Avenue and Lincoln. According to McMechen, "it was the second fashionable residential terrace erected in Denver, antedated only by La Veta Place." For its first quarter century, Brinton Terrace was occupied by notable business, civic and professional people in Denver. Life in the Terrace had a strong social and intellectual emphasis.

Brinton Terrace apartments at 18th and Lincoln Streets (1919), Denver Public Library Western History Collections

Its "golden era as an art center," according to McMechen, began about 1906. He wrote that "the honor of having conceived 'a Bohemian retreat'" was due to a Margaret S. Van Waganan, whom he described as "a protégé of Miss Anne Evans, daughter of Colorado's second Territorial governor, one of the founders of the Denver Art Museum and the Central City Opera Association." This is one of the few specific examples we have of a quiet, but important, activity of Anne Evans, that of supporting talented young artists financially, to which reference is often made in accounts of her contributions. One newspaper article said, "She grubstaked young artists as her father grubstaked miners."[15] Anne Evans helped Miss Van Waganan to obtain her art education at the Chicago Art Institute and in New York. After her return to Denver, Miss Van Waganan launched a plan to assemble local artists under one roof "where they might unite in a common cause and derive inspiration from one another." A similar idea had been tried during the early eighties when J. Harrison Mills and associated artists took over the entire fifth floor of the new Tabor Grand Opera House, but that center never attained the cohesion and camaraderie of the Brinton Terrace Center. Credit for the success of Miss Van Waganan's venture is given by McMechen to her "blithe and shining spirit" which, he wrote in 1947, "has kept her memory verdant among Denver artists to this date."

Among the extraordinary roster of artists and architects who had studios at one time in Brinton Terrace were R. L. and Cyril Boutwell, who opened a lively art gallery there in 1906; the architectural firm of Maurice Biscoe and H. H. Hewitt, designers of many of Denver's early mansions; George Elbert Burr, nationally famous etcher and water colorist, whose later studio and home at 1325 Logan is now the club house of the Denver Woman's Press Club; Waldo Love, a portrait and landscape painter, miniaturist, and the staff artist for the Colorado Museum of Natural History, responsible for its first large dioramic backgrounds; and Allen True, whose talents Anne Evans called upon many times. True started his career as a successful illustrator, specializing in Western Life motifs, and went on to become famous as a painter of murals depicting Western pioneer and Indian life.[16] Also in Brinton Terrace were jewelry and metalwork artists Alice Best and Helen Dougall, and portrait photographers Wilma Wallace and Anne Dailey. Miss Van Waganan married Dudley Carpenter, a talented mural painter. The couple became well known for their leaded windows. One of the leading firms of interior decorators, Carstens and Timm, also had their studios for a time in Brinton Terrace.

Many of Denver's pioneer musicians had studios in Brinton Terrace, including Dr. Wilberforce J. Whiteman, Supervisor of Music for the Denver Public Schools and father of big band leader Paul Whiteman. He opened a studio in the Terrace in 1925. Another musician, Horace E. Tureman, arranged for the first chamber music recitals in the city. He directed the Elitch Gardens Orchestra, in addition to being a capable composer, an outstanding music teacher, and a founder and long time Director of the Denver Civic Symphony. Much later, he was honored, along with Anne Evans, for his many contributions to the cultural life of Denver.

One of the last gifted occupants of Brinton Terrace was Dr. Antonia Brico, who had her music studio there from 1939 to 1955. For many of these years, she served as Music Director of the choir of Trinity Methodist Church, as well as conducting her own choir and the Brico Orchestra. Dr. Brico was a close friend of Anne Evans' niece, Margaret Evans Davis. There is a family story that the fine Steinway piano that used to be at 1310 Bannock Street somehow ended up in Dr. Brico's possession, and was quietly replaced by a Chickering of lesser quality.

To encourage easy sociability between the talented tenants and their patrons, Miss Belle Herzinger and Miss Alice Fisher operated the Teacup Inn at Brinton Terrace. They were "graduates in domestic science" according to McMechen, who adds the intriguing phrase that this was "about the time that calories and vitamins were embryonic."

In the early 1920s, another school important in the development of art education in Denver opened in two of the Brinton Terrace houses. The Denver Academy of Fine and Applied Arts was the brainchild of Dr. John Cory, a well-known New York newspaper cartoonist and yet another talent drawn to Denver for health reasons. He became a cartoonist for the *Rocky Mountain News,* in addition to heading up his new school staffed by a faculty of gifted artists. The best known of these was John Thompson, one of Denver's earliest modern painters who maintained his own studio in the Terrace for a number of years. Thompson, a native of Buffalo, spent time in New York before moving to Paris in 1905 where his work was greatly influenced by the Fauvists. Moving back to the U. S. in 1914, he taught for three years in Buffalo. In 1917, he moved to Denver and became an active participant in the development of its art institutions.

In 1925, Jack Manard bought the Cory School and moved it to Chappell House at 1300 Logan St. This school developed into the *University of Denver School of Art*, in which Anne Evans was deeply involved.

Many other talents—photographers, commercial artists, sculptors, and teachers of elocution and the dramatic arts—had their studios in Brinton Terrace over the years, contributing to its stimulating atmosphere as well as to the cultural life of Denver. There is little doubt that Anne Evans was a welcome guest at many openings, exhibits and celebrations at Brinton Terrace, because of her close connection with Miss Van Waganan and many friends among the occupants. Perhaps she found much to discuss with Dr. John Gower, who moved to the Terrace in 1917. McMechen described Gower as "one of the most interesting and best loved characters among Denver's cultured people."[17] Originally from England, he became "an organist of international fame, a distinguished composer and the personal friend of such students of psychic phenomena as Dr. William James of Harvard, Sir Oliver Lodge ... and Sir Arthur Conan Doyle." Anne Evans had by this time become a member of the Theosophical Society. There is no evidence that Anne Evans was interested in the spiritualist aspects of theosophy, but she was keenly interested in exploring the outer limits of human experiences, especially those with transcendent aspects.

Brinton Terrace was razed in 1956, to make room for a parking lot.

A New Home for Art in the Carnegie Library

Securing of the actual first home for the exhibitions of the Artists' Club was a tribute to the vision and negotiating skills of Anne Evans. In 1907, she was appointed as a member of the Denver Public Library Commission and was therefore privy to the plans to build a new central library for the city, stimulated by the offer of significant financing by Andrew Carnegie.

In 1904, Anne Evans had been appointed to the new Municipal Art Commission and was an enthusiastic proponent of Mayor Speer's ambitious plans for a new Civic Center for Denver, a centerpiece for its transformation into a City Beautiful. It became quite clear to her that the proper place for an eventual art museum was as part of the proposed Civic Center; and, that an excellent first step would be for the Artists' Club to have gallery space in the new Carnegie Library Building. Not so incidentally, this arrangement, if it could be achieved, would for the first time present the Artists' Club with the opportunity to create some legal and financial ties between itself and the city. It must have seemed obvious, by this time, that only with financial help from the city of Denver would there ever be a viable art museum in the city. The literary arts were tax-financed through the public library, and the Museum of Natural History enjoyed considerable city support both for its building construction and operating expenses. Elisabeth Spalding wrote, in her paper of recollections about art history in Denver,

> It was a great forward step when the gallery was planned in the new Public Library. We knew at that time how much we owed to Anne Evans, whole-hearted member as she was of both Library and Artists' Club Boards.[18]

In the valuable 1996 history of the Denver Art Museum, Marlene Chambers similarly wrote, "Anne Evans, who sat on the Library Commission as well as the board of the Artists' Club, was generally credited for working out the agreement that allotted space for the club in the city's new library on Civic Center."[19] It was no small achievement. There had been many ambitious plans and dreams before, but this practical plan came to fruition without great fanfare and laid the foundation for the art museum we have today, with its successful combination of municipal backing and extensive private support. It must be admitted, however, that progress towards that ultimate ideal of an art museum building on the Civic Center proved slower and more obstacle-filled than anyone could have foreseen.

The gala opening of the new art galleries in the Carnegie Library took place in February 1910,[20] arranged to coincide with the debut of the 16th annual juried exhibition of the Artists' Club. The centerpiece of the exhibit was the same design for a fountain by Elsie Ward that had so delighted visitors to the 1899 exhibit offered by four women artists.[21]

The Artists' Club Becomes the Denver Art Association

By 1917, it was apparent that the name, Denver Artists' Club, did not convey the breadth of the group's mission, so it was changed to the Denver Art Association. Elisabeth Spalding noted that

> the old name had hindered growth, for although there had been from the start members who were not artists as associates, and although the club had always worked for civic art and civic education through exhibitions and lectures, still the idea persisted that if it was named 'Artists' Club' it must be for artists only, and it needed constant explanations.[22]

Incorporation papers for this new not-for-profit corporation were filed on February seventh of that year. The objectives echoed those of the Artists' Club: to cultivate and promote a general interest in art; to establish and maintain a permanent art collection; to acquire real estate and to erect thereon a building or buildings for an art museum. There was one significant addition: "to co-operate with the City of Denver or with any other body corporate or any individual in the establishment and maintenance of such an art gallery."[23] Yearly dues of the new Association remained at $2.00 for artists, teachers, and students, and $10.00 for sustaining members, but were raised to $5.00 for other regular members. The President, Horace G. Wetherill, declared in the annual bulletin, "The Association will work in close union with the public schools, art extension work of the Public Library, and all art interests of the city."

First Art Director Makes His Debut

An important step towards a more active role for the new Association in the cultural life of Denver was taken with the hiring of the first paid Director. This was Reginald Poland, who came to the city highly qualified and mainly through the persuasion of Anne Evans' good friend and tireless co-worker, Marion Hendrie. Poland, the son of a distinguished art historian, had been educated at Brown, Princeton, and Harvard, and had served on the staff of the Boston Museum of Fine Arts. Although hired in 1917, Poland volunteered in the armed forces in World War I and did not come to Denver until 1919. But when he did arrive, according to Spalding, he inspired a great and energetic increase in the activities of the Art Association. In the new galleries at the Library building,

> Exhibitions were increased to a continuously filled gallery, and constant talks were given. The Atelier, a branch of the international Beaux Arts, was strengthened and encouraged. Mr. Poland worked with the students ... to guide and help; he gave everywhere of his best and his unflagging efforts met with real reward.[24]

Poland authored a weekly art column in the *Rocky Mountain News*, championed the cause of Western art, and campaigned energetically for an art museum building on the Civic Center. Indeed, he put forward an interesting though unsuccessful proposal. It was that two memorials, which were being widely debated at the time— one to commemorate the unique contributions of Mayor Speer to Denver, the other to acknowledge those who died in the recent world war—should be combined in the form of an art museum.

George William Eggers' Contributions

Poland stayed in Denver only for two years, leaving to take up a post as Director of Education at the Detroit Institute of Arts. Attracting the next Director to Denver was again due to the efforts of Marion Hendrie. To persuade a man who had headed up the Chicago Art Institute for the previous four years to come west, to a city that did not even have premises to call its own, was quite a feat. George William Eggers had a broad and democratic view of the functions of an art museum and many important advances took place on his watch. He carried forward the impetus to make the Art Association the official partner of the City of Denver in art matters, negotiating the first financial support to the Art Association from the city—a grant of $3,000 in 1923. Elisabeth Spalding summarized his vision for the future of the arts in Denver in her memoir.

> Mr. Eggers had visited Denver and felt that here was a larger opportunity even than in Chicago. He appreciated its need for civic beauty to be guarded and developed, the need for distinguished and distinctive character to attract and to hold the tourist and the resident, its need for an art building which should give needed inspiration to the industries and arts rapidly developing here and its need for good examples for educational purposes, all of its needs meaning great opportunities.[25]

The Gift of Chappell House

While the Art Association was enjoying its first taste of a presence on the developing civic center with its galleries in the Library building, and ideas for the eventual location there of an art museum building were part of most plans, an unexpected gift temporarily changed the course of the organization's development. Art patrons Delos Chappell Jr. and his sister, Jean Chappell Cranmer, wife of George Cranmer, who later made his mark as one of Denver's most effective Managers of Parks and Recreation, gave to the Art Association in 1922 the home they had inherited at 1300 Logan Street, in memory of their parents.

Chappell House was a Denver mansion with a history. Built in the 1880s by Horace W. Bennett, who made a fortune in Cripple Creek mining and "plowed the proceeds into Denver real estate,"[26] the 20-room sandstone mansion in Capitol Hill was sold around 1900 to David May, founder of the May Company department stores. May in turn sold it to Delos Chappell, Sr.

The gift of Chappell House came with conditions. The house was to become a center for the creative arts. The upper floors were

Totem poles in front of the Chappell House located on 1300 Logan Street. (c. 1930) The Chappell mansion became the Denver Art Museum in 1922 until it was razed in 1970. Denver Public Library Western History Collections

to be used as artists' studios and the main floor as headquarters for the Art Association and for a group headed by Jean Cranmer, The Allied Arts Inc. This organization was formed in 1920 by Jean Cranmer, Anne Evans, Ida Kruse McFarlane and Burnham Hoyt, "for the purpose of awarding scholarships and enlivening the Denver art scene."[27] According to the pamphlet on the history of the organization by journalist and art critic Allen Young, it was born "at a time of surging growth in Denver" by a group which believed in "encouraging the energy and intelligence of the young in determining a luminous future for Denver."[28] The guiding spirit behind this enterprise was Jean Cranmer, who was herself a talented musician. Young observed, "As an artist, she knew that the arts needed the nourishment that only money could bring."[29]

The acquisition of Chappell House gave to the Art Association a kind of solidity and reality that it had previously lacked. The building's atmosphere and many rooms encouraged the development of art classes and served as headquarters for art-related organizations. Its living rooms were fine settings for small musical recitals and social occasions. It was not, however, a suitable facility for exhibitions. So its maintenance and expansion proved to be quite a drain on the limited financial resources of the Art Association, which remained convinced that its ultimate goal was a museum building on the civic center.

Debut of the Denver Art Museum

At the Art Association's annual meeting in 1923, Director Eggers' recommendation to change the name of the organization to the Denver Art Museum, thus recognizing its expanding role in the community, was adopted. The three major goals of the organization remained the same as in the 1897 incorporation of the Art Association. One specific goal was added, that of holding and conducting art exhibitions, which had always in fact been one of the major activities of the group. It was not long before the new organization had to drain most of its funds, as well as raise new monies, to add a 2,000 square foot gallery to Chappell House. This provided some minimal exhibit space. Anne Evans, as Executive Secretary, wrote about the history of the Art Museum in 1931 and characterized Chappell House as "the first great acquisition." She noted that, by the mid-1920s,

> as the Library had become greatly pressed for room and now needed the gallery for its own use, it was decided to add a fireproof wing to the original Chappell residence and to move the Association bodily into the new quarters. Here the various collections which had gradually accumulated were gathered together, and with a permanent abiding place and visible possessions there came a new sense of identity. Once again, the old name was felt to be inadequate and outgrown, and when a new constitution was framed and adopted, the Art Association emerged therein as the full-fledged Denver Art Museum.[30]

Interior of the Denver Art Museum at the Chappell House (1930), Denver Public Library Western History Collections

In this article by Anne Evans, and another in the same issue of the *Art Register* by Walter C. Mead, President of the Board of Trustees of the Art Museum, an optimistic scenario for the future of the Museum was projected. George Eggers resigned as the Art Museum's Director in September of 1926, but because of the construction of the addition to Chappell House and a serious possibility of having an art museum site included in the latest civic center plans, he delayed his departure until the end of October.

Problems with Eggers' Successor

Arnold Ronnebeck (1885–1947) a sculptor whose work had been showcased in a Chappell House Exhibit, succeeded Eggers. Ronnebeck had given a public lecture on his own work, and on modern sculpture in general, sponsored by the Cooke Daniels Lecture Foundation. This had drawn a favorable review by Eggers in the *Rocky Mountain News* (April 4, 1926), and an offer to Ronnebeck to serve as art advisor to the Museum. Ronnebeck had studied in France under Auguste Rodin, Aristide Maillol and Antoine Bourdelle. He brought a prestigious Maillol exhibit to Denver soon after becoming associated with the Museum, and persuaded the Board of Trustees to purchase a cast of a life-size Maillol bronze nude. Thus, the Denver Art Museum was the first public museum in the country to acquire a major Maillol work.

After Eggers' departure, Ronnebeck, with no change in his title of Art Advisor, was placed in charge of the Museum. In March of 1929, the Board appointed Samuel Heavenrich, formerly curator of the Fogg Museum at Harvard University, as executive secretary to take over museum operations. Unfortunately, the two men proved to have totally incompatible ideas about the function of an art museum, and the kind of art a museum should be collecting. Their arguments spilled over into the press. Their short-lived joint direction of the Denver Art Museum was terminated.

Anne Evans Becomes Interim Director

The Board turned to fellow-trustee Anne Evans to take over as interim director until they could find a qualified successor. Lewis Story, in his history of the early years of the Denver Art Museum[31] noted, "Her energy and vision often assured a viable future for the organization, and she was always ready to serve in any capacity, from hostess at the 1894 opening of the club's first rooms, to interim director."[32] Anne Evans assumed this directorial role at a crucial time in the long development of the Denver Art Museum from a small non-profit artists' club to a bold and handsome public art museum in the heart of the city. "Over the years," said Lewis Story, "she assumed a dominant role in the cultural affairs of the city and sat at various times on both the Library Commission and the Art Commission."

The Denver Artists Guild

Anne Evans continued to support artists, even when her plate was already very full. The Denver Artists Guild was another of her affiliations aimed at supporting Denver's artists. According to Deborah Wadsworth,

> In 1928–29, as the United States slipped into the Great Depression, an adventurous group of Denver artists banded together to form the Denver Artists Guild. Their goals were "To encourage the practice and appreciation of the fine arts and to promote the highest professional standards in original art." They believed deeply in the redemptive powers of art, and the joy of the creative process.[33]

Denver Artists Guild, Denver Public Library Western History Collections

Like so much of the history of art in Colorado in the first half of the twentieth century the activities, even the existence, of the Denver Artist Guild had been virtually forgotten. In the summer of 2009 an exhibit of work of most of the fifty-two original Guild members in the Western History department of the Denver Public Library vividly brought the Guild and its mission to life. The exhibit was a labor of love on the part of its two volunteer curators, Deborah Wadsworth and Cynthia Jennings.[34]

According to the brochure accompanying the Exhibition, the distinctive characteristic of the Guild was that "in contrast to the cut-throat competition of many art associations, the founders encouraged, taught and even hired each other."[35]

Many of the fifty-two founders have already made an appear-ance in the pages of this book—Donald Bear, Laura Gilpin, Vance Kirkland, Paschal Quackenbush, Arnold Ronnebeck, and Elisabeth Spalding. By 1928, Anne Evans had long since ceased her own painting activity, so her role in the Guild was one of support—primarily drawing people to and publicizing its events. A happy surprise was that for the 2009 exhibit, Deborah Wadsworth managed to find a small, hitherto unknown original oil painting by Anne Evans. Deborah Wadsworth discovered it in the course of her major volunteer effort for the Western History Department, categorizing every original piece of art in the Department's collection, with digital images and a full description of each.[36]

The Eccentric Cyril Kay Scott

A new Director for the Art Museum, Cyril Kay Scott, was installed in August, 1930. Described by Lewis Story as an eccentric, his back-ground more than qualified him for that description. "According to his own account, he had multiple careers and lived much of his life under an assumed name."[37] Born in 1879 in Missouri, Scott trained as a doctor, married, had four children, divorced, and married again, this time to a concert pianist. As young Dr. Frederick Creighton Wellman, he worked in Angola and Honduras. An authority on tropical medicine, he returned to the U. S. to join the faculty first of Oakland Medical College and then of Tulane School of Medicine.

When he was forty-four, Dr. Wellman met an enchanting and highly original young twenty-year-old woman, the daughter of a friend, and eloped with her by freighter to London. They reinvented themselves as Cyril Kay and Evelyn Scott, and soon moved to Brazil, fearful of being traced and arrested in England. After his plans to make an income by collecting specimens for the British Museum fell through, Cyril eked out a living as a baggage porter. Next, he worked for the Singer Sewing Machine Company, moving up from bookkeeper to district supervisor. Later, he became successively a homesteading rancher and a mining engineer.

Evelyn Scott gave birth to one child, after which she became quite ill. To secure medical attention for her, the couple returned to the United States, where they lived in Greenwich Village and became writers. Both of them, but more especially Evelyn, achieved critical acclaim. This did not translate into an adequate income. Their marriage became an open affair. The couple traveled widely in France and North Africa, hooking up with a New Zealand artist named Owen Merton, who stimulated Cyril to start painting. Merton also became Evelyn's lover. This did not sit too well with Owen's young son Thomas, who had lost his mother at a young age to cancer. He was to go through many dark nights of the soul before becoming, in his later adult years, the beloved Cistercian monk, prolific writer, and Catholic theologian Thomas Merton.

Now an artist, Cyril Kay Scott finally divorced Evelyn, started to hyphenate his name, and moved to Santa Fe. There he started an art school and embarked on a fourth, rather unpropitious marriage.

New Goals, New Challenges

It was from Santa Fe in 1930 that Cyril Kay-Scott came to Denver to be the director of the Denver Art Museum. He had twin goals for the rising young museum. First, to be a major educational resource for the community, "essentially a center of civic service," where art objects would be installed so as to "count day by day for the enjoyment and cultural education of the largest number of people, both young and old."[38] Second, he wanted to see the Museum's collections both enlarged and broadened, to include not only sculptures, paintings and prints but also art objects usually designated as crafts, such as rugs, furniture, and ceramics. This policy fit in well with long-established beliefs and practices of the Museum's leaders from the early beginnings of the Artists' Club, and certainly, with their decision to include American Indian Art in their collections, an area intimately associated with Anne Evans' interests and contributions.

Kay-Scott realized, as did the Trustees of the Museum, that the de facto acquisition policy, which had been pursued for at least ten years, of accepting virtually all gifts that were offered would no longer do. New standards for the acceptance of donations were drawn up. Even with new limitations, the collections continued to grow. Two collections, already conditionally bequeathed to the city, still needed a home. One was a group of twenty-eight late nineteenth and early twentieth century paintings donated in 1917 by Junius Flagg Brown, as a result of Mayor Speer's "Give While You Live" campaign. It was given on condition that a suitable building in which to display the collection would be built within fifteen years. That time limit was fast approaching. The other was a collection of Chinese and Japanese bronzes donated to the city, at about the same time as the Brown bequest, by Walter C. Mead. Both were being housed and displayed at the Colorado Museum of Natural History, which began to make it quite clear that the space was needed for their own exhibits.

The needs of the Denver Art Museum for display space had outgrown Chappell House, even with the new gallery addition, and the ideal of having a space of its own on the Civic Center had never gone away.

To understand the next chapter in the story of the Denver Art Museum, it is necessary to look at two of Anne Evans' parallel commitments, the Denver Public Library and the Denver Art Commission.

Anne Evans, *Untitled* (Portrait of Territorial Governor John Evans),
ca. 1890 Oil on board, 22.6 x 26.6, Courtesy History Colorado

Anne Evans, *Margaret,* n.d. Watercolor 27.25 x 17.5 Courtesy History Colorado

Anne Evans, *Winter Scene,* n.d. Oil on board, Denver Public Library
Western History Collection

Alfonso Roybal, *Harvest Dance,* Denver Art Museum, 1932.207

Abel Sanchez, *Man and Buffalo,* Denver Art Museum, 1932.232

Guadaloupe Montoya, *Corn Dance*, Denver Art Museum, 1932.235

Edmund Tracey, *Father Sky and Mother Earth*, Denver Art Museum, 1932.156

Elisabeth Spalding,
Anne's Cabin, Courtesy
Jan Mayer

Elisabeth Spalding, *Anne Evans Living Room,* Courtesy Ethelind Elbert Austin

Vance Kirkland (1904–1981, American) *Central City Opera House*,
1933 Watercolor on paper, 25 X 19 Collection of Kirkland Museum of
Fine & Decorative Arts, Denver. VK1933.01

Vance Kirkland (1904–1981, American) *Moonlight in Central City,*
1935 Oil on linen, 29 X 36 Collection of Kirkland Museum of Fine &
Decorative Arts, Denver. VK1935.12

15

A Center of Public Happiness: The Denver Public Library

When the announcement was made that you had resigned from the Library Commission we felt as if the main prop had fallen from our library, and when I talked with Dr. Wyer about it the next day I wept. Perhaps I realize more than anyone else what you have meant to us; how you have worked for us, what you have contributed of your heart and strength and dauntless spirit through the years.[1]
  —Helen Ingersoll to Anne Evans, April 23, 1940

Denver Public Library Commission

Anne Evans played a major role in the development of the Denver Public Library, another pillar of Denver's cultural life, to which she gave more than half a lifetime of devoted service. Appointed to the Commission in 1907, and reappointed by a succession of Denver mayors, she served without interruption until her resignation on health grounds in 1940, a year before she died.

Anne Evans took her place on the Commission at a troubled time for the Library. The 1904 Home Rule charter for the newly created City and County of Denver provided for an 8-member Library Commission appointed by the mayor. Members were to serve for staggered terms without compensation. Part of the reason for Anne Evans' appointment was that a clause in the new Charter required that two of the Commission members be women. The first two women appointed by Mayor Speer were Mrs. Lucy M. Hughes and Mrs. Mary E. Fisher. On Mrs. Fisher's resignation in 1907, the Mayor appointed Anne Evans to replace her. Later, Mrs. Jasper Writer was appointed to replace Lucy Hughes. According to an engaging memoir by Helen Ingersoll, a long-time member of the Denver Public Library staff, when these "two women were appointed on the Library Commission, Miss Anne Evans, daughter of the second Territorial Governor of Colorado, and Mrs. Jasper Writer, things began to happen; they were both public-spirited, interested women. They felt the pulse of the community ..."[2] To understand some of the problems facing the library, a little history is necessary.

Three Hundred Saloons and No Public Library— Library Services in Early Denver

Rena Reese, a long-time member of the Library staff, wrote a history of the Denver Public Library. The most interesting document in all of its collections is an old blank-book containing the constitution, by-laws, regulations and list of members of the Denver City and Auraria Library and Reading Room Association. It is dated February 10, 1860.

Reese notes that ninety-nine men signed the roll of the Reading Room Association, all but thirteen of whom "have been identified among those pioneers of Denver who contributed to its culture and progress." An unknown writer had penciled in a few notes about the less fortunate or less admirable subscribers, such as one man who "Died on the plains, August, 1860. One of nature's noblemen. A more perfect gentleman never trod the earth." Another is described as "Dead. Lynched and hung for horse-stealing, August, 1860." At least he had paid his dues. Among the admirable majority were five for whom Denver streets were later named: Bayaud, Blake, Curtis, Lawrence, and Wynkoop. One became Chief Justice of the Territorial Supreme Court and later Mayor of Denver; another a future Speaker of the House of the Territorial Legislature. In addition, there were: a future post-master, five physicians, three lawyers, six editors and printers, five who helped found Masonic lodges, and ten who helped organize the first Episcopal Church. The secretary was O. J. Goldrick, the first superintendent of public schools in the Territory, who became, at one point, associate editor of the *Rocky Mountain News* and later founded the *Rocky Mountain Herald*. In spite of its auspicious start, the Association soon faded for lack of funds to sustain it.

Historian Tom Noel wrote that virtually the only places for the public to read books and newspapers for the next few years in Denver were in some of the numerous saloons.[3] "In the town's early days, saloons competed by offering goods and services, including reading rooms." In 1874, another attempt was made to provide a reading room open to the public by a membership organization calling itself the Denver Library Association. When it ran out of money four years later, the collection of books was donated to the Denver School Board in the fervent hope that "at no distant day it may become the nucleus of a grand public library for our city."[4] The books were placed in the Arapahoe School in downtown Denver and were available to Denver citizens. In 1882, when the original Arapahoe School was replaced by the new East Denver High School, located at 19th and Stout Streets, the collection was placed in the west wing of the new school, which was planned as a public library. Unfortunately, because of construction and other delays, the school was not occupied until 1889. It was in these years that the *Rocky Mountain News* lamented, "The shame of having 300 saloons and no public library in Denver has been borne too long already."[5]

The Mercantile Library

In 1886, because there was still no free public library in operation, the Denver Chamber of Commerce decided to sponsor a subscription library called the Mercantile Library in their new building at 14th and Lawrence Streets. It opened in November with Charles Dudley as Librarian and 3,000 volumes. This library was supported by subscriptions, but offered borrowing privileges also to those who made a deposit or who were guaranteed by a subscriber. In 1891, the City Council of Denver started to make yearly contributions to this library, renamed City Library in 1893. By 1898, the holdings of the library had increased to 30,000 volumes, with a circulation of more than 160,000.

John Cotton Dana and the Public Library

Meantime, with the opening of the East Denver High School in 1889, the Public Library opened in its West Wing, with funding provided by a one-tenth property tax mill levy. Hired both as librarian and secretary of the School Board was a dynamic innovator, John Cotton Dana, destined to revolutionize the entire concept of what constituted a successful public library in the United States.

Dana was yet another of those who came to Colorado because of ill health. He graduated from Dartmouth College and was a class-mate of the brother of Aaron Gove, Denver School Superintendent.

For his first two years in Colorado, Dana led an outdoor life, working with a surveying party in the mountains. He studied law, being admitted to the Colorado bar in 1880. According to Ingersoll, Dana described himself as a "philosophical anarchist" and a "scholar and liberal thinker" who "read the classics with pleasure all his life."[6] One of his major innovations as a librarian was to put most of the books on open shelves and encourage the public to browse among them. He is also credited with creating the first classroom libraries in the country, the first children's library, and the first circulating collection of reproductions of famous paintings.

To provide a supply of trained library workers, Dana organized training classes in librarianship, the first one starting with six students at the East Denver High School Library in 1894. Dana wrote a little *Public Library Handbook, 1895* to use in the class, in which he advised, "The library is not a business office; it's a center of public happiness first, of public education next … The library reaches its highest degree of usefulness when its shelves are empty and all its books are in the hands of readers." Dana believed in advertising the library, with the object of attracting the average person and making books a part of their lives. He wrote in his training manual,

> Of all possible advertising, the best, perhaps, is a cheerful and accommodating atmosphere in the library itself … Treat boy and girl, man and woman, ignorant and learned, gracious and rude with uniform good temper, without condescension, never pertly. Anticipate all inquiries when possible and especially put the shrinking and embarrassed at ease.[7]

In his library, Dana set aside a special Woman's Room, with comfortable chairs, wall-to-wall carpeting and "books and magazines to cheer and help the housewife."

Dana was good to his staff, inviting them weekly to his home for discussion about books and a lot of laughter, and a delicious dessert served by his wife.

> When (the actor) Booth came to the Tabor in Hamlet, he saw that his 'girls' went. He bought their tickets. He took a great interest in his staff but he expected a lot from them. If hair straggled or if

heels were run over, or if he heard a mistake in grammar, he would write a note calling attention to the dereliction.[8]

In spite of this, Ingersoll notes, "his staff adored him" and after he left they "tried to carry on his traditions that were later to make him one of the foremost librarians of the country." This was not easy, because after he left, things changed.

The Two Libraries Merge

This did not happen immediately, for Dana's successor was a man recommended by him. John Parsons became Librarian of the Denver Public Library in 1898. He had been a Congregational minister but had left the ministry because of a conflict of conscience: he found he could not believe in immortality.[9] He came to Denver for his wife's health "and was a man of great scholarship and learning and a very fine gentleman."[10]

Following the passage of a new library law by the Colorado General Assembly in 1893, which enabled municipalities to establish and maintain public libraries, a general public consensus arose to merge the two libraries. Both were being partially financed by the City of Denver. In August, 1898, an agreement was made to consolidate the City (formerly Mercantile) Library and the Denver Public Library. "The tax payers were murmuring about the upward trend of taxes. They protested against the upkeep of two libraries ... The consolidation of the two libraries would mean an appreciable saving of money, and the City agreed to provide a tax levy to support a larger institution."[11]

It was decided to move the books belonging to the Denver Public Library to the Chamber of Commerce building but there was no room for most of them on the shelves, so the vast majority of the collection remained in boxes on the floor. The City had to find new quarters immediately for the doubled collection of books—35,000 in the City Library and 43,000 in the Public Library. A contract was worked out for a 2-year lease on a two-story building to be constructed by the Prudential Insurance Company at 15th Street and Court Place. There the newly consolidated Denver Public Library opened its doors in 1899.

The question as to who should be appointed as the City Librarian—Charles Dudley of the former City Library or John Parsons of the former Public Library—was not a simple one. The two libraries had operated from completely different philosophies. John Parsons admired and followed John Cotton Dana's convictions. The Mercantile/City Library was characterized by Ingersoll as the brainchild of Roger W. Woodbury,

> a member of the Mercantile library board, a man of authority, of outspoken opinions, and a stern believer in a closed-shelf system … All books in this library were behind iron cages and no one was allowed to enter and browse among the books. Book selection was made from the printed catalogues, which were chained to the rough wooden tables … If a patron owed a dime or more on an overdue book and could not pay the fine, he was not allowed to take another book, but his card was held until the entire amount was paid.[12]

According to Ingersoll, Mr. Parsons was the most beloved and had the finest ideals of library service, but Mr. Dudley was well known to influential social circles in Denver and had a fine presence. Dudley was named City librarian with Mr. Parsons as assistant librarian. "This was a very difficult and sad situation and Mr. Parsons met it with fine character and devotion to duty."[13]

New Denver Public Library Goes on the Dewey Decimal System

The former Mercantile/City Library had been catalogued on the Poole system, and the Public Library on the Dewey decimal system. It was decided "to recatalog all the books using the Dewey system. John Parsons supervised the massive project."[14] "He also did reference work and was an able research man with a wonderful knowledge of books. He had an admiring and appreciative following among the library patrons," wrote Ingersoll.[15] According to Ingersoll, Charles Dudley went out of his way to humiliate Parsons, and this was noted and resented by the staff.

The Commission originally decided that the newly merged library should be operated on the open shelf system. The policy was changed at the end of 1902 on the advice of Librarian Dudley, who reported that 3,000 books had been stolen and that there was not enough space to operate anything but a closed-shelf system. Dudley also made quite arbitrary decisions about which books were suitable for children to read.

A huge controversy arose, which reached national proportions, over *Huckleberry Finn*. Dudley "instructed the staff that no youngster was to have the book."[16] Unfortunately, a young man who worked for one of the newspapers asked for the book and was refused. "Articles came out in the paper and all over the country. *Harper's Weekly* called the barring of *Huckleberry Finn* a practical joke on the Denver Public Library, and said it was an offense against our national common sense which ought quickly to be removed."

Denver Public Library in La Veta Place (1907). The new Carnegie Library construction is visible in the background. Denver Public Library Western History Collection

The Library soon outgrew its "light and airy" location at 15th St. and Court Place. By 1902, when the lease on that building expired, library funds from a tax levy had been adequate to set aside $98,000 to purchase property on which to build a brand new library. In January of that year, La Veta Place was bought for this purpose. Once the fashionable L-shaped terrace of units faced Colfax Avenue and, turning the corner, ran part way along Bannock Street to Court Place. The property was built in the 1880s by David Moffat. He sold it to silver baron H. A. W. Tabor who gave it to Augusta Tabor as part of their divorce settlement.[17] By 1902, the property was run-down and had fallen into decay.

Support from Andrew Carnegie

Ingersoll told the story that, at this point, a well-meaning gentleman took it upon himself to write to Andrew Carnegie requesting $200,000 to build a new library in Denver. The Commission was mortified: they had planned to ask for $400,000. They received the $200,000 at the beginning of 1903. The City of Denver had to come up with the rest of the money to construct the building they were planning, in addition to signing an agreement with Carnegie to provide a minimum of $30,000 a year for the operation of the library and to pay off the amount still owed on the building site.

Storeroom in basement of Denver Public Library in La Veta Place (1907), Denver Public Library Western History Collection

To save money, the Library Commission decided to demolish only that part of La Veta Place fronting on Colfax, and to fix up minimally the remaining four residences to house the Library until the new building could be completed. This move "was very hard on the staff. The once fashionable place was grimy, and there were bats, and there were bedbugs crawling out of the layers of old wallpaper … All the books were still behind cages and the rooms were crowded and small. The Children's Room was in a dingy old basement …"[18] The Library was moved into La Veta Place in 1903, and was located there far longer than originally anticipated.

Anne Evans Joins the Library Commission

This then was the condition of the Denver Public Library in 1904, when its governing structure was changed as a result of the adoption of the home-rule city charter. On January 7, 1907, Anne attended her first Commission meeting. As already noted, she was reappointed from then on by successive mayors until 1940, a year before her death, when she resigned for health reasons. She was the only woman to have served as the Commission's President until 1987. On becoming a member of the Commission, she was put to work promptly. "On motion duly carried, the President appointed Mr. Moon, Miss Evans and Mr. Ross to revise the rules of the Commission and formulate an order of business to govern the meetings." The committee must have gotten down to work immediately, for the revised rules were submitted and adopted at the meeting of May 13.

There were many delays in getting the construction of the new building under way. The Commission held a national competition for its design and received 28 submissions. The commission was awarded to architect Albert Ross of New York City for an elegant neo-classical proposal. Andrew Carnegie was less than happy about the design. "I am sorry to have my money wasted in this way," he wrote on a newspaper clipping featuring a drawing of the proposed building. "This is no practical library plan. Too many pillars."[19] Ground was broken on August 7, 1906. The Chicago contractor chosen for the project proved to be unsatisfactory and, after quite bitter legal actions, had to be replaced. At last, on April 11, 1907, at 4:30 p.m. the site had been cleared, construction was underway, and all was ready for the elaborate ceremony of the laying of the cornerstone. Anne Evans was on the small committee named to arrange the program for the cornerstone exercises "for and with the Governor."[20]

The Carnegie Library was the first new building to grace Mayor Speer's Civic Center and so was of interest to the entire Colorado community. Seated on the platform for the ceremony were Henry Buchtel, Governor of the State; Robert Speer, Denver Mayor; Dean Martyn Hart; Rabbi W. S. Friedman; W. B. Tebbetts, President of the Library Commission; Frederick R. Ross, Chairman of the Building Committee; John McIntyre, contractor; and Charles Dudley, Librarian. "There was also a crowd of spectators, small boys perched on the iron structure, reporters, camera men, besides a goodly number of state and city officials and prominent citizens."[21] Among the latter were the other members of the Library Commission besides Tebbetts, Friedman and Ross—Judge A. Moore Berry, Anne Evans, William A. Moore, Lucy M. Hughes, John K. Mullen. "The honor of laying the stone fell to William B. Tebbetts as president of the Library Board. Dr. Friedman invoked a blessing on the enterprise. A telegram of congratulation from Andrew Carnegie was read. Frederick R. Ross read a list of the contents of the cornerstone ... Addresses were made by Governor Buchtel and Mayor Speer and the benediction was pronounced by Dean Hart."[22]

Galleries for the Denver Artists' Club

It was almost three long years before the new building opened for business. During that time, an agreement between the Public Library Commission and the Denver Artists' Club was worked out by a committee consisting of Anne Evans and William Moore for the Library Commission, and William Smiley, Henry Read, and Edward Ring for the Artists' Club. After examining the plans for the building, already under construction, the joint committee made its recommendations on May 10, 1907. They found

> that the central room on the second floor, immediately below the sky-light, and measuring approximately 59 x 26 ft. with a height of 18 ft. could be adapted to the purpose of an art gallery without structural or permanent change, and at comparatively small expense ... Being fully convinced of the pressing need of an Art Gallery in Denver, and of the manifest advantage to the community that would be derived from its location in the Public Library, we earnestly recommend that steps be taken to carry out the project.

The recommendations were adopted, and the necessary modifications incorporated into the building plans.

The Denver Public Library located in Civic Center Park, the Greek Revival style building features gray Turkey Creek Sandstone, fourteen fluted columns with Corinthian capitols. The inscription along the frieze reads: "Erected in the year of our Lord nineteen and nine and dedicated to the advancement of learning." Denver Public Library Western History Collection.

Library Spaces in the Carnegie Building

The building, looking like a Greek temple, had three floors and a basement. In the center of the imposing main floor was a long desk for registration, book return and checking books out. On the west end was a spacious open-shelf room named for John Cotton Dana; on the east, the Children's department and story room. Two stairways led to the second floor. There the Art Gallery occupied the center with a 300-seat auditorium at the east end and the magazine room on the west. The book stacks had the capacity to hold 225,000 books and potentially 300,000 with planned expansion. The existing book stock was moved into the new premises by catwalk from La Veta Place, through the west windows of the new building. The 125,000 volumes looked quite lost. One patron complained, "You will never have enough books to fill all those shelves. The wastefulness of it!"[23]

After waiting for more than 10 years for a permanent home, the Denver Public Library finally opened the doors of its new Carnegie building "to the public for inspection at two o'clock in the afternoon on February 15th. It was a very stormy afternoon, but

The Art Gallery located on the second floor of the Denver Public Library (c. 1911),
Denver Public Library Western History Collection

probably fifteen hundred people were in attendance."[24] That same evening, the formal dedication of the building took place in the second-floor auditorium. The program included interludes of music by Mozart, Hadyn, Mendelssohn and Beethoven, addresses by Mayor Speer and the Senator Charles Thomas, and a Historical Sketch of the Library by Librarian Charles Dudley. The audience filled the auditorium, overflowing into the adjacent Directors' Room and Art Gallery. "The lending of books began on the following morning, at nine o'clock." There was not an elevator for the use of either patrons or the poor librarians who had to run up and down stairs for books from the closed stacks. "Once someone counted the number of times Helen Ingersoll ran up the stairs for books for patrons. It came to twenty-three times in one hour."[25]

Dissatisfaction with Library Director— Anne Evans Listens

The Library staff's dissatisfaction with Dudley's administration had been brewing ever since the consolidation of the two libraries and the selection of Dudley over Parsons to head up the new institution. Apparently, there was no trust that anyone on the Library Commission would really listen to their grievances until Anne Evans was appointed. It appears that the staff got some idea, from her actions as a Commission member, that she would be a person who would get things done as a part of her determination to help the Denver Public Library become as good as the best in the country.

A courageous employee concluded that there was hope, and that an attempt to get the situation changed must be made. The employee was Mrs. Galbreath, working at the time as Parsons' assistant in the Catalogue Department. Subsequently, she became the Librarian at Denver University and later at the State Library. A meeting with Anne Evans (and possibly also with Mrs. Writer, the other woman member of the Library Commission) was scheduled at Helen Ingersoll's home, with Galbreath, Ingersoll and two other Library staff members present. Mrs. Galbreath "did most of the talking" according to Ingersoll's account. The list of grievances included the fact that all book ordering was done from published lists, so that there was no opportunity for book selection by the staff to meet the specific needs of Denver patrons.

In another area, Ingersoll noted, "I cannot tell you how unhappy we all were. All the women felt that Mr. Dudley showed favoritism to the men on the staff, even when these men did not bother to wait on the public at all. He did not encourage his staff to go to library school. He gave no recognition to those who did go."[26] Mrs. Galbreath did her level best to convince Miss Evans "that Mr. Dudley was not suited to be librarian." She apparently succeeded, and the wonderful result, from the point of view of Ingersoll and the rest of the staff, was that things changed.

The first of these changes was introduced at the Commission meeting of February 10, 1910, when a general plan was adopted "intended for the best interests of the library, which plan, in addition to other matters, provided for the substitution, so far as practicable, of trained women assistants upon the library staff, in place of men, such substitution to take place July 1, 1910." At a May 27 meeting, the date for termination of the men in question was postponed to Feb. 1, 1911.

The second, and major, change was that Librarian Dudley was forced to resign in 1910, though he was retained as consultant librarian for a year while the search for a replacement was undertaken. The *Denver Republican* noted, "There had been friction and dissatisfaction, too much 'dead wood' around, not enough 'get up' to meet the ideas of the progressive members of the board."[27] Perhaps the action was partly rationalized as a further move to employ only those with training in librarianship, for the dismissal of "untrained men" also applied to John Parsons. This was very upsetting to many staff members, according to Ingersoll,[28] but a heartfelt and publicly supported movement to have him retained was rejected by the Commission.

Search Finds a Dynamic New Director

Anne Evans and Mrs. Writer were promptly delegated by the Commission to go to Chicago where the American Library Association had its headquarters. Their mandate was to find a young, qualified librarian with the potential to mold the Denver Public Library, in its handsome new quarters, into a first-class institution. They succeeded admirably with the choice of Chalmers Hadley, who served with distinction as Denver City Librarian from 1911 to 1924. A graduate of Melvil Dewey's Library School in New York, Hadley served as Executive Secretary of the American Library Association. He proved to be an efficient businessman as well as a superb Librarian. In his first year in Denver, through the establishment of rigorous business practices in the conduct of the Library's financial affairs, he had paid off the Library's debt of $32,000.

Chalmers Hadley, Librarian of the Denver Public Library (1911), Denver Public Library Western History Collection

Hadley fortunately was not discouraged in his efforts to improve service in Denver by an early misfortune. This literally hit him as he walked in the Library door soon after taking up his new post ..." a man hit him over the head with a sharp instrument making a gash ... that bled profusely. He fell, striking his head against the lower step ... When he regained consciousness, the man was jumping on his chest. Two page boys jumped over the counter to his aid ... They grabbed the man." The attacker was later judged to be insane. "Mr. Hadley wore a scar ever afterward."[29]

During his tenure, Hadley was credited with many successful innovations in library service. Direct access to books through open shelving was increased. Patrons were encouraged to request information by telephone. For the first time they were allowed to reserve books, and the number they could check out increased from two to ten. A system of interlibrary loans was instituted, and the entire library was organized into what we today would call user-friendly departments. In addition to his professional abilities, Hadley had a "most pleasing personality of mingled dignity and kindness."[30] He also "had a fine appreciation of good books which he communicated to his staff, and an appreciation of people that made him warm hearted and generous."[31]

Chalmers Hadley became a member of a circle of like-minded friends of Anne Evans, those devoted to expanding cultural opportunities for the people of Denver. He served with her not only on the Library Commission but also on the Denver Art Association Board and on the Municipal Art Commission. His marriage to a sister of Marion Hendrie, Anne's good friend and indefatigable co-worker on behalf of Denver's art interests, helped to cement the friendship.

Anne Evans Becomes Commission President and Heads Up Move to Build Branch Libraries

Anne Evans became president of the Library Commission in 1910, and served, during a busy period of the Library's development, for four years. It was said at the time that she was the first woman to become head of a municipal Public Library Commission. One of the accomplishments of Librarian Charles Dudley during the last years of his tenure was to make preliminary arrangements with Andrew Carnegie's office for a second grant with which to build branch libraries. In this respect, Denver at the time was lagging behind other cities of the same size.

Outlying areas of the city were served after a fashion by traveling boxes of books and some small library "stations" located in rented rooms. There was a rising demand from Denver citizens for neighborhood branch libraries. Chalmers Hadley took up this matter enthusiastically. A committee on branch libraries, headed by Anne Evans, was formed to work with Hadley to evaluate the needs and make recommendations about size, cost, and locations. Carnegie offered a grant of $80,000 for four branch libraries. There were certain conditions, including one that required the City of Denver to pay for the land required. At the Commission meeting on June 16, 1911, "the Librarian reported that the City Supervisors had formally accepted Mr. Carnegie's gift of $80,000 for branch library buildings."

Matters then proceeded with quite elegant precision and dispatch. On March 11, 1912, "Miss Evans submitted to the Commission a report from the committee appointed to investigate sites for branch library buildings." The report recommended that two sites be purchased, one for $2,050 and one for $2,060, and that the other two branch libraries be built on sites in Denver parks, one in Highland Park and one in Platte Park. Total cost of the four buildings would be $84,000, two to cost $20,000 each and two $22,000. Four architectural firms were recommended for the commissions—Marean and Norton, Maurice Biscoe, Fisher Brothers, and J. J. Benedict—and the award of which buildings were to be designed by which architect would be decided by lot. Miss Evans announced the decision at the April 18 meeting. As plans proceeded, an attempt by architect Benedict to have the budget for his building increased was firmly rejected by the Commission. He was instructed to redraw the plans, without reducing the size of the building, to come within the budget.

Recognition of the value of the dedicated efforts of Anne Evans to fulfill the mission of the Denver Public Library was given in an unexpected public announcement at the cornerstone-laying exercises for one of the new branches. "Miss Anne Evans Honored at New Library Exercises" was the headline of an article in the *Rocky Mountain News* on September 12, 1912.

> More than three hundred persons witnessed the laying of the corner-stone of the Charles E. Dickinson branch Carnegie library on West Colfax by Frederick R. Ross yesterday afternoon. (Ross was Chairman of the Building Committee for the branches.) The surprise of the occasion centered about the reappointment of Miss Anne Evans to succeed herself as member of the library board of Denver. Her term of five years expires October 1 and her re-appointment and the glowing tribute paid her service by the mayor were greeted with applause.[32]

When the four buildings were completed, the costs came in just $38 over the $84,000 budget.

Art and Ceremonies for the New Buildings

In this era of Denver's development, the embellishment of public buildings with art of high quality was taken for granted. There existed no need for an ordinance requiring that 1 percent of construction costs be spent on art. Sculpture, decorative murals, and paintings, specially commissioned for the purpose, were believed to be essential to the satisfactory completion of new schools, libraries, and other civic buildings, as well as such important private construction as banks and insurance company headquarters. The Carnegie Library Building had vivid murals by Allen True, as well as "valuable collections of framed etchings by modern masters." Art elements were commissioned for the four new branches. On September 12, 1912, for example, the Commission considered the question of commissioning two wall paintings on canvas for the Decker Branch Library. A vote to secure the services of Dudley

Four libraries were constructed with the first Carnegie grant.

Warren Branch   Woodbury Branch

Decker Branch   Dickinson Branch

Denver Public Library Western History Collection.

Carpenter was passed, and a committee consisting of Miss Evans, Mr. Norton and Mr. Hadley appointed to secure sketches from the artist. All the proposed artwork had to be approved by the Municipal Art Commission, and on May 13, 1913, the Library Commission learned that a letter had been received notifying them of the Art Commission's approval of the designs for the decorative paintings in the Sarah Platt Decker, Henry White Warren, and Charles Dickinson branch library buildings.

The question of how to conduct appropriate opening ceremonies for each of the four new libraries was discussed by the Library Commission. It was decided to rely heavily on input from the neighborhood committees that had been appointed for each of the branches, and a motion was passed that "the question of opening exercises for the four branch library buildings be left to a committee composed of Miss Evans, Dr. Friedman and Mr. Hadley." These all took place in 1913.

Anne Evans Passes Presidential Gavel to Frederick Ross

The following year, Anne Evans' term as President expired. A unanimous motion to re-elect her for the office was passed early in 1915. However, at the next meeting on February 16, she announced that she would like to resign the office and recommended that Frederick Ross be elected in her place. There is no way of knowing just why she took this step. Possibly, it was because this was the time when she was beginning to make many trips to the Southwest in connection with her developing interest in southwestern Indian art and the preservation of mission churches, which would necessitate her being absent from a significant number of Commission meetings. More likely is that she recognized an invaluable leader for the library in Frederick Ross and was happy to encourage his contribution and slip out of the limelight.

Frederick Ross, according the Frederick J. Yonce, "was a successful, 41-year-old real estate investor and civic activist in 1906, when Mayor Speer appointed him to the Library Commission."[33] He gave his time and talents unstintingly on behalf of the Denver Public Library until his death in 1938, he served the last 18 years as president of the Library Commission. He made the library the major beneficiary of his will. This action of Anne Evans revealed one of her major talents which she demonstrated several times throughout her public life: she knew how to recognize and encourage effective leaders.

More Library Branches

The four new branches were an immediate success with the public. However, large areas of the growing city were still without adequate neighborhood library service. According to the minutes of October 23, 1913, library services were offered in the following locations, in addition to the main library and four branches: Valverde Station, Elyria Station, Lindquist Cracker Co. Station, Denver Dry Goods Co. Station, and Daniels and Fisher Station. Carnegie approved a second grant of $80,000 for four additional branch libraries in 1916. The process of building them followed the efficient model of the first four: site selection, appointment of four local architectural firms, and strict adherence to budget. The Byers and Smiley libraries were completed in 1918, and Elyria and Park Hill libraries in 1920. They were

The second Carnegie grant included four more branch libraries.

Smiley Branch

Elyria Branch

Byers Branch

Park Hill Branch

Denver Public Library Western History Collection.

designed respectively by architects Ernest and Lester Varian, Park French, Harry J. Manning, and Burnham Hoyt. Anne Evans continued to work on the building committees needed for the new branches, serving on one to select the architect for the Park Hill Branch, and another to consult on plans for the Elyria Branch. "All the Carnegie branches were small buildings designed by Denver architects. They combined fine architecture, murals, and sculpture. The buildings attracted national attention for their artistic charm and effectiveness."[34]

Malcolm Wyer replaces Chalmers Hadley

When Chalmers Hadley resigned in 1924 to head up the Cincinnati Library, he was succeeded by Malcolm Wyer. During his long tenure, 1924 to 1951, Wyer made major contributions to the development of the Denver Public Library as a "regional and national resource."[35] Before coming to Denver, Wyer had headed up the libraries of three universities: Nebraska, the State University of Iowa, and Colorado College. His accomplishments at the DPL included the establishment of a Bibliographic Research Center, which became a model for many other regional systems; a great expansion of the art and music collections; and the founding of the School of Librarianship at Denver University, where he served as Dean in addition to his responsibilities as Librarian for the DPL. Probably his major contribution was in establishing the Denver Library's Western History Department.

The Denver Public Library Western History Department

In 1950, Wyer wrote a brief history of this endeavor.[36] He traced the origin of the collection to a decision in the early days of the library to set aside a separate section for books by Colorado authors, with special interest in publications about Colorado. There was at that time no systematic effort to collect materials about the state, or the West generally, in spite of a growing interest in the subject throughout the twenties. The first attempt to meet this demand was a special staff project to prepare "an annotated bibliography of books relating to the Rocky Mountain West."

In 1929, Wyer raised the issue officially with the Library Commission, pointing out that no library in the region was making a systematic effort to build up a comprehensive collection of books and other source materials. "The Historical Societies were gathering what they could with the limited financial resources granted them," wrote Wyer, but each was concerned only about materials for one state. The Commission, after careful discussion, agreed that "There is no library which could assemble such a comprehensive collection as logically as the (Denver) Public Library or which could make it so easily available to students, writers, and research workers as this library." The DPL agreed not to compete with the State Historical Society "for the collection of manuscripts, letters, and family papers relating to the state of Colorado." The Commission then authorized the Librarian to forge ahead with building up the collection. Initial funds were granted from the City Council in the fall of 1929. On the advice of Professor Archer Butler Hulbert of Colorado College, the collection began to include a pictorial record of the Rocky Mountain West, including drawings, photos, reproductions, paintings, and engravings, which grew rapidly. Additional grants were secured from the Carnegie Foundation and by 1934, the collection had increased so much that it was elevated to the status of a separate Western History Department.

In several brief biographies of Anne Evans, it is stated that she played an important role in the establishment of this department. However, there does not appear to be any evidence to support this claim. While she undoubtedly supported the concept, and was always concerned that the efforts of the early Colorado pioneers be honored, her individual efforts in this area seem to have been limited to acting as liaison and possibly negotiator between the Library Commission and the Board of the Colorado Historical Society. For example, the minutes of the Library Commission meeting of September 1, 1925, included a discussion about the fate of the CHS book collection since they had "released" their librarian. "The librarian was advised to request Miss Evans to discuss this subject with Mr. John Evans, a member of the State Historical Society Board."

DPL Outgrows its Carnegie Library

As generous as the space in the Carnegie Library appeared in 1910, there came a time when the Public Library Commission had to inform the Board of Trustees of the Denver Art Museum that it needed the space occupied by the Art Galleries for its own use. For the DPL, taking over the space occupied by the Art Galleries could grant only a temporary reprieve from the pressure to secure more space. By 1940, when Anne Evans resigned from the Library Commission after 33 years of service, it was clear that the steady growth in demand for services from the central branch would, in the not-too-distant future, require a building much larger and better suited to the changing needs of a dynamic mid-twentieth century library. However, the Second World War loomed ahead, and it would be 1947 before Denver voters authorized a $2.5 million bond issue for a new central library building. In September, 1956, the handsome contemporary structure, designed by Burnham Hoyt in cooperation with the architectural firm of Fisher and Fisher, opened to the public.

To understand the difficulties of settling on a site for this new library building, as well the challenges for the Art Association in finding interim new space for its public Art Galleries, it is time to trace the slow, uneven progress towards the realization of Denver's dream of a Civic Center.

16

The Dream of a Civic Center

Denver's immensely practical and intensely idealistic mayor, Robert W. Speer, adopted the City Beautiful after his election in 1904. Speer championed a panoply of City Beautiful reforms, including a park and boulevard system, a magnificent mountain parks system, ornamental tree lighting, a tree-planting program, flood control, and playgrounds. His greatest ambition for Denver was a civic center.[1]

—William H. Wilson

"There were giants in those days."[2] No public figure in Denver's history better illustrates this assertion than Robert W. Speer, Mayor of Denver from 1904 to 1912, and again from 1916 to his untimely death while in office in 1918. Surprisingly little was written about Speer between a laudatory but informative monograph, *A City Builder*, by Edgar C. McMechen in 1919,[3] and *Denver's Mayor Speer* by Charles A. Johnson in 1969. Johnson's book is subtitled "The forgotten story of Robert W. Speer, the political boss with a rather unsavory political machine who transformed Denver into one of the world's most beautiful cities."[4]

Perhaps the reluctance to examine Speer's contributions is rooted in the reality that Johnson's subtitle reveals: Speer's tenure in office left Denver an almost unbelievably rich legacy and yet he was, in every sense of the word, an old-style political boss. He built a loyal cadre of followers in each ward of the city, and made accommodations with kingpins of gambling and prostitution, as well as big business enterprises. He did this in order to push through his wide-ranging agenda for the improvement of his adopted city and the enrichment of the lives of its citizens. We would like our heroes to be without blemishes. It is uncomfortable to acknowledge that Speer achieved his projects, which created Denver as a City Beautiful, not in spite of, but perhaps because of, his power as a political boss.

Speer's Early Years

Robert Speer, Courtesy History Colorado

Robert Speer was born in Pennsylvania in 1855 to a father who had been a Colonel in the Civil War. Robert had a good education, and as a youth was something of a hero when he rescued his sister and her school friend from drowning. Much later, in 1882, he married that friend, Kate Thrush. When his sister contracted tuberculosis, Robert took her to Pueblo hoping for a cure, but she found life too unsatisfying and said she would rather die at home than stay there. Speer worked for an express company in Pueblo and started reading law in the office of an uncle. However, he too developed tuberculosis and, after a violent hemorrhage, went to live on a ranch outside Denver until he recovered his health.

He then tried earning his living in Denver as a carpet salesman for Daniels and Fisher Department Store but finding that the lint and dust irritated his lungs, opted for an outdoor life as a real estate salesman. At this point, he began to take an interest in Democratic politics. According to McMechen, Speer had an open, frank and winning nature. He made friends quickly and was soon counted as one of the up-and-coming young men of the Democratic Party.

Speer never considered returning to the east. He said frequently that the city that had given him back his health was good enough for him. At a time when Republicans were entrenched in City Hall, Speer became influential in Democratic politics. In a rather dramatic election in 1884, he was elected City Clerk by secret ballot, ousting a Republican incumbent. The next year, he was appointed Denver Postmaster by President Cleveland. He held that post for four years and then returned to the real estate business. In 1891, Republican John Routt, who had been Mayor of Denver when Speer was City Clerk, became Governor. The Legislature had just passed legislation creating a fire and police board for Denver and giving the Governor power to appoint the three board members. Routt appointed two Republicans, and Speer. The Governor soon began hearing complaints that young Speer was running things by working one of the Republicans against the other.

Speer began building his powerful Democratic machine, which became widely known as the *Big Mitt*. Under the next three governors, all Democrats, he was appointed continuously to municipal offices in Denver. Alva Adams made him Police Commissioner for two years, and then he became Fire Commissioner under Governor Charles Thomas until 1901. James Orman appointed him President of the Board of Public Works of Denver, in which office he served until 1904. All of these offices gave Speer an unparalleled experience of the detailed workings of three of the most important municipal departments in Denver—public works, police, and fire—as well as an intimate knowledge of the physical condition of the city and of its diverse inhabitants, from the social elites to its shadiest entrepreneurs.

In these twenty years, stresses between the State of Colorado and the City of Denver had been growing, with the city straining against the amount of control over its destiny exercised by the State Legislature. The simple narrative goes something like this: Amendment XX to the State Constitution, adopted in 1904, divorced Denver from Arapahoe County, consolidated five or six communities into a single governmental unit and granted the new City and County of Denver home rule. A charter convention was called and the people of Denver adopted the new charter by a vote on March 29, 1904. Speer ran for mayor in the subsequent election. It proved quite a test of his political machine, since he was opposed by all the Denver newspapers that favored a business candidate. Speer bought up all the prime billboard space in the city and won.

The much more complex story, probably best told by Phil Goodstein in *Denver From the Bottom Up: Volume I: from Sand Creek to Ludlow,* was a tale of murky political struggles between many factions and voting fraud of awesome dimensions. Among the major players were the four powerful utility companies, whose interests were in the franchise agreements they would be able to make with the new city/county entity. These were led, though quietly (since he preferred to remain behind the scenes) by Anne Evans' older brother, William Gray Evans, head of the Denver Tramway Company and de facto head of the Denver Republican Party.

The other three utility companies were the Denver Union Water Company, headed by Walter Cheesman; Denver Gas and Electric, part of a national chain headed by Henry Doherty and managed locally by another astute politician, Dennis Sullivan; and the Colorado Telephone Company. This company became a part of the burgeoning Bell Telephone system under the leadership of Edward Bell Field, an Alexander Graham Bell relative and another of those who came to Colorado suffering from tuberculosis.

The City Beautiful

Robert Speer knew how to operate his new City and County of Denver to accommodate its major business interests and, at the same time, to promote projects and programs for the benefit of the ordinary citizens of the community. He also understood how to combine both of these objectives with his passionate interest in reshaping Denver from a lively but rather unlovely place into an example of that turn-of-the-century ideal, a City Beautiful.

In this area of municipal planning, Speer was not an original thinker: his ideas were those in general circulation after the immense impact of the Chicago Columbian Exposition of 1893. Daniel Burnham, the architect whose ideas shaped the character of that exhibition, took his inspiration from the Renaissance in Europe. He favored particularly the Baroque era, with the creation of open plazas, elegant landscaped boulevards and monumental public buildings. In the plan they developed for Chicago, Burnham and Bennett—the latter was later involved in the planning for Denver's Civic Center—wrote,

> There is a need ... for an orderly arrangement of public and semi-public buildings, and for proper approaches to such structures, to express the power and dignity of the city. One thinks of Paris, not as a place of so many millions of people, but as a beautiful capital in which the artistic sense of the French people has found the fullest expression.

They also wrote of the necessity of making plans on a grand scale.

> At no period in its history has the city looked far enough ahead ... Rather let it be understood that the broadest plans which the city can be brought to adopt to-day must prove inadequate and

limited before the end of the next quarter century ... Therefore no one should hesitate to commit himself to the largest and most comprehensive undertaking.[5]

The Denver Art Commission

One idea central to Burnham's conception of a well-designed city was that of the civic center, a handsome central plaza functioning as the hub of municipal government. When Robert Speer became the first Mayor of the City and County of Denver in 1904 and made his first appointments to the newly created Denver Art Commission, he welcomed enthusiastically one of their early recommendations. In fact, he probably stimulated the suggestion that a city plan be drawn up, and that the plan should include a civic center. The first commission appointees included artist Henry Read, Mrs. W. B. Tebbetts, William A. Smiley, Albert Norton, Seth Bradley, and Anne Evans. The hand-written minutes of the Commission's meetings from July 20, 1904, to January 14, 1919, are in the Western History Collection of the Denver Public Library. They document a no-nonsense group that got right down to the tasks at hand, did their homework between meetings, and made confident judgments about aesthetic matters— feeling as free to reject what they saw as poor design as to approve their perceptions of the good. At the first meeting, Henry Read was elected "permanent chairman," and Mrs. Tebbetts, Secretary. One of the first items of business called for the selection of a design for a seal for the new City and County of Denver. Of the some 200 ideas submitted, the Commission chose one by Arthur F. Willmarth. This was a design quite conventional for the period—a strong and virtuous young woman, with eyes fixed on the future, carrying a banner with FORWARD emblazoned on it, the banner's standard pointed downward at the word DENVER embossed at the bottom of the Seal.

Plans for a Civic Center

At its November 30, 1904 meeting, the Commission voted to address a letter to Mayor Speer recommending the adoption of a city plan for Denver. At a subsequent meeting, Henry Read reported on a letter received from Mayor Speer requesting the Commission to seek information from other cities about their procedures relating to civic improvements. The Commission did so, "and in July 1905, made a short report to the mayor, advocating the preparation of some consistent plan of city development ..."[6] Speer promptly responded and authorized the Commission to hire a consultant to make recommendations on needed civic improvements. On December 13, 1905, the Commission officially decided to engage Charles Mulford Robinson of Chicago, who had published his thoughts on the subject of city planning in his 1903 book, *Modern Civic Art, or the City Made Beautiful.* "He was invited to make a full report on civic improvements in Denver for an inclusive fee of $550." Robinson arrived in Denver on January 8, 1906, and made his report to the Commission on January 18. His recommendations were published by the Commission and included a diagrammatic proposal for the development of a civic center.[7]

Robinson's plan centered on a diagonal park from the north side of the State Capitol to the Court House. As Robinson recognized, this was plainly an awkward arrangement, with access to the park interrupted by traffic on both Colfax and Broadway. Robinson's plan also provided for four small parks on the south side of Colfax, west of the Capitol, and incorporated the site for the proposed Carnegie Library which fronted on Colfax. Robinson dealt with a number of other needed civic improvements in his report, including recommendations about more rigorous smoke abatement efforts and a practical suggestion about trees.

> I recommend for Denver a city forester, who shall have control of the trees on all streets that are not under the care of the Park Commission: whose duty it shall be to plant trees in front of vacant or other land where trees have not been planted; who shall conserve uniformity in the planting on each separate street; whose employees shall cut out the dead wood, shall trim the trees and water them, and who, on petition of a majority of property owners of a street, shall take care also of the parking, the cost to be assessed ... on the property.

Robinson was obviously charmed by Denver and enthusiastic about its potential. He ended his report with the following: "Denver is so beautiful already, so marvelously developed in its short life, so well worth saving and making the very most of." He saw the city "at the parting of the ways"—further growth was either going "to make it commonplace" or its citizens could "turn to account the city's natural opportunities ... and make it one of the fair cities of the world."

Approval of the plan, and authorization of taxes needed to carry it out, foundered on unexpectedly virulent opposition from real estate interests. In part this was simply because the proposal involved an increase in real estate taxes. But also, it was because the plan required that the tax burden for the civic center be borne solely by the East Denver Park District and not the entire city. At that time, the city was divided into four park districts. The other three districts had each paid for their own parks, but all the open space in the East District, including City and Cheesman Parks, had been paid for by the entire city. Since this area had most of the valuable commercial real estate, it was argued that the East District could well afford the costs involved. So the first phase of the long and painful process of birthing Denver's Civic Center ended.

The Many Concerns of the Art Commission

In the meantime, the Commission kept on with its other tasks. At its second meeting on September 10, 1904, it took up a vexing problem that was to recur frequently: "Discussion occurred about over-hanging street signs and the disfigurement of public highways by advertising." Concern over the adverse impact of billboards on the cityscape had already been a matter of public discussion before the creation of the new City and County of Denver. The Municipal Art League, of which Henry Read was an active member, had always strongly supported the right of the city to regulate billboards, against the legal objections of billboard companies.[8]

At its third meeting on December 5, 1904, the Commission formed five committees to deal with specific areas of its work: Press, Parks and Boulevards, Street Fittings and Lighting, Public Buildings and Monuments, and Designs and Competitions. Anne Evans sat on two of these—Parks and Boulevards and Street Fitting and Lighting. The latter appointment was no doubt made in the light of her close connection with the head of the Tramway Company, since the Commission had already been considering the proposition of requiring the company to place its electric wiring underground and to combine its electric poles with those used for street lighting. The aesthetic standards set by the Commission were quite demanding. At its meeting on October 30, 1905, they discussed designs "for use by the Tramway Company on 16th Street. Miss Evans moved that none of the designs be accepted as they stood." It took a number of subsequent meetings and lengthy negotiations with manufacturers before acceptable designs were approved.

The meeting of February 27, 1905, must have been quite refreshing: Mayor Speer attended and "spoke of his plans for cleaning and washing the city." He described new trash containers ordered for the city "to be placed at street corners in the business part of the city hoping that the papers and trash would be thrown in them rather than on the street to be blown about by the wind." On April 22, design proposals were opened for "an arch to be erected at the foot of 17th Street." The prize of $100 was awarded to Marie L. Woodson. This would be the welcome arch for visitors coming to Denver via Union Station, which stood for many years, adorned with the Hebrew word MIZPAH.[9] The design of bridges also concerned the Commission, and a committee was appointed to meet with the department of public works to determine how more ornamental bridges could improve the Denver environment.

Sculptor MacMonnies Has Some Thoughts on the Civic Center Plan

In 1907 came the next phase in the Civic Center saga. The defeat of the Robinson Plan had not discouraged a small group of civic leaders from pursuing the goal of securing a civic center for Denver. With their encouragement, Mayor Speer appointed "a special committee of twelve influential citizens to consider acquiring real estate in the vicinity of the State Capitol."[10] Their report, *Proposed Improvements in Denver*, was published by the Art Commission in 1907. It essentially followed the lines of the Robinson plan for the civic center, while trying to deal with the prospect of the city condemning some valuable business properties. Although the report was a

> definite step in the right direction, it was not felt to be altogether satisfactory, because it did not properly reconcile the discordant angles created by the location of two important public buildings, the State Capitol and the Court House.[11]

Meantime, the Public Improvements Committee of the influential Real Estate Exchange had commissioned a nationally known sculptor, Frederick MacMonnies, to create a monument honoring Colorado's pioneers. MacMonnies came to Denver in 1907 to confer on the exact site for his proposed Pioneer Monument. After studying the entire area, he met with the Art Commission and recommended a new solution to the civic center problem—placing the axis of the proposed center in a line directly west from the State Capitol, instead of northwest towards the existing courthouse as in the Robinson plan.

Beginning to Clear the Site—
The MacMonnies Plan Advances

With a few modifications, the Art Commission endorsed his concept and submitted them to Mayor Speer, who emphatically approved. The Commission prepared a new plan based on MacMonnies' ideas, and the citizens' special committee agreed to substitute it for the plan they had recommended. Part of its appeal was that the property, which would have to be purchased, was much less expensive than under the Robinson plan. Disadvantages were that the plan pretty much dictated that any replacement for the old Court House building would have to be at the west end of the new axis and not on the old site, and, that the planned Carnegie Library building would have its back to the new civic center. The city attorney and the Park Commission agreed that the land acquisitions should be made by a bond issue on the East Denver Park District, as part of its packet of purchases for parks and parkway purposes.

The proposal generated wide support from the professional and business organizations. Early in 1909, the Park Commission designated which parcels of land were to be acquired. An organized opposition, headed by an "Anti-Civic Center League," delayed the process of land acquisition for more than a year. Even after the last legal hurdles were overcome, it proved impossible for the Park Commission to come to a negotiated settlement with affected property owners. Action to acquire the property by right of eminent domain was initiated in July of 1910 and not completed until February of 1912. By April of that year, the city had sold $2,700,000 of East Denver Park District bonds to a firm in New York City. It looked as if the civic center might actually become a reality.

There were twenty-two influential citizens serving on the three organizations leading this effort to achieve a Civic Center for Denver—the Art Commission, the Park Commission, and the Special Committee appointed by Mayor Speer in January 1907. Among them were such memorable figures as David Moffat, J. K. Mullen, Stephen Knight, Jacob Fillius and of course Henry Read, who served both on the Art Commission and the Special Committee. Anne Evans was the only woman. Mrs. Adelaide C. Tebbetts, an original member of the Art Commission, was succeeded in 1909 by Frank Shephard.

Other City Improvements Accomplished at Breathtaking Pace

Denver elected Mayor Speer to a second four-year term of office in 1908. Most of his major improvements to the Denver environment forged ahead much more speedily than the Civic Center project. During the first few months of his first administration, starting in 1904, a bond issue was passed to build the Municipal Auditorium (now remodeled into the Ellie Caulkins Opera House). Work commenced on the improvement of Cherry Creek. As we saw earlier, Cherry Creek was "a demon stream"[12] subject to periodic disastrous floods, the first in May of 1864. In between the floods, the creek banks were used as city dumps. "They were the repository of tin cans, rubbish, manure piles, and were unsightly and unsanitary to an alarming degree."[13] Overcoming serious opposition, Speer began walling in the stream and creating a boulevard along its banks. With the aid of Dutch-born landscape architect, S. R. De Boer, Denver's boulevard and parkway system took shape, streets were paved and sidewalks put in place. Sanitary and storm sewers were systematized and enlarged. Telephone and telegraph lines "that had previously cobwebbed the streets" of the business section were placed in underground conduits.

The Element of Design

Speer and his supporters on the Art Commission placed high value on decorative elements, which they felt added greatly to the city's texture and attractiveness. Speer's first two terms saw installation of the elegant Cheesman Memorial in Cheesman Park, designed by architects Marean and Norton and contributed to the city as a memorial to Walter Cheesman by his wife and daughter. Two ceremonial entrances to City Park—the Sopris gateway and the Esplanade entrance—were completed.

A Children's Fountain, the work of French sculptor M. Blondat, enlivened the south shore of City Park Lake. Speer had been so enchanted with the original, which he saw in Dussledorf, Germany, during an influential trip to study European municipal government sponsored by the Boston Chamber of Commerce, that he got permission to have a marble duplicate carved for Denver by the sculptor.

A spectacular "electric fountain," installed in the City Park Lake, was completed in 1908 and operated in connection with nightly concerts given by the Denver Municipal Band. "During intermissions, the fountain leaps from the bosom of the lake like a glowing jewel. It throws 4,000 gallons of water a minute, has one hundred and twenty-five water formations and nine color combinations."[14] It cost almost $20,000, paid from general revenues. After many years of disuse, the fountain was completely rebuilt and had a spectacular debut in the summer of 2008.

Trees, a City Auditorium, Golf Courses, and Playgrounds

While Speer cooperated with the major utility companies, he insisted that they pay the city for the franchises granted to them, using the revenues so generated for services that benefited people. For example, $5,000 of the Denver Tramway Company's franchise fee was used to purchase the tree saplings that the mayor gave away to Denver citizens every year, along with instructions on how to care for them. Between 1905 and 1908, he distributed 110,000 trees. He also required the railroads to build viaducts in the interest of safety for the people of Denver.

Of all Speer's projects, perhaps his most cherished was the City Auditorium, which he regarded as "a medium for bringing to the masses a higher culture." He was especially enthusiastic about programs catering to young people, and was caught more than once letting children in free through side doors. Completion of the building was rushed so that it could accommodate the 1908 National Convention of the Democratic Party. It would be exactly 100 years before Denver was chosen to host this affair again.

Speer inaugurated a bathing beach system in a number of Denver's parks.

The history of the bathing beach movement in Denver is exceedingly interesting, for when the city was founded there was nothing in the form of a lake on its site. Every lake was scooped from the dusty prairie, or water from the streams was diverted to fill some natural depression in the ground. No city ever overcame such obstacles to secure so simple and desirable a landscape feature as did Denver in securing her park lakes.[15]

Speer was responsible for initiating Denver's system of municipal golf courses; the first opened in Berkeley Park in the fall of 1910. He also created a playground system from scratch: between 1904 and 1912, a dozen new playgrounds were built, equipped and supervised, as well as quite a number located within existing parks.

Denver Experiments—Briefly— with Commission Government

Speer decided against running for a third term as mayor. He had been bitten by the bug of political ambition and decided to run for the office of U.S. Senator from Colorado. Rumblings of opposition had developed to Speer's wielding so much power under Denver's strong mayor system, and these were magnified by opposition to the policies of his successor. Mayor Henry J. Arnold, without having a detailed plan for construction, decided to erect four buildings on the Civic Center site, similar in size and scale to the Carnegie Library; he promptly started to raze existing buildings that were yielding substantial rents to the city. Dissatisfaction with Arnold's plan added fuel to the movement to convert the city to a Commission form of government.

This was the era of Denver's muckrakers. Reformers like Judge Ben Lindsey believed that Speer and his administration were too closely identified with the utility companies and large exploitative industries and lenient toward the gambling houses, saloons and prostitutes thriving in the community. An amendment to the City Charter approving a switch to a Commission form of government was passed by the citizens in 1913, before the end of the first year of the Arnold regime.

Frederick Law Olmstead Jr. Works on a Plan for the Civic Center

Under the new Commission system of government, the fate of the Civic Center became the responsibility of the Commissioner of Property. Commissioner Otto Thum hired Frederick Law Olmsted, Jr., of Brookline, Massachusetts, the son of the planner of Central Park, to work on a comprehensive plan for the Civic Center. His design generally followed MacMonnies' concept. It provided, for the first time, that the badly needed new municipal building be placed between Bannock and Cherokee, outside the area already purchased. Olmsted wrote, "Studies for completing the design entirely within the limits of the present holdings ... on the east side of Bannock Street, prove conclusively that the western end would appear cramped, congested ..."[16]

Olmstead's plan also provided for the facility long dreamed of by the Artists' Club—an arts building right on the civic center, a counterpart to the Carnegie Library. In hindsight, it is astonishing to reflect that the artists' group and their staunch supporters had to wait for 36 more years until their ambitions for an art museum building on the civic center were realized. Not a small share of the credit for this extraordinary persistence and eventual success must go to Anne Evans. As Lewis Story writes in the Denver Art Museum's book, *The First Hundred Years*,

> Her name is woven into the fabric of the museum's history from its inception as the Artists' Club until her death in 1941 ... Her energy and vision often assured a viable future for the organization, and she was always ready to serve in any capacity, from hostess at the 1894 opening of the club's first rooms to interim director.[17]

Under Commissioner Thum, all the buildings remaining on the main body of the Civic Center were torn down, and the ground planted in grass. No progress on developing the Civic Center occurred under the next two Commissioners.

Art Commission Re-Constituted

The old Art Commission ceased to exist and a new one came into being, with members appointed by the Commissioner of Improvements. The *Denver Republican* newspaper reported on June 25, 1913, that Henry Read had been appointed president of the Commission for a term of six years. Miss Anne Evans, "who has been a member of the art commission since the Speer administration," was also appointed for six years. Artist Charles Partridge Adams and architect Albert Norton were appointed for four years each and Frank Shephard and George Van Law for two-year terms.

Anne Evans resigned her seat on the Art Commission in 1914. The announcement in the Commission minutes is simple, with no explanation. At the February 10, 1914, meeting of the Art Commission in the Public Library

> It was announced that the resignation of Miss Anne Evans as a member of the Art Commission had been handed to Commissioner Hunter and by him accepted, and that Mr. Hunter had appointed Mr. Alex C. Foster to be a member of the Commission in her stead.

This was about the same time as she resigned the presidency of the Public Library Commission, though remaining as a board member. Lacking any written explanation for these actions and failing to find any family members or others who have relevant memories about this time in Anne Evans' personal life, a biographer is left only with speculation.

There are several possible factors that could have entered into her decision. This was quite a traumatic time for the beloved family with whom she lived. On the official level, with Speer no longer driving civic improvements, and a rather ineffective city government in his place, she may have felt that the role of the Art Commission was greatly diminished and that she could trust Henry Read, still the Commission's head, to see that sound decisions were made on any matters coming before it. Also, as previously noted, this was the time when she started to travel extensively in the Southwest, in connection with her increasing interest in the life and art of the Native Americans there. This unique aspect of her life and activities is taken up in the next chapter.

Mayor Speer Creates His Civic Center

Speer lost his bid for a Senate seat. Citizens from all walks of life in Denver urged him to run again for mayor. People had grown tired of seeing nothing accomplished towards developing the city, especially the Civic Center, and contrasted the lack of progress with the spectacular achievements of Speer's administrations from 1904–1912. The proposal by Mayor Arnold (1912–1913) to clutter up the proposed Civic Center with four buildings had angered many. Speer agreed to run, but only if the city charter were returned to a strong mayor system, and only if passage of the amended charter were linked to his election. In 1916, the citizens approved another charter amendment giving complete executive power back to the mayor and electing Speer to that office. "The Speer Amendment made

Denver's mayor one of the most powerful city officials in the United States."[18]

Speer got to work immediately. He did not approve of many aspects of the Olmstead plan and brought Chicago landscape architect E. H. Bennett to Denver, charging him with the task of developing a Civic Center plan acceptable to all. The plan eventually implemented was substantially the one drawn up by Bennett. It included a strong transverse axis, bisecting the main axis at right angles, and incorporated Speer's idea for a Colonnade of Civic Benefactors and an open-air theater on the south side of the Center. Speer had made a striking speech in 1909 to the Chamber of Commerce in which he stressed the importance of the more fortunate Denver citizens donating to their city.

> At best, life is short. We want the good opinion of our fellowmen while here, and to be kindly remembered when we have passed on. I know of no better way than to cultivate and unfold some blossoms along life's path, add rest stations, play stations and beauty spots along the way. The time will come when men will be judged more by their disbursements than by their accumulations. Denver has been kind to most of us by giving to some health, to some wealth, to some happiness, and to some a combination of all. We can pay a part of this debt by making our city more attractive.[19]

This theme of Speer's came to be known as his "Give While You Live" campaign. To encourage the spirit of public giving, Speer planned to place upon the Colonnade the names of people, living or dead, who enriched the cultural or artistic life of Denver by a substantial gift.

Within a few months of the acceptance of the Bennett plan, work was under way on the Colonnade and the defining stone balustrades of the Civic Center. Plans for the Open Air Theater, frequently called the Greek Theater, were finalized. To balance these structures on the south side, the Voorhies Memorial Gateway was being designed by architects Fisher and Fisher as a ceremonial entrance to the Civic Center from the north. J. H. P. Voorhies, a Colorado pioneer, left a bequest to the city for a memorial structure memorializing his wife and himself. Speer arranged that the other Civic Center improvements would be funded by back payments from the Telephone Company for use of the city streets. The Bennett plan still included a proposed art museum building, balancing the Carnegie Library. It also proposed placing a colossal fountain in the center of the plaza. According to McMechen, Speer made it clear that he hoped to finish the Civic Center before his term ended in 1920. "But, at least, I have got it so far defined that nobody will be able to change the main plan," he said.[20]

Robert Speer died unexpectedly in 1918, but the main outlines of his Civic Center were secure and his legacy of other civic improvements to Denver is still unsurpassed.

Site for a City and County Building

The major question still left unsettled by the Bennett plan was just how and when a new municipal building to replace the aging Court House and City Hall would be built at the western end of the Civic Center. This would balance the State Capitol Building at the eastern end and complete the classic design. The process leading up to the purchase of the land on which the City and County building now stands was described in an article, "Completion of Civic Center by Voters," in the May, 1923, issue of *Municipal Facts*.[21] When Speer died, there still existed a great deal of opposition to the Civic Center site from downtown business interests, who feared that the move would shift the business center and damage their property values. Those who favored the Civic Center location concluded that, unless a strong and organized effort was made to get the matter settled, "the civic center would never be completed." At the end of 1922,

> a voluntary committee was formed, composed of many of the most prominent people in Denver in every walk of life. Representatives of the trade unions sat with representatives of big business interests, and ministers of various denominations all united for the civic advancement of the city.

The group's consensus was to submit to the voters a $500,000 bond issue to purchase the land and also to put on the same ballot the question of whether the new municipal building should be located on the Bannock Street site or the existing Court House site.

A Civic Center Extension Committee was formed headed by Roblin Davis, the husband of Anne Evans' niece, Margaret, with Anne's nephew, banker John Evans, as Treasurer. Henry Read actively participated, even though he too had resigned from the Art Commission, due to a disagreement with Mayor Mills over the removal of a lamp standard on Champa Street.[22]

The Civic Center Committee had representation from every improvement association in Denver, and proceeded to see that "the voters were enlightened by a whirlwind campaign." The Fine Arts Committee of the City Club of Denver later paid tribute to Anne Evans' success in heading up this vital drive.

> We remember her splendid organization of the effort of several hundred civic-minded citizens to assure selection of the present site for the new municipal building and the block-by-block canvas of the city for the sales of bonds to help in acquiring of that site.[23]

At the election of May 15, 1923, the Bannock Street site was decisively selected, and the bonds to purchase it authorized by a somewhat lower margin. The issue of where to put the new municipal building was now settled. The decision was certainly helped by the fact that the Court House site was estimated to be worth at least $1,250,000. The questions of raising the money to pay for the building, and of who should design it, were left for another day.

Civic Center Sculpture

In 1916, Mayor Speer had renewed his extraordinary campaign, directed primarily at the wealthy, to "Give While You Live." Thousands of dollars in different forms of giving to the city resulted from this campaign, some of which materialized as sculptures on the Civic Center. The two popular nostalgic bronzes by Alexander Phimister Proctor—*The Broncho Buster* and *On the War Trail*—were funded by Stephen Knight and J. K. Mullen in response to Speer's appeal.

Proctor, regarded as one of America's most important sculptors of the late nineteenth and early twentieth centuries, started his artistic career in Denver. Born in Bozanquit, Canada, in 1860, he arrived in Denver as a young man and took his first art lessons from an immigrant Dutch painter. He became an enthusiastic hunter, alternating hunting wild animals in the mountains with sketching them. From Denver artist J. Harrison Mills he learned wood engraving skills. His first paid art commission was for illustrating a book, *Hands Up*, by Sheriff Dave Cook.

Proctor left Denver to study at the Art Students' League in New York. His first bronze, *Mule Deer*, was modeled at the New York Zoo.

A photograph of it appeared in *Harpers' Weekly*—his first national publicity. In 1893, Proctor's commissioned sculptures of thirty-five western animals, as well as two large equestrian monuments of American Indians, were exhibited at the World's Columbian Exhibition in Chicago. They earned him international recognition and a scholarship to study in Paris where he won a Gold Medal at the 1900 Paris Exposition. He returned to the United States as an accomplished and famous sculptor, locating his studio in New York City. With his wife, Margaret, he traveled widely in the West, living for a time in 1914 with the Crow Indians on their reservation. Deciding that his heart belonged in the West, he moved to Oregon in 1915, where he was living when commissioned to do the Denver Civic Center sculptures.

Preston Powers and the Closing Era

Speer was undoubtedly aware of the long-drawn-out and unsuccessful efforts to raise funds to pay sculptor Preston Powers (1842–1904) for the first purely artistic sculpture to be located on the grounds of the State Capitol. *The Closing Era* is easy to miss on a routine visit to the Civic Center because it is peacefully located at the east entrance to the Capitol building, and not at the west entrance facing the Civic Center. The sculpture was originally designed for a group of real estate promoters who were developing Perry Park, four miles west of Larkspur. It was to be carved in the red sandstone of the site, depicting a Plains Indian standing over the body of a bison dying from a bullet wound.

In a *Rocky Mountain News* article (April 10, 1988), Frances Melrose told the story of the sculpture and the sculptor. Preston Powers spent some years in Denver at the end of the nineteenth century, becoming for a short time the director of the University of Denver Art School. He was born in Italy in 1842, the son of a famous American sculptor, Hiram Powers. Preston Powers made his final model for the Denver sculpture in Italy, and decided to fashion it in bronze rather than sandstone.

The deal with the realtors fell through, at which point the ladies of the Denver Fortnightly Club entered the picture. They were determined to obtain the sculpture for Colorado and tried to raise $10,000 in bonds at $10 each to pay for it. They sent it for display at the 1893 Chicago World's Fair but only managed to raise $5,000. "Powers, who understandably had grown somewhat temperamental over the whole mishmash, refused the money and instead presented the statue to the state." This version is somewhat at odds with that of Elisabeth Spalding, a long-time Fortnightly Club member, who wrote, "The Denver Fortnightly Society, through its members, has always had much to do with Denver's art progress ... Through their interest and subscriptions years ago, the first public statuary was placed; Mr. Preston Powers' 'Indian and Buffalo.' "[24] In any event, upon its return from Chicago to Denver, the statue was placed on the Capitol grounds.

The Art Commission Reappears

After the resignations of Anne Evans from the Art Commission in 1914 and of Henry Read in 1919, the level of activity of the Commission is not clear. The minutes seem to have disappeared. Both Anne Evans and Henry Read continued to maintain an active role in promoting the development of the Civic Center as envisaged by Mayor Speer. The Voorhies Memorial, designed by architects Fisher and Fisher, was completed in 1920. Its serene reflecting pool is enlivened by Robert Garrison's sea lion sculptures, to the cost of which, according to Spalding, the Fortnightly Club contributed. When the one major public controversy in which Anne Evans was involved erupted in 1937, an article in the *Denver Post* (June 6, 1937) seemed to indicate that she had never left the Art Commission.

> Since the day when the late Robert W. Speer, then mayor of Denver, decided to make the city safe for good art, Miss Anne Evans has been a member of the art commission created by charter. It would be as easy to imagine her off the commission as to imagine the dome sliced from the state capitol.

A partial clue to this mystery surfaced among some miscellaneous papers of Anne Evans found in the Denver University archives. These are drafts of minutes, in Anne Evans' handwriting, of several meetings of the Art Commission held early in 1931, when she took on the role of secretary. On September 23, 1931, she wrote,

> At the request of Mayor Begole, the newly appointed Art Commission of the City and County of Denver met in the Mayor's office

on Tuesday Sept. 22nd at 4 p.m. The entire Commission was in attendance, as follows: Mr. Frank Shephard, Chairman, Mr. Willis Marean, Architect Member, Mr. Cyril Kay-Scott, Artist Member, Mr. Arnold Ronnebeck, Artist Member, Mr. George Cranmer, Miss Anne Evans, and Mayor Begole, Ex-Officio.

This introduction seems to indicate that either the Art Commission had lapsed into inactivity, or that the terms of all its members had been terminated. In either case, Mayor Begole, on assuming office in 1931, was apparently free to appoint the entire Commission. This was an important time for the art interests of Denver, because the plans for the new City and County Building, which would complete the Civic Center design, were being finalized.

A Presence for the Denver Art Museum on the Civic Center

The supporters of the Denver Art Museum, in spite of the acquisition of Chappell House and the addition there of a gallery space, needed more room. They had never given up their long-term intention to have the main location of the Museum be on the Civic Center. Anne Evans is credited with helping to achieve the next phase of this plan, persuading the City authorities to make room in the new City and County Building for art galleries.

It is rather astonishing to remember that at this time, Anne Evans had taken on the responsibility of being the Executive Secretary of the Art Museum; was in the thick of organizing efforts to save the Central City Opera House and develop a public summer program there; and was still involved with architect John Gaw Meem's labors to restore mission churches in New Mexico.

At the September 22 Art Commission meeting, Roland Linder, Supervising Architect for the City and County Building, explained reallocation of space within the new building,

> [Roland Linder] was asked to show the plans of the Civic Building, and to expound the changes recently adopted. He explained that, through elimination of the auditorium space which had been provided for certain departments on the lower floors ... The Mayor had thereupon suggested that the entire south end of the top story might be used for an art gallery ... pending the erection of the future museum building.

One major impetus for this development was the fear that Denver might lose the valuable gift of paintings donated in 1917 by Junius Flagg Brown, inspired by Speer's "Give While You Live" campaign. The donation was made on the condition that the city must provide, within 15 years, an appropriate building in which to display the collection.

Linder requested the help of the Art Commission in selecting an artist to

> ... have charge of the interior decoration and of a sculptor to design and execute the pediments over the entrance—He pointed out the prime necessity of securing the best possible men in their respective fields, as the ultimate beauty of the building depended upon them.

Two committees were appointed: Anne Evans, Cyril Kay-Scott and George Cranmer "to confer with Mr. Linder and to recommend an artist for the interior decoration," and Cranmer and Kay-Scott "to collect data concerning the finest architectural sculptors."

This earnest search for the highest standard of design in every aspect of the city environment was evident in Anne Evans' minutes for the October 15 meeting, when the Commission heard a presentation on "an electric light standard to be installed on 13th Street. After full discussion it was thought best to ask for another drawing, conforming as did the one under consideration to the requirements of standardization, but with greater insistence on fine proportion and grace of form." Mr. Ronnebeck was asked to write to certain German and Scandinavian cities for pictures of their street lighting.

The minutes of the decisive October 22 meeting were admirably brief. Walter C. Mead was present by invitation. This was in his capacity as Trustee of the Brown Bequest, another significant gift to the city. Architect Linder

> presented the blue print of the proposed galleries on the fourth floor of the new civic building to the Commission for consideration and approval. Commendation was enthusiastic and the plans were formally endorsed and signed by Mr. Begole as Mayor of the city, Mr. Shephard as Chairman of the Commission, and Mr. Mead as representative of the trustees of the Brown bequest. Hearty thanks were tendered to the Mayor for this great step forward in the advancement of Art in Denver.

Gallery Space for Art Museum
in Planned City and County Building

The importance of this step for the Art Museum was not only the acquisition of new and spacious galleries on the Civic Center, but the definitive recognition of the Denver Art Museum, a private corporation, as the city's art agency. The Museum had been receiving a modest annual allocation of city funds from 1923 and had in effect, by virtue of being the custodian of the Mead Collection and the Brown Bequest, "established its claim to art works promised to the city when and if it constructed a suitable building."[25] With the opening of the new galleries in the City and County Building, two important agreements between the City and County and the Denver Art Museum were signed. The first, a two-party agreement, outlined the "respective obligations" of each party wherein the city agreed to employ the museum as "its art agency" and the museum agreed to exercise full responsibility over all gifts of art to the city and administrative control over the galleries in the City and County Building and—in a very important clause—"oversee the new Art Museum Building to be erected as provided in the contract with the Dill Trustees and the Schleier Trustees." It was the requirements of these two bequests that prompted the drafting of the second, four-party, agreement.

The Schleier will left funds to the city to be used for the completion or beautification of the Civic Center, or for the purchase of land and/or the erection of buildings in or near the Civic Center, as long as these became public property owned by the City and County of Denver. One of the purposes of the four-party agreement therefore was to satisfy legal challenges to using Schleier funds for needs of the Denver Art Museum, a private corporation, by establishing it as "the authorized art agency of the city so that funds left to the city might be considered properly spent in erecting a building to be occupied by the museum ..."[26]

The Dill bequest came from Denver schoolteacher Helen Dill. "An astute Denver real-estate investor, Helen Dill left about $128,000, which was then a considerable sum, to the city for 'the beautification of the Civic Center.'[27] Dill died in 1928, but agreements with the trustees about the use of the funds were not signed until 1932. These provided for $40,000 to be allocated to the cost of the new galleries in the City and County Building, and the remainder for art museum purchases. Lewis Story, in his chapter on the formative years of the Denver Art Museum's history, noted that, though acquisition funds from the Dill bequest theoretically became available in 1933 during the tenure of Cyril Kay-Scott, some questions about just how they should be spent delayed the process. Kay-Scott resigned in 1934, and was succeeded as DAM director by Donald J. Bear, a man already on the Museum staff as an educator and curator of paintings. To Bear fell "the agreeable task of expending the bulk of the fund ..."[28]

Anne Evans, as acting Executive Secretary of the Denver Art Museum in 1932, a position she held again from 1934 to 1940 during the negotiations over the provision of galleries in the new City and County Building, and the terms of the relationship between the Museum and the City, is credited with being a quiet but potent voice in getting the agreements signed and thus moving the Museum a giant step forward towards its ultimate but still distant goal—a separate Art Museum building on the Civic Center.

The new galleries in the City and County Building opened to the public on December 12, 1932. Their range revealed the extent of collecting that had started with a few acquisitions and had accelerated through the years as a result of bequests. There were two rooms devoted to old-master and contemporary paintings; one to sculpture and drawings; two to Asian sculpture, paintings, prints, and ceramics; one to American colonial textiles, furniture, and china; and a minute space to southwestern (Hispanic) folk art. This space was for materials owned by Anne Evans,

> who began to acquire the religious folk art of southern Colorado
> and northern New Mexico before the material was catalogued, pub-
> lished, and brought to the attention of art historians and collectors
> by the American Index of Design.[29]

As a last minute addition to the plans, there was a gallery showing a selection of the Museum's American Indian art collection. The majority of the collection, so much a tribute to Anne Evans' long-time passion for valuing and collecting this material, was still housed at Chappell House. These two aspects of Anne Evans' contribution to the art sensibilities of Denver are covered in more detail in a later chapter.

Arnold Ronnebeck, Anne Evans, 1932, bronze, Denver Art Museum

Because of her significant bequest, one of the major galleries was named after Helen Dill in a special dedication ceremony in May of 1933. On this occasion, a bronze bust of Anne Evans by sculptor Arnold Ronnebeck was presented to the Museum. The sculpture was paid for entirely by friends in recognition of Evans' extraordinary and long-time dedication to the advancement of art in Denver.[30]

There is an ironic aspect to this particular honor: it was over the design of a proposed sculpture by Arnold Ronnebeck that Anne Evans resigned her seat on the Art Commission and made a rare appearance as a controversial—and combative—figure in the headlines of the Denver newspapers.

Controversy over Speer Memorial Sculpture

Almost as soon as Mayor Speer died, sincerely mourned by the city that owed him so much, there was talk of the need for a monument to commemorate his achievements. Many ideas were put forward, one of the most popular being to carry out Speer's dream of a large and elaborate fountain in the middle of the Civic Center. Leadership to move this project forward was lacking until the stimulation of a $100,000 bequest for the construction of a memorial to Robert Speer, left by Vaso L. Chucovich, who died in 1933.

Chucovich was born in a seaside town on the Dalmatian coast, which was in the Austro-Hungarian Empire at the time but became part of Yugoslavia after the First World War. He emigrated to the United States as a young man and found himself penniless in Carson City, Nevada, in the middle of its mining boom. There, he held a variety of jobs and found that he had a particular talent as a dealer in its gambling establishments. He moved to Omaha, continuing to profit from working in gambling halls. Having accumulated a tidy sum of around $75,000, he arrived in Denver in 1886.

He worked briefly for the man who was known as the gambling czar of Denver but soon decided to go into business for himself. He purchased an interest in one of the popular gambling halls on Larimer Street. According to Speer's biographer,[31] "Despite his flamboyant occupation, Chucovich was regarded as a 'square shooter' and his integrity was never questioned." Mayor Speer and Chucovich developed a long-lasting friendship. After the Mayor closed Denver's gambling establishments in 1907 to conform with new state laws, Chucovich turned his energies to real estate investments with great financial success.

The trustees of Chucovich's estate decided to commission the internationally known Yugoslav sculptor, Ivan Mestrovic, to create a suitable piece of sculpture. His design was approved by the Denver Art Commission. Like Chucovich, Mestrovic, of Croatian background, was born into the Austro-Hungarian Empire. He started life as a shepherd; he was then apprenticed to a stonecutter who became aware of his talent and found a sponsor to send him to study in Vienna. From there he traveled widely, living and working in Paris, Belgrade, Rome and Zagreb. But the year in which he was considered for a sculpture commission in Denver was 1933, and America was suffering from the Great Depression. The director of the federal PWA (Public Works of Art project) publicly disapproved of the idea of paying a foreign sculptor $100,000 when so many American artists were unemployed.

The Denver Art Commission, which had the responsibility of accepting or rejecting any proposed addition to the Civic Center, was forced to withdraw its approval of the Mestrovic design. The Chucovich estate trustees then commissioned Denver sculptor Arnold Ronnebeck to come up with a proposal. His design was published in the *Denver Post* and the *Rocky Mountain News* on May 2, 1935. It consisted of a granite base and five bronze figures. The completed composition was to be 24 feet high and was to rest in a water basin 48 feet in diameter. Fountain effects would be in the base with the outline of the water supporting the outline of the group. Night illumination would be supplied from the rim of the water basin. An inscription in memory of Mayor Speer would be placed on the base. Ronnebeck suggested in addition a quotation from Walt Whitman's *Leaves of Grass*, "Give me men to match my mountains."[32]

The trustees enthusiastically applauded the concept but the Art Commission, apparently spearheaded by Anne Evans, turned it

Arnold Ronnebeck, sketch for proposed Speer Memorial, Courtesy History Colorado

down. As her later comments indicated, she considered it a "sculptured atrocity." While the *Rocky Mountain News* article was a factual report, the *Denver Post* was quite scornful, headlining its article "New Speer Statue Design, Fortunately, Still Just a Sample."

The next chapter in the Speer Memorial saga came with the announcement of a national competition, open to all the major sculptors in the nation, which garnered fifteen submittals, including another one by Ronnebeck. The Art Commission selected the entry jointly shaped by a nationally known sculptor, William Zorach, and

Denver architect Burnham Hoyt. Now it was the trustees' turn to differ with the Art Commission's choice and they requested the mayor to appoint a separate advisory committee to review the options, which he agreed to do. This committee chose an artist of international reputation, Maurice Sterne, to make the definitive judgment. He also opted for the Zorach/Hoyt design. This failed to persuade the trustees, who were still wedded to Ronnebeck's concept.

It is difficult to assess the artistic merit of Ronnebeck's proposal from the photographs reproduced in newspapers. Was it too avant-garde and was Anne Evans too conservative in her tastes? This seems unlikely; her major preference seems to have been for high quality in artistic works, whether from western European cultures or from those of Native Americans of the southwest. It appears that she was quite open to new ideas. In their portrait of her, the Jameses found that "she tried to keep an open mind and defended serious work in more advanced modes."[33] A painting of her living room in her mountain home by Elisabeth Spalding, done in the mid-twenties, shows a Bauhaus-style tubular steel chair alongside the Indian rugs and baskets. Katharine Davis, in her paper on Anne Evans, noted that Anne kept the tubular steel chairs at her home in spite of the "endless chiding" she received about them, especially after one of the "more portly males of the family" bent one of them out of shape.[34]

It was now 1937. Mayor Begole had left the scene with the election of 1935, and the former Mayor Benjamin Stapleton (1923–31) had been returned to office. According to Johnson, "By this time, the atmosphere was charged with accusations and counter accusations."[35] Stapleton apparently wanted the Art Commission, to which Anne Evans was still acting as secretary, to go along with the Chucovich trustees' preference. Although it was well known that she was the major opponent to this course, he chose not to remove her—her term was up in June of 1937 anyway—but to fire two other Commission members who were supporting her stand. She was furious.

It was the only time in her long career of volunteer civic service that she went public with her anger and frustration. It was the removal of the two fellow Commissioners that irked her the most: "Fine reward for honest, efficient service," she said as fire flashed in her blue eyes. "The charter by which the art commission was created sets forth the rules for its operation. Appointment under these rules is made upon recommendation of the Board of Directors of the art museum. If we have laws and ordinances, let's obey them"![36] "I try to keep an open mind to respect the views and opinions of others," she said, "but I want the fight to be fair—no striking below the belt. If a person who has been honored with appointment to a responsible position, as were these two of my colleagues on the commission, is dropped for no reason whatsoever and contrary to law, I propose to ask 'WHY?' as loud as I can and keep on asking. How else can we expect to hold the respect and trust of the public?"

The *Post* article, headlined "GOVERNOR EVANS WOULD BE PROUD OF DAUGHTER ANNE," is illustrated with four photographs of Anne Evans, with a caption under each. Under the first, "I don't care what the mayor or the governor or anyone else says. The art commission must be kept free of political wire-pulling." Under the second, as she is on the phone, "You needn't shout. I can hear you. Whether I'm on the commission or off, the civic center is going to be kept free from sculptured atrocities." The third, smiling, "Oh, well. It's all in a day's work. You have to get angry with people sometimes or they'll think they can run over you, especially if you're a woman." And the last, philosophically, "Fortunately, tho, there is some work you can do all by yourself. You can sit down at your desk alone and get it done quietly and the way you want it."

Denver Public Library Western History Collection

Anne Evans resigned from the Commission. Under the overall headline, "ANNE EVANS TO CONTINUE VALIANT FIGHT FOR GOOD ART"[37] appeared an article which was a major tribute to her long years of energetic service to Denver's cultural development. There are two segments of text. One, headlined "City Likely to Lose Her as Commission Member" has the subheading "'Colorado's Outstanding Woman' Adheres to Her Sound Judgment With Almost Fanatical Zeal Altho Views Clash With Mayor's."

> Not only has she been a faithful, always active, member of the art commission, but of the library commission and of the board of directors of the Denver Art Museum. If she has received a 5 cent piece or any other sum for her services, neither she nor anyone else can remember the passing of the coin. Financial independence and a zeal to serve the city makes her a most valuable public servant and citizen, and she brings to her task what amounts to a fanatic's consecration ... Scores of young, struggling artists have found in her a generous friend and honest critic. She believes in the exercise of tact when it doesn't interfere with principle ... 'I never went into anything in my life on a pass' ... a great lady is Anne Evans. Thousands of women in organizations have voted her Colorado's outstanding woman. This she declaims with a smile and a wave of the hand and the assurance, 'I like work. I like people. I love Colorado'.[38]

There is still no statue on the Civic Center commemorating its creator. Mayor Stapleton persuaded the Chucovich trustees that, in the middle of the depression, it would be more appropriate to spend the bequest on a sorely needed Children's Wing for Denver General Hospital. In memory of Mayor Robert W. Speer, who loved children, the completed Wing was dedicated in the summer of 1941.

17

Anne Evans and the
Theosophical Movement

*During my last visit (I was taken) to see Miss Evans and I
am grateful to have had this privilege. I have never had
in one brief visit such an intense impression of spiritual
and intellectual vitality and beauty.*[1]
—Chancellor Caleb Gates, Denver University

About Theosophy and Theosophical Organizations

The modern theosophical movement in this country began with the
founding of the Theosophical Society in New York in 1875 by Helena
Petrovna Blavatsky, a dynamic woman from an aristocratic Russian
background. Her associates in founding the Society were Americans
H. S. Olcott and W. Q. Judge. Since that time, there has been a mind-
numbing proliferation of theosophical organizations in America.
Some lasted for a while and then faded, others survived through
changes. All, however, were based on the teachings of Blavatsky,
which were expressed in books, articles, and speeches, as well as in
what we today would call mission statements. The principal aim and
object of this Society is to form the nucleus of a universal Brotherhood of Humanity without distinction of race, creed, sex, caste or
color. The subsidiary objects are: the study of ancient and modern
religions, philosophies and sciences, the demonstration of the importance of such study; and the investigation of the unexplained
laws of nature and psychical powers latent in man.[2]

Blavatsky held that the reasoning faculty, which deals in verbal
expression and detached logic, is only one aspect of human consciousness. Another important aspect is what is true for each individual. It
is not the reasoning, writing, or talking about different elements of
human life, but the actual experiencing of them that counts.

Blavatsky believed in the existence of an ancient and continuing
wisdom tradition, exemplified especially in oriental philosophies

and religious teachings that point to an underlying interconnection between all things in the universe. The power or energy that sustains this connection is what people over the centuries, and in hundreds of different cultures, have named as deities or as God.

For herself and her followers, Helena Blavatsky rejected all creeds and dogmas, believing that each spiritual seeker should continually widen his or her own horizons by study and action. She wrote, "All must strive for freedom of human thought, for the elimination of selfish and sectarian superstitions, and for the discovery of all the truths that are within reach of the human mind."[3] Blavatsky believed some day this striving will flower into a universal human culture that will be without war or violent conflict, but open to a wide variety of beliefs that are all different aspects of universal truths.

The aspect of Blavatsky's teachings and writings that generated controversy, and sometimes ridicule, was her insistence on the reality and importance of occult phenomena. She was not alone in her fascination with this subject. Interest in spiritualism, with its séances and mediums, its messages from the dead or from Wisdom Teachers or Masters, was widespread in the last half of the nineteenth century. Respected professionals, such as psychologist William James in the United States, Carl Jung in Switzerland, and Sir Arthur Conan Doyle and Sir Oliver Lodge in England, were deeply interested in exploring the significance of spiritualist manifestations.

Later, spiritualism faded, though never disappeared, as a serious pursuit of mainstream intellectuals, perhaps because a great deal of fraud connected with séances and other spiritualist activities was revealed over the years; or perhaps because science itself began to deal in such unimaginable mysteries as relativity, black holes, the uncertainty principle, and the "100th monkey" hypothesis. Western spiritual seekers continued to find profound meaning in a serious exploration of eastern traditions, especially Hinduism and Buddhism. There they found a blending of challenging spiritual principles, exercises like the Zen koans to disturb the reasoning brain, and experiential disciplines such as yoga, meditation, and breathing exercises.

Unraveling Anne Evans' Connections to Theosophy

It was the diversity of Theosophical Societies that frustrated our first attempts to follow a tantalizing lead. Many short biographies of Anne

Evans listed her, without comment, as the author of an article on Norse Mythology in the *Theosophical Quarterly*. Our original enquiry to the headquarters of the Theosophical Society of America in Wheaton, Illinois, brought a cordial response, but no information as to whether the author Anne Evans was from Denver, or whether she was a member of the Society. Late in 2009, an unrelated search by Kevin Gramer, Director of the Byers- Evans House Museum, for biographical information about Anne Evans' friend Mary Kent Wallace, set into motion a series of discoveries.[4] These established, without a doubt, that Anne Evans was a leading, active member of a Theosophical Society branch in Denver. When she joined is not certain, but her documented membership lasted from 1913 to 1938.

Later enquiries to the Wheaton headquarters elicited valuable information from a new archivist, Janet Kerschner[5]:

> The fact that you found references to Anne Evans in *Theosophical Quarterly* tells me that she was active in a different Theosophical Society than ours. In 1898 a Theosophical Society in America was formed, headed by Ernest Temple Hargrove, J. D. Buck and others. It dropped the 'in America' in 1908, but was headquartered in New York City until 1942. It was never a very big group, but was very dedicated, and had lodges in Cincinnati, Providence, Denver, Los Angeles, a few other cities, and several foreign countries.
>
> Our society has been called the Theosophical Society in America since 1934, but previously was the American Theosophical Society or the American Section of the TS—Adyar. Yes, it is confusing. The Theosophical Society now based in Pasadena has an even more complicated history.

Janet Kerschner scanned issues of the *Theosophical Quarterly*, marking all references to Anne Evans, Mary Kent Wallace and the Denver Branch. She forwarded a copy of the marked pages, noting "The references span the years 1907 to 1937 for the branch, and Anne Evans is mentioned in many of those years. Assuming that it is the same Anne Evans, she was very active in the theosophical movement."[6]

Further study of the contents of the *Theosophical Quarterly* Magazines revealed that in addition to her involvement with the Denver branch, Anne Evans wrote at least five well-researched articles for the *Quarterly* on a surprising variety of subjects, including "Norse Mythology."

The emergence of this new information, of course, raised questions for a biographer. What influences, in the development of the well-educated daughter of two dedicated Methodists, might have caused her to espouse such a radical life-view as Theosophy? What aspects of Theosophy particularly appealed to her? How did its values fit her own?

Background for Anne Evans' Involvement in Theosophy

Some experiences mentioned previously in this text help to explain Anne Evans' openness to more spiritual paths than the Methodism that her mother and father found so compelling. One was the spiritual journey of Cousin Nina, with whom Anne spent a crucial, formative year in her teens. In her memoirs, Nina described one of her mentors as a "revered Guide, Philosopher and Friend!" He introduced her to what he said was the source of all religions, and taught her "something worth while about the Saints and Sages of the Far East." For a while she was enchanted with the

> splendid philosophy that the real man was not the visible body; that it was only a suit of clothes that the spirit had put on, and could take off from time to time; that as instruments we must be finely tuned so as to respond as they put it, to the touch of the hand of the Master.[7]

Nina marveled later that, "I ever came safely through a maze of doubt, mystery, and peril"[8] and attributed her spiritual survival to the fact that she was not free to immerse herself indefinitely in visionary ideas and spiritual practice: the little events of each day, and frequent travel, served to break up such large enterprises and scattered them into a kaleidoscope of small fragments. Perhaps Anne gained from Cousin Nina an ability to stay grounded, and to carry on effectively with her many involvements, while also exploring the spiritual paths taken by different human cultures over the centuries.

Another potentially liberating influence was Anne's exposure to the exhilarating atmosphere of student life in Paris, Berlin and New York in the last decade of the nineteenth century.

While Anne's mother, Margaret, seems to have been satisfied to be contained within the Methodist faith, there are indications that her father was more open to the value of other religious paths.

As mentioned in Chapter two, Knittel characterized John Evans' religious outlook in the following terms:

> His enthusiasm was tempered by a broad tolerance and a kindly regard for all religious expression, which brought him much respect and personal admiration.[9]

We noted earlier that John Evans became disenchanted with the Quaker sect in which he had been raised, reacting particularly against such narrow-minded tenets as condemning marriage outside the Hicksite community.

Anne's older brother, William, demonstrated a similar openness, at least to alternate Christian doctrines, in a newspaper article he wrote during an early "evolution vs. Scripture" controversy. Defending the faculties of the Iliff School of Theology and the Denver University Department of Religion and Philosophy against criticism from the Presbyterian Church hierarchy, he concluded, "I have no doubt, myself, the Presbyterian route leads straight to heaven. Restrictions on travel that way make more roads necessary for the multitude."[10]

Significant also was Anne Evans' ability to appreciate the spiritual beliefs of the Pueblo communities she came to know in New Mexico. She admired the integration of these beliefs into every aspect of their lives—their art, ceremonies, agriculture, child raising—seeing a great contrast between this and the typical, rather perfunctory, religious experience of most Americans.[11]

Finally, there is the frequently quoted ambition of Anne Evans: "*All* the world's religions, I want to know about *all* of them."[12]

Documenting Anne Evans' Theosophical Activities

The materials on which to draw for a discussion of Anne Evans' particular interests, within the wide range of theosophical concerns, are some reports of the Denver branch's activities, written by her for the annual conventions of the Theosophical Society, and her five articles: "Norse Mythology" (1913–14); "The Eastern Church" (three-part article in the 1913–14 volume); "The Renaissance," (p. 45–52, July 1915); "The Foundations of the Moravian Church,"

1917–18; and "The Bhagavad-Gita," 1923–24; (Vol. XXI, No. 4, April, 1924).

The Virya Branch Meetings in Denver

The Denver branch was named Virya, which is a Sanskrit word, etymologically connected to virility. It signifies fearless, brave activity, which supports people in overcoming the various obstacles that invariably present themselves in life. The Virya branch was founded in 1907. Blavatsky had definite ideas about the duties of a Branch President. Believing that every member of the Theosophical Society should "contribute his part, small though it may be, in mental or other labour for the benefit of all"[13] she ordained that "The duty of Branch ... Presidents will be to see to it that the Theosophical beehive is kept free from those drones which keep merely buzzing."[14] In most of her reports, Anne Evans noted the reading and discussion of the Denver branch was mainly used by members to work out their own decisions about "right conduct" of their individual lives and their contributions to the community.

The first year in which Anne Evans wrote the annual Branch report was 1913, she noted that although the membership was small, meetings had been held every first and third Sunday afternoon since October. "The most valuable feature has been that the work has proved so helpful to the members personally ..."[15]

In 1916, in the middle of World War I, she reported that no matter what subject they had chosen to discuss, the discussion always came back to the war,

> so finally we took war in general as our topic, and tried to see in past wars what the spiritual heritage had been. Sometimes we took a personal hero like Joan of Arc ... we took the Crusades and ... our own Civil War, trying to link them with the present European war. With the aid of the *Gita* and the *Quarterly,* we have been able to bring out some vital and interesting aspects of the situation. Several of our members are working together in the same church, and so have the opportunity to discuss their problems in the light of Theosophy, and to carry the theosophical spirit into their work.[16]

In 1923, Anne Evans signed the annual report as President of the Branch, for the first time, with Mary Kent Wallace as Secretary. Since there were no visitors other than one quite regular in attendance, she reported that all the meetings were conducted as study classes, with members doing a great deal of outside reading. They discussed the doctrines of Karma and the Seven Principles, and the meaning of various theosophical terms. "The greatest amount of our time has been given to the basic principles of action and conduct, the more theoretical subjects having been studied purely with the idea of clarifying and elucidating the problems confronting us all."[17]

Reporting in 1925, Anne Evans noted the branch had met regularly all winter. In addition to studies of materials in the *Quarterly*,

> We have taken up several of the current popular movements, religious, social and charitable, and have analyzed them theosophically, to try to distinguish just where they are working for righteousness, and where they fell short or were harmful. The Youth Movement; the Young Women's and Young Men's Christian Association; and several religious sects have been so considered. The interest of those present has been steady and vital.[18]

In the 1929-30 *Quarterly*, Anne Evans reported, "We have studied continually *The Crest Jewel of Wisdom*, reading a few verses in rotation and analyzing them as fully as possible."[19] These readings were supplemented by "articles from the *Quarterly*, parts of the *Yoga Sutras*, selections from the Bible, and other contributions to the subject."[20]

The author of *The Crest Jewel* is said to have been Sankara (510–478 B.C.) whom Blavatsky described as the greatest of the esoteric masters of India.

> *The Crest Jewel* consists of 580 verses in Sanskrit ... However; it has the dialogue form of the *Gita*—here, between the Master and the disciple ... It is comprehensible in its scope and covers a variety of subjects, *viz*, preparation to fit oneself, learning to discern the real from the false, controlling the personality to liberate oneself, and final union with the One.[21]

It is likely the most appealing aspect of the book for the Virya branch were passages such as, "Sankara says that it is not enough to listen to his words ... Sickness is not cured by saying 'Medicine' but by drinking it ... the Teaching must become part of our life and character if it is to bear fruit; it is futile to contemplate the virtue of freedom in the abstract, without living the higher life."[22] For again in the 1929–30 report Anne Evans wrote, "The discussion has turned largely on practical questions of conduct and right living."[23] In 1935, Mary Kent Wallace, as Branch Secretary, submitted a brief report, noting "This year, the interest has been less intellectual, centering more on conduct."[24]

Norse Mythology

The religion of a people was a "vital factor in any just estimate of a national character and of the part it has played in the world's history,"[25] stated Anne Evans at the beginning of her article on Norse Mythology. For Americans, she wrote, this subject was "a real task of self-study,"[26] either because they had Northern European ancestry, or from "the forced imprint of marauding Vikings and the irresistible hordes of the great Northern Exodus"[27] on Anglo-American culture.

Evans contrasted the methods of introducing Christianity into different parts of Europe. Christian missionaries swept over France and Germany "with so militant an attack that save for obscure traces in folklore and superstition, all literary evidence of the supplanted faith was irrevocably destroyed …"[28] From Anglo-Saxon Britain, there remain the Beowulf epic and the Traveller's Song, fragmentary remnants of a whole body of myth. Iceland, she wrote, was a different story. In "a marked contrast to the usual vandalism of zealous bigotry with which we are only too familiar, the tolerant priests aided and abetted the conservative loyalty of their converts."[29] The nature of the Norse mythical saga—which she described in considerable and poetic detail, from the "period before the veriest beginnings of time"[30]—lent itself to a blending of its gods and heroes into the Christian story.

> … The Valfadir was quietly metamorphosed into the Father Almighty; Odin and his sons merely declared to have rounded their life cycle, and already to have met their defeat in the long prophesied … cataclysm of Ragnarok … The apostles of the new faith had but to declare the Risen Christ and the tidings were acclaimed as the joyous fulfillment of the prediction that Balder the Good, incarnation of light and peace, would in good time return to rule with the Valfadir over a regenerated world.[31]

Describing her efforts to disentangle the "skein of imaginative brooding and concrete folk-lore"[32] by studying the text of the Icelandic "Sagas and the Eddic Lays,"[33] and then canvassing the work of the many commentators on, and interpreters of, these sagas, Evans revealed a real depth of research, and a genuine quest for understanding of the "primitive concepts of a race's childhood."[34]

The Eastern Church

In this ambitious treatise, divided into three articles and covering twenty-five pages, Anne Evans recognized that she was tackling a huge segment of the development of Christianity. She acknowledged that she was "appalled by the vastness of the panorama. The field is so wide, both geographically and chronologically ..."[35] She chose to deal in the first part with a lively description of the Council of Nicaea, which she described as "the culminating event of the early church, of the time not only before the West had divided from the East, but even before the so-called national churches of the East had adopted distinctive color and form."[36]

Before the Nicene Council was convened by Emperor Constantine, she noted, the Church did not exist. There were scattered churches and small groups of Christian believers in both the East and the West, but no common acknowledged authority, no recognized body of doctrine. Evans described the makeup of the assembly, from the "motley rank and file"[37] to the "polished logicians"[38] who held the floor in lengthy debates about such abstruse but intensely partisan subjects as the Arian controversy. She expressed admiration for "the breadth and genial temper of the Emperor" in contrast to the severity of intolerance displayed by later councils, and quoted from an account of his farewell speech:

> Let them avoid their party strifes; let them envy no one distinguished for wisdom, but regard the merit of every single individual as common property. God only could judge who were superior. Perfection was rare, so allowance must be made for the weaker brethren, slight matters forgiven, human infirmities allowed for, concord prized above all else ... in all ways, unbelievers must be saved; let them be like physicians, and accommodate the medicine to the disease, the teaching to the different minds of all.[39]

Anne Evans wondered, "if in all the intervening centuries we have progressed far beyond the gentle commonsense of these admonitions."[40]

In the second article, she dealt with the long and tortuous history that led to the eventual separation of the Eastern and Western branches of the Christian Church in 1054.

The third and last segment of her study she devoted to the development of the Russian Church from the time of the earliest missionaries. She described the process by which Prince Vladimir, beset by delegations from Rome, from the Mussulmans, and from Constantinople, and also listening to the reports of emissaries he sent to bring back information about the different faiths, finally made up his mind. The Mussulmans, who gave him a "long dissertation on God and the Prophet,"[41] also told him that taking on their religion would require that he give up vodka. He sent them away, exclaiming, "Drinking is our great delight, we cannot live without it!"[42] Likewise, he sent the Roman Catholic representatives home. His emissaries had returned from Constantinople, singing the praises of the splendor of the service and the unrivalled richness of the Cathedral of St. Sophia.

Vladimir was finally persuaded by "a philosopher from Constantinople"[43] who crowned his presentation with an actual picture of the Last Judgment. This showed the saints on the right hand ascending into a heaven of golden glory, while the sinners on the left descended into a painful flaming hell. Anne Evans believed that this story was a "foreword of the vast influence sacred pictures were to play in the religious and national life of Russia … a passion, not for works of art as such but for pictorial emblems and visual instructions" which "became the consecrating element."[44]

In the rest of the article, Anne Evans chronicled the history of the Russian Church through the ordeals of the Tartar dominion and the Polish invasion, in which she described the Church as emerging "as the impregnable fortress, a living centre of courageous inspiration."[45] After a period of moral decline, the ecclesiastical reforms of the Patriarch Nikon ushered in what she described as "the Russian Reformation,"[46] culminating in the pro-western programs of Peter the Great. She noted approvingly the new provisions that were introduced into the ceremonial oath taken by bishops at their consecration:

> I will not, for the sake of gain, suffer to be built superfluous churches, or ordain superfluous clergy. I promise that there be erected no tombs of spurious saints. I will diligently search out and put down all impostures practiced under the show of devotion,

and will provide that honor be paid to God only, not to the holy pictures, and that no false miracles be ascribed to them.[47]

Evans ended her article with a plea for tolerance from Western Protestants in evaluating the contributions of the Russian Church. We find it hard, she said, "to brook conservatism or the abrogation of the liberty of private judgment."[48] With tolerance, we "can grant (the Russian Church's) uninterrupted succession back to Apostolic time; and can honor an unsullied body of Christianity in its primordial completeness ..."[49] Obviously, the fact that in a very few years this Church would be shaken to its very roots by the Russian Revolution was totally unforeseen by Anne Evans when she wrote this article.

The Renaissance

In this article Anne Evans writes about the exuberant flowering of human creativity in the Italian Renaissance, for which she expressed the passionate appreciation of a woman who had been deeply involved with art all her adult life. Opening with the rather enigmatic statement that,

> Any and all human achievement may be considered as theosophic documents, and thus a period of consummate achievement, such as the Italian renaissance, holds for us a very special significance.[50]

She went on to say,

> Here a great spiritual force seems at work so near the surface that one can fairly see its tumultuous surge-seeking outlet through every possible channel. The whole of Italy seethed with an over-endowment of energy, of passionate hearts and eager intellects and lofty souls, all contributing their quota toward a unified movement; princes were super-princes in brilliance and magnificence, poets burned with the divine afflatus, saints were carried to heights of ineffable ecstasy, and artists were the recipients of an unexampled tide of inspiration.[51]

She expressed the belief that poets, painters and musicians have done as much as saints and ethical leaders towards "the awakening of the world, the deepening of consciousness and the heightening of aspiration."[52] When we hear the words of great teachers like

Savanarola or St. Francis, she wrote, "our argumentative mind meets it on a common ground, accepting or confuting it point by point."[53] But in the presence of great art, we become receptive to the "direct inrush of life itself ... there is an immediate sympathetic enkindling of our higher powers, those above the reasoning intelligence."[54]

The experience of listening to great music, or studying some masterpiece of painting or sculpture or architecture, directly influences our ability to "go forth to meet our daily tasks with renewed sense of high courage, of other-worldliness, of essential unity ..."[55]

The main body of the article is devoted to observations about the life and work of the greatest artists of the Renaissance—Giotto, Botticelli, Leonardo da Vinci, Michaelangelo. She contrasted the impact of their "power of vision"[56] with the barren products of "the lesser man, the merely talented, who observes, combines and invents."[57]

Evans ended her meditation on the Renaissance with a questioning about the possible universal laws that may underlie these products of artistic genius. She concluded,

> ... the pictures of genius, those having truly the life-enhancing power, are not only representations of objects or scenes or events, though this is a prime function and of value in that it bestirs memory and thought; they are more even than the penetrating interpretations of character and emotion and event, though it is their high privilege to so widen our sympathies and enlarge our horizon; these powers they do indeed possess to our exceeding great joy; but moreover and above this, they hold a direct appeal through the creative use of color and form, to our love of high truth, and of the laws, not man-made and partial, but divine and universal, another manifestation of the same law of magnetic energy which holds the stars to their courses and draws after it the tides of the sea.[58]

The Foundations of the Moravian Church

Anne Evans wrote in the opening of her article on the history of the Moravian Church, "The story of the United Brethren is one of the most essentially romantic volumes in the whole library of religious movements ..."[59] She went on to note, "... the succession of heroes and martyrs, resolutely defending their faith against armed force or subtle craft is almost unbroken. It is so monotonously rich in tragic events that one can scarcely grasp the consecutive story as a whole."[60] She told this story in something of a snapshot form, starting with the year 1457, when a small group under the leadership of one Gregory the Patriarch "shook the dust of wicked, gay old Prague from its feet and fared forth to lay the foundations of the new faith." They established a peaceful little community of simple worshippers in the obscure hamlet of Kunwald.

Then Anne Evans went back to the middle of the ninth century when "the reigning duke had thrown off the Frankish yoke."[61] He decided to reject the Roman Catholicism of the former conqueror, and "import his Christianity from the East."[62] Constantinople sent two beloved missionaries.

Forward next to the early 15th century, when the primacy of the Roman Church had been reasserted, to tell the story of the life, teachings, and death at the stake, of Wycliffe follower, Jan Huss.

Anne Evans returned then to where she started, in 1457, to recount the subsequent torture of Hussite Patriarch Gregory, and the persecution and scattering of members of the peaceful little religious community which had so rejoiced in their "liberty to read their Bible in their mother tongue."[63]

> For the ordering of their communal life, they depended on the explicit letter of the gospel. They would take no oath; they would not go to law; they would offer no resistance to evil; and they would live to the best of their ability honest, industrious and God-fearing lives.[64]

The scattering of the Brethren proved fruitless. It meant "more and more people were witness of their simple goodness and piety. The little band shone as the clear light in the darkness of the land."[65] They won more and more recruits, and finally "from very shame, King George called off his soldiers."[66] Evans' account of the early history of this remarkable little band ended with the official establishment of the new Church of the Brethren.

The Bhagavad-Gita

The first part of this essay is a testimony to Anne Evans' desire to transmit an understanding of the most fundamental concepts of Eastern philosophy and religion: Karma, re-incarnation, and Nirvana.

The paper was originally written for the Fortnightly Club. Its members would not have been as knowledgeable about these ideas, nor as necessarily sympathetic to them, as would readers of the *Theosophical Quarterly*. To begin with, she assured her readers that

> there is one thing which Nirvana is *not*, and that is annihilation … Nirvana is on the contrary the very fullness of life, purified and spiritualized and raised to the highest power of consciousness. It is the ultimate goal of an evolution which, starting in the lowest mineral kingdom, gradually ascends through the vegetable, animal human and divine planes to the height of supreme consciousness."[67]

When the human level is attained, a special endowment comes into play—that of self-consciousness—which is the beginning of personal immortality. In life as conscious choices are constantly made "between good and evil, between better and best, between calls of conscience and selfish desire, this self-consciousness is increased and enriched and solidified."[68] At death, the more or less developed self-conscious soul passes for a sojourn into a realm the Indians call Devachan. However, most people are very rudimentary souls. She noted that the *Gita* and the older *Upanishads* teach that even many long lifetimes are too short a time to master the lessons of earthly life—and that the law of evolution *"demands* a complete mastery."[69] So we are drawn, according to an immutable law, into re-birth—by "the calls of unsatisfied desires, of unexpiated wrongs, of neglected opportunities."[70]

> Now again he lives his life for better or worse, and at its end he will be wiser and stronger by a tiny degree … will be happy in the realm of the spirit for a longer time, but not for ever … there comes again the inevitable moment when the desire for separate earthly life grows too strong to resist, and once more he is attracted to a material body. This briefly stated is the theory of Re-incarnation.[71]

The law of Karma, the next concept which Anne Evans tackled, "is intrinsically a part of the law of Re-incarnation; it is often defined as the law of cause and effect."[72] When an ego reincarnates, it is "not a free and untrammeled being, gathered from nothing out of nowhere; but a very real person who has earned by hard effort every advantage of brain and character and physique to which he is heir, and who has many sins and omissions to atone for."[73] The sum of these advantages, virtues and sins constitute a person's Karma. To explain the concept further, she used her favorite quotation on the subject from a source she named as *The Book of Golden Precepts*.

> Learn that no efforts, not the smallest, whether in right or wrong direction, can vanish from the world of causes. A harsh word uttered in past lives is not destroyed but ever comes again. The pepper plant will not give birth to roses, nor the sweet jessamine's silver star to thorn or thistle turn. *Thou canst create* this day thy chances for thy morrow.[74]

With the doctrine of Karma, wrote Anne Evans, the "old philosophy"[75] explained inequalities of birth while believing that, "equally for all, there stretches upward the gradual ascent through hierarchies of heroes and saints, to the perfect peace which is Nirvana, where all life is essentially one, inevitably shared."[76]

These basic doctrines, said Evans, the *Bhagavad Gita* holds in common with the other great scriptures of the East. One of its special aims was to reconcile the philosophic teachings of many different groups, demonstrating how all were just different paths to the same destination. "Above this, the *Gita* may be especially designated as the great exhortation on unselfishness, a clarion call to disinterested work."[77] She introduced the *Bhagavad Gita* as a text that has stood as one of the great scriptures of the East for more than twenty-seven centuries.

> It is a very little volume, but if one wishes to get the flavour of its quality and the true essence of its meaning, it has to be read slowly, little by little, to be absorbed by unhurried thought, its lessons tested by application to practical situations and problems.[78]

The *Gita* is in the form of a dialogue between Arjuna, a young army commander doubting the righteousness of undertaking "the stern duty of a fratricidal war,"[79] and Krishna, speaking as an "avatar or Master"[80] to a beloved disciple. Anne Evans wrote that the method used in the book is to illustrate great ethical precepts through Krishna's answers to Arjuna's doubts and questions. Arjuna's struggle ..."

comes very soon to symbolize the eternal warfare between the forces of righteousness and the forces of evil, and every direction can and should be read in this light."[81]

Evans proceeded to summarize the major wisdom principles brought out in the book, including the destructive role of Desire and the necessity to overcome a "wavering mind"[82] through "assiduous practice and detachment."[83] She found especially appealing Krishna's emphasis on doing good works without attachment to the reward of the work.

> This is a very satisfactory verse to ponder over—it takes in so many of the finest people we know—self-sacrificing doctors, and artists who refuse to paint pot-boilers, and all sorts of men who care more for what they are trying to do than for the personal reward.[84]

After apologizing for stopping short of "a complete and exhaustive study of the *Bhagavad Gita*,"[85] Anne Evans reiterated its enduring value. "It stands as one of the imperishable counsels of perfection, so based upon the eternal verities that the mind cannot outgrow it nor new discoveries undermine its truth."[86]

Theosophy and Anne Evans' Values

What emerges from this review of Anne Evans' reports of her experience of Theosophical meetings, and her articles written for the *Theosophical Quarterly*, that throws light on her own beliefs and values?

It is not possible to know, from the written record, how much of Eastern spiritual beliefs Anne Evans adopted as her own. For example, in her article on *The Bhagavad Gita* she gives a knowledgeable and sympathetic account of the concepts of a soul's progress through many reincarnations, of the law of Karma, of the eventual attainment of Nirvana. But she does not directly express her personal beliefs in this area.

Anne Evans does not seem to have had the slightest interest in spiritualism, a prominent and controversial aspect of theosophy in her time. There is not a single mention of the subject in any of her writings.

The focus of the Virya Branch meetings was the study of a wide range of spiritual traditions, in accordance with Blavatsky's second object of the Theosophical Society, expressed in her book, *The Key to*

Theosophy, "To promote the study of Aryan and other scriptures, of the World's religion and sciences, and to vindicate the importance of old Asiatic literature, namely, of the Brahamanic, Buddhist, and Zoroastrian philosophies."[87] This study certainly fulfills Anne's expressed wish, "*All* the world's religions, I want to know about *all* of them!"[88] What stands out clearly, from the branch reports, is that the primary purpose of studying and discussing this literature, in the Denver branch, was to use its wisdom as guidance for members' conduct of their own lives.

It seems clear from Anne Evans' articles and other writings that her embrace of Theosophy did not entail a rejection or belittling of her parent's Methodist beliefs. Her approach to the myriad varieties of religious experience was to honor each one in its setting and to learn as much as she could about as many as she could. Judgment came into the picture only where members of one faith sought to impose it on others by persecution and torture. In Anne Evans' five articles there were many different prescriptions for living a worthwhile life. Of these, three seemed particularly important to her.

First was the conviction that whatever good one seeks to do in life must be done for its own sake, and not for money or honors or rewards of any kind. The precept Anne Evans certainly carried out in her own life and works, as was frequently mentioned in articles about her in her lifetime, and in tributes to her after her death.

The second was that anything which inspired an expansion of human consciousness, whether it was a new level of free thought and free speech introduced by Jan Huss, or spiritual truths revealed in the subtle dialogue between Krishna and Arjuna, or the brilliant explosion of artistic creativity in the Italian Renaissance, was to be celebrated, studied and, where possible, experienced personally. Living out this prescription is perhaps exemplified in the enthusiasm with which Anne Evans approached new travel experiences, in her ability to appreciate the spiritual dimensions of Native American life, her optimistic efforts to expand the scope and offerings of Denver's young cultural institutions, and in her zest in taking on the challenges of a totally new venture like the rescue of the old Opera House in Central City and the founding of a high quality Summer Festival there.

Finally, there was the emphasis on laboring for the benefit of the community, "If one does not work for others one has no right to be called a Theosophist."[89] This maxim could almost sum up the lifework of Anne Evans. In the areas to which she gave her time, energy and resources, her vision was always of something that would benefit others who would be nourished by the cultural enrichment of her beloved Denver and Colorado.

In her theosophical connections, as in most areas of Anne Evans' life, the destruction of all personal materials, after her death, leaves a biographer with unanswered questions. The fact that her reports of Denver meetings were published, as well as her articles, does not support a notion that she made any great effort to keep her Theosophical Society affiliation a secret. Yet it does not seem to have been widely known within the family. It is not mentioned in any publicity about her, nor in any of the surviving obituaries. We learn from the 1916 report to the Annual Convention of the Theosophical Society only that the Denver Virya Branch was meeting on the first and third Sundays at four in the afternoon at 1045 Clayton Street. Aside from her lifelong friend, Mary Kent Wallace, no information has surfaced to date about who, in Denver, were Anne's companions in the Virya Branch's quiet search for wisdom through Theosophical studies.

18

Anne Evans, Mary Kent Wallace and the Kent School

A best friend is a sister destiny forgot to give you.
—Unknown

Friendship is a strong and habitual inclination in two persons to promote the good and happiness of one another.
—Eustace Budgell (1711)

Anne Evans and Mary Kent Wallace— A Close, Lifelong Friendship

Anne Evans and Mary Kent Wallace were virtually the same age. Just where and when they met is not known. Possibly, it was as early as student days at Wolfe Hall. The close friendship between them was apparent in the active interest each took in the other's activities. They were both active members of the Denver branch of the Theosophical Society. Mary Kent Wallace accompanied Anne Evans on many of her trips to New Mexico when she was working for the restoration of Mission Churches. When Anne became absorbed in preserving the Central City opera House and creating a summer festival in the city, Mary Kent Wallace became a participant in that work also. She spent part of many summers with Anne at the Evans Ranch. Similarly, when Mary and her closest associates became disenchanted with the operation of the school where they were teaching, Anne Evans was totally available to help in any way she could.

MARY KENT WALLACE

Mary Kent Wallace, The Kent School Archives

Perhaps the most productive of all gatherings at Anne Evans' summer home was one that took place in the spring vacation of 1922, when Mary Kent Wallace, Mary Bogue and Mary Louise Rathvon—who became known as the Three Marys—"retired for a time to the Evans Ranch, where Miss Anne Evans, a friend of Miss Wallace, gave them shelter."[1] There they laid plans to open their own school in Denver in the fall.

The Last Years of Wolfe Hall

To understand just why Kent School came into existence, it is necessary to take up again the development of Wolfe Hall. As was noted earlier,[2] construction of a large and costly new building for that Episcopalian school, a pioneer in the education of young ladies in Denver, was completed in 1889. Wolfe Hall soon ran into severe problems, both financial—because of the expense of the building in difficult economic times—and educational due to an antiquated and over-ambitious curriculum. A new Head Mistress arrived from Boston, who "brought to the whole school vigorous administration and modern methods and curricula."[3] This was Anna L. Wolcott, an 1878 graduate of Wellesley College. In spite of her successes, Wolfe Hall's future was sabotaged by poor financial management and "exacerbated by a long-smoldering quarrel between Bishop Spalding and that magnetic British personality, the Very Reverend H. Martyn Hart, Dean of St. John's Cathedral."[4]

Miss Wolcott's School

Miss Wolcott resigned in the spring of 1898, and immediately proceeded to establish her own school in attractive though still unfinished premises in September of the same year. In this, she had the support not only of Dean Hart but also of her two brothers in Denver, both of them successful businessmen and powerful figures in the Republican Party. The Wolcott School occupied land on both sides of Marion Street at 14th Avenue, where Miss Wolcott "erected in stages the congeries of buildings, gardens, and playing fields which grew into an unusually attractive campus." The school had a rich and varied curriculum, expected high academic performance from the students, and also placed great emphasis on physical education and creative activity. Music was so important that in time a separate Wolcott School of Music came into being. Students of the school were frankly drawn from the upper levels of Denver society, and Anna Wolcott expected her school to prepare them to assume social obligations and civic responsibilities. She herself actively participated in the social and artistic life of the Denver community and became the first woman regent of Colorado University, serving from 1910 to 1916.

The Wolcott School at 14th and Marion Streets in the Cheesman Park neighborhood (c. 1900–1920), Denver Public Library Western History Collection

Then, in 1913, as she reached age fifty-five, Miss Wolcott shocked the parents and students of her school by getting married—to J. F. Vaile, a 65-year-old widower with grown children. Leasing out her school, she moved to Hawaii with her husband. Soon dissatisfaction arose on two fronts: on the part of parents, because of a decline in academic standards, and on the part of faculty, because of low salaries. The situation reached a crisis in 1920. Mrs. Vaile returned to Denver, her husband having died in 1916, and took back the school. She appointed as Head Mistress a faculty member who had joined her years before in the move from Wolfe Hall.

Mary Kent Wallace Becomes Head Mistress of Wolcott School

Mary Kent Wallace graduated from Wolfe Hall and returned there to teach Greek, Latin and English Literature, after obtaining her degree from Colorado College. She continued to teach these subjects at the Wolcott School.

> ... when college entrance requirements no longer included Greek, she initiated a course in the History of Art, and about this time made her first trip to Italy and Greece. She had always been interested in Greek and Roman art; a second trip to the Eastern Mediterranean made it possible for her to acquire a fine collection of prints of classical sculpture and architecture ... to enrich a course highly popular with students.[5]

Wallace was fifty-one years old when she took up her duties as Head Mistress of the Wolcott School in 1920. She had the support of the existing faculty, especially of Mary Bogue, who had taught French at the school since 1917 and who was named Assistant Head Mistress in 1921, and Mary Louise Rathvon, who had taught at the school before the war, served in the Red Cross in France, and returned in 1919 to teach mathematics. Unfortunately, Mrs. (Wolcott) Vaile proved incapable of giving Wallace the authority she needed to do her job well. Serious problems arose in the spring of 1922, when Vaile threatened to dismiss the dean of residence, whom Rathvon had persuaded to leave her position at another school to join the Wolcott staff. The Three Marys—Wallace, Bogue and Rathvon—protested Vaile's actions and resigned.

Off to the Evans Ranch

It was at this point that the women accepted Anne Evans' offer of a retreat in the mountains. Amid the serious discussions about establishing a school of their own, the Marys acquired nicknames for each other: Wallace became Kentia, a name which Anne Evans called her thereafter. (For example, in a letter in 1937 to her young protégée, Ann Matlack, Evans wrote, "Kentia's affairs are still unsatisfactory but I am trying to bring about a solution."[6]) Because she had exploded in anger in an interview with Anna Vaile, Rathvon was dubbed T.N.T.; Bogue became known as Kingpin.

Birth of the Kent School

From the spring vacation until June, in Rathvon's living room the three teachers taught three students who had also withdrawn from the Wolcott School. Meantime, they made plans for their new school and chose a name. It was a spur of the moment thing, happening as they were getting incorporated. Their interim name of "The Three Marys School" did not seem appropriate and nothing else in any of their names sounded as good as Mary Kent Wallace's middle name. They incorporated the Kent School Association with themselves as trustees and a strong advisory committee of prominent business-men. Money to buy the former Berger mansion at 933 Sherman Street, to remodel it, add additional space, and buy adjoining lots for athletic fields was raised by an intensive summer fund-raising campaign, spearheaded by Rathvon. Much of the money was raised through the sale of interest-bearing bonds.

The Kent School for Girls at 933 Sherman Street (1940), Denver Public Library Western History Collection

The three founders assembled a "brilliant faculty"[7] and had enrolled eighty-two students by the end of its first year. Mary Kent Wallace served as Head Mistress, while Mary Rathvon and Mary Bogue were Associate Head Mistresses. All three were also teachers. The educational philosophy of the new school was articulated in its first catalogue:

The Kent School is established to further the development of character, which it believes to be the ultimate purpose of a true education. In thus laying stress upon character, the word must be taken in its broadest sense, including the growth of personality in grace and loveliness as well as in poise and strength. School life rightly ordered creates an atmosphere in which these qualities naturally unfold, and becomes thoroughly enjoyable.

Every activity of the School is directed towards this end. Truthfulness, simplicity, unselfishness, fidelity, perseverance, respect for elders, and the recognition of duty as the supreme obligations are made the foundation of all other instruction.

In a 1972 history of Kent School, Headmaster Michael Churchman commented that, while the catalogue expressed the beliefs of all three founders, "certain paragraphs stand out as the work of Miss Wallace."[8] Among these, he cited,

Courses are arranged to embrace the training of every faculty of the child's nature, the imagination, the reason, the will, and not merely the memory. The habit of accurate and sincere work is the definite goal of every exercise. Nothing is acceptable which is not a serious effort and the best the student can offer. The subjects taught are both fundamental and cultural … Five years are recommended for college preparation … giving opportunity to include those subjects which … awaken an interest and a 'kinship with what is great and permanent and beautiful.' … Such an attitude should be understood as the opposite of an aristocracy of materialism with its narrow and selfish pleasure in privilege and personal possessions. Rather it will stamp those who come under its influence with the generous qualities which admit them to a community with all who seek true cultivation and the fellowship of gentle service.

The Wolcott School continued until June, 1924, when Vaile abruptly closed its doors and sold the buildings. The separate Wolcott School of Music continued for a while and then metamorphosed into the Lamont School. This eventually became part of the University of Denver. Many, perhaps most, of the Wolcott School's remaining students transferred to the Kent School, which added a large north wing designed by architect William Fisher to accommodate them. The beauty of the old mansion was complimented by a walled garden, with lawn and flowerbeds shaded by large maples and apple trees.

Art, Music, and Sports
in a Pleasant Capitol Hill Environment

"The building was filled with art and the first two yearbooks record many gifts of works of art, which the presence of Miss Wallace attracted to the school."[9] These included paintings donated by Elizabeth Spalding, Italian prints given by Anne Evans, and gifts of Pueblo Indian pottery from Evans and others.

A former student, who attended Kent while Wallace was the Principal, remembered another aspect of Anne Evans' involvement with the school. In an interview, Prue Grant was asked,

> Did you know Anne Evans? 'Of course, she had blue eyes and tremendous enthusiasm for anything she was interested in ... She was the best friend of Mary Wallace who started Kent. [As a reward for some school achievement at Kent] I was allowed to spend the night up at the Evans Ranch with Anne Evans ... She was charming. If she wanted you to like her you couldn't help it.'[10]

The school flourished in its attractive Capitol Hill environment. An active sports program was enhanced by the acquisition of additional land for a tennis court, playground and hockey field. Musical recitals, in which Margaret Evans (Mrs. Roblin) Davis, Anne Evans' niece, figured prominently. She enlivened the life of the school, as she did dramatic productions; many were directed by Anne Evans' young protégé and friend, Ann Matlack who taught in the upper school. Artist Josephine Hurlburt, who carved the unique gable wood sculptures on Anne Evans mountain home, joined the faculty in 1923 as an art teacher and taught for 25 years until her retirement.

1929 Depression brings Hard Times to Kent

The Depression of 1929 affected Kent School as it did almost every aspect of American life. Enrollment was stagnant. Rathvon, who handled the financial side of the school's operation, was proud of a decision the school principals made. "We let people stay whether they paid or not so we'd have a school. If you let everyone go who couldn't pay the tuition, you'd have no school. I think that's how we survived."[11] Faculty salaries were reduced. The three principals took a 25 percent pay cut.

Unwilling Retirement for Miss Wallace

In the midst of all this turmoil, the advisory board insisted that an issue relating to the performance of Wallace as Head Mistress—namely, her increasing deafness—be confronted openly. Just how great a problem this had become is clear from memoirs left by Bogue and Rathvon.

> Mary Kent Wallace had one great misfortune. She was deaf and had to wear a hearing aid. While that didn't matter in the teaching, when she had to deal with the public it was a tremendous handicap. The difficulty was that when people came they wanted to talk ... but if you're deaf you can't let them talk—you must control the conversation. So they always went away disgruntled.[12]
>
> Unfortunately, Miss Wallace was very deaf even during her last years at The Wolcott School. She was very sensitive about the limitation this imposed. Misunderstandings would arise and leave the impression that she was unduly stern. However, in easy situations her pupils, faculty and friends were well aware of her fairness, her friendliness and her sense of humor.[13]

The advisory board wanted Miss Wallace to stay on at the school as a "sort of principal emeritus" but have the day-to-day administration, and especially the contact with parents and the public, turned over to Rathvon and Bogue. The new allocation of duties was not satisfactory from Wallace's point of view, and she resigned in the spring of 1936. Bogue and Rathvon took over as co-principals. Unfortunately, the finances of the school were going from bad to worse at this point, the three principals' salaries had taken a further cut, and the school could not offer Wallace a pension.

By 1940, the Kent School's financial situation was so dire that its closing was seriously considered. Instead, it was totally restructured into a non-profit corporation. Rathvon and Bogue agreed to cancel notes against the School for back salaries. "After a very delicate and pressing negotiation with Miss Wallace"[14] she accepted a settlement of $3,500 for her notes and was granted a pension of $100 a month "subject to the provision that the school make a profit."

This settlement, however, came after Anne Evans' death. Anne was deeply concerned about her friend's financial well-being (as is indicated by the letter to Matlack quoted above) and did her best to assure it, within her limited means, by leaving a lifetime monthly stipend to Wallace in her will.

The Late Years of Mary Kent Wallace

Mary Kent Wallace continued her civic and cultural activities in Denver after her 1936 retirement until her death in the spring of 1948. In his fifty-year history of Kent School, Churchman wrote, "Miss Wallace gave The Kent School her own high standards of scholarship, her love of art, music, and poetry, and the teaching and administrative experience which had launched the School."[15]

19

New Mexico: Advocate for the Art of Native Americans and the Preservation of Mission Churches

Surely if the Art teachers of the country, USA, especially of the West, could only fix it firmly in their minds and hearts that here is Art, a true and beautiful expression of a people's ideals, they might do something to help preserve it. By understanding it they could teach others to choose the good rather than the tawdry—the bit of sincere workmanship from among the potboilers, so to speak, and they might bring some influence to bear in Washington so that the Government teachers should be required to learn something of reverence for the achievements of these people which they are so zealously striving to replace with those of a nation which we may frankly concede is as little sensitive to beauty as any in the world.[1]

—Anne Evans

Almost by accident, the role of Anne Evans as an advocate for the Indian art of the southwest area is more richly documented than any of her other contributions.

For a sense of the quality and depth of her understanding of pueblo art and culture, thanks are largely due to the Denver Fortnightly Club, of which Anne Evans became a member in 1919. Each member was required, from time to time and in her turn, to prepare an original paper. Evans wrote four papers on different aspects of her experiences visiting the pueblo communities of New Mexico.[2] Only two of these are preserved in the Fortnightly files in their entirety, while some hand-written notes and descriptions in the minutes give an idea of the contents of the other two.[3]

Information about Anne Evans' role in the movement to restore and preserve the Mission churches of New Mexico is included in two biographies of the Santa Fe architect John Gaw Meem.[4] In these, we also gain some insight into exactly how Anne Evans went about helping talented young artists to develop their potential and advance their careers.

The significance of Anne Evans' role as a collector of both Pueblo Indian art and of New Mexican Santos is later described as part of the unique history of the Denver Art Museum's Native Arts Department.

Hopi Land

> I understand that many good Americans, when they die, are going to Paris—I'm secretly hoping that when one American dies she may alternate Paris with Hopi land—about half and half, with a slight preponderance in favor of the latter ...

So Anne Evans expressed her delight in being a visitor in the land of the Hopis. She was writing about "The Art Impulse of the Hopi Indians" in 1920 and made it clear from the beginning that in this paper she was not going to deal with their actual artifacts, but with "the art impulse and the conditions which produce it."

In her paper, Evans contrasted the reception that she and her party found among the Hopis with what they experienced from the Navajos. The party had driven across the Navajo reservation to reach their destination.

> The ride had been wonderfully beautiful, with the wide stretches of desert grass, the long curves of the prairie, the abrupt buttes. We met with no whites at all, but occasionally there had been a solitary summer hogan, with the inevitable weaving frame outside, and ever and anon a slim little herder ... zealously guarding his mixed flock of sheep and goats ... In spite of an entire willingness to parley and barter, to joke with and about us and to accept our gifts ad infinitum, we had been aware all the time of an alien and essentially hostile people. But the moment we crossed over into Hopi land, ... there was an absolute change of atmosphere. Smiling babies ran out to greet us, old and young welcomed us with gentle

cordiality. They helped us with campfire and cookery, and with the innocent curiosity of children examined us and our belongings. So inherently courteous were they that we felt no embarrassment, nor resentment, of a minute observation which continued almost without a break ... until our departure.

On this occasion, Anne Evans and the group of people traveling with her were staying in the Hopi village of Walpi. She reminisced about her first visit there,

I wish you might see the village of Walpi as I first did. It was late in the afternoon of a glowing August day and high on the mesa the terraced houses of grey adobe were silhouetted against the sky. The flocks had already been driven home from pasture and were huddled on the ledges of the almost sheer cliff-sides. And spreading about its base, like a garland, were the tiny-tiny little fields of corn, the wee little patches of melons and beans and the wonderful old gnarled trees of the prized peach orchards, the seeds for which were brought in by the Spanish invaders.

The Potter Nampayo

By telling the Fortnightly Club members about the life of the famous Hopi potter Nampayo, Evans tried to express her understanding and admiration for the culture that produced the art works she so appreciated. "She is very old now, with children and grand-children about her, but she is still busily creating lovely pieces of pottery, modeling and firing and painting in unhurried peace." When Nampayo was young, "the potter's art had reached a very low ebb among her people." The clay they were using was brittle, "while the design had fallen into meaningless repetition of the old motives—which I suppose is always the danger when art is bound very closely to tradition and symbol." But the young Nampayo noticed that the shards of ancient pottery, scattered on the sands all around the settlement, were much more beautiful in design and texture. "... she had the brain to consider and compare and determine just wherein the superiority lay—and the will and determination to discover a remedy." She searched a wide area around her village to find better clays, and ground up shards of ancient pottery to analyze their ingredients. She experimented with different ways of firing "till she finally reached a satisfactory result not quite as fine even yet, as the best of the old pieces—but hard and firm and pleasant to the touch, giving forth a fine metallic ring when tapped."

Then the potter turned her energies to design, and with a skillful blending of the traditional symbols:

> ... of bird and beast and Katzina,[5] they were once again freely adapted to shape and purpose and were so distinctly individualized that one can recognize a Nampayo pot as surely as one can recognize a picture by Manet or Corot. It is her own expression of the art of her race.

Perhaps the strongest witness to the "inherent freedom of her spirit," theorizes Evans, was the fact that Nampayo taught the art of pottery to her husband, Lastzu, "for no man may be a potter in that tribe, and to break a convention is an almost inconceivable audacity."

Evans went on to explain all of this lifetime effort on the part of Nampayo:

> ... with no ulterior object in view. It could not possibly profit her aught, in fame or money; it was pure, unadulterated love of beauty and fine workmanship. Her modicum of corn and melons and mutton, her moccasins and ceremonial robes, were the end of her material wants and were insured her in any event, save in time of famine, when no amount of money would be of the slightest avail.

Her house was hers, for in the Hopi social system, Evans wrote that the dwelling places were owned and controlled by the women. Yes, Nampayo had become famous. She had been taken to the 1904 St. Louis Exposition where she was part of the Indian exhibit.

> ... and many efforts have been made to coax her to live at Albuquerque or the Grand Canyon for the luring of tourists—but she smilingly insists on dwelling in the adobe house on the summit of the East Mesa.

This decision was hard on "the dealer, who, though he may purchase her pots for a mere pittance, must transport them by wagon across those many miles of sand and sage brush through alternations of parching drouth and suddenly flooded arroyos ..."

For the "uncommercial traveller" however, Evans reported that Nampayo's choice of dwelling offered much: an insight into a Spartan interior—

> its walls glistening white from the fresh coat of gypsum—for decoration only the Katcina plaque on the wall and one or two water ollas on the wainscot edge—for furnishing only the heap of gay blankets and the baby's cradle swung from the ceiling.

The door was always open, looking out on the adobe oven and

> the broad polished black stone on which is spread and baked the pretty piki bread—gossamer sheets of cornmeal of a texture resembling a wasps nest—and immediately beyond, the cliff drops away six hundred feet to the plain, so that always by raising her eyes from her work she can see the marvelous view across the desert, shimmering with all the iridescent colors of a ring-dove's neck, to the blue Navajo mountain on the far horizon, peopled with all the spirits of the Hopi mythology.

During the visit, Evans reported that they selected a jar of a lovely shape and asked Lastzu

> to paint the decoration. He cheerfully acquiesced and bringing his pots of color, made of ground clay, red, black and white, and his brushes of yucca fibre, arranged them carefully on the floor and then sat down cross-legged with the bowl in his lap. For a full half hour he sat, perfectly motionless, intently regarding its smooth untouched surface, evidently conceiving and mentally picturing the design. Finally, he reached for his brush and steadily, surely, without a pause, an erasure, or mistake of any kind, completed it to the last detail.

The Hopi Art Impulse

This little episode demonstrated, said Evans, what she thought were the mainsprings of the Hopi Art Impulse—Contemplation, Concentration, and Vision. Perhaps, she admitted, this was true of the wellsprings of art in every culture, but it was seen with more clarity in the Hopi:

> Conditions are singularly free from the complications which confuse and confound us when we try to lay bare a central motive force in the modern everyday world. Here is no mesh of mixed native and foreign influences to be disentangled—no quarrel between the proper spheres of painting and literature—no allowances to be made for the technique of differing schools—no need to discount the effect of premature criticism or praise. It is all stripped down to the bare fact that a primitive though far from barbaric people are such beauty lovers that their joy lies in their arts; in the patient production of pottery and textiles and baskets—in the songs which they sing at work and play and ceremonial—and in their dances and dramaturgies—all springing from a spontaneous desire of creation, so universal that no dividing line exists between audience and actor, between artist and creator.

Because the Hopi potter worked wholly within a familiar culture, he "may use his symbols of rain and lightning, or water and earth, his prescribed colors for North, South, East and West, sure of the instant comprehension of every man, woman and child of his world. His problem is so to fit the symbol to the form, either of jar or rhythm that it shall be lovely; that all may find the joy in beholding that he does in production."

Evans went on to speculate about what it was that had raised the art of the Indians of the Southwest "so far beyond that of the Eastern, Southern, and Mountain tribes, where the beauty of the location is so much more obvious, the changes so much more rapid, the colors so much more crude." She believed that it was in part due to "the months and years of almost unbroken contemplation" during their "gentle tasks of flock-tending, of ploughing and planting the precious corn, of grinding the meal on the stone metates." It may have been part, also, to their environment, where

> in the quiet of the days and of the nights, their eyes rest lingeringly on the beauty around them and grow always more sensitive to the subtle suggestions of form and color ... to all the finer gradations of grays and violets, to the appreciation of the noble simplicity of the landscape ...

The contrast could not be due solely to something distinctive about the pueblo peoples, because products of the same high artistic quality were also produced by the nomadic Navajo,

> whose best baskets and blankets—not the ordinary commercial blanket of the curio shop and the bungalow floor, but the old chief and ceremonial blankets—are real works of art showing a fine sense of color, a quite distinguished sense of space division and a sincere execution.

Returning to the distinctive character of the Hopi art impulse, Evans stressed the importance of their "perfect community of interest." Having withdrawn to the top of a mesa so that they might live in peace and "according to the tradition of their name—Hopi, the Good People," they were cut off from the outside world and totally dependent on themselves for all their needs.

> The abundance of the crop in one field means so much assurance against famine for the entire village; the achievement of a master artist is just so much added to the common fund of shared pleasure, the good fortune of one is the good fortune of all ... Hard and fast division between work and play, between use and ornament, between religion and life are unknown, since each component part exists for and because of the others.

To the Hopi, according to Evans, the concept of "art for art's sake" would be incomprehensible. She told a story which beautifully illustrated this. There was a musician who was trying to collect traditional Hopi songs. He asked a woman to sing for him a typical cradlesong, and was "confronted with a perfect stonewall of incomprehension." She told him that her child had grown too old to be sung to sleep by a lullaby; she was totally unable to imagine that a song "could exist except as it was needed." In the same way that the music of the Hopi was integrated into everyday life, Evans explained, so was their religion. Utterly different from our

> usual perfunctory once-a-week-and-well-over concession ... it is bound to every function and daily need; it governs their hours and seasons and lends an otherworldly consciousness to their

commonest acts. In turn, it draws to itself the utmost possible richness
of expression in song and legend and symbol.

Anne Evans became an ardent student of the rituals and ceremonial festivals of the Pueblo Indians, often making travel arrangements to coincide with occasions which were open to visitors, or
to which she had a special invitation. She studied the legends and
symbols embodied in the different ceremonies, diligently read and
analyzed books written about them, and wrote papers on the subject
to read to an appreciative audience at the Fortnightly Club.

Pueblo "Dramaturgies"—The Snake Dance

In the last section of the 1920 paper on the "Hopi Art Impulse," Evans
described the character of their "dramaturgies"—a term she preferred
to dances, because it included the dramatic telling of a story as well
as that of choreographed movement. She focused especially on the
Snake Dance, "which was the objective point of our expedition."
Descriptions of other Pueblo rituals are contained in a hand-written
draft of part of her 1924 account of "The San Francisco Missions of
New Mexico".[6] She opened her most widely read 1927 paper on "A
Christmas Pilgrimage in the Southwest" with a vivid description of
a Christmas Eve ceremonial in the Pueblo of San Felipe, following
the midnight mass. About her 1929 paper, "Social Customs and
Government of the Zuni Indians," we have only some brief minutes.
But together these accounts are enough to illuminate the profound
impact of these unique ceremonials on Anne Evans, familiar as she
was with all the bustle and pageantry and religions of the centers of
western civilization—London, Paris, Berlin and New York—and with
the conflicting crosscurrents of twentieth century culture.

Among the Hopi, Evans noted that there were many ceremonial
dances or dramaturgies "following the round of the years in a steady
succession of special supplications, of which the Snake Dance ... is
the best known." Contrary to the prevalent idea "that it is a wild
and barbaric rite, working itself up to a climax of fanatical fury,"
she described it as "a solemn and sustained effort of prayer and
concentration, extending over nine days of self-denial, fasting and
mystic ceremonial; a prayer for rain that 'our crops may ripen and
our children have to eat, and afterwards we too may have to eat.' "

The Snake Dance is a reenactment of one part of the Hopi
creation myth which Evans described as "a true myth, handed down

orally from generation to generation of a people without written literature." All people originally emerged through an opening to the underworld, a si-na-pu. Morning Dove guided the Hopi clan "to the edge of the Colorado Grande where the clouds were thin, the rain came seldom and the corn was weak." The son of the Chief embarked on a long river journey, carrying prayer sticks given to him by his father. Seeking the knowledge needed by his people to survive and flourish, he visited first the lodge of Spider Woman, the Earth Mother "who spins the fateful thread of life." With her guidance and instruction, he then visited four Kivas or Lodges, in each of which he received further enlightenment.

First, he came to the Snake-Antelope Kiva, whose Chief "causes the rain clouds to come and go, the ripening winds to blow and who directs the coming and going of the mountain animals." Next, he visited the abode of the woman of the Hard Substance, whose sphere is wealth and precious stones. Thirdly, he descended to the lowest underworld where "a host of eager toilers work with anxious haste making the seeds of all vegetation, of all animals and men." Finally he enters the palace of the Sun, "rosy red in color, where he was taught to make the great Sun Pa-ho or prayer stick—by this his eyes were so opened that thence forward he knew all people and by looking into their hearts could comprehend their thoughts."

The Snake Dance dramatized the lessons learned in the Snake-Antelope Kiva. Its purpose was to attract the gods who dwell afar, "that the dry river-beds may be swollen with water and the farmers hear the pattering of rain." The first seven days of the ceremonial were not open to the public, although Evans noted that a good many white men had been initiated over the years into the mysteries of the underground Kiva and had written descriptions of the rites in great detail. For the waiting visitor, there was plenty to do and see "in simply watching the village life; in making friends with the people and playmates of the bare brown babies, in watching the grinding of the meal on the stone metates, or the baking of the piki bread, or the weaving of the firm blue cloth."

On the eight and ninth days, the village and the visitors were awakened before dawn

> by the call of the crier far above in the housetop, announcing the races which would occur at sunrise. We hurried out in time to see the runners slip by in the dusk, silent, intent, and absolutely

oblivious of our presence. The Snake race ... was participated in by about forty youths, who gathered at a point about five miles out on the plain.

The race starter drew the rain-cloud symbol four times across the trail with sacred corn meal and then, exactly at sunrise, the runners were off.

In the splendor of the level morning light, these tense brown bodies straining steadily forward to the base of the cliff and then up, up its sheer sides, was a never-to-be-forgotten sight. It was Greek—it was Homer and the beginning of the world.

In the late afternoon of the two final days came the "spectacular public dances." First, there marched a solemn procession of priests around the court, with the Antelope priests arrayed in costumes and paint of white and blue, and the Snakes "rich in threatening red and black." Then, for more than half an hour, "the contrasting lodges drew up in opposing lines ... engaged in intricate antiphonal songs and dance steps, rhythm and melody suggesting much which words fail to convey." The ceremony on the ninth day culminated with the introduction of the

wild dramatic element of the living serpents. The Snake priests divided into groups of three. In turn, each group approached the *kisi*—a kind of loose basket made of cottonwood branches—where the serpents, the 'Elder Brothers,' were 'confined and concealed.'

One member thrust in his hand, seized a snake, placing it between his teeth "stoically disregardful of its writhing protest, marched once about the court, when a second was seized and, replacing the first, was treated in a like manner." The second member of the priestly trio put his hand around the shoulders of the first, and tried to calm the snake by stroking it with an eagle feather. The third gathered up the serpents as they either wriggled free or were dropped at the end of each circuit.

When this part of the ritual was completed, a group of ceremonially dressed *Manas*—"charmingly picturesque maidens," with long black hair wound high on their heads and decorated with squash blossoms—sprinkled the snakes with sacred meal. Then a circle of meal was laid down, and all the snakes poured into it, whereupon the priests seized them in "double handfuls," hurried down the rock trail and set them free on the plains.

Describing the reaction of herself and the rest of the visiting party to this "unbelievable sight," Evans said, "We accepted it with a strange lack of concern. The spirit of the place—remote, unworldly, primal, had gripped us too forcibly to permit the domination of twentieth century standards." In common with the Hopi, their "real excitement came with a glow of conscious gratitude at the sudden crash of thunder, flash of lightning and drenching torrent which fairly flooded the court. The gods had given quick proof that the sacrifice had been accepted, that they had found 'no hearts to be bad nor thoughts to have left the straight path.'"

> General rejoicing and merry making followed. The long fast was broken by a Homeric feast and from every side came the laughing *Manas*, bearing great wicker trays piled high with melons and corn, with roasted kid, with piki and tortillas.

Zuni Culture

"Miss Anne Evans gave us a delightful talk on the cosmogony and creation myths of the Zuni Indians, dwelling particularly on the story of the birth of the corn," wrote Carla Denison Swan, recording the minutes of the Fortnightly Club meeting of March 19, 1929, at which Anne Evans read her paper on "Social Customs and Government of the Zuni Indians."

> First she described the Indian's inherited and innate feelings about his environment—a feeling that he was the 'here,' the center of an egg-shaped universe in which the other 6 directions (north, south, east, west, up and down) were all intrinsically associated with very definite and separate concepts—of pure color: of warmth and seasons: of animal and vegetable totems: of precedence in time and rank: of varying religious mysteries—so associated that his whole life, especially his art and his many festivals and dances, was saturated with the symbolism he evoked from such congenital beliefs.

Next, Evans read what Swan described as

> 'a beautiful word picture, full of poetry and imagery,' a translation
> of parts of the Zuni creation story. This contained 'surprising bits
> of inexplicable knowledge about evolution and world history,' and
> many interesting correlations with the creation myths of other lands
> and times.

The paper ended with a telling of

> the exquisite story of the creation of corn, which came about
> through the unified and combined magic and 'potencies' of the
> Brothers of the Dawn and (the Brothers of) the Dew, two mythical
> tribes who, in search for the perfect center of the Universe, met in
> the Arizona desert, and amalgamated into the Zuni people.

Evans brought with her some "intriguing Indian paintings" and,
before the meeting adjourned for tea, she talked briefly about their
meaning. The group, Swan wrote, was "reluctant to leave this subject
which she had made so vibrant and illuminating." So, "as our time
was up and still so much left to be said on the subject of these Zuni,
it was suggested that it be continued at our next [meeting]."

A Christmas Pilgrimage to the Southwest

Without doubt, the widest circulation of Anne Evans' impressions
of Pueblo Indian ceremonials was the account in her paper entitled
"A Christmas Pilgrimage to the Southwest," the story of a trip she
made in 1925. She read the paper to the Fortnightly Club on January
18, 1927. Originally titled "Primitive Ceremonials," the paper was
read again at the Club meeting of March 6, 1973, more than thirty
years after she died. There were introductions by four Club members,
which included their vivid personal memories of Anne Evans. "It
was Christmas Eve in the Pueblo of San Felipe." So Evans began her
story, telling how she, along with other companions, had been making a pilgrimage to the Old Franciscan Missions of New Mexico—
Acoma, Laguna, Isleta—carefully planning to "reach San Felipe at
this exact moment to be present at the curiously beautiful rite
which the Indians present annually at the close of the midnight
Mass." As they drove into the village, a "broad path of light" from the

open doors of the church invited them "to enter and pay reverence to the Creche arranged so reverently and with such naïve simplicity upon the altar." After a little while spent admiring the "bare beauty of the interior," the "simple spaces of the thick adobe walls, alive with flickering candle-light from the hand-wrought sconces" and the "heavy, carved ceiling beams, high up in dim obscurity," they took a little stroll around the moonlight-bathed Pueblo, the ground "covered with a fresh fall of sparkling snow." Soon they were back in the church, watching the "picturesque in-gathering" of Mexicans and "blanketed Indians," slowly filling the entire sanctuary.

> There is a gentle ripple of pleasure and a gesture of reverence as the padre enters, and as he pronounces the sonorous Spanish sentences of the service there is the complete hush of concentrated attention.

She observed that, although many of the listeners did not understand either English or Spanish, the

> representation there on the altar of the stable at Bethlehem speaks plainly to them all. More directly perhaps, than to the people of our modern cities, for the miracles of nature and the intimate companionship of burros and cattle are the very warp and woof of life in an Indian pueblo.

Deer and Buffalo Dance

When the mass was over,

> like wind over the corn, comes a general rustling movement and a new orientation of the entire congregation. It flattens itself into a dense mass against the walls, it crowds up into the gallery, it swarms up the pulpit steps, and all eyes turn expectantly toward the open doorway ... Now there comes to our ears, at first far off and faint, but increasing in a rapid crescendo the exciting beat of approaching drums in an insistent intricate rhythm, and in an irresistible onrush through the door, and into the center of the church itself, a bizarre company of Indians in full ceremonial garb, who have come according to long custom for the annual enactment of the Deer and Buffalo dance before the Virgin and Child.[7]

This was not, explained Evans, a dance as understood by the white man, an occasion for recreation and pleasure, but "a most earnest prayer of supplication, a visualization and presentment of the tribal needs, and it is performed in a spirit of consecration prepared for by fasting and ritual."

As the ritual proceeded,

> one is at first stunned by the weird strangeness of the sights and sounds and it seems like confusion confounded; then gradually we realize that there is order and precision in the mass of multi-colored movement; that between the two lines of dancers there is a sort of antiphonal interaction, and still more gradually we become more familiar with certain steps and phrases which are repeated over and over again.

Slowly, she said, they began to distinguish one group from another, noting the differences in headdresses, costumes and ornaments.

> First, we observe the Buffalo—black-horned, dark-browed, and heavy-set. Never for one moment do their personalities lose the character of the powerful lumbering beasts who once made all the western plains thunder under their stampedes, and (who) were the chief sources of food and shelter and raiment.

The Deer had "wide branching antlers and wreaths of green spruces around their necks." Each carried a strong, short stick,

> and one of their characteristic poses is to lean forward on this, with bended back and lifted head, producing the effect of startled bucks peering out from a thicket ... All their movements have the light strength and alert poise of real deer, and we watch their springing step with sheer delight.

The Antelope group was equally distinctive, "true to type in color and marking, and the sharp spike-like horns ... and ... in front of them all, with downcast eyes, steps the modest Buffalo Maid with such contained, suppressed steps that her tiny feet scarcely leave the ground."

The last stage in the ceremony was that

each and every beast must needs make obeisance before the Crèche. One by one the Buffalo tramp up, drop heavily to their knees, and the dark heads are bowed in submission; the Deer bound up the shallow steps, and the high-spreading antlers make their reverence in all humility. The Antelope scurry forward in a very panic of nervous timidity.

"We watch it all with a breathless feeling of exaltation—it seems too wonderful to be true, that here and now, in this prosaic every-day world, in the year of our Lord 1925, there can be so sincere and unspoiled a survival of this old, old rite." After the last dancer leaves the church, the audience turned together towards the altar.

... kneeling together in unison, Mexican and Indian and White man murmur in unison the words of the closing prayer, and as we rise to our feet we stop for a moment to give thanks that we have been privileged to take part in the most uniquely beautiful Christmas service in all the length and breadth of the land.

Father Steele's Commentary on Evans' Paper

Colorado History, a publication of the Colorado Historical Society, printed the paper in full in a 1997 article, "Anne Evans's Christmas Pilgrimage," by Father Thomas J. Steele, S.J. Born and raised in St. Louis, Steele studied literature at the University of New Mexico and fell in love first with its Santos—of which more a little later—and then with everything New Mexican. He taught in the English Department at Regis University in Denver, and even after retirement served as the curator of their Santos collection.

Father Steele noted that Evans' paper

provides an excellent example of how the Pueblo Indians fulfilled their two religious commitments, the one to their native religion and the other to Catholicism. The two religions remain always distinct, but they are juxtaposed quite frequently, and the Pueblos move smoothly and surely from one to the other—from the Latin Mass and the congregation's veneration of the image of the new-born Savior in the crèche on the sanctuary floor, then to the animal dance that Evans describes so vividly, then to the dancers' veneration of the Christ Child image, and finally to the dances that continued on the plaza outside.

Steele also commented on Anne Evans' basic attitude towards the Pueblo Indians, remarking that, "she may seem supercilious and patronizing by contemporary standards." He is picking up no doubt on her frequent comments about their belonging to "the child-hood of the race," her characterization of them as primitive, and her indulgent description of their children as "bare brown babies." At the end of her paper on the Hopi, she writes,

> One can describe foreign cities with some degree of success, for after all they are of our time and age and are full of people much the same as ourselves. But Hopi land and its villages are of the far, far past—the stone age almost. One finds oneself thinking in biblical language—trying to quote Homer—digging up half-forgotten scraps of knowledge about Assyria and Ancient Egypt—always pressing back into the primitive beginnings of great nations, the childhood of the race.

However, Steele noted,

> We must recall the times in which she lived and wrote. In the 1920's, for instance, the Ku Klux Klan exercised great influence in Denver and Colorado and would have had nothing but contempt for both the Catholic Mass and the religious dances of the Pueblos.

He makes the interesting comment that Evans' "respectful interest in the dances" is "surely more aesthetic than religious—'New Age,' perhaps, seventy years before its time."

Steele did not comment on another aspect of her perception about the Pueblo Indians, which seemed to echo much earlier gen-eral attitudes of the westering settlers towards the Native American population: that in their exposure to our more complex civilization, they are somehow doomed and will inevitably pass from the scene. Of the Hopi, for example, she wrote,

> I would advise you all most strongly to make a pilgrimage while you yet can get to this fountainhead, for it can't last very long. The

people are dying out, they are not very robust and our method of civilizing them is apparently quite disastrous even to their bodies.

Early Travels to the Southwest

How did Anne Evans develop such an intense interest in the Southwest and its peoples? When did she first visit there, and who introduced her to this land? How often did she travel to New Mexico, once she discovered its beauty and its magic, and who are included in the "we" she refers to in her surviving writings about her journeys? A diligent search of available sources yields a patchwork of answers, some well-documented, many fragmentary. In a hand-written draft of her Fortnightly Club paper on "The Missions of New Mexico," given on November 11, 1924, she wrote,

> I had the good fortune to make my first wanderings down that way before the automobile had shortened the journey, and before I had any smattering of history or archeology to forewarn me—I just sallied forth on a lark one August day unprepared for anything of extraordinary interest aside from the Indian Dance-Drama with which a friend had baited an invitation to Hopi-land.

This would seem to indicate that her first visit was quite early in the twentieth century and probably involved a train journey to Santa Fe and a trip on horseback to the pueblos. She was an accomplished horsewoman, having grown up with riding as part of every summer on the Evans Ranch. Because of her acquaintance with most of the early artists in Colorado, several of whom were fascinated by the landscapes and peoples of New Mexico, they no doubt discussed the subjects they painted and photographed there. Evans also befriended Canon Winfred and Dr. Josepha Douglas and frequently visited Camp Neosho, their Evergreen summer home which is now the Hiwan Homestead Museum. Both Douglases were dedicated collectors of Pueblo Indian art, especially of pottery and baskets, and it is more than likely that she traveled with them from time to time.

Historian Caroline Bancroft, in her article about Anne Evans titled "She Created an Indian Cult,"[8] wrote about a "little early group of artists" that included Anne Evans and Canon Winfred Douglas. Bancroft said, "It was perhaps he [Douglas] ... who first insisted upon the authenticity of Indian work as a native folk art, as a fine contemporary contribution, as a *going* thing." She went on to quote Anne Evans:

> This was almost twenty years before the Santa Fe artists' colony began to insist upon the same evaluation, and while they have been able to do much more effective working publicizing the idea, it was our little group who first believed that the Indian work should become a part of the national art consciousness. As much as the art of Greece, say ...[9]

We know for certain that Anne Evans made a number of her trips to New Mexico in the company of her lifelong friend, Mary Kent Wallace, because Wallace left behind some typewritten notes she took on expeditions in 1925, 1926 and 1927.[10]

Preserving the Mission Churches

There were several other aspects to Anne Evans' activities in New Mexico in addition to her interest in Pueblo Indian culture and ceremonials. It was probably early in the twentieth century that Anne Evans started to buy objects of Native American art which appealed to her taste. She always made sure that these were genuine expressions of the particular tribe or Pueblo, and not gimmicky reproductions created for the tourist trade. Anne also exhibited a firm dedication to the restoration and preservation of the Franciscan Mission Churches.

In her Franciscan Missions paper, Anne wrote that as a result of those "first wanderings down that way ... to all intents and purposes I discovered for myself the oldest and most deeply significant architecture in America—the Franciscan Missions of New Mexico—a 'chain of monuments to a great and heroic venture.' She wrote about her first impression of "Acoma ... the city in the Sky whose great church is perhaps the most noble and the most sternly tragic of them all and of how, on that first visit, she and her companion were not allowed inside the church.

> They wouldn't let us inside it—they wouldn't let us photograph or sketch it—and being two lone women, the only white people thereabouts, the only English-speaking people in all that high world—

we minded the Governor's mandates in every least particular! We
were just pitifully subservient—and we fairly showered cigarettes
and fairly sugared the rock with largesse of candy!

When she came back into the world of books and libraries, she read
everything she could lay her hands on about the history of Acoma
and the other Mission Churches, finding that the "story led us back
and back almost to Columbus himself."

The rest of her paper, less than half of which survives, apparently
discussed the almost inconceivable hardships involved in the original Spanish explorations and the building of the Mission Churches.
After the occupation by the Spanish in 1540, "New Mexico became
the advance line of the Mexican Vice-Royalty and the Catholic
Church. By 1616, there were 14,000 Indian converts in New Mexico;
eleven churches had been erected, with sixteen priests to guide their
spiritual lives."[11] By 1639, there were 66 priests, but then the number
began to decline due to conflict between the church and the civil
government. Dissatisfaction also rose between the Indian population and the Spanish authorities, exploding in the Pueblo uprising
of 1680.

Some of those first churches built in the region under the super-
vision of Franciscan monks were destroyed in that Pueblo Rebellion
and never rebuilt. In other villages, however, "where an energetic
priest could inspire the parishioners to action, the building or
rebuilding went forward once again."[12] What distinguished the New
Mexico churches from others built by the Spanish in the Americas
was that they were designed using the materials at hand and the
building techniques of the native population.

> The typical church was constructed of thick-walled adobe with a
> low, earth-hugging profile relieved by twin towers at each end of
> the façade. There was a single nave and projecting apse. The
> width of the nave was determined by the length of available pine
> logs to serve as roof beams.[13]

These peeled logs were known as *vigas* and sometimes decorated
with chiseled patterns. The wooden entrance doors to the church
were set between the two towers of the façade, usually with a small
chapel to the right of the entrance used as the baptistry.

With the independence of Mexico from Spain in 1821,

> the traditional support of the Spanish crown had been withdrawn. Mexico had taken no interest in the upkeep of the seventeenth and eighteenth century churches which the Franciscan friars had built, and adequate clergy were so lacking that most Indian and Spanish parishes were left without a priest. By the 1920's, after a century of neglect, almost all the colonial churches had deteriorated dangerously.[14]

The deteriorating condition of many of the surviving mission churches became a common concern of those who loved them. Further, attempts at repair and remodeling were often totally inappropriate. "When gable roofs began to appear on some old mission churches in the state, there was general lamenting over what was felt to be an historical and artistic sin."[15]

"This Energetic Lady" Heads Denver Rescue Effort

> The sad condition of these churches caught the attention of a group of Denver citizens who frequently visited New Mexico. Prominent among them was Miss Anne Evans, the daughter of a former governor of Colorado; this energetic lady determined to try to rectify the situation. Miss Evans raised funds (mostly in Colorado).[16]

This group secured the financial support of William McPhee, a Denver businessman with timber interests in New Mexico, along with the professional support of Denver architect Burnham Hoyt and the enthusiastic cooperation of concerned New Mexicans. These included representatives of the Museum of New Mexico and the School of American Research in Santa Fe, artist Carlos Vierra and Dr. Frank Mera. Together, they set up an informal organization called the Committee for the Preservation of New Mexico Mission Churches. "To raise funds, Anne Evans interested many friends and associates in her cause, often taking trips to New Mexico—usually with an interested party in tow."[17]

Hoyt and Carlos Vierra took photographs and made notes on the old missions in need of repair. "Where no money was available for restoration, the people of the villages were encouraged by the preservationists to use inexpensive, temporary repairs with traditional materials at hand."[18] However, starting in 1922, the Preservation

Committee undertook a renovation project each summer in a different village, with the understanding that the Committee would provide the tools, materials and a foreman while the villages would volunteer the labor.

Watching all this with keen interest, John Gaw Meem, a young tuberculosis patient, would be destined before long to take the lead in this effort.

John Gaw Meem

Born in Brazil, where his parents were missionaries, John Gaw Meem received his education in engineering at the Virginia Military Institute and served in the armed forces in World War I. He survived a bout with the vicious 1918 influenza but fell ill with tuberculosis. Of the treatment options offered by the army, he selected, almost on a whim, the Sunmount Sanatorium in Santa Fe. This proved to be a most fortunate choice. It was run by a remarkable physician, Dr. Frank Mera. According to Meem's biographer,[19] Mera was not only an expert in the treatment of tuberculosis,

> but even more important, perhaps, he was by instinct a good psychologist and a man of broad culture. The brother of the anthropologist H. P. Mera, Dr. Frank Mera was much interested in the traditional culture and art of the Southwest and had assembled a collection of Indian pottery and weaving.

Mera's sanatorium was designed to look like a series of pueblo buildings "with flat roofs, blunt corners, and earth-colored stucco."
Dr. Mera was interested not only in the lungs of his patients but

> realized that their minds had to be occupied and their spirits kept high if they were to respond to his treatment. He was constantly on the alert for an interest or talent ... that he might encourage.

Mera was interested in all the historic preservation activities beginning in Santa Fe at the time, and encouraged his patients to mingle with members of the group involved in these efforts when they visited him at the sanatorium.

One of these, artist and photographer, Carlos Vierra, became a close friend and colleague of Meem's. Vierra, who had come to Santa Fe in 1904 suffering from tuberculosis, "was one of the first newcomers to discover the charm of the mission churches, which he recorded in paintings and photographs, along with the vernacular architecture of Santa Fe, the Spanish villages and the Indian pueblos." Meem, too, became fascinated with New Mexico, its arts and architecture. In his first year at the sanatorium, be bought his first *retablo*—a New Mexico religious painting in tempera on wood. Through the years, he acquired a valuable collection of this type of art, which he eventually presented to the Museum of New Mexico. As his health allowed, he began exploring the rural areas of New Mexico.

Meem soon developed an interest in architecture, making sketches and experimenting with simple designs. As requests for design help came in from friends, Mera assigned Meem a small building on the campus to use as an architectural office. Meem soon realized, however, that he needed more training. At this point, one of his new Santa Fe friends, Lura Conkey, came to him with a suggestion. She would be going by train to Denver to visit an old friend, Anne Evans, whose circle of close friends included the well-known Denver architect, Burnham Hoyt. With Mera's approval, Meem went with her. In Denver, according to Beatrice Chauvenet, "Meem made two more friendships that were to influence his life."[20]

Meem in Denver

From Lura Conkey's point of view,

> Anne Evans was known as the patron saint of Colorado artists long before she became interested in New Mexico Mission churches. The daughter of parents who were both well-educated and wealthy, she had grown up in the West and had the vision to see that it provided a stimulating setting for artists ... Her method of enlisting the aid of others was quiet and self-effacing. She did not stage a big well-publicized campaign for support, but talked with intense enthusiasm across the tea tables and polished office desks of her influential friends.

Conkey, already working with Anne Evans in the informal committee trying to save what remained of the state's mission churches, believed that Evans

> knew how to enlist the right people in a crusade. Of her, it might be said that she had the four cardinal qualities needed for a great

patron of the arts: vision to recognize and plan; a cultivated taste; persuasiveness to stir the support of others; and a generous purse. Her concern was to promote other people, not herself, and Meem was always grateful that the friendship came early in his career.

Anne Evans Introduces Meem to Burnham Hoyt

Burnham Hoyt is known as one of Denver's finest architects and a long-time friend of Anne Evans. He had worked with her on the remodeling and expansion of her mountain home, and they worked together in a succession of social and civic enterprises. Born in Denver and a graduate of North High School, Burnham Hoyt had an older brother, Merrill, who practiced architecture in Denver. After serving an apprenticeship with a Denver firm, Burnham travelled to New York to study at the Beaux Arts Institute. He became an outstanding student and won many awards. He worked in the office of one of the foremost architects in New York until the outbreak of World War I, when he joined the army. In 1919, Burnham returned to Denver and formed a partnership with his brother in the firm of Hoyt and Hoyt. The practice prospered, producing mainly buildings designed in historical revival styles. Burnham also taught at the Denver Atelier, an affiliate of the Beaux Arts Institute of Design.

Burnham Hoyt, (1941), Denver Public Library Western History Collection

In 1926, Burnham Hoyt returned to New York to undertake "the ultimate commission of the first phase of his career, the interior design of the Riverside Church, commissioned by John D. Rockefeller." When he returned to Denver ten years later, after his brother's death, he began the final stage of his career as one of Colorado's pioneer modernist architects.

Anne Evans' connections apparently worked their magic. Meem met Hoyt, who had a direct approach and simplicity that endeared him to Meem. They discussed Meem's future. His engineering degree gave him good basic training, and he had already discovered a liking for architectural sketching, With Dr. Mera's blessing, Meem moved to Denver to gain the fundamentals of design that he lacked; as Hoyt's protégé, he took an apprentice job with the architectural firm of Fisher and Fisher. At the same time, he enrolled for night-school courses at the Atelier.[21]

Eventually, this schedule proved too much and the tuberculosis recurred. Meem returned to the Sunmount Sanatorium to convalesce, but his interest in his new career persisted and "he was soon sitting up in bed with a drafting board across his knees." Even while recovering, he became a key link between the Denver and Santa Fe groups increasingly concerned about the future of the deteriorating mission churches. As soon as his health permitted, he began to serve as the coordinator of their activities.

Work Begins on the Zia Restoration

The actual work of restoration started in 1923 at the Zia Mission. The money was largely supplied by Denver businessman William McPhee. The work was done by forty-three Zia Indians. Josef Bakos, an artist and member of Los Cinco Pintores of Santa Fe, supervised along with assistance from the Santa Fe Museum, which offered the services of a carpenter and a truck and tools.

There were enormous difficulties. Roads turned to treacherous bogs in the rainy season, supervisors lacked a local supply of food and water, and problems persisted with restoration of the roof. These were solved, apparently at Burnham Hoyt's suggestion, by using a two-inch layer of concrete reinforced by chicken wire. This solution proved to be effective, though controversial among architectural purists. Meem, though not directly involved in the Zia restoration, followed its development with keen interest.

In the fall of 1924, Dr. Hewett, a member of the Preservation Committee and of the Museum of New Mexico governing board, wrote a letter to McPhee in Denver. He remarked that after attending a recent meeting of the Preservation Committee, and hearing a report on the Zia accomplishments and the plans for future work,

> I felt moved to write you this letter of congratulation on the great success of the work that you have so generously supported. Miss

Evans will doubtless have much to say to you in person on her return from her recent tour through northern New Mexico ...

The letter gives some idea of the role Anne Evans played in keeping the Denver donors informed and interested in the preservation campaign.

Frustration at Acoma

The next project undertaken by the Committee proved ambitious and challenging—the restoration of the ancient and sadly deteriorated church of Acoma. At this time, the committee named Hoyt as architect, and Meem as assistant architect. Meem would have liked to supervise the work himself, and live for a few months in or near the pueblo, but Mera felt this would be too much of a strain. So Meem located a capable supervisor who agreed to travel with him to the site.

Meem wrote to Anne Evans outlining the plans and asking that the Committee approve his rental of a car for the journey from Santa Fe to make the preliminary survey. They needed to secure the cooperation of the Acomas in providing the labor, and to set up a schedule for accomplishing the work.[22]

The Pueblo Acoma Mission (c. 1915), Denver Public Library Western History Collection

San Jose de Gracia de Las Trampas (c. 1885), Denver Public Library Western History Collection

He promptly received a telegram informing him "that the Committee authorized the expenditure for the car and was delighted that he could go."

The work proceeded slowly and with even more difficulties than had been encountered at Zia. A tough and conscientious man named Reuter replaced the original supervisor. There were constant delays due to

> a scarce labor supply during the planting and lambing season, in-fighting between factions at Acoma, and a dislike of Father Fridolin (the Acoma Catholic priest) by some leaders. The work was backbreaking, and if Reuter did not like a finished product, he made the men take it down and start over. At first water was scarce, and then the summer rains came and the mud was so deep on the road to New Laguna that it was impossible to haul supplies from the railroad.[23]

A further complication for Meem was that he needed to spend time working on his own first big architectural commission, an addition to the La Fonda Hotel in Santa Fe, and would not be able to spend the time he would have wished on the Acoma project. Since the Preservation Committee was also running short of money, Meem decided to suspend the work at Acoma until another season, and send Reuter to work on an easier assignment. In fact, a great deal had been accomplished at Acoma. The North Tower had been rebuilt.

> With the roof in sound condition, the worst of the outside wall damages repaired, and the portion of the façade that had collapsed restored, it was safe enough to leave the job until a more auspicious time, even though they hated to leave it lopsided, with the south tower stripped down to roof level.[24]

Reuter, frustrated by all the difficulties at Acoma, moved on to Santa Ana, "glad to end the season in more productive work."[25] By mid-December, the Governor of Santa Ana wrote to Meem thanking the Society and the contributors for re-roofing the old mission and repairing the clerestory. When cold brought the construction season to a close, Reuter wrote his annual report to the Preservation

Zia Pueblo Mission Church (c. 1885), Denver Public Library Western History Collection

Committee recommending that, in spite of the enormous difficulties involved, the effort should be made to completely restore the church at Acoma, calling it "this remarkable building whose gigantic proportions must have cost a previous generation the best efforts of their existence."[26]

John Gaw Meem, Anne Evans and the other members of the Committee agreed. They were ready and willing to raise the funds needed to complete the job, but only if they could get the full cooperation of the Acoma people. Prospects for this looked better when Governor Juan Pablo Garcia wrote to Meem in early December, inviting him to bring Anne Evans for the Christmas dances on December 24 and 25, 1927.[27] Meem's commitments to his La Fonda commission made it impossible for him to attend, but he telegraphed Anne Evans encouraging her to go. He wrote to the Governor telling him that Anne Evans and a friend would be there and requesting that someone from Acoma meet "the lady who has raised all of the money necessary to carry on this work."[28]

In 1928, Reuter returned to Acoma, but difficulties prevented any more work being done that year. An opposition movement had emerged, suspicious of the motives of the Preservation Committee. The Governor of Acoma Pueblo wrote to Meem, asking, "Who are these business men, bankers, merchants, professions [sic]? What desire have they? ... Who is Anne Evans? ... Please look into this and why the money comes so freely?"[29] Meem by this time was the architect in charge of the Committee's work, Hoyt having left for New York. Disturbed over the Acoma suspicions about the Society's motives, Meem recognized that Native Americans had so often suffered from dishonest dealings in the past that their fears were understandable. He prepared the affidavits requested, but made it clear that the Society would not raise any more funds until the people wanted to complete the restoration and asked for help. This did not come until the following year, but in 1929 and 1930 the South Tower was rebuilt and some repairs were made to the old priest's house.

Responsibility Passes to John Gaw Meem

Over an 11-year period from 1921 to 1932, in spite of numerous difficulties in what Anne Evans liked to refer to as the "Land of Poco Tiempo," (translated as the land of "pretty soon" and the title of a popular 1893 book by Charles F. Lumis, the Committee repaired the roofs of five churches—Zia, Acoma, Santa Ana, Laguna, and Trampas. It furnished, through the work of John Gaw Meem, plans for two new churches, at McCarty's and Abiquiu, and bought the Sanctuario at Chimayo, presenting it to the Archdiocese of Santa Fe. The Preservation Committee had by this time spent about $16,000, a considerable sum at that time.

In 1932, the informal committee was incorporated as the Society for the Preservation and Restoration of New Mexico Mission Churches with John Gaw Meem as Architect and Secretary. The impetus for incorporating was to raise funds for an addition to the cathedral in Santa Fe. The death of the archbishop and the difficulty of raising money in the deepening economic depression forced the suspension of these plans. From 1932 on, Anne Evans's own fundraising efforts were directed primarily to the enormous challenge of saving the Central City Opera House and building a successful summer theater season there. John Gaw Meem, whose talents she had helped to flourish, went on to become a nationally-known pioneer in historic preservation and "the Southwest's preeminent architect."[30]

Anne Evans as Collector

The final aspect of Anne Evans' involvement with the arts of New Mexico is the building up of her own collection of Native American art. When her achievements are remembered, a major contribution that is usually cited is her early recognition of the value of Southwestern art, not just as colorful craft items with which to liven up a kitchen or a summer cabin, but as a valid aesthetic genre of the highest order.[31] She had a sensitive appreciation for the symbolism embodied in Native American arts. Some hand-written notes survive from a talk she gave on this subject:

> Tell first that the Indian thinks in images and pictures rather than logical words—that he has a gift for rhythm—and for observation— that a symbol is a synthetic thought—it bears a meaning that cannot be put into words, carrying meaning within meaning—for instance, with the Indian, take lightning—it means many things—force— power—speed—the arrows of the thunder bird—it is connected with rain—it and the hissing serpent are almost interchangeable symbols—so it is seldom safe to attach too specific a meaning to a symbol—one must use the imagination—an imagination which the

Indians use, which does really *feel* relationships and likenesses that he can't express orally.[32]

The effect of Anglo-American civilization on the culture and art of Native Americans remained a source of great anxiety for Evans. At the end of her paper on the Hopi, she lamented that

our method of civilizing them ... is terribly disastrous to their art. The tourist who passes by a fine water-olla and seizes on a soap-dish especially produced for his delectation is only too common ...

She wondered what she might possibly say, "that would stay this devastating influence a little."[33]

City Club Assesses State of Art in Denver

The City Club of Denver organized in 1922, is still very much alive today. In the original statement of the Club's purpose are a number of specific goals, all contributing "to the end that, in Denver, public administration, commerce, the arts and the sciences may thrive."[34] In *Art in Denver*, an interesting pamphlet published jointly by the Club and the Denver Public Library in 1928, the Fine Arts Committee of the Club made a broad inventory of the city's art resources. They included a brief description of the four active art schools in Denver and a listing of Private Fine Art Collections. Six names are listed as collectors of American Indian Art, including Anne Evans and Rev. C. Winfred Douglas.

At first, Anne Evans' purchases were used to enliven her two homes—her rooms at 1310 Bannock and her mountain cabin. Gradually, however, more and more were transferred to the Denver Art Museum, and that relationship is the subject of the next part of the Anne Evans story.

20

Introducing Native Arts at the Denver Art Museum

So we began to collect—blankets, pottery, basketry, jewelry and the like. We did not collect them as curios nor for any archeological interest. We collected for the beauty of design and form. We believed ... that they had real art value. Of course people thought us a little mad. In those days there was no difference in a buyer's mind between a beautiful blanket and a good woolly one. They were just bright things for somebody's den. But gradually our movement took hold.[1]

—Anne Evans

The building up of the Denver Art Museum's permanent collections proceeded in fits and starts. As described in the well-documented history of the Denver Art Museum, *The First Hundred Years,* there was a chronic shortage of funds. This resulted in an over-dependence on gifts of art works, without a clearly-defined policy to ensure a high quality of acquisitions. However, in 1925 a new category was added to its collections, a step which might best be characterized by the words of Robert Frost: the museum "took the one [road] less traveled by, and that has made all the difference."[2]

Museum Director Thomas Maytham (1973–83) described the decision which proved to be so significant as follows:

Although the new museum's first directions paralleled those of most art museums, one of its founders, Miss Anne Evans ... expressed her conviction that the art of the American Indian should figure in its collections. Her generosity and efforts established the foundation of the collection ...[3]

Evans was not alone in her appreciation of Southwestern Indian art works as art, worthy of being set alongside art of any other culture, and not to be considered merely as anthropological or archeological artifacts. A small group of artists and connoisseurs in Denver, like Evans, appreciated this unique part of the American heritage. In 1925, this view was distinctly that of a small minority, and almost non-existent among major art museums. It would ultimately prove revolutionary in its impact on museum art collections.

The Denver Art Museum showcased an exhibition of American Indian Art in its Chappell House quarters early in 1925. Putting this exhibition together revealed to the trustees the hitherto unsuspected "richness of local private collections."[4] The board, "perennially in debt during this period," voted to spend $3,100 to acquire a group of Navajo textiles. Anne Evans and her supporters among the trustees must have been singularly persuasive on this issue, because the museum could only make the purchase with the owner carrying a 6 percent note. Two years later, the entire budget for Denver Art Museum acquisitions was only $1,500 with $1,550 still owed on the note.[5] The trustees "made another commitment toward building strong holdings in American Indian art when it decided to devote a room at Chappell House to a permanent Indian art collection."[6] Anne Evans immediately began to donate gifts of American Indian objects from her own collection. These showed up in the museum's documentation of acquisitions beginning in 1925.

At this point, Anne Evans did something rather rare in the history of her organizational involvements: she made a formal request, in writing, to be named head of a standing committee— one charged with the responsibility "to upbuild a fine Indian Art Collection." Her request was read, in her absence, at a meeting of the Museum's Executive Committee on November 14, 1926.[7] The committee elected her unanimously to chair a committee which apparently already existed, perhaps as an ad hoc group formed to help with the exhibition mentioned above.[8]

The first curator of the new collection was Edgar C. McMechen, a man well-known to Anne Evans, as he had just published an affectionate biography of her father.[9] McMechen established a catalog system for the new Native Arts collection and made many trips to the Southwest and to the Great Plains area to acquire some choice additions to the collection.

Eric Douglas—First Full-Time Curator of Native Arts Department

Frederic H. Douglas, curator of American Indian Art at the Denver Art Museum in 1929, Denver Post, March 11, 2001, Denver Public Library Western History Collection

Perhaps the single most valuable contribution made by Anne Evans to the development of the Denver Art Museum Native Arts Collection was her introduction of Eric Douglas to succeed McMechen, who left the Denver Art Museum to become involved with the Colorado State Museum. Starting as a volunteer docent in 1929, Eric Douglas was hired the following year as the first full-time curator of its Native Arts Department. He brought to the job a deep knowledge of the field, a unique imagination and boundless energy that propelled a rather small museum, poor in resources, to the top of an emerging area of art collection.

Canon Winfred Douglas

The depth of Eric Douglas' expertise in the area of Indian art came from his unusual background. Eric's father, Canon Winfred Douglas, was yet another of that large company of immigrants to Colorado who came in search of a cure. He was born in 1867 in Oswego, New York, where his father, Virgil Douglas, served as superintendent of schools. Winfred was one of two surviving children born to his mother, who died of tuberculosis when Winfred was six.

To help him regain his health, his rector arranged for him to receive an invitation from Henry Martyn Hart, Dean of Denver's St. John's Cathedral, to take up a post as minor canon. And so, "frail and impoverished"—his own words—he arrived in Denver in the fall of 1894.

There he met Dr. Josepha Williams, a graduate of Denver's Gross Medical School and a staff physician at the Marquette-Williams Sanitarium on Pearl Street. Soon Canon Douglas was among the many guests invited to enjoy the mountain climate and plentiful sunshine of Camp Neosho, the summer home of Dr. Jo's mother,

Mary Neosho Williams, located thirty miles west of Denver in the little foothills settlement of Evergreen.

One of the "founding mothers" of Evergreen, Mary Williams, a devout Episcopalian, was largely responsible for the Episcopalian presence there. She also took an active role in the development of St. John's Cathedral in Denver. Sometime in the 1880s, Mary Williams found 1200 acres of beautiful land for sale in Evergreen, including most of the land on both sides of Main Street and the acreage eventually occupied by the Evergreen Episcopal Conference, as well as the area surrounding what is today the Hiwan Homestead Museum. On this site stood a small log building which Mrs. Williams enlarged by the addition of a kitchen, living room and upstairs bedroom for the rather frail Dr. Josepha. Mary Williams herself, like all the other guests, slept outside in a rather luxurious version of a tent, with a wooden floor and wood stove to warm up the space on cool mountain evenings.

To carry out her plans for the building of Camp Neosho, Mary Williams secured the services of Jock Spence, who developed into Evergreen's master builder.

Douglas Family Life

Canon Douglas and Dr. Jo married in June of 1896. They had many interests in common, including their devotion to the expansion of the Episcopalian mission in the west and an intense interest in the art and artifacts of the Indians of the Southwest. Josepha apparently began her own collection of Indian art as a young girl while visiting her uncle, a doctor in Taos.[10]

The couple had just one child, Frederic Huntington Douglas, born in 1897 and known to everyone as Eric. In the early years of their marriage, the Douglases spent much of their time in Evergreen. Canon Douglas served on the local School Board. For the care of their son, they developed a rather unconventional arrangement—a separate little house, built for him and whoever was taking care of him, which at different times could be Canon Douglas' sister or a housekeeper. In later years, as Canon Douglas's activities and responsibilities in different areas of church music developed, the family lived in many places—New York, Wisconsin, England, Denver—but they returned to Camp Neosho almost every summer.

When in Evergreen, the young Eric Douglas grew up surrounded by magnificent examples of Native American art. He traveled with his father, who "toured the Indian country of Arizona, New Mexico and Utah by pack train, covered wagon, and, later, automobile." The younger Douglas developed his own familiarity with the cultures and people, and with the intricacies of trading in Indian artifacts. Eric Douglas listed the dates of his "Trips into Indian country of S. W. as: 1911, 1913, 1916, 1918, 1923, 1925, 1926, 1927, 1928, and 1930."[11]

Mary Neosho Williams died in 1914, leaving to her daughter a considerable inheritance. This enabled the family to hire Jock Spence to add to Camp Neosho, making it into a comfortable home. There the Douglases continued the easy summer hospitality in Evergreen, with guests as varied as prominent New York musicians Kurt Schindler and Walter Damrosch, Indian friends from the Southwest, members of the Evergreen summer community like Anne Evans and others from the Evans Ranch, and visitors from Denver. Freddie Lincoln, an Evergreen summer resident, remembered Camp Neosho as a sort of continual open house. When you were invited to dinner there, she said, "You never knew who would be there and there were no introductions ... You were just supposed to talk with whoever was there."[12] Her most vivid memories of Anne Evans came from attending the Hiwan "cow camp suppers" given by the Douglases. "Anne was a very vital person there. So was Canon Douglas. He used to go around in his plus fours, greeting everyone and talking. I used to ride my horse there. I had a crush on Eric Douglas—thought he was very handsome."[13]

The resources they inherited allowed the Douglases to continue their generous gifts to the Episcopalian summer institutions growing up in Evergreen, including a six-week summer church music school organized by Canon Douglas. Douglas devoted himself wholeheartedly to the study and teaching of church music, especially plainsong, and took on the controversial but rewarding responsibility of revising the Episcopalian Church Hymnal. This task he undertook twice in his lifetime, completing the first major revision in 1919 and the second shortly before his death in 1944.

When the inheritance passed on to Eric Douglas, it did nothing to diminish his formidable capacity for work. However, it did enable him to approach his work with an independent spirit, and to make constant quiet contributions to the collections of the Denver Art Museum.

Eric Douglas' Contributions to the Denver Art Museum

Eric Douglas graduated from the University of Colorado, completed a year of postgraduate study at the University of Michigan, and then spent four years at the Pennsylvania Academy of Fine Arts where he developed his own considerable artistic talents. When he returned to Denver, he was recruited by Anne Evans as a volunteer docent at the Denver Art Museum. Recruiting capable docents was apparently one of the many services Anne Evans performed for the Art Museum. Donald Bear, who became the Museum Director in 1934, "recalled Anne Evans first hiring him (Bear) as a docent on the strength of two articles on French painting she had assigned to test his skill as a critic." Eric Douglas proved so valuable that he was asked to join the paid staff in September of that year—at the princely salary of $125 a month. In May of the following year, he was appointed curator of Indian art.

By this time, Anne Evans' Indian Art Committee had made considerable progress in acquisitions. In 1928, the Committee undertook "a concerted effort to enlarge its base of contributors by forming a permanent support group to study and build the collection."[14] Sixty-five interested patrons attended a recruitment dinner held in May. They elected artist Allen True, a collector himself, chairman. The museum felt a sense of urgency for collecting by this time, as other museums and collectors had begun to realize the aesthetic value of Indian art. McMechen emphasized this urgency when he was still the Native Arts Curator as well as Assistant Director of the Museum.

In a communication to the museum's executive committee at a September, 1928, meeting he wrote, "It was important to complete the Southwestern and Plains Indian-Pueblo collections ... before the disappearance of these objects from the market."[15] When money was not available to meet McMechen's proposed purchase of some desirable Navajo blankets, the trustees agreed to borrow $400. "Anne Evans suggested the board find twenty people willing to give $100 every three months until the Indian art collection had been placed on a more satisfactory basis."[16] By 1930, when Douglas took over, more than 800 works had been acquired and he could claim that the collection "in some phases ranks with the best."[17]

What Douglas accomplished in the next ten years was astonishing. Personable, charming, and self-confident, he invested himself wholeheartedly in his new career. Although he had trained for a vocation of painting and wood carving, he is quoted as saying that he became so interested in his museum work with Native Arts that, from the day he started, he "forgot all about painting and hasn't touched a paintbrush since."[18] We might say today that he "pushed the envelope" in four areas: expanding the collections, building a unique library of books related to Native American art, educating the public about the significance of this area of art, and developing arresting and innovative ways of displaying the materials.

Douglas learned much from watching his father's dealings regarding the challenges and excitement of collecting. He also felt that luck had a great deal to do with his successes, but those who knew him well noticed he also had a tremendous capacity for hard work. He prized

> his own super-charged good luck charm, a Crow Indian Sundance doll. The little lady, about eight inches long of elkskin trimmed with beadwork, fell into his hands in his early collecting days. Indians on the Crow reservation in Montana told him that he would always have good luck as long as kept the rare doll.[19]

One lucky example occurred when he heard about the existence of two Alaskan raven screens, each 7 feet by 14 feet," taken from a great wooden house built by a tribe of Tlingit Indians." He called an agent and urged him to try to buy them immediately, and heard back that the agent had arrived "just in time to save the partitions from being sawed into fence boards." In fact, when the shipment arrived in Denver, one of the pieces had a small section sawed out of it, and only after much frantic letter writing would the piece be found, months later, on a "dump pile."[20]

> These carved and painted panels proved to be brilliant masterpieces of Alaskan aboriginal craftsmanship and hence were priceless, because nothing of the sort was ever known to have survived thru time.[21]

These practically priceless partitions had cost the Denver Art Museum $100. Another lucky "coincidence" came after his service in World War II, when Douglas had become interested in adding native arts of the Pacific Islands to the Denver collection. He set his sights on acquiring a wooden roof ornament from a native hut in New

Caledonia. The problem was that exporting such ornaments, believed to represent the family's ancestral spirits, was absolutely forbidden. A friend, who had also served in the Pacific, asked Douglas casually one day, "By the way, I picked up some sort of roof ornament in New Caledonia. Do you suppose the museum would like it?"[22]

For Douglas, "collecting was a hands-on, grassroots activity ... He maintained contacts with virtually every dealer and private collector in the region as well as many artists."[23] During his time as Curator, Douglas

> acquired literally thousands of objects with his own funds. Most were given outright to the museum, others placed on long-term loan with the intention that they would enter the collection later.[24]

In his collecting, he followed the same aesthetic criteria as did Anne Evans and his father and mother. Reviewing the Denver Art Museum collection in 1934, he wrote of it as "very probably the only one in existence which is designed primarily to display the artistic side of Indian life."[25]

"The collection was given a new dimension in the early thirties when Anne Evans and Mary Kent Wallace donated 143 paintings by contemporary Pueblo artists."[26] According to Churchman, in his history of Kent School,

> The collection of Indian watercolors is an interesting chapter in the history of Southwest Indian art. About 1920 a group from Denver, notably Miss Anne Evans, the good friend of Mary Kent Wallace, was encouraging the Pueblo Indians to portray their dance and other rituals in watercolor, a comparatively new art to them. 'Miss Evans gave to the (Kent) school a large collection of these paintings,' ... It was later decided that the collection was too valuable to hang in the School and that it should be given to the Denver Art Museum.[27]

Museum Director Cyril Kay-Scott acknowledged receipt of the collection in a letter dated September 21, 1932.

Before she donated the collection to Kent School, Anne Evans asked art dealer, Cyril Boutwell, to pack up a large selection of the paintings and ship them to Nice, France. There a portfolio of reproductions was made, which is now in the possession of the Hayden family. Mag Hayden reported seeing an identical one for sale in an antiquarian bookstore in Santa Fe, so perhaps more than one portfolio was produced, or perhaps some time later a meticulous "copy of the copy" was made.

When he announced this new acquisition, Douglas pointed out that many of these artists had been influenced by the School of American Research in Santa Fe and its educational philosophy of developing young artists "without subjecting their creative sensibilities to undue Anglo-Saxon influence."[28] In 1951, Douglas started a series of yearly exhibitions of the work of contemporary Indian artists. "More than 250 pieces were acquired from these shows to add to the Evans-Wallace nucleus."[29]

Otto Karl Bach, Director of the Denver Art Museum from 1944 to 1974, wrote about Douglas' ongoing contributions in a newspaper article in 1954.[30] He wrote that when Douglas started work in 1929, "there was one volume in the native arts library ... The library at present includes some 30,000 volumes." Douglas assembled one of the finest collections of books on native arts, particularly the arts of Native Americans, in existence at that time. Undoubtedly, he paid for most of them out of his own pocket, and he deeded the entire collection to the museum shortly before his death from cancer in 1956.

Douglas' "Indian Style Show" and Other Innovations

The other two areas of Douglas' unique contribution are really different facets of the same passion—to increase public awareness of the quality and variety of Native American art and to appreciate it in its own context. To educate people about the aesthetic value of objects in the Denver collection, and about how they were made and what they were used for, he wrote a series of attractive and inexpensive leaflets. Requests for these materials came in from all over the world.

To showcase the Museum's fine collection of Indian costumes, he developed the concept of displaying them in an Indian Style Show, using as models the members of whatever group he was invited to address. The idea came to him after an invitation to speak about native arts in 1942 at the Art Museum in Phoenix, but was admonished, "Please, no lantern slides. Something different perhaps?" The show he developed would be seen across the country—in New York's

"21", at the Surf Club in Miami, in Beverly Hills, where his models were the daughters of movie stars, and at the Brooklyn Museum, where they were chorus girls from Billy Rose's Diamond Horseshoe.

Douglas' concepts of exhibiting Native Arts were startling for their time. They first garnered national attention after his appointment in association with Rene d'Harnoncourt, director of New York's Museum of Modern Art (MOMA), to organize a major exhibition of American Indian Art for the 1938–9 Golden Gate International Exposition in San Francisco. The same team mounted a second exhibition at MOMA in 1941. Rather than exhibiting objects in traditional archaeological fashion, crowded in rows and marked with academic labels, Douglas chose to exhibit relatively few carefully chosen, dramatically-lighted pieces, and to show them in appropriate native settings. MOMA published a handsome catalogue and description of its exhibition, later republished as a book and widely distributed.[31] These two events "did a great deal to increase public awareness of Indian art and, coincidentally, gave Douglas and the collections of the Denver Art Museum national visibility."[32] Approximately one-third of the items exhibited at the San Francisco Exhibition came from the Denver Art Museum collection.

Anne Evans' Santos Collection

One category of the Southwestern Art collection merits special attention: the assembly of objects called Santos, which Anne Evans collected over the years. She donated her collection to the Denver Art Museum in 1936.

Santos are an integral part of the history of the Franciscan Mission churches in New Mexico. When the churches were built, traditional paintings and statues from Europe or Mexico were brought in by congregations that could afford them. Yet they were far too few to supply the needs. Franciscan monks learned to use ornamental pieces produced by local artists who became known as *santeros*, literally "saint-makers." They produced two main types of religious art: *retablos*, paintings on a flat surface, usually on wood but also on treated hides of elk, deer or bison; and *bultos*, painted wooden sculptures. A few of the *santeros* were priests, but most were lay artists who created their own individual versions of biblical characters. According to author and Jesuit Father Thomas Steele, the ordinary people in New Mexico Catholic congregations felt that

Priests, in performing the sacraments and other official liturgical actions of the church, relate human beings to the Trinity ... The laypeople, by contrast, do not tend to reach so high, focusing instead on the saints, the angels, and Our Lady, who seem more human and thus more accessible than God.[33]

He explained that, in the minds of New Mexico Catholics, a *Santo* "shares in a small way the being of the heavenly saint." Therefore, they were "not merely inert objects, for they served as the focal points of sacred interpersonal relationships between the devotee and the holy personages."[34] In a later age, when the Franciscan monks were no longer in charge of the churches, having been replaced by "various French diocesan clerics, Italian Jesuits, and other pious gringos from back East," the *Santos* "were exiled from town churches and from village chapels." The people clung to them, but sometimes they had to be hidden and slowly many of them fell into the possession of private individuals or were lost.

There grew to be a strong connection between the *santeros* and the Penitentes, the Penitente Brotherhood of Our Father Jesus the Nazarene, originally introduced into New Mexico in 1598. Both were eventually rejected by the Catholic Church and both had strong roots among the population, especially in the rural areas of New Mexico. The art work produced by santeros for the buildings of the Penitentes focused on figures exemplifying the sufferings of Christ and of Mary. According to Father Steele, the creation of *Santos* "started out as a provincial and shoddy imitation of European Renaissance art" but "progressed back to a true religious folk art."[35]

In the 1920s, a new attitude toward the *Santos* began to appear, due largely to the appreciation of artists, writers and art connoisseurs who valued them as authentic expressions of "vernacular art and vernacular Catholicism"[36]. Whether Anne Evans' attitude was purely aesthetic, as Father Steele believed, or whether it included also a religious dimension, is impossible to know. It is certain, from what remains of her paper on "The Franciscan Missions of New Mexico" and from some paragraphs of "A Christmas Pilgrimage," that she developed an enormous respect for the courage and endurance of the Franciscan friars and for the church that sent them forth. She had accumulated quite a valuable collection of *Santos* in her years of frequent travel to New Mexico. There is no documentation of exactly

why she decided, in 1936, to donate virtually her entire collection
to the Art Museum, but it is clear that at this time of her life her major
energies were focused on Central City. Quite a number of Evans'
Santos are still on display at the Art Museum.

Eric Douglas was made Acting Director of the Denver Art Museum
in early 1940 when Donald Bear left Denver to become head of the
new Santa Barbara Museum of Art. In 1941, Douglas became director of the Denver Art Museum. In late 1941, he was called up for
active duty in the South Pacific as an officer in the Army Medical
Corps. At the time he requested that he be given leave-of-absence
as curator of Indian Art until the war ended. While in the South
Pacific, Douglas became intensely interested in the native art of
the region and began to collect extensively. When he returned to
Denver, the scope of the Museum's Native Arts collection was
broadened to include art from the South Pacific and from Africa.

Balancing Collections at the Denver Art Museum

It was probably inevitable, given "Douglas's extraordinarily energetic
ambitions for the American Indian collection"[37] which had "begun
... to assume the status of a separate institution"[38] that the post-
war emphasis of the Denver Art Museum would be on building up
the other major areas of art collection—Asian art, Mediterranean
and European art, and American art. Since there were virtually no
funds for new acquisitions, Otto Karl Bach, who came to be Art
Museum Director in 1944, realized that "the primary avenue open
for collection enhancement was the sale or exchange of works
owned by the museum."[39] This policy was not new in the Indian
Arts collection—Douglas had for years engaged in a vigorous program of exchanges and sales. Under Bach, however, a systematic
evaluation of the Indian Arts collection was undertaken and "near
duplicates and lesser materials" were sold outright or traded for
"top-flight art objects." This policy has continued, more or less
rigorously at different times, right down to the present day.

Relatively few of the art objects donated by Anne Evans to
the Museum to start its Indian Arts collection, or that were given as
memorials to her, remain in the possession of the Denver Art
Museum. A visit to the impressive Native Arts exhibit early in 2008
revealed just seven items donated by her on display: two kachinas,
four of the Indian paintings which were a joint gift from Anne
Evans and Mary Kent Wallace, and a piece of Zia pottery. Yet this

in no way diminishes the importance of her pioneering efforts to have American Indian art recognized as a unique and significant aesthetic category worthy of placement in art museums alongside that of any other culture, nor of the consequent elevation of the Denver Art Museum to national recognition because of the strength of its early collections in this area.

In an article written after the opening of the spectacular new Hamilton Building designed by Daniel Libeskind, Tom Noel wrote, "Far ahead of her time and despite that era's prejudices, Anne Evans realized that the native peoples of Colorado [and the Southwest] had a culture and history to celebrate. The DAM's greatest boast is not the new wing, but the Indian and Hispanic art therein."

21

You *Must* Have a Good Time!
Summer Life on the Evans Ranch

*You girls must get to know Anne Evans. She is simply fine
and the more you know her the more good points you see.*[1]
—Marion Hendrie

*Darling Aunt Anne came for us shortly, and, bag and
baggage, we piled into two cars and headed for the
ranch. It took about two hours to come up through the
mountains, and we struck a sudden and dramatic
hailstorm on the way. But it cleared off, and when we got
up to the ranch we had a splendid view of the valley and
the mountains beyond, from Aunt Anne's terrace. It's a
sweet place. I love the air, I love the mountains, and I
love Aunt Anne.*[2]
—Mary Walker

Anne's mountain home quickly gained a reputation for warm
hospitality and spirited discussion of substantive issues. John
M. Rosborough wrote,

The more beautiful one's experience the less possible it becomes to
express ourselves—in words. The hospitality of your friendly home
quite overwhelmed us all ... Dr. Steiner said 'in some homes one
sees only wealth and material plenty, but in Miss Evans' home
one sees love and a great spirit.'[3]

There are many versions of Anne Evans' typical instructions to
guests arriving at her mountain home on the Evans Ranch, especially
to young guests.

> A young niece and nephew, aged 11 and 12, were sent to spend a summer on the ranch with their Great Aunt. They were interviewed. Wide-eyed and apprehensive, they were told that one rule and one rule only must be obeyed. They trembled. 'You *must* have a good time!'[4]

Anne Evans' sheer zest for life, for putting enthusiastic energy into creative projects in cooperation with friends or family and for thoroughly enjoying the results, had its freest expression in the summer life up on the Evans Ranch above Evergreen. This is documented in a number of delightful papers, diaries, interviews and newspaper clippings.

An earlier chapter reported some stories about Anne Evans' life on the Ranch as a child and young woman.[5] With the completion of her studies at the Art Students' League in New York by 1900, Anne's energies were focused on family and friends and contributing to Denver's art and culture. Her winter home was with her brother, William, and his family at 1310 Bannock Street. Summers, however, were spent at the Evans/Elbert Ranch.

Death of Samuel Elbert and Changes in Ranch Ownership

By 1900, there were important changes in the ownership of the ranch. When Governor Evans ran into financial difficulties in 1896, he turned to his close friend and son-in-law, Samuel Elbert, for help. Elbert lent him almost $5,000, with Evans' half-ownership of the Evans-Elbert Ranch as security. As we have seen, Governor Evans died without a will in 1897 and with his financial affairs in total disarray.

Samuel Elbert died in 1899 in Galveston, Texas. With him at the time of his death were his brother, Ben, and Evan Evans. Elbert had developed Bright's disease, but the hope that moving to a lower altitude might bring some relief was not fulfilled. His body was returned to Denver for a Masonic funeral service, and he was buried in Riverside Cemetery next to his wife, Josephine Evans Elbert, and their infant son. Flags at the State Capitol flew at half-mast in mourning for his passing, and the Denver newspapers ran lavish obituary tributes.

> Territorial governor, justice of the supreme court, member of the territorial legislature, president of the Chamber of Commerce and

chairman of the Republican central committee, pioneer, citizen and jurist, Samuel H. Elbert was one of the giant figures in the up-building of Colorado. Few men in the history of the state and the territory were better known and few left a deeper impress on the progress of the young commonwealth.

Elbert's name is remembered in the town of Elbert, in Elbert County, and Mount Elbert, the highest of Colorado's 52 "Fourteeners" (mountains over 14,000 feet).

In his will, Samuel Elbert left a life interest in his portion of the ranch to Margaret Evans, Governor Evans' wife. After Margaret's death, the property went equally to Anne Evans and William Evans' wife, Cornelia. To these two ladies, Elbert also bequeathed the promissory note signed by Governor Evans, in effect canceling the mortgage on the ranch, which had grown, through purchases over the years, to over 4,000 acres. Thereby the property passed into the sole ownership of the Evans family.

With such a large share in the ownership of the ranch, Anne Evans began to take a leading role in its development. She incorporated the Kuhlborne Ranch Company on June 19, 1916, in cooperation with her brother, Evan Evans, and her nephew, John Evans. Purposes of the company were to

acquire and own ranch and farm lands and to carry on ranch and farm operations; to buy, sell, mortgage, encumber, grant, lease and exchange ranch and farm lands and all other kinds of real estate; to buy, sell and deal in cattle and other live stock; to lend money with or without security therefore; to borrow money and to encumber any or all of the property of the Company as security therefore; to cause to be built houses, barns, fences, corrals and other kinds of permanent or temporary improvements on real estate; to cultivate the soil and to market the products thereof and to do all thing pertaining or incident to the operating of a farm or farms or of a live stock ranch or ranches.[6]

Anne Evans served as President of the three-person board of the Company. The board began to develop irrigation systems and other improvements. By 1927, the Clear Creek County Assessor's statistics on the agricultural characteristics of the land revealed that the Kuhlborne Ranch covered 4,573 acres used as follows:

Cultivated acres: irrigated 55; non-irrigated 60; acres in oats: irrigated 50; acres in spring wheat: irrigated 2; acres in potatoes: irrigated 2.5; wild grass to be cut for hay 60 acres; acres in pasture: non-irrigated 4,450.

The overseeing of the ranch operations fell into the hands of successive foremen who lived in the original Vance homestead house.

Summers at the Cottage

The summer gatherings at the Cottage still included some of the Elbert family as well as members of Governor Evans' family. William Evans, who loved to spend time at the ranch, was increasingly preoccupied with political and financial challenges related to his leadership of the Tramway Company and later with his continuing efforts to support David Moffat's almost impossible dream of constructing a railroad tunnel through the Continental Divide. William's wife, Cornelia, and their four children, John, Josephine, Margaret and Katharine, however, were lively participants in all the activities that this then remote and beautiful land offered. Evan Evans and his wife, Kathryn, seem to have enjoyed being up in the mountains as much as his conscientious stewardship of the estate of Governor Evans allowed. Kathryn was the sister of Evan's late first wife, Anne Ferrell. Anne Evans spent as much of the summer at the ranch as her growing commitments permitted. There were still long visits from the Lunt family in Colorado Springs and from more distant Evans, Gray and Lunt relatives. Friends too were easily invited and included in the pleasant summer routines.

The Building of Separate Family Homes— The Dodge Ranch

The first of a long process of setting up separate summer households on properties that were either carved out of the Evans Ranch or adjacent to it began in 1903. In that year, Regina Lunt and her husband, Clarence Phelps Dodge, from Colorado Springs bought 160 acres of Newman property "along with other additions of land" adjoining the Evans Ranch.[7] This property is now owned by the Jefferson County School District and operated as one of its two Outdoor Education Laboratory Schools. Regina was the daughter of Judge Horace Gray Lunt of Colorado Springs, a nephew of Gov. Evans' wife, Margaret. Regina and her brother, Horace Fletcher

Lunt, spent a great many summers on the Evans Ranch as children and teen-agers. Horace left a delightful letter of reminiscences about those early years, written for Regina and Clarence's son, Phelps Dodge.[8]

Born in 1877 in Hawaii, where his father was a Presbyterian minister, Clarence Dodge was educated at Phillips Academy and Yale University. He moved west to Colorado Springs soon after graduating, rapidly becoming a community activist and marrying into the well-known and respected Horace Lunt family. Dodge owned and published the *Colorado Springs Gazette* for eighteen years. In 1904, he was elected to the Colorado House of Representatives and later, in 1918, ran unsuccessfully for governor.

The Dodges first built a small home on the Newman land, and then went on to plan a spacious home on the same site used by pioneer John Newman for his own small cabin. That building was moved to the site it still occupies, and was converted for use as an office by Clarence Dodge. Later, Regina had a room added at the back, with skylights to make it suitable for use as her painting studio. Regina Dodge was an artistic and confident young woman of twenty-three when she developed the plans for their cherished summer home. The couple secured the services of Evergreen's talented and hard working builder, Jock Spence. Spence was the builder of many fine original homes in Evergreen, including the one that is now the Hiwan Homestead Museum.

Besides being a superb and well-trained craftsman, Spence had the gift of working with clients to help them secure exactly the kind of spaces and finishes they had in mind. Horace Lunt noted that

> Unlike most competent workmen, (he) was perfectly willing to do things the way his employers wanted them done rather than insisting on his own ideas. I remember his spending hours, if not days, patiently putting up and taking down various designs of paneling in the living room until Regina decided which one she liked best.[9]

The house consisted of three levels, constructed mostly from materials on the site. The wood came from the Kirby Mill on Peedee Creek, one of the last remaining mills in the area. Cutting the virgin timber was a major source of income for the first settlers, and in the early days of white settlement, there were many sawmills in the

Upper Bear Creek area. In less than forty years, however, most of the valuable timber in the entire foothills area accessible to Denver and other Front Range cities disappeared. The number of sawmills diminished rapidly.

Fireplaces and woodstoves were the only way of heating homes built on the Evans Ranch at that time. Every room in the Dodge home had its own stone fireplace. Lighting came from candles and oil lamps, and "... the dining room was lighted by forty-eight candles in wall sconces, a candelabra and a large chandelier, which hung over the dining table." The living room had exposed wood ceiling beams, an entire wall of bookcases, diamond-paned windows and "a concert grand piano ... hauled by wagon over the Squaw Pass road."[10] After the house was finished in 1907, the small home the Dodges first lived in was moved some way down the hill to become the servants' quarters and laundry. An icehouse was built nearby. Each spring, ranch hands would cut ice with handsaws from the creeks or beaver ponds for the growing number of homes, pack them in sawdust and transport them to icehouses for summer use.

The Dodges had two children, Clarence Phelps Jr. and Regina. This family and their many interesting guests were an indispensable element in the activities of the vibrant Evans Ranch summer colony, even after they moved from Colorado Springs to Washington D.C. in 1930. This was true right up to 1938, when Regina and Clarence left for California after the summer season was over. There Clarence Dodge developed pneumonia. He died the following July at his son's home in Denver.

The ranch property passed into the hands of Phelps Dodge Jr. After serving in the armed forces in World War II, Phelps and his wife, Eileen, chose to make it their year-round home. They converted the guesthouse, servants' quarters and studio into cabins for paying guests, and tried to operate the relatively small acreage as a working ranch, with Angus cattle, Palomino horses and chickens. But it was a constant struggle financially. When Phelps Dodge injured his back, they decided to sell 424 acres of the property to the Jefferson County R-I School District to be used for nature education.[11] Since 1961 literally thousands of sixth grade school children, from all over this largest of Colorado's school districts, have spent what many of them subsequently describe as the most memorable week of their entire school careers, studying all aspects of "natural science" in this glorious setting.

Wind-in-Woven—the Elbert-Everett Austin Estate

The next summer home to take shape belonged to Louise Elbert Everett and her husband, Leonard. They were married in 1901.[12] Leonard was some thirty years older than Louise and according to her niece, Ethelind Elbert, he "adored his attractive young wife, showering her with gifts and always 'letting her have her way.' "[13]

Anne Evans and Louise, as was noted in an earlier Chapter, were already great friends as children and teen-agers. It is not quite clear what financial arrangements were made for the Everetts' acquisition.

One source simply notes:

> Governor Evans daughter Anne made it possible for Governor Elbert's niece, Louise Elbert Everett, and husband, Leonard Everett, to regain possession of the central portion of the original ranch.[14]

Another suggests, "Sam Elbert's niece, Louise, bought a portion of the ranch from Anne Evans." However, Anne was fully aware that if it had not been for the generosity of Samuel Elbert in leaving his half of the ranch to Cornelia and herself, and also in effect canceling the mortgage he held on the Evans' half, most of the property could have ended up in the hands of Elbert rather than Evans descendants. There was also Anne's long-time friendship with Louise. So there is no doubt that she was happy to arrange for the Everetts to take title to a generous spread on which to build a summer home and have horses.

In J. Christopher Jensen of Council Bluffs, Iowa, Louise found an architect sensitive to the environment and to her tastes and needs. Like the Dodges, she secured the services of Evergreen's master builder, Jock Spence. She chose as the site for the house

> an exceptionally fine stretch of woodland, meadow, and pasture-land and it was her intent to place the house in the meadow and have it look as if it had grown there ... She ordered the exterior of the house to be done in pine slabs with the handsome Ponderosa pine bark intact.[15]

The house is a single structure, two stories in height, with a U-shaped floor plan. It has a number of hipped roofs with deep overhangs.

The roofing material is wood shingles. Both the large formal dining room and the living room, essential to Louise's love of entertaining guests and hosting imaginative dinner parties, open through French doors to the shaded west porch. Both have massive fireplaces of native stone. The unique wood finish in these rooms seems to have been a special innovation by Spence to fulfill Louise's desire for a dramatic interior: the paneling was on 25" wide boards placed vertically, their joints covered by board battens. The ceiling also was of wide pine boards, supported by 5" beams.

> Beams, ceiling, vertical panels, battens were all finished uniformly by a wood-scorching process done with hot irons; the result is a warm, dark, velvety luster, particularly lustrous in candle or fire light. This permanent sheen is superior to any polish obtainable with stain and wax.[16]

Barns and corrals for horses were built at a considerable distance from the house to minimize the impact of flies on family and guests. The Everetts were fortunate in having two year-round springs on their property that "permitted the contrived, but nevertheless natural touch of developing a small waterfall as a feature of the north patio of the house."[17]

In the summer of 2003, the charming house looked very much the same as it did when newly completed in the spring of 1909, perhaps even improved by the weathering of almost 100 years. Its vigorous 90+ year-old owner, Ethelind Elbert Austin, as a young girl traveled from Iowa every summer to enjoy care-free holidays as a guest of her memorable Aunt Louise. When Ethelind and her husband, Holcombe Austin, became owners of the property, re-naming it the Elbert-Austin Ranch. It was listed on the National Register of Historic Places on September 11, 1992.

When Margaret Evans died in 1906, she left her half of the ranch to her three children, William, Anne, and Evan, with the stipulation that each of William's four children should receive a 20-acre site.[18] Daughter Josephine chose to take possession of a secluded log cabin on the ranch, originally built by homesteader "Dutch John" Walsh.

Fire Destroys the Cottage Yard

A shocking event precipitated the next round of home building on the ranch. In the summer of 1909, the Cottage, which had sheltered so many family members and numerous guests for almost forty years, burned down. Everyone staying at the Cottage that day, which included the Everetts, Anne Evans, and a number of others, went out riding, with the exception of Anne Evans' friend, Mary Kent Wallace, who did not ride. Suddenly the house erupted in flames and smoke. The caretaker saw the fire and ran to do what he could to douse the flames, but his efforts were in vain. When the riding party returned, they could see that the situation was hopeless.[19] The cause of the fire was never officially determined, though according to one source[20] "rumors credited Wallace's cigarette smoking as the cause." If this were suspected, it certainly did nothing to change the relationship between Mary Kent Wallace and Anne Evans; they remained good friends and lifelong traveling companions.

Between the time of the fire and the construction of new summer homes, stays at the Ranch apparently continued unabated. There were still a number of small cabins on the property, some of them built by hopeful miners, which were used by family and guests.[21]

Anne Evans Builds Her Mountain Home

Anne Evans had always regretted that the Cottage was situated down in the meadow without taking advantage of the magnificent views of Mount Evans and the Continental Divide that were visible from so many sites nearby. When she decided to build her own house after the fire, she knew exactly where she wanted to locate it. The Evans and Elbert families, quite early, had named many of the small and larger hills on the ranch. According to Horace Fletcher Lunt,

> Mt. Susan was named for ... Aunt Margaret's mother. The Captain was named for Uncle William Gray (Cornelia Gray Evans' father) and the Judge for Judge Elbert. A little hill, just ... west of Mt. Susan was called Mt. Anne and a larger knob beyond it Mt. William; (they) were so named because Anne was a little girl and Cousin Will a big boy.[22]

Anne Evans decided on a site on Mt. Susan, just up the hill from the ranch headquarters, with fine mountain views in all directions.

Anne's mountain home received a good deal of favorable publicity over the years for its magnificent site, its unique vertical log structure, its distinctive artistic treatment of the gable ends, its striking use of Native American materials in the interiors, and other unusual features. The design is usually attributed to Colorado's famous architect, Burnham Hoyt, and because he was a very good friend of Anne Evans, it is indeed possible that he had some informal input into the design from the beginning. Lacking any written records or plans of its initial construction, however, it seems more accurate to say that the original building, completed in 1910, resulted from a combination of Anne Evans' creative design ideas and the skillful execution of builder Jock Spence. Thereafter, in alterations and additions carried out in 1924 and at various time between 1910 and 1930, Burnham Hoyt was the official architect, as evidenced by the original drawings to be seen in the Western History Collection of the Denver Public Library and by contemporary published materials.[23]

According to the most straightforward and detailed description of the house, and its evolution over the years,[24]

> the site is a prow of land dropping away sharply to the northwest, down a hundred feet to Metz Creek below. The formal entry ... is on the high side southeast, and the house cascades down in two levels, plus a basement opening out ... at the third level, to capture the fall of the land.

Anne's cabin living room, Courtesy Margaret E. Hayden

The location is high up in the Bear Creek watershed, at an elevation of 8,200 feet above sea level.

> ... views from the house to the west are spectacular, and include Mount Evans ... The fitting in of the building to the rugged site with stonework terraces and steps around the house is distinguished, and locks the house to the land as an integral element of the larger landscape.[25]
>
> The construction technique of this building is rare if not unique ... Walls are constructed of 15" diameter vertical logs sandwiched between a grade beam on the stone foundation and upper eave beam. These beams at the perimeter measure a full fifteen inches square in cross section. The vertical log structure of the exterior is repeated on both sides of the interior hall. Other partitions separating formal from service spaces are half-logs.

The authors of this report, prepared for registration of Anne Evans' house on the National Register of Historic places, noted that,

Anne's cabin living room, Courtesy Margaret E. Hayden

> A perusal of the literature of the period reveals no equal. There are examples of half-log vertical siding, but no full log expression consistently expressed on the inside. No examples were found of the full grade beam in wood as base for the log infill. This building is of a weight and permanence a quantum step beyond the expectation of rustic construction. Even the roof sheathing is in the form of timber: 8" x 12" members laid side by side on 10" x 12" rafters.

This unique feature of the Anne Evans house was undoubtedly due to the combination of her vision for an innovation in construction, using local materials, and the skill of Jock Spence to execute her ideas. "The beams are adzed true to a remarkable craftsmanship, and the building is constructed with a demanding precision."[26] An appreciative critic, Theodore Fisher, commented on the original elements of the summer home's design:

> ... (in her) designs for the decorative gable panels, Miss Josephine Hurlburt has carved from ash some highly effective conventionalizations of eagles, with the wood oil-treated to prevent climatic damage. The entrance panel depicts eagles flying through the lightning flashes of a storm.
>
> Small stones were used for foundations and retaining walls, for fireplaces, chimneys, and terraces, and even the roof utilizes stone slabs laid shingle-fashion on a binder of asphaltum. Logs of yellow pine, selected with care to an almost identical size of 16 feet in diameter, were peeled and set on sills of rough-hewn native logs. The whole place fairly breathes substantiality, frankness and ease in relation to its woody mountain setting of superb pines and gigantic spruces.[27]

The house contains 3,200 square feet on two levels, following the contours of the site, with a small basement at a third level down. The overall footprint of the house is in the shape of the letter T, with entry hall, four bedrooms, two baths and two sleeping porches on the upper level (the "stem" of the T) and living and dining rooms on the second level down (the top, or crossing, of the T), with kitchen and, originally, servants' quarters tucked back under the "stem." The eight-foot entry hall runs the length of the upper level, ending in a most unusual staircase of the same width, fashioned of whole peeled logs, which leads to the living room below.

A Setting for Drama

Anne's cabin staircase, Courtesy Margaret E. Hayden

What is unique about this staircase, besides its unusual width and fine craftsmanship, is its potential as a setting for drama and entertainments. As visitors descend the staircase their eyes are drawn to the view straight ahead, which is of a substantial stone fireplace enhanced by two works of art created specifically for the setting: a painting commissioned from artist Allen True, and a metal cutout fire screen designed by Josephine Evans, telling a Native American folk story. Plays, pageants and a great variety of programs could be—and were—presented in this setting in one of two ways: either the audience sat on the stairs, with the production taking place in front of the fireplace, or the audience was seated in the living room as the action unfolded on the staircase and the hallway above it.

A Fortnightly Club member wrote a vivid account of one of the more ambitious performances staged in this setting, which involved a weekend's effort by almost a dozen people, elaborate costumes, and an original play written by Anne Evans. Miriam Washburn Adams wrote about the event, which took place at the time she was an art student from Colorado Springs, taking classes at the Denver Atelier headed by Burnham Hoyt.

> The crowning glory of my connection with the Atelier was a Medieval House party at Miss Ann (sic) Evans. Miss Ann told Burnie she had written a medieval play she wanted acted on the stairway in her Mt. Evans home. She wanted ten members of the Atelier to come up Friday and give the play Sunday evening. So Burnie sent word to us to be at Willie Mead's studio by 4:30 Friday afternoon. They had medieval costumes we could be squeezed into, and it wouldn't be fair to bring any modern clothes—except perhaps a coat and our night clothes ... by the time I got there, there were only two brocade dresses left; but Burnie was sure I looked regal in a brilliant red brocade and some lace on my head— and ... long flowing sleeves which hid the three safety pins it took to hold the dress on. The men wore tight Robin Hood costumes. One of the women had on a most glorious wimple—streaming through the air as she drove. We had food of some sort at the studio—got into two cars in the alley and started for Miss Ann's. I assure you as we drove through Denver in the then popular open cars we were gazed at—catcalls, boos, etc. But we didn't care. We were on a big mission.
>
> We arrived about 8 o'clock—Miss Ann all but expired when we tumbled into her house all dressed in these costumes! We looked wonderful that evening in her out-of-this-world house with the enormous logs that made the inside as well as the outside ... At breakfast, I will admit, we were a wild sight—especially me in the low-neck red brocade.[28]

"Burnie had us working all day Saturday," Adams recalled. Gray gauze was fitted over the entrance to the stairway. She regretted that she could not really describe what it was like,

> working for dynamic Burnie—making all kinds of necessary crowns, swords, horses, stars, etc., out of cardboard; and, believe you me, they had to be perfect—we were working for a perfectionist—but luckily one who could point the way to perfection!

One development almost brought the project to a halt. After the "most delicious lunch Saturday—the biggest bowl of, mushrooms, rice, etc." it turned out that a poisonous toadstool had been "lurking in the bowl." Sunday produced "a sorry lot of actors. Burnie was the color of chalk. I was all right if I could sit down." By three in the afternoon, most had recovered and they started rehearsing. At six, they gave the play.

> Margaret Evans Davis read the words on the other side of the screen as she wove her tapestry. Most of us were holding positions and draped up the stairs—Burnie and another man having a big tilt or joust on wooden horses at the top of the stairs. It really must have been fantastically lovely.[29]

The audience for this intense effort was small ("Miss Ann, Miss Wallace, Roblin Davis, their sons and daughter, and Miss Ann's cook") as it was for many other efforts on the ranch over the years. The reward apparently was more in participating in the production than in the applause.

Burnham Hoyt's Modifications

The 1910 house had broad overhangs and shingled roofs. When Anne Evans decided on some alterations in 1924, she commissioned Burnham Hoyt, then in partnership with his brother Merrill, to rebuild the roof above the eaves "with heavy timbers, lower slopes, and locally quarried stone roofing tiles." It is an understatement to say that this aesthetically interesting and unusual roof never worked well. Just who was responsible for its failures is a little unclear. The facts are not in doubt: the stones, quarried from the ranch and, by some accounts, hauled to the site by Anne's nephews and nieces, were laid in coal tar on a roof slope much shallower than the original. The new roof construction was well designed to support the great weight of the stone roof but it was impossible to cut the stone to fit tightly enough to prevent leaking. The coal tar, applied around the roof stones, was prone to melt in the hot sun and penetrate into the house. Was this failure due to Burnham Hoyt's design? The practical and hard-working Evans Ranch foreman at the time, Bryan Schwartz, certainly thought so.

"I don't know where they got that Burnham Hoyt. He was the instigator of the stone roof. I know he was a friend of Aunt Anne's and all that ... The stone roof leaked ... They forgot and they mixed coal tar instead of asphalt."[30] But Long Hoeft, the architects who did the research in preparation for having the house placed on the National Register of Historic Places, maintained that the Hoyt design called for a slate roof, and not native stone. Slate has long been used successfully as a roofing material. So it seems probable that the use of local stone was Anne Evans' brainchild. In other areas of construction, foreman Schwartz paid tribute to Hoyt's meticulous specifications.

> Well, he drew a picture of all of the logs that had to be cut. In other words, every dimension. And I worked from that and selected the trees, and we got them all out.[31]

The new roof design created gables on the eastern and western ends, opening up two areas for artistic embellishment. Striking woodcarvings, with an eagle motif, were created by another of Anne Evans' artist friends, Josephine Hurlburt. Hurlburt was a long-time art teacher at Kent School and was one of two friends to whom Evans left a small monthly stipend in her will. The artist for the later woodcarving on the third gable is not clearly established, though many people believe it was Arnold Ronnebeck. The story of the highly public controversy between Anne Evans and Arnold Ronnebeck, over his design for a Civic Center sculpture honoring Mayor Speer, has been told earlier.[32] The lingering discomfort over this split could account for the elimination of any reference to Ronnebeck in national publicity about the art works for Anne Evans' ranch home.

In 1931 and 1936, Hoyt designed further modifications for the house, including the enlargement of the west patio, addition of a winding stone staircase at its west end, and alterations to the living room, dining room and kitchen. None of these changed the fundamental character of the house, which received a considerable amount of favorable publicity from 1917 on.[33] The first article, written by Edgar C. McMechen and published in the *House Beautiful* magazine of June 1917, was titled, "A Forest Home in the Mountains of Colorado." The subtitle gives a clue to the home's design, "A Log Cabin that is Wind and Frost Proof—No Chinks and No Plaster—A Staircase of Solid Logs and Solid Tree Trunks for Porch Pillars." Nationally, McMechen placed the building of "a multitude of hunting lodges or log bungalows ... either on privately owned ground in the woods or in the national forests" into the context of a world war "that has served to introduce to their own country many thousands who have been afflicted with the foreign travel habit." In the Denver area, he attributed the building of "hundreds of forest homes" to the development of the Denver Mountain Parks system, and the "splendid sixty-five mile road built by the city to connect its mountain playgrounds." Finally, he wrote, "The mountain home par excellence, in this region, was built by Miss Anne Evans."

McMechen singled out three aspects of the house for comment, including the application of what he called "the cabinet maker's art" to the construction.

> Instead of having the logs placed horizontally Miss Evans directed that they be set in a stone foundation, vertically. By a flawless tongue and groove arrangement, cut into the logs themselves, the building has been made proof against the lowest temperature.

This is a tribute to Jock Spence, even though his name is not mentioned. McMechen admired the way the building related to its magnificent surroundings

> From the porch, supported by the colonnades of solid tree trunks, a view opens down Bear Creek above which the mountains, heavily timbered, rise in graceful curves. Rough stonewalls extend from either side of the porch, like the nippers on a pair of ice-tongs, and a spring of crystal water, issuing from beneath the porch, trickles along one of these walls and drops with a musical tinkle into a little pool.

Knowledgeably and eloquently he described the beauty of the surrounding trees, shrubs and wildflowers. Finally, he noted the use of

Native American artifacts in the cabin's furnishing, using the curious term "barbaric" to describe them.

> A barbaric touch has been given the interior by the introduction of Navajo rugs, woven in fantastic patterns of rich, warm colors. Indian baskets stand about, and skins of grizzly and black bears, mountain lions, gray wolves, deer and mountain sheep, serve as rugs.

A 1934 *Rocky Mountain News* article[34] rather fulsomely stated,

> The mountain home of Miss Anne Evans on the Evans Ranch in upper Bear Creek is perhaps the most notable example of the use of native materials, which unerring good taste and visualization have transformed into a unique and most charming retreat. The house

Waterfall outside Anne's cabin, Courtesy Margaret E. Hayden

> in which Miss Evans lives most of the summer and sometimes far into the winter, has been pronounced by architects of two continents as perhaps the most distinctive example of its type extant. It literally has grown out of the soil of the Evans domain ... As a true daughter of Colorado, Miss Evans has used only material indigenous to the hills of her native state and has employed only native craftsmanship to rear this gem of architecture from them.

It is interesting to find that Evans' unique use of vertical log construction was picked up by New Mexico architect John Gaw Meem.

When Anne Evans died in 1941, she divided the 21+ acres she owned into two parcels. She left her mountain home and 10 acres of land surrounding it to her nephew, John Evans Sr., and 11+ acres to her niece, Margaret Evans Davis.[35] These were part of the Kuhlborne Ranch, undergoing the process of liquidation at the time of Anne's death.

Exterior of Anne's cabin shows the intricate woodcarving by Josephine Hurlburt, Courtesy Margaret E. Hayden

Most of the art making the interior of Anne Evans' home so striking and unique has had to be reconstructed in the imagination. When the house came into the possession of John Evans Jr., the son of Anne Evans' nephew, John Evans, most of the Native American objects were gone, bequeathed to the Denver Art Museum. Evans undertook considerable remodeling of the house, including re-doing the leaking roof. He had the stone tiles replaced with roll roofing, widely recommended at the time for waterproofing low-slope roofs. The living room was expanded into the former porch area and the two former servants' rooms became a den, a bar and a storeroom. Evans Jr. was married three times. Over the years of his ownership it appears that most of the remaining art objects were disposed of.

Anne Evans' Mountain Home Sold to Fred and Jan Mayer

Art connoisseurs and collectors Frederick and Jan Mayer bought the Anne Evans mountain home in 1990 from John Evans Jr. (1915–

1993). By this time, little remained of the bounty of art pieces, so vividly remembered by those who wrote about visiting Anne Evans in her summer environment. The mural *Free Trappers*, by Allen True, still hung there, though it had been removed from its original position as an inset above the fireplace and reframed as a hanging picture. At his death, John Evans Jr. willed back to the Mayers a wooden sculpture of St. Hubert, patron saint of hunters, which had been in the house in Anne Evans time. The Mayers understand it to have been carved by Anne's friend, Josephine Hurlburt. The uncommon fire screen, designed by Josephine Evans, still decorated the fireplace. Ethelind Austin showed us a picture of the screen and told us what she had heard about its subject, an Indian legend of "How the Robin Got His Red Breast."[36]

> The Indians had a fire going, and they had to go off on some expedition, all except one little boy. They told the little boy he *must* keep the fire going, because if it went out, they wouldn't have any more fire. The little boy … kept it going for a while, and then he fell asleep. A robin came by, and … saw what was happening. So the robin fanned the fire with his wings. That's how he got his red breast. It's a lovely legend, and there it is. There's the little boy asleep, and there is the robin fanning the fire.

It is hardly possible to imagine new owners for Anne Evans' mountain home better suited to the task of restoring it, and enjoying it, than the Mayers. Frederick R. Mayer and his wife, Jan, were avid art collectors and generous benefactors of the Denver Art Museum, as well as of other organizations supportive of the arts.

Unique Arrangements Preserve the Evans Ranch

The Mayers' first investment in the Evans Ranch was not Anne's cabin but one of the five, 500-acre "ranches" into which the Ranch was being subdivided. The size of the Ranch had already been reduced in 1858 by the sale of 1,126 acres to the State of Colorado, to form part of a State Wildlife Management Area. The remaining 3,200 acres were held in trust for a growing number of Evans family descendants. The property had considerable theoretical value but yielded virtually no return to the trust beneficiaries. However, if the Ranch had been sold on the open market, it's zoning would have permitted the building of some 1,600 units on 5-acre lots.

Many organizations and individuals desperately wanted the Ranch to be preserved since it covered mountain landscapes of great beauty and "contained some of the best wildlife habitat on the Front Range, including a large trophy elk herd and its calving area"[37] However, no public money for preservation existed at that time. Finally a new organization, Colorado Open Lands, decided to make the Evans Ranch its first preservation project. With the help of a $4.5 million, low-interest loan from the Gates Foundation, COL bought the Ranch in 1984 and developed an imaginative and well-publicized plan. This divided the majority of the land into five ranches, whose owners were required to accept serious limitations along with deeds to their properties. They would form an association to retain and staff the original ranch headquarters and to oversee the balance of the ranch property, place conservation easements on their properties, and agree that they would only build one home and related structures on a designated 40-acre site, selected for view, ease of access, privacy and visual separation from each other.

The Mayers originally planned to build their own summer home on the ranch they bought, but when they heard that John Evans Jr. was selling Anne Evans' house with 40 acres—zoned for 2-acre sites that could conceivably be chopped up for 20 new homes—they decided to buy it. They placed a perpetual conservation easement on the 40 acres. The Mayers did eventually build a house on their ranch property for the enjoyment of their children and grandchildren.

A Sensitive Restoration

The Mayers undertook a rare and exemplary restoration and updating of Anne Evans' mountain home, which in 1990 sorely needed much loving attention. Their approach to this task is exemplified in a statement by Frederick Mayer:

> Jan and I knew of Anne Evans from our association with the Denver Art Museum, Central City Opera, and Kent School. We respected and admired her for creating the Native American and Santos Collections at the Denver Art Museum. When we purchased the mountain cabin in 1990 we felt like we were stepping into history. We made every effort to carefully restore the cabin and its interior as it was in Anne's time.[38]

The Mayers commissioned Long Hoeft, a Denver architectural firm experienced in historic preservation, to investigate the state of the building and prepare the necessary documents to have it listed on the National Register of Historic Places. They drafted plans and wrote specifications for work to update the building in accordance with the Mayers' ideas and needs, while still maintaining its historical integrity. The house achieved listing on the National Register on January 28, 1992.

The house that the Mayers bought had been little occupied for years and had been allowed to deteriorate. Exterior walls, especially on the south side of the house, were damaged by exposure to the weather. The various sealants applied from time to time had not been noticeably effective. Shrinkage between logs on the interior had been packed with hemp. The character of the interior had been significantly changed by painting surfaces in white and green, and by the installation of carpeting.

Anne Evans had been consciously determined to keep her mountain home in a rustic condition—to introduce a minimum of modern technology and have the ranch environment remain a genuine contrast to the busy, noisy tempo of city life. She refused to install telephone service, relying in emergencies for messages to be delivered from the ranch headquarters. Originally there was no electricity in the house. Even when the need for some electric service became imperative and a generator was installed at the ranch headquarters, quite near to her home, she only provided for service in the kitchen, bathrooms and servants' quarters. As long as she lived, candles and kerosene lamps remained the source of lighting, and fireplaces and wood stoves the only means of heating.

After World War II, REA electric service became available in the Bear Creek valley and John Evans Jr. took advantage of this to install electric heating and electric outlets throughout the house.

The Mayers elected to restore the house in general to its character between 1912 and 1920, though inconspicuously providing for ample electric outlets, telephone and cable TV connections, and propane heat. Work on the restoration started in 1991. The roof needed the most extensive work. Pictures taken during removal of the roofing show extensive deterioration; the entire structure almost had to be rebuilt from scratch. A new slate roof was installed, with copper flashing. The leaded glass windows and the logs have been replaced or restored in harmony with the original design. Originally with two bedrooms, a bathroom and a sleeping porch on each side of the expansive hallway on the upper level, a master bedroom has been fashioned from Anne's bedroom and outdoor sleeping porch. Additional space each for the new owners—an office for Frederick Mayer and a small art studio for Jan Mayer—is provided. Opposite are two guest rooms and two bathrooms. The attic, originally for storage only, "is arranged for overflow of family and guests with sleeping bags and futons."[39] Downstairs, on the living room level, the kitchen was completely remodeled.

The Mayers received several awards honoring the successful restoration and remodeling of Anne Evans' mountain home. A bronze plaque at the entrance marks an award for Interior Rehabilitation from the *Magazine of Historic Preservation*.[40]

Aspenwood—
the Summer Home of John and Gladys Cheesman Evans

The fourth home to take shape on the Ranch was that of John Evans Sr. and Gladys Cheesman Evans. This was a larger, more formal building than the other three, constructed in the early 1920s.[41] For its design, they turned to Fisher and Fisher, the same respected and experienced firm of Denver architects who had designed their Denver home, a Mediterranean-style building at 2001 East Alameda, which they called "Hilltop."

Gladys's mother, Mrs. Walter Cheesman, did not much care for informal mountain living. There is a story that she was invited to the Evans Ranch when the Cottage Yard was still the family summer home and guest quarters. She was quite horrified when she found there was no lock on her bedroom door. She had to push a small bureau in front of it before she could feel secure enough to fall asleep. Apparently her daughter was not kindly disposed towards rustic living either. It was probably in the hopes that she would come to enjoy summers in the mountains more that John Evans had Fisher and Fisher design "Aspenwood." The effort must have succeeded to some degree; the children loved their time up there and one of the animated diaries about summer life on the Evans Ranch in the 1930s describes the home of "the Evanses" as a welcoming and enjoyable environment.[42]

The Margaret and Roblin Davis Home

Margaret Evans, the oldest daughter of William and Cornelia Evans, developed into an accomplished and multi-talented young woman. A superb athlete and a fine musician, she studied in Paris in her late teens. Some of her contemporaries said that her contralto voice was so hauntingly beautiful that it became their criterion for evaluating the voices of others. Ethelind Austin, for example, in a memoir of her summers on the Evans Ranch, wrote, "Cousin Margaret's singing was so lovely that I do believe her voice has been the standard by which I measure all other singers to this day."[43]

In 1914, Margaret married Roblin Davis, a capable businessman who became president of one of Denver's major banks, the Denver National. Margaret's brother, John Evans, presided over one of the others, the First National. Margaret and Roblin had four children: Roblin (who died young), Margaret, David, and William, and this family became one of the liveliest nodes of the interactive summer colony. In 1935, they became the official owners of what had been known as the Devlan/Metcalfe Cabin.

In 1913, a piece of land homesteaded by brothers Charles and Will Devlan attracted the attention of civil engineer Leonard Metcalfe, then visiting the Evans Ranch with his college friend, John Evans. By this time, John Evans was in charge of Cheesman's Denver Union Water Company, which had invited Metcalfe to help them in appraising the worth of the Company. This became one episode in the long, drawn-out drama in which the City and County of Denver finally acquired control over its water supply, with John Evans insisting on a fair price for the Cheesman holdings.

Metcalfe soon made up his mind to buy the Devlan property. His proposals were turned down until he came up with an offer the brothers could not refuse: he would contract with them to build him a mountain home of timber and native stone. Charlie Devlan could incorporate his own design ideas into the house, and he could stay on the land afterwards as caretaker. The brothers agreed to sell, and set to work to build the cabin, which they finally completed in 1924. Metcalfe brought his two unmarried sisters from the East coast to visit him at his new summer home, but they did not stay long, finding the mountain environment too isolated and inhospitable. When Metcalfe unexpectedly became ill and died the following year, he left the property to his sisters. Not wanting anything to do with it, they sold it to John Evans in 1928. John used the place as a guest cabin and hunting lodge for relatives and friends before selling it to the Roblin Davises.

The Walker Diaries

For a vividly detailed account of the summer life on the Evans Ranch in the late 1920s and early 1930s, including information about daily activities, annual ritual events and memorable one-time extravaganzas, there are the Walker diaries. These were written by Mary Walker, the oldest of four sisters invited to the ranch several years for summer vacations by Anne Evans. Sometimes their mother, Mona, came with them. Perhaps Anne met the Walkers while she was a student at the Art Students' League, or perhaps there were other family connections.[44] The girls—Mary, Dina, Challis, and Rhoda—were totally accepted by the summer ranch community, staying with different families and participating wholeheartedly in all the activities. They were by all accounts unusually attractive, vivacious and outgoing young women.

1927: Walker's Account of a Month on the Ranch

Mary Walker made an entry in her 1927 diary virtually every day from August third until reluctantly leaving on August 30.

> We spent the morning unpacking and getting fitted to horses and saddles. I was given a big homely bay named L. C., nothing to look at, but strong, willing, and pleasant to ride. After lunch, the four of us rode a little way down the valley. It was good to be once more riding a horse through mountains.

This was the beginning of a treasured month. After the ride, the sisters walked over to the Everetts' for tea.

> I have fallen in love with Mrs. Everett ... She has a crowd up there consisting of Ethelind and Sam Elbert, Dorothy Moulton from Lexington, Mass., Mayo Harris, an infant from Yale, and Alice Bemis from Boston.

This gives a good idea of the numbers of visitors that could be in residence at any one time in each of the five hospitable households on the ranch.

The next day saw the first of many daily expeditions with which groups of young people, sometimes accompanied by adults, happily occupied the days. The "Everett gang" and the "Evans gang" plus one of the Davis children

> rode about sixteen miles to Echo Lake and had lunch there, at a typical mountain hotel. Some of us danced between courses to a victrola. We had lots of fun … The ride took up most of the day. We got back to the ranch just in time for tea.

Other days, they took simple lunches with them, no doubt prepared by the cooks in the various households, and rode to different destinations, some on the ranch and others on adjacent properties up on the slopes of Mount Evans.

> A large gang of us rode up to the Mount Evans rest cabin … We ate lunch beside a brook—or *in* it, I might say, since some of us sat on a big rock and had food thrown at us.[45]

Often, as well as riding, the groups stopped to fish.

> Rhoda, Challis and I rode to Beartrack Lake with the whole Everett household. We started at seven, and after a beautiful ride got there at 10:30. Then we fished—and fished *and* fished.

On this occasion, Mary had little luck, but described how Louise Everett, an expert in casting, caught sixteen trout.

> But the lake was so beautiful and the people so sweet and the ride such fun that I didn't mind coming home with icy, wet feet and only one fish.[46]

Mary Walker had more success later in the month when, after lunching at the Dodge's, "Mr. Davis came for me shortly and took me down to Mr. Cranmer's meadow to fish."[47] (Mr. Cranmer was George Cranmer, the husband of Jean Chappell who has been mentioned earlier as a long-time ally of Anne Evans in efforts to advance cultural causes in Denver.)

In an interesting memoir, poet and journalist Thomas Hornsby Ferril, characterizing Cranmer as an early ecologist, described how he built his 1922 home. It was on the beautiful Yankee Creek property he and his wife bought for their summer residence, with a sod roof for insulation. This was apparently less than totally successful. In one of her 1930 diary entries, Walker noted being taken over to the Cranmers in a rain storm to pay a "good-will call." "We found them sitting in a very wet living room, surrounded by basins and bowls to catch water from the many leaks in the roof."[48] Cranmer also experimented with self-sustaining trout ponds. These experiments must have been successful, for describing the day Walker was taken to fish there, she wrote,

> I've never known such good fishing ... they were biting like mad, so often that it was really exciting, but they were quick as lightning, and got away from me again and again.

While she only caught six, two of which had to be thrown back because of size, the total haul, between herself and Mr. and Mrs. Davis, numbered twenty-six.

On another day,

> Young Everetts, young Walkers, Judge Symes and Virginia rode out to find the P. D. Falls this morning. We succeeded, but we had hardly got there when it began to pour. We Walkers had no slickers, and had to snuggle up under a little pine tree till it stopped.[49]

Expeditions to the Summit of 14,000 ft. Mount Evans

Ethelind Austin remembered her first trip to the top of Mount Evans as a child of nine or ten—probably around 1918—in the company of her Aunt Louise, Uncle Leonard and the second Anne Evans, daughter of banker John Evans Sr.:

> I believe we got up at 3 a.m., reached the summit about 11 a.m. and got home about 7 p.m. That was a thrilling ride and an amazing new world above timberline. Aunt Louise regaled us with tales of how she had ridden there once when it was so cold that she began to shrink, and her feet wouldn't reach the stirrups and her hat spun around on her head! And she told of another occasion when she and (Aunt) Anne wanted a fire so badly that they burned the wooden stakes that marked the trail.[50]

Mary Walker described a special trip on August 14, 1927. "The John Evanses took all our household to Mount Evans in their two cars, a stunning ride over the highway." At that time, the road went only as far as Summit Lake. Mayor Speer, in his years of office,[51] did not succeed in his dream of having all of Mount Evans included in the Denver Mountain Parks system, but two areas were included, one around Summit Lake and another around Echo Lake. Speer lobbied for funds for the daring project of building a road to the summit of Denver's signature Fourteener. The laborious process of construction from Echo Lake almost to the summit began in 1917 and was completed around the end of 1927. Work was only possible in the summer, and even then weather conditions were often harsh and changeable, especially as construction crews reached higher elevations. The road was paved in the 1930s and is the highest paved automobile road in North America. It is still closed every winter.

Above Summit Lake, the party from the Ranch looked up at over a thousand feet of mostly rock.

This was what you were supposed to climb, but when I saw it, I said "No, thank you!" But after we had a copious picnic lunch and time to contemplate that highest peak … I decided to try it and see what happened. We started up behind Mr. Evans—all of us, Alice (Evans), Betty Knode (a friend of Alice Evans from Chicago), and Miss Wallace—and climbed very slowly, stopping for breath constantly on account of the altitude. Betty, who had just come from sea-level, turned blue in the face before she's gone half way, and decided not to go on. Mona stayed back with her. It was two hours before we reached the saddle, but by that time I had got my second wind and was climbing easily, so I followed the others up to the summit and looked over what seemed like half the state from the height of 14,400 feet. It was cold up there and very windy, so that I only *kneeled* on the highest point, while bolder ones stood. The view was gorgeous on every side. I thanked my stars that I had made the climb.[52]

Going down was much faster: "we scrambled, slid and fell down in half the time it took us to go up."

Another day, "We went down to the Douglas' for tea[53] and were shown their place and their Indian things."[54] On another visit to the Douglas', Walker wrote, "Father Douglas and I sat right down to playing two-piano music—Bach, Brahms, Debussy, and more besides, all heavenly stuff." Considering that Canon Douglas was a nationally recognized church musician, Mary Walker must have been quite a confident and talented pianist.

The parts of the days not taken up with rides or other expeditions were spent in an easy round of informal activities: grooming the horses, visiting different households, conversation, reading aloud, letter-writing and playing games. The two favorites among the older young people, in the years covered by the Walker diaries, were poker and bridge, played fast and furiously. Pencil and paper games were also enjoyed, including an invented guessing game. Among the books shared in reading aloud, Walker mentions *Lazarus Laughed*, *San Michele* and *Experiences of an Irish R.M.*

Elaborate Dinner Parties

Several times during the summer, one or other of the five households would plan an elaborate dinner party, often involving music, decorations and costumes. Mary Walker describes several of these events, including two hosted by Anne Evans.

Eighty years later, 98-year-old Ethelind Austin vividly recalled the night when Anne Evans brought a group of Native American dancers to perform at the Ranch. Mary Walker also described the occasion. Mary, along with Alice Evans and her Chicago friend, Betty, spent the morning building a large bonfire "up on the hill beyond the driveway." Such an activity would horrify our fire authorities today, but it is clear from the daily accounts of weather in the Walker diaries that heavy rain in August was an almost daily occurrence at that time. Anne, noted Mary in her diary, had arranged for the Indians to come up to the ranch from Indian Hills.

Just how a group of Indians happened to be in nearby Indian Hills is a story told by two highly intelligent women residents, who decided to write a thoroughly researched history of their community. In *Indian Hills: the Place, the Times, the People*, Helen Brush and Catherine Dittman described how the NaTeSo Pueblo was built in an Indian Hills meadow in the mid-1920 as part of a promotional project designed to attract more visitors to the area.

> Designed by Jean A. Jeancon [who figures later in this chapter as one of the guests at the Evans Ranch], an authority on American

Indian culture, the adobe walls were laid by members of the Navajo, Tesuque, and San Ildefonso communities in New Mexico, and the name combined a syllable from each of the three tribes.[55]

One of the Indians involved recalled his experience many years later:

> I went to a place called Indian Hills in 1925 and 1926 with Lucy (his wife.) This Anglo hired us to go up there and make pots, paintings and bead-work ... We went by bus. When were got there ... there was nothing. We had to build the whole pueblo ... We made adobe ourselves mixing the straw and mud with our feet. We plastered the insides with our hands.
>
> The pueblo was in part two stories high. We also built a kiva: no outsiders were allowed in it ... Lucy and I made pots and I painted. We could keep the money we made from selling these, and we were also paid a salary. The man made money by charging admission at the gate of the Village.[56]

Visitors could come from Denver on buses that ran twice a day, watch the Indians demonstrate their crafts, purchase craft items in a little store and buy lunch. Mary Walker wrote about an expedition to the Indian Hills pueblo a few days before Anne Evans' party.

> Miss Katherine [sic] Evans drove our house down to the Indian Hills pueblo, about sixteen miles from the ranch. We met the Everetts there and Father Douglas. When we learned that they were going to give the Eagle Dance in the afternoon, we bought an impromptu lunch at a grocery store in the 'white' village and ate it under the trees on a hillside.

For Aunt Anne's party, "All the families on the ranch turned out in full force ... All the Indians in their bright blankets made a lively picture as they grouped there in the woods."[57] Before dinner,

> they did the basket dance ... and then three of the little boys danced and won everybody's hearts. The biggest of them, who solemnly and earnestly led the dance, chewed gum steadily all through it.

The four Walker girls

> turned waitresses at this point, being dressed in our drill uniforms
> of blue and white (these had been made for the annual Circus
> event, described below) and served mutton stew to the whole party,
> while Mr. Davis acted as head-waiter and commander-in-chief. We
> all sat around in a circle on the ground—at least, everyone but
> ourselves—and ended up with huge pieces of water melon.

After it grew dark, the bonfire was lit.

> As it blazed, the two eagle dancers came out and did their dance.
> The scene was indescribable—weird music, fantastic figures, strange
> light, cool, dark air, and the strong motion of those dancing bodies.
> It was all too beautiful, and unlike anything in the world.[58]

As Ethelind Austin remembered this evening, she too remarked on
the brilliance of the night, and the color and excitement of the
dancers.

Another evening, in 1930, Aunt Anne hosted a Chinese supper.

> She had her house all fixed with Chinese things, and outside and
> in were some seventy-five paper-bag lanterns, all decorated with
> Chinese characters, thanks to Mona and Aunt Sapphira's unflag-
> ging labors for the past few days. Aunt Louise and Mrs. Dodge,
> dressed as gorgeous Chinese princesses, and Aunt Anne as a coolie,
> served the food, and afterwards we played 'Murder.'

A few days later,

> Aunt Anne had a charade party after supper. Most of the ranch
> came, and displayed surprising talent till quite late. The high spot
> was a melodrama with Dina as Our Nell, Mr. Davis as the naïve
> hero, Phelps as the villain and Mr. Richardson as the old father.[59]

For Aunt Louise's French-themed party, Mary Walker came as a
man. In a tuxedo borrowed from Phelps Dodge, a mustache and
goatee fashioned from "some ends of my own hair and glue," and
with a wide red ribbon across her chest, she became le Marquis de
la Facon de Parler. When she arrived with the party from Anne's
house, they found that Wind-in-Woven had been transformed into

the Café aux Vents Entrelaces, with guest Mrs. Richardson, "whose French is flawless and acting superb" as the maitre d'hotel,

> wearing a tail coat much too large for her, and a black wig. Aunt Louise, much be-bosomed and be-capped, was the patronne, Ernestine, and Mr. and Mrs. Davis, a hot-tempered chef and harassed waiter respectively.

The action developed noisily and with much laughter—"the chef swore and threatened and had to be pacified, the customers demanded service and lost patience, the waiters hurried and scurried." Outrageous flirtations led to a duel. Finally, "we adjourned to the other room, and sat about and sang songs, helped by Mr. Dodge with his banjo while Mr. and Mrs. Davis donned suitably elaborate costumes for their skit, written by Milt Gross, a New York humorist, about Mokky and Klippy—Mark Anthony and Cleopatra."[60]

"Blahs"

Afterwards, Mr. and Mrs. Davis sang some of the Ranch's unique inventions called "blahs." These were doggerel verses, usually referring to a recent event or activity in the life of the summer colony, and composed and sung on the pattern of the Whiffenpoof Song. Some of these were written down. One for Aunt Louise's French party went:

> The other night at a gay café
> Blah! Blah! Blah!
> Georges' manners were quite parfait
> Blah! Blah! Blah!
> He'd kiss her hand—Oh he knew how 'twas done
> Then his face it shone like the red summer sun
> He's kissed, not Louise, but the fat patronne,
> Blah! Blah! Blah!

On several occasions, Walker described how she and other youngsters were tutored in the art of writing blahs by Mr. Davis.

The Circus

Two special annual events, in which all the households and their guests invested much time and effort, were the Circus or Gymkhana,

Circus Chariot, Courtesy Margaret E. Hayden

and the Scavenger or Treasure Hunt. Both were essentially horseback-riding exercises, though many additional games and rituals were added to the Circus.

It became a tradition to hold this Circus on August 11, the birthday of Peggy Davis (later Peg Hayden). Mary Walker chronicled the event for the years 1927 and 1930 in her diaries. A few days after the arrival of the four sisters in 1927, she wrote,

> Mrs. Davis came over (to Anne Evans' house) to talk about plans for the circus ... Everyone is giving some kind of stunt, and Peggy and David are going to be in costume.[61]

For the next few days, the girls

> practiced the drill that the four of us are going to do in the circus ... In the afternoon, we shut ourselves in our rooms and sewed on the banners which we are going to carry in the drill and unfurl at the last minute. It's our one surprise.[62]

That evening, she noted, "The whole community—in other words all the ranch families—had a barbecue, for which Mr. Davis roasted a whole side of lamb most deliciously."[63] The next day,

> It rained all day, but in spite of it, we put on our slickers and diligently practiced our drill ... In the afternoon we sewed and painted our banners with surprisingly good results.

On August 10,

> This morning we practiced our drill diligently, and swore at each other with almost equal diligence,
>> 'Rhoda, make Cinderella come up!'
>> 'Dina, you *always* come too far up!'
>> 'You're supposed to keep even with me, you know!'
>> 'But, Mary, you have a much faster horse!'
>> 'Oh, shut up, and let me ride for myself!'
> And so forth ...

On August 11 was,

the great and important day of the circus, and no one for a minute was occupied with anything else. All morning we drilled and groomed and braided our horses' manes and tails with blue and white ribbons (Aunt Anne's colors are blue and white). We had made blue and silver brow-bands for all our bridles, and our uniform was all planned out in the same color scheme—

Challis Walker Training Horse for Circus Performance, Courtesy Margaret E. Hayden

white shirts, broad blue bands over one shoulder, blue and white bands on our hair, and all wearing silver belts ...[64]

At 2:30 we assembled to go to the ring, all dressed alike, including Mona and Miss Wallace, and Aunt Anne carrying a handsome white banner with a blue figure on it.

Just as they met up with the rest of the circus participants, it began to rain heavily, and

we all took refuge under Aunt Anne's sheds. We were a very gay group. Every house wore its own colors as conspicuously as possible— all the Everetts, for instance, wore red coats, but no group looked as well as ours, if I do say so. Mr. Davis, encrusted with gold braid, with a tall hat and a yellow and green cockade, was a wonderful ring master.

The rain let up and the procession to the ring in the meadow formed, led by Peggy Davis celebrating her ninth birthday.

... then came the rest of us with our banners and gay colors, making the prettiest cavalcade I've ever seen outside of a medieval painting. We began with a parade around the ring, with each family in turn dropping out to watch the others.

The group from Aunt Anne's house was first on the program.

The others tied their horses and formed an audience, and Mr. Davis introduced us as 'the four Incomparable Walker Sisters, who will now give you the drill they have performed before all the crowned heads of Europe.'

The Circus Knight, Courtesy
Margaret E. Hayden

It went well, including the "surprise" ending,

that we had been working on for days and that everyone knew about. After we had charged in close formation down the field, we unfurled our banners and galloped around the ring, holding them high above our heads.

This act was followed by

Various stunts ... Johnny Evans and Bobby Taylor rode round the ring in the red bug, with costumes that covered themselves and gave the appearance of two people sitting backwards with their legs dragging behind. The legs (overalls stuffed with hay) fell off at one point, and were picked up the next time around ... Bobby Davis did a skit as a clown, Mrs. Davis dressed up as 'Why Men Leave Home'—some sort of 'Gay Nineties' costume, Ethelind [Elbert] and Alice [Evans] danced as what Mr. Davis called Troglodytes [in] an ingenious costume with a broomstick for arms, and collars around their waistlines. Their hands, crossed over their heads, made wiggly ears, and they danced to a victrola.

Then came games—"a potato race for the youngsters where they galloped around the ring holding a potato in a wooden spoon," a two-team competition for older participants "where they speared potatoes out of a wooden bucket and ran back to drop them in boxes," and finally a costume race "which held for me the one blot to the afternoon." Mary twice fell off her horse while dismounting to "put on the horrible garments," which "did awful things to my opinion of myself and my riding ... Oh, I was *mad*! ... but I tried to make a joke of it. If I don't know how to ride, at least I know how to fall off." Nevertheless, "The circus drew to a glorious close and we all had a marvelous time. I'll always remember the gay pageantry of it."[65]

In the summer of 1930, the Walker sisters followed a similar routine, but with a different theme which involved rigging up "Aunt Anne's express cart as a covered wagon" and hunting for a

"Gentle Cow who was to act as our team of oxen ..." They were told that there was such a creature on the ranch but that

she was turned out in the little Bear pasture which runs up to Mount Evans ... we would know her imme-diately because she was 'black and white, like a magpie,' and would be the only cow in the herd that we could walk right up to.

Costumed Horse in Circus Performance, Courtesy Margaret E. Hayden

Fortunately, they found the cow close to the nearest gate

and easily put her halter on. She was a little timid, so Dina led her on foot, Ethelind rode behind to remind her to keep moving ... and I kept at a safe distance on the impatient [horse] Dingle.

After a few minutes,

the rain and hail began to come down and worked up to terrific violence. All of us were, for one reason or another, unable to put on our slickers, and so we came home thoroughly drenched—but we got our cow! So we all disrobed and dried in front of Aunt Anne's fire ... After lunch we drilled again.

Circus day started with a morning of continuous rain.

Just before lunch Aunt Anne sent me dashing over to the Davises to find out their plans ... They were counting on having the circus at any cost ... at length some of us assembled in the barn and watched the rain. To our surprise it stopped toward three, and after some hurried collecting of ranch folk, the procession was formed and the circus was under way.[66]

The circus that year was shorter than usual, due to the rain delay, but included drills on horseback, stunts and skits, including the one from Aunt Anne's house which they called, "Early Settlers in Colorado or How Bear Creek got its Name."

'It was brief, but our costumes and properties were quite wonderful, and the skit made a hit.' Games followed—a potato race, 'an egg tossing contest, messy but amusing, and tilting for rings. And a happy afternoon was over ...'

Scavenger Hunt

The Scavenger or Treasure Hunt usually came near the end of the summer. To Mary Walker, her first experience in 1927

> was even more fun than I thought it would be. We all assembled in front of the Everetts' house and were paired off—Ethelind and I together. Then they gave the first clue, which we opened feverishly.

The hunt involved riding from one location to another, following clues and making a guess at each successive destination. "Never have I ridden so hard and so fast in my life! We simply *tore.*" Hours were wasted on false leads. After a clue led back to Aunt Anne's, to which "the whole troop galloped at top speed," they were told to stop for the day and go over to the Davises for supper. There Mr. Davis cooked sausages and scrambled eggs, over two small fires, for all the treasure hunters. The grown-ups had dinner at the Everetts and then came over to join the gathering at the Davis's home, where a large bonfire was lit.

> It was the biggest assemblage we've had at any party so far, with all the Dodges, all the Everetts, all Aunt Anne's household ... Later we went into the house for coffee, and the Blahs were sung by Mr. Davis with great success.

Perhaps this was one of that evening's Blahs:

> This scavenger hunt is a strange kind of dance
> Blah! Blah! Blah
> Live trout in our buckets, pismires in our pants
> Blah! Blah! Blah!
> Deebray from the dump, gravestones and horseflies –
> While searching for these we are dodging cow-pies—
> No wonder the horses gave us all a wild glance
> Blah! Blah! Blah!

The Ranch this summer no danger lacks –
Blah! Blah! Blah!
From fast charging cow elks to coyote packs—
Blah! Blah! Blah!
Porcupine quills and soupcon of bear,
Bad enough to give everyone a scare;
Gosh—the only safe ride is from here to Jack's!
Blah! Blah! Blah!

The treasure hunt was concluded the next morning, when "the treasure hunters assembled again at Aunt Anne's, and set to work to find the next clue. It was up on her terrace, hidden in a chink in the wall." After guessing this one right, "the next clue led to the treasure, and we went wrong for the first time—a fatal mistake which cost us the treasure." The 1930 hunt proved more challenging, with some clues proving impossible for the whole group, and everyone cold and tired and wet from "two terrific downpours in the middle of the day, when we were pelted with hailstones the size of mothballs."[67] At 6:30 in the evening, the group quit without finding the final clue, although "Bobby and Challis found the treasure." In the evening, over supper at the Dodges, they

> went through the whole treasure hunt, reading out the clues that none of us had seen. There were appropriate remarks, humorous and otherwise. Afterwards we sat around the fire and talked, and of course sang.

A Medley of Summer Guests

Much of the richness of the summer ranch experience owed to the character and variety of guests staying at the various households or visiting from their own mountain summer retreats. Mary Walker mentions a few of Anne Evans' house guests in her diaries.

> Miss Foot arrived today as a fellow guest. She is 75, has grey bobbed hair, a sharp old face, wears grim, bleak tailored suits and is bright and spritely, and very gay and funny. She was full of stories and recollections, and tales of her various studies, especially that of the cootie in Paris during the war.[68]

Then there was a Miss Whately, a Member of Parliament from England.

> I quite fell for her. She's a lively and forceful lady, very dignified, very English, and very entertaining. She loves to talk, but fortunately she always seems to have something to say.

In 1930, in addition to Mary Kent Wallace, who seemed to be at Anne's home much of the summer, there was also the artist Elisabeth Spalding, known for some reason as Aunt Sapphira, who spent a good deal of the time out painting. Walker described her as "a bright, sweet person, full of fun and enthusiasm."[69]

How much Anne Evans' summer visitors enjoyed her unique hospitality is summed up in a letter from John Rosborough:

> Everyone there in the home with you—Miss Wallace, Miss Hurlburt, the young man and that culinary artist in the kitchen—like a beautiful chord in music—all in tune! And the House—a place filled with things beautiful and thoughts that elevate living. We shall never forget yesterday.[70]

On August 3, Walker wrote, "the Jeancons and the Proctors came to lunch. Later many people came over and Mr. Jeancon read his paper on Santa Clara Indians." Walker noted mischievously "Aunt Louise counted five people who went to sleep" during this reading. Jeancon, both a musician and a scientist, was eulogized in 1936 as "one of the foremost authorities on the Indians of the southwest."[71] He worked in the bureau of ethnology at the Smithsonian institution before coming to head up the Colorado State Museum from 1921 to 1927, and "was well-known as a writer and lecturer on Indian subjects." Among those who came to the Jeancon reading were Evergreen neighbors—the Douglases, junior and senior, and some of the Cranmer household. Walker noted, "Eric and Freda [Douglas] were the bitter enders. I thought they'd never go home!"

Another summer neighbor who spent much time with the members of the Evans Ranch summer colony was Judge J. Foster Symes. Walker mentions his participation, along with that of his daughter, Virginia, in a number of events, including the Circus. In 1922, at the age of 44, Symes had become the youngest United States District Judge in the Federal service. Born in Denver in 1878, he graduated from Yale and Columbia Law School, served in the infantry in World Ward I and returned to Denver to continue practicing law. As a federal judge, Symes became an authority on patent law and, at a crucial time, supervised the reorganization of the Denver and Rio Grande Western Railroad.

A Party in Denver and the End of Another Ranch Summer

There was a general reluctance on the part of the summer residents to leave the Ranch for any reason, and especial resistance to going down into the summer heat of Denver. But some of the adults had to return from time to time—Walker notes on several occasions that Anne Evans had left to escort house guests on their way home, or to meet other commitments. Mary Walker's sisters occasionally left for visits in town, with their mother or with members of the John Evans family. Mary was the most resistant, but she did describe leaving for one special occasion, a grand party on August 20, 1930, at the Hilltop home of John and Gladys Evans to celebrate the engagement of Alice Evans to Hudson Moore Jr.

> When we struck Denver and its heat, I wilted like a flower. I left Mona and Ethelind at Daniels and Fisher, hurried to the John Evanses' to collect two evening coats, back to pick them up, and finally to Aunt Anne's house [1310 Bannock] and had tea with her and Katherine. [sic]

The party, Walker wrote, "was lovely—a huge dinner dance with tables in the dining room and all around the ball room." Anne Evans' paper bag lanterns were transported down from her mountain home for the occasion and, along with Japanese lanterns, lighted

> all the gardens and terraces ... and the whole effect was stunning. The evening was clear and warm and spicy, all the people were nice, the music was good and the floor was excellent—what more can one ask?

Later, she and Ethelind were taken back to Anne Evans' home "where we lay on my bed and talked till four o'clock." The following day, Katharine Evans drove Aunt Anne and Mary to lunch at the Cosmopolitan Hotel with Mona Walker and other friends. "I went afterwards to Chappell House with Aunt Anne, and she showed me all around." But city offerings were nothing compared to life on the ranch. "Oh, it was good to get back!" When the time came to leave for home, Walker wrote, "Our last night here, and I can hardly bear it!"

With such a rich variety of activities, and freedom to enjoy them, it is no wonder that the successive generations of Evanses, Elberts, Lunts, and Dodges, and their guests valued their golden summers on the Evans Ranch so highly. The next addition to the texture of their lives in the mountains would be the inauguration of a summer drama season at the restored Opera House in Central City. The story of that unique accomplishment, and Anne Evans' leading role in it, is the subject of the last chapter in this biography. First, however, it is time to tell the "boom and bust" story of the development of the University of Denver, to which many references have already been made—for the tale of Central City is bound up with the fortunes of Denver University.

22

The Evans/Denver University Connections

He (Governor Evans) was president of the D.U. Board of Trustees until his death in 1897 ... Since that time, the name of Evans has continue to be linked closely with the development of D.U. ... William G. Evans, son of the governor, served as president of the board of trustees for almost a decade, until he was succeeded by his son John Evans, a Denver banker, who headed the board until 1943. The third John Evans, also a Denver business man, is now a member of the D.U. board, carrying on the tradition of service to the university in the fourth generation. Miss Anne Evans, daughter of the founder and one of Colorado's outstanding women, played a prominent role in the university's development as well as in Denver cultural activities generally.
—D.U. Press Release regarding establishment of
Evans Award, © 1955

Some of the story of the Evans family's involvement in the development of the University of Denver has been told in earlier parts of this book. This chapter will amplify these associations, outline the University's development up to the end of Anne Evans' life in 1941, and detail her own connections with DU.

Of all the institutions which Governor John Evans helped to found during his long and productive lifetime, the one for which he had the most direct, and at times virtually the sole, responsibility was the University of Denver. He had it in mind when he first arrived in Colorado in 1862, gathered support to get it started, nurtured its potential when it foundered, and played a leading role in its development until his death. His legacy of leadership passed down to his son, grandson and great grandson. His daughter, Anne, served DU in the cultural areas in which she had both interest and expertise, service that would be honored by the University.

The Colorado Seminary

On July 18, 1862, Governor Evans presented his message to the Territorial Legislature, including recommendations about education. Within a few days, the legislature introduced a bill "to enable trustees of colleges, universities and other institutions, societies and companies to become bodies corporate." It was passed, and signed into law by Governor Evans.

In his single-minded drive to found a private, Methodist-sponsored institution along the same lines as Northwestern University, Evans realized he needed "a capable fiscal agent who would perform the same functions as Orrington Lunt had … capably carried out in the development of Northwestern."[1] He settled on the Rev. O. A. Willard, who had been called by the Kansas Conference of the Methodist Episcopal Church "to come to Denver in October, 1862, to take charge of the small Methodist Church, to build it up and take a hand in whatever educational opportunities there were to be exploited."[2] A small board of Trustees was formed, and enlarged the following year to include twenty-five of the most influential citizens of Denver. Their task was to move forward with plans for a building and to raise the necessary funds. Governor Evans purchased six lots at the corner of "E" (later 14th) Street and Arapahoe, across from his own home, to be given to the Seminary. Construction began in July, 1863,[3] with the cost something over $6,000. The building went ahead, and was substantially completed by October, 1863, in spite of the city's major setback in the disastrous fire of April 19, 1863, and before an agreement had been reached on the new institution's name and exact mission.

Although everyone agreed that the eventual goal was to found an institute of higher learning, it grew obvious that college preparatory classes would have to be offered initially. William Byers' preference was for the name Denver University, but a consensus favoring Colorado Seminary was reached. There arose considerable discussion as to whether one more denominational school was needed, in view of the fact that the Episcopalians and the Roman Catholics were already making plans to sponsor religious educational institutions. Rev. Willard, however, countered with the persuasive argument that, even though only ten of the Trustees were Methodists, the Seminary's best chances of survival were by attaching it to the Methodist Conference, an organization already well-established in the community. More-over, more than three-fifths of the entire funds raised for the venture had come from Methodists, who had demonstrated their support for the Seminary by postponing the building of a church and donating money raised for that purpose to the Seminary coffers.

An act of the Legislature officially incorporated the Colorado Seminary on March 5, 1864, naming twenty-eight individuals as the initial Trustees of the institution. The list was headed by John Evans and included Samuel H. Elbert, W. N. Byers, D. H. Moffat, J. M. Chivington, Amos Steck (then Mayor of Denver), J. B. Chaffee, O. A. Willard, and W. A. H. Loveland. The Charter mandated that "No test of religious faith shall ever be applied as a condition of admission into said Seminary." Another clause, which Evans insisted upon, based on his previous experience with private institutions of higher learning, provided that "Such property as may be necessary for carrying out the design of the Seminary in the best manner, while used exclusively for such purposes, shall be free from all taxation." This provision became invaluable in the long struggle of the institu-tion to survive financially. Though the term Seminary included the intention of training students for the ministry, it was by no means limited to this function. Seminary was used in the generic sense of "a place of education": the Charter noted that the Trustees "shall have full power to confer all degrees and emoluments customary to be given by similar institutions." At its first meeting, the board of trustees elected Amos Steck, President; Samuel Elbert, Vice-President; D. H. Moffat, Treasurer; and William Byers, Secretary. Evans was elected to the executive committee.

Full of expansive optimism for the new school, Governor Evans predicted that, for young scholars, it would soon "make a journey to the States not only unnecessary but unpopular."[4] The Seminary opened in November, 1864, with a President and two faculty mem-bers. By December it had enrolled about fifty students, no mean feat in view of the fact that the number of schools in the area was increasing. "By the time the Seminary opened there were some eleven schools to which parents could send their children, though some of these were small and had but a short life."[5] One of the students in the classical curriculum of the new Seminary was the Evans' oldest son, Willie. Many years later, in 1921, when he had inherited the mantle of his father as President of the Board of Trustees of Denver University, William G. Evans recalled,

Though I am not listed among the members of the Denver University Alumni Association, I am not sure but that I am entitled to be a member. Something more than fifty years ago I attended school in the Colorado Seminary, when the institution first began its existence ... In that long ago it seemed a strange thing to be setting up a school here to teach Latin and Greek. Denver was more than five hundred miles from a railroad. There were about four thousand people, drawn by the gold excitement. It was away out on the far border of the Great American Desert.[6]

The Seminary Fails to Thrive in Denver's Darkest Days

The first incarnation of the Colorado Seminary lasted only three or four years, during which time it went through four Presidents. The 1860s, as described earlier, were years of great hardship in Denver. "The middle sixties were the darkest years in Denver's history."[7] It seemed entirely possible that Denver was on track to becoming just one more ghost town.

The failure of the infant Colorado Seminary to thrive in such circumstances was understandable, especially when combined with the lack of interest, on the part of most of the population, in anything more than the most elementary schooling for their children. There was nothing remarkable about the closing of the Colorado Seminary; it was "a common frontier experience ... An analysis of colleges founded before the Civil War shows ... an average mortality of 81 percent."[8] What was surprising was the preservation of its legal entity and building, and the reopening in 1880.

The University of Denver

The transformation of Denver's fortunes began with the persistence of Governor Evans, ably supported by citizens like William Byers, David Moffat and Samuel Elbert, in forging a connection with the transcontinental railroad by 1870. The major new discoveries of silver in Leadville in 1879 brought immense wealth to Denver. The 1880 Census showed an increase in Denver's population to almost 40,000. Before the Colorado Seminary closed in 1867, Governor Evans, aided by Samuel Elbert and other trustees, took on the role of securing title to the building and grounds. By 1874, Evans "had acquired sole title to the building and lots, but there was a $5,000 mortgage on the property."[9]

Colorado Seminary located in downtown Denver at 14th and Arapahoe Streets across from Gov. John Evans house. Denver Public Library Western History Collections

In June of 1879, Evans' offered to return the property to the Methodist Conference, on the condition that they re-open the school. The offer was accepted. A new board of trustees was appointed, with the understanding that the institution's name would be changed to the University of Denver. Evans was elected president. A little research revealed that a new institution could not obtain tax-exempt status from the Legislature, and so a rather awkward but necessary arrangement emerged. The University of Denver was incorporated in 1880 as the degree-granting body, but all property was held in the name of the Colorado Seminary. Evans donated the Seminary property back to the institution and gave an additional $3,000 to equip science laboratories. A third story was added to the original building, as well as a four-story addition of a dormitory wing.[10] The building was not yet completed when the new University opened in October, 1880, with an enrollment of some fifty students. Before the end of the first year, this had increased to one hundred and fifty.

By this time a home-grown supply of high school graduates became available. Boulder High School graduated its first class in 1876; the Denver East High School followed in 1877. Other institutions of higher learning also competed for students. Congregationalists had opened the Colorado College in 1874, closed for six years and reopened in January of 1880. The Colorado School of Mines, building on the foundation of an Episcopalian School in Golden, had opened in 1874. The University of Colorado, authorized by the Territorial Legislature in 1861, finally opened in September of 1877.

The University's Programs

The University of Denver opened with a College of Liberal Arts, a College of Music, and a College of Fine Arts. The Seminary consisted of a Collegiate Preparatory Department and a Junior Preparatory Department.[11] By 1881, an important new University department had been added—a medical school. This was the first of a bewildering variety of new academic and professional departments opened up by the University in its almost 130 years of existence. Many of them ended quite abruptly. They were started in good faith as the University constantly adjusted its mission to meet changing times. The closures were predominantly for financial reasons, but sometimes because it seemed more feasible for a state-supported institution like the University of Colorado to offer education in a specific area.

In 1911, the CU Medical School absorbed its DU rival, with the result that "a strong school replaced two comparatively weak ones."[12]

Denver University kept the college preparatory school open for some years, and at another time it operated a forerunner of the community college.

Contributions of Margaret Evans to Denver University

It is difficult to trace the wayward fortunes of art courses in the early days of Denver University. Chancellor Duncan in 1939 stated confidently that the University of Denver opened in 1880 with a College of Liberal Arts, A College of Fine Arts and a College of Music.[13] Margaret Evans, Governor Evans' wife, took a great interest in the Art Department. From 1885 to 1892 she offered annual student prizes "and her gifts of well-selected plaster casts of famous works of art formed the nucleus of their teaching collection."[14] The 1882–83 "Circular of Information of the University of Denver and the Colorado Seminary" (DU Archives) listed a College of Fine Arts, with Ida DeSteiguer serving as Dean and teaching courses in Drawing and Painting, and one other faculty member offering Woodcarving and Designing. The circular includes a short article on the requirements to earn a Bachelor of Painting degree through the courses offered by the Fine Arts Department. Illustrated with a sketch of "The Art Department—Studio," the article announces that the studio is supplied with "designs and antique casts," and has added other features that promote the efficiency of this very popular and flourishing department of the University. The gift of "a furnace for burning decorated China" by Mrs. Gov. Evans and a Mrs. Frank Church is acknowledged.

In their monumental *History of Colorado* published in 1927, James Baker and LeRoy Hafen wrote:

> In 1892, the Denver School of Fine Arts (The Art Department of the University of Denver) was given exclusive use of the old University building at 1330 Arapahoe Street ... *The Prospectus for 1892–3* stated that the department sought to instruct in the fine arts and establish a museum. Mrs. John Evans ... was the patron spirit. The faculty included Preston Powers, sculpture; Ida De Steigeur, drawing, life and casts; George W. Platt, painting; and John Henderson, design and wood carving.[15]

The 1892 reorganization created a Board of Control for the Fine Arts Department, with Margaret Evans serving as President.

According to Elisabeth Spalding, the generosity of Governor and Margaret Evans "equipped the art school for the University."[16] Ida De Steiguer's name continued to appear in the bulletins through 1893 and then disappeared. The 1892–3 Bulletin listed "Annie" Evans as a Special Student in the Art Department, taking classes in Painting and Drawing. Special students were defined as those who "are unable to meet the entrance requirement of the School" but are "permitted to register for such courses as their previous training qualifies them to undertake."[17] It seems possible that Anne Evans had some instruction from Preston Powers during this year. Elisabeth Spalding, close to the art situation in Denver at the time, wrote, "Preston Powers modeled and taught all one year in Denver and gave a real impetus to art." At the time of the formation of the Artists' Club, forerunner of the Denver Art Museum, in 1893,[18] Margaret Evans was still President of the DU Art Department's Board of Control. She was thus able to secure the use of the Fine Arts building for the new group's first art exhibition.

In 1884, Margaret Evans headed a committee of twenty women to raise $30,000 to establish the Woman's Chair of Belles Lettres at the University of Denver. Mary Lowe Dickinson was the first incumbent from 1888–91. In 1891, Gov. Evans gave the University property valued at $100,000 to add to the endowment of the president's chair and the Woman's Chair, reserving to his wife the right to name the Woman's Chair. She requested that it be called the Mary Lowe Dickinson Chair of Belles Lettres. It was occupied by three women before the title lapsed in 1923. Ida Kruse McFarlane, later Anne Evans' close associate in the creation of the Central City Festival, was the last of the three, holding the chair from 1910–1923.

Margaret also served for a number of years on the Board of Trustees of the Colorado Seminary/University of Denver. Some of the early records are difficult to locate, but it seems clear from available University Catalogues that she served at least from 1890 to 1900.

University Park Campus

The creation of a new campus for the University, way out south on the far fringes of the city, was precipitated by the prospect of a large gift—promised in 1884, then withdrawn—from Elizabeth Iliff Warren. A woman of great energy and a devoted Methodist, Warren had come from Canada to Denver in 1868. Here she met, and in 1870 married, widower John Wesley Iliff, popularly known as the Cattle King of the West. He died young and unexpectedly in 1878, leaving his fortune in cattle and real estate to his wife and son. Five years later, Elizabeth Iliff married Henry White Warren, the first resident Methodist Episcopal Bishop of Colorado, in the little Evans Memorial Chapel built by Governor Evans in memory of his daughter, Josephine.

Bishop Warren became one of the most effective and vigorous supporters of Denver University in its early years, sharing "in the burden of raising money and erecting buildings for the university."[19] Bishop and Mrs. Warren were influential community benefactors in Denver.

The gift that Elizabeth Iliff Warren offered to the Trustees of Denver University in 1884 would be used to build a School of Theology. She withdrew the gift later in the year, believing that the board had not met her conditions. The trustees, however, did proceed to act on one of her stipulations—that they should look for a permanent home for the University away from the increasing noise and smoke of downtown Denver.

A committee headed by John Evans investigated three sites in 1885, finally settling on the one offered by a colorful character named Rufus "Potato" Clark. Connecticut-born Clark had an adventurous life on whaling ships before coming to Colorado in 1859 and growing potatoes along the Platte River. He earned his nickname "Potato" after raking in $30,000 for one crop. After reaching a low point of his life, he confessed to being "a confirmed drunkard, a slave to drink, so deep in the mire of sin and drink I never cherished a hope of getting out."[20] Then he underwent a sudden conversion, "and began a life of prayer and service to his church and community."[21]

A group headed by Clark offered Denver University 150 acres of land, with water rights on most of them, situated three miles to the south east of Denver's then city limits at Alameda Avenue. The gift came with three conditions. By May, 1886, 200 acres adjacent to the university site had to be platted as a town site, with lots, streets and blocks. Within a year, the University had to plant 1,000 trees along the streets and in new parks on the site. The Board of Trustees began immediately to raise funds and make plans to build on the new campus.

The University Park Colony soon began to take shape. The east-west avenues were named for Evans, Methodist Bishops Asbury and Warren, and John Wesley Iliff. Initially the north-south streets were numbered, except for University, which ran along the eastern border of the proposed campus. Although already 76 years old, John Evans took up the task of promoting the new development with energy and imagination. Rail and tramway connections to the new residential area were developed. A pair of lots cost $300–$400, depending on location.

Evans brought prospective buyers out on the railway and took them to the highest point on the campus, where he extolled the benefits of living in the area. He called it a "superbly healthy location," where "the dominant controlling idea shall be conscience and culture, the two essential elements of a great civilization." Yet sales were slow. It took a great deal of imagination to see this empty, inhospitable prairie land as a desirable residential community. The first two houses in the area were built by a trustee and by the Warrens. To encourage development John Evans built a Sunday School, a post office, and a store at Milwaukee and Evans, which still stands today.

Roeschlaub Designs "Old Main"

The cornerstone for the first campus building, University Hall, was laid on April 3, 1890. Designed by architect Robert S. Roeschlaub, the Hall used the same Castle Rock rhyolite stone he had selected for Trinity Methodist Church in downtown Denver. With the new building under construction, the trustees made a concerted effort to put the University on a better financial footing. "In January, 1891, a drive to collect $100,000 in contributions was announced. Evans pledged $25,000 as a starter."[22] In April, Evans donated some downtown property to the University. This brought his total donations to the University of Denver to more than $130,000. University Hall, now known as "Old Main," was completed in 1892. It provided for offices for the chancellor and other administrators, a chapel on the ground floor, lecture halls and laboratories on the second and third floors, and "parlors for entertainment and meeting rooms for the two Greek letter groups."[23] The building and furnishings cost $80,000 which, even with the 1891 drive for funds, still left the University in debt. For several years it was the school's only campus building.

Old Main, the first building on the Denver University Campus designed by Robert Roeschlaub, 1890. Courtesy History Colorado

Iliff School of Theology

In 1892, the Iliff School of Theology finally made its appearance to the south of University Hall. It was built with a gift of $50,000 from William Seward Iliff, Mrs. Warren's stepson. After an auspicious start, it too began to suffer from a financial shortfall. As the debts of Denver University mounted, the Iliff School tried to separate its financial fortunes from the University in an effort to protect its own investments. In 1900, Elizabeth Warren made the decision to close the Iliff School "temporarily." It did not reopen until 1910, and then under private ownership, having been legally separated from Denver University in 1903.

Brief Period of Prosperity

The first few years of the 1890s were years of optimistic expansion of curriculum and programs and of increased student enrollment. The University "had ten departments, several graduate programs, and assets of one million dollars, largely in pledges backed by real estate in the University Park."[24] For many years to come, the University also maintained departments in downtown Denver in a variety of locations.

The Depression of 1893

In spite of its optimistic paper assets, the University remained quite heavily in debt, and the situation materially worsened as a result of the Silver Panic of 1893 and its long aftermath.[25] William Fraser McDowell, DU's energetic Chancellor from 1890–1899, later reminisced about this difficult period, "It was not a sudden storm that came and went, leaving devastation in its wake. It was sudden enough in its coming, but showed no haste in its departing. The University shared the experience of individuals and institutions."[26] While this depression still had the University fortunes in its grip, John Evans, who had rescued it so many times from looming catastrophe, became incapacitated. He died in 1897, still nominally Chairman of the Board of Trustees.

The debt mounting, faculty salaries went unpaid and lawsuits were filed threatening to foreclose on mortgages. McDowell, who later said, "I marvel that we did not all go to pieces," knew that he had done all he could, resigning in mid-1899. The search for a new Chancellor willing and able to take on the immense challenge of rescuing an institution on the brink of collapse led to a man who had already made great contributions to the Methodist cause in Denver.

Buchtel Becomes Chancellor

Henry Augustus Buchtel came to Denver in 1884 to be at the bedside of his seriously ill brother. A minister, Buchtel took time out to preach a few sermons in the Evans Chapel, next to Grace Methodist Church. His intense, lyrical sermons drew large crowds. John Evans and other Methodist leaders in Denver tried to persuade him to stay in Denver, but he chose to serve out his term at a church in Indiana. A few years later, Bishop Warren succeeded in bringing him back to Colorado. He took over the ministry at the old Lawrence Street Church and shepherded its congregation through the process of building the impressive, and expensive, new church, Trinity Methodist, at 18th and Broadway. Buchtel proved to be both an inspiring pastor and an able fund-raiser. He served for five years at Trinity before moving on to pastorates in Indiana, New York and New Jersey.

The persuasive Bishop Warren traveled to East Orange, New Jersey, to ask Buchtel "to have the spirit of sacrifice in sufficient measure to come and get under our load."[27] Accepting the offer to lead Denver University meant a decrease in salary for Buchtel and limited educational opportunities for his four children. Yet he came back to Denver in 1900 full of confidence

> that with great sacrifice and determination his vision of a sig-
> nificantly improved campus and further development of a solid
> liberal arts curriculum would prevail. From the beginning he
> looked toward a library building, a science hall, and a chapel of
> commanding proportions. He was convinced that money could
> be secured for them. The professional schools were almost inde-
> pendent on the downtown campus; the focus of development would
> be at University Park ... Here should be the 'Harvard of the West.'[28]

Buchtel began an astonishing round of visits to virtually every community in Colorado—forty-five in his first year—preaching or lecturing on topics from "Success" to "Practical Values of the Christian Faith," even giving poetry readings. In some towns he came away with pledges for $200, from others amounts as much as $10,000.

The William Evans/Henry Buchtel Partnership

In all of his efforts, Buchtel had the invaluable support and help of many benefactors, including the Methodist churches of Colorado, Bishop and Mrs. Warren and, most notably, John Evans' oldest son, William. Elected to the Board of Trustees in January of 1902, William Evans soon became a staunch ally and personal friend to Buchtel.

"With the entrance of William G. Evans on the scene, things began to change," according to Buchtel's biographer.[29] As we have seen, William Evans was by this time a prominent and successful businessman in Denver, as well as a powerful behind-the-scenes figure in the Republican Party. He also proved to be a devoted and generous supporter of Denver University. Evans became President of the Board of Trustees in 1905 and continued to serve in that capacity—even after his serious breakdown in 1913, when he resigned from all of his other official commitments—until his death in 1924. As Buchtel wrote to Evans, commenting on their success as a team in appealing to the business community, "You can meet people I have no ways of knowing." By 1903, the last mortgage was paid off, and Buchtel's energies could be directed towards building up the faculty, strengthening the curriculum and planning new buildings.

Throughout his twenty-year term as Chancellor, Buchtel relied on Evans' steady support, both financially and in terms of backing his policies. This is clear from the extensive correspondence between them and from the records of Trustee meetings.

Andrew Carnegie offered to give $30,000 for a library building provided that the University could match his contribution. The money was raised in two years and the building completed in 1909. In January of that year, planning started for a science building. Buchtel again approached Carnegie, who offered the sum of $50,000, subject to a match to be raised by the University. Pledges were secured from five individuals, including Evans, who gave $15,000.

Buchtel Becomes Governor of Colorado

What historian Breck described as "An interesting interlude in the affairs of the University"[30] (a considerable understatement) occurred in 1906, when Buchtel ran for election as the Governor of Colorado and won. The campaign unleashed quite a barrage of accusations in some sections of the press that Evans, the effective head of the Republican Party at the time, had coerced Buchtel into running. As Governor, the critics charged, Buchtel would act in the interests of Denver University, the Denver Tramway Company, and the other corporate monopolies perceived to be running Denver and Colorado. "Evans owns the university, the University owns Buchtel, and will you please tell me who owns the state if Buchtel should happen to be elected governor?" wrote the *Boulder Daily Camera*.[31]

Buchtel's entry into politics and his affiliation with William Evans also brought him into collision with Judge Ben Lindsey, Denver's fiery "muckraker" and champion of the city's poor and under-privileged. Lindsey publicly accused Buchtel and Evans of trying to corrupt him by giving him an honorary degree. Buchtel's reply was printed in a four-page leaflet, dated January 10, 1910.

> It seems from reading his (Judge Lindsey's) story that everybody he meets is wishing to corrupt him. My experience is directly the opposite. I accepted the nomination for Governor of Colorado on the 20th of September in 1906. From that day until I retired on the 12th of January 1909, no one ever proposed to me, directly or indirectly, that I should do anything out of harmony with my character as a minister and the head of a great Christian school.

Lindsey's reply, with which the exchange closed, "was that the Chancellor was an innocent simpleton with infinite capacity for self-delusion."[32] In the early 1900s the term of office for Colorado Governors was two years. Buchtel served his term as Governor, and continuing to serve as Denver University Chancellor, all while still living in his modest home at South Columbine and Evans.

Scriptures vs. Evolution

One other controversy during Buchtel's term as Chancellor, in which both Evans, as President of the Board of Trustees, and Buchtel were involved, occurred over the strangely familiar issue of Evolution and the Bible. In 1919 it was reported that the hierarchy of the Presbyterian Church in Denver objected to the failure of the Iliff School of Theology and the Department of Religion and Philosophy at Denver University to uphold the authority of Scriptures; they were teaching "the advanced theory of evolution." Buchtel defended the departments, asserting that the professors were competent scholars and teachers. Evans, having experienced much distortion in the press when he gave interviews, asked that he "be quoted in his own exact words." The *Express* printed them:[33]

> I regret most sincerely the attack published yesterday ... upon our Denver University. I feel it deserves the most helpful and kindly support, particularly from Denver people to whom its greatest service is rendered. There has been built up at Denver University

a most valuable institution, and to do it has required such great struggle and sacrifices as only the expanding and inestimable value of such an institution could warrant. Inquiry about the already long list of graduates ... men and women, noting their generally fine spirit and activities and prominence in the professions ... proves its great value.

I think I had best leave theological discussions ... to Chancellor Buchtel ... I have no doubt, myself, the Presbyterian route leads straight to heaven. Restrictions on travel that way make more roads necessary for the multitude.[34]

End of the Buchtel Era

Looking at where the university stood in 1920, compared with 1900 when Buchtel became Chancellor and Evans joined the Board of Trustees, the Buchtel-Evans team had much to celebrate. From one heavily-mortgaged building, Old Main, the University Park campus had expanded to six debt-free structures including the Library, Science Hall, the Chapel—later named Buchtel Memorial Chapel— given by the Methodist Conference Churches, a gymnasium paid for by alumni, and a small History Building. The student body had expanded from just over 550 to almost 2800, and the number of course offerings grew from 185 to 385. In addition to Schools of Law, Pharmacy, and Dentistry, DU opened a Business School (officially named the School of Commerce, Accounts and Finance), and a School of Engineering. William Evans knew that this progress resulted largely from the unremitting, year-round efforts of Chancellor Buchtel. Buchtel acknowledged Evans' indispensable contributions in a moving letter written at the end of 1917:

> Eighteen years ago when I came into service as Chancellor, the University was considered by many to be hopelessly embarrassed. The situation was most depressing, as our deficit was large and our income small. The University debt had grown large and larger each year.
>
> You were elected a Trustee of the Colorado Seminary in 1900. In 1905 you were elected ... President of the Board of Trustees of the University of Denver. But for your timely assistance again and again we could not have kept the University alive and in a state of high efficiency. During these eighteen years we have collected

in cash around a million dollars. Fully eleven percent of that gigantic sum has been given by you without any solicitation from any one. Your knowledge of our distressing needs has always moved you to make great personal sacrifices.

In an outstanding manner you have honored your Father and Mother by your devotion ... in the lists of thousands who have cared for the University and have made sacrifices to keep it alive and efficient, your name, like that of Abou Ben Adhem, leads all the rest.[35]

Buchtel's last major contribution to the development of the University was to spearhead the creation of an endowment fund. In 1912, backed by the Board of Trustees, he persuaded the General Education Board—which later became the Rockefeller Foundation—to make a pledge of $100,000 for this purpose. In return, there were serious conditions to be fulfilled by the University. The entry of the United States into World War I interrupted the fund-raising campaign but finally, in 1921, the last payment by the General Education Board was matched by the University.

In September of 1920, Buchtel suffered a major stroke, leaving him deaf and partially paralyzed. He ended his letter of resignation as Chancellor with a brave and forward-looking quotation, "The old days never come again, because they would be getting in the way of the new, better days whose turn it is."[36]

The Board appointed the Vice-Chancellor, Dr. Wilbur Engle, as Acting Chancellor and searched for a successor who could fill the huge void left by the loss of Buchtel. In the meantime, Evans and Engle announced the beginning of a campaign to raise $2,500,000 to attract qualified new faculty members, raise salaries, and enlarge the University's endowment.

Heber Harper, Chancellor, from 1922 to 1927

The Board of Trustees settled on Dr. Heber Reece Harper as the new Chancellor. Born in Manchester, England, Harper had come to the United States as a boy of five. After being ordained as a minister, he studied for his doctor of divinity degree and became a member of the faculty of Boston University's School of Theology. After war service with the YMCA and its Liberty campaign, he returned to Boston University as Executive Secretary. He helped to raise four million dollars for that institution and so was very much in the sights of universities looking for new leadership. He later explained how William Evans persuaded him to accept the position as Chancellor of the University of Denver:

> Challenging as some of these other openings were, early in my
> visit to Denver I had the feeling that *this* was the place I wanted
> to work. It may have been due to the wonderful week I spent in Mr.
> William G. Evans home, [1310 Bannock] I remember vividly the
> first night. After dinner, when the ladies had retired, Mr. Evans
> took me to his study and showed me a map of the Rocky Moun-
> tain region ... up to that time I had very little conception of the
> magnitude and significance of the Rocky Mountain region ... Mr.
> Evans said, "Young man, this empire that I am showing you is as
> large geographically as Germany and France combined, and
> some day, in my opinion, it may be as significant as either of those
> two countries—politically and economically."[37]

Harper finished his obligations to Boston University and came to Denver in November, 1922. Harper and Evans formed a strong bond in working together for the development of the University. They made a particularly determined effort to improve its image among the citizens of Denver, too many of whom spoke disparagingly of DU as "tramway tech."[38]

Death Comes to William Evans and Henry Buchtel

William Evans died in October of 1924. He had made his last trip to Washington in April of that year to give testimony about a possible railroad consolidation, but he became ill and had to return to Denver. He recovered, resumed work, and suffered a relapse in September, pulling through that only to come down with influenza. He thought he was recovering well, but on October 21, he died. Anne Evans was at his bedside along with his four children. Cornelia, his ever attentive wife, was absent; she was in Mercy hospital recovering from an emergency appendectomy.

William Evans' longtime friend, former Chancellor Buchtel, died the following day. The two funeral services were conducted on the same day, October 25. The services for Buchtel drew a large crowd of Denver University students, faculty, and Denver citizens. Services were held that morning in the University Chapel. Chancellor Harper, following the wishes of William Evans, conducted the simple services at the Evans home at 1310 Bannock Street that afternoon. "Probably there never before has been a funeral of one of Colorado's really great men of such simplicity as that for Mr. Evans."[39] There was no music, just a single prayer and a brief address by the Chancellor. One member of the family was absent; William's wife, Cornelia, remained in Mercy Hospital.

Harper's Chancellorship

Harper served as Chancellor for only five years, his term marked by significant successes and failures. Among the successes must

Margery Reed Hall, Denver University (1929), Denver Public Library Western History Collections

be counted the establishment of the Social Science Foundation, generously funded by businessman James H. Causey. A much-needed new liberal arts building, financed by Verner and Mary Reed, helped to alleviate the serious over-crowding on the University Park Campus. In 1928, the Margery Reed Mayo Hall opened housing seventeen classrooms, five large general purpose rooms in the basement, and a theater seating 300 on the first floor. The building served as a memorial to the Reeds' daughter, Margery.

Among Harper's failures included the building of an enormous stadium on the campus, seating more than thirty thousand. The successful campaign to raise funds for this effort was led by William's son, John Evans, who became chairman of the Board of Trustees in 1925. He pledged $100,000 for the project and helped to convince the City of Denver authorities to float a stadium bond issue. However construction costs exceeded expectations and ticket sales were lower than anticipated making the stadium a money-loser for the University. Another serious problem came with the denial of accreditation of the University by the Association of American Universities on grounds of high professor-student ratios, excessive class sizes and other problems. Then there was the failure to secure grants for a new building for the Dentistry School and for the support of the liberal arts program. Overall, however, the picture by the time Harper resigned was not all discouraging. Student enrollment in 1926–7 reached almost 3,500.

Frederick Maurice Hunter, 1928–35

Hunter became the first non-Methodist and the first layman to be named Chancellor of Denver University. Hunter arrived in Denver in 1928, determined to make a realistic evaluation of the University's resources and potential so the school could become "a true urban university."[40]

The Suzzalo Report

A three-man committee of prominent educators, headed by Henry Suzzalo, President of the Carnegie Foundation for the Advancement of Teaching, and including the Presidents of Stanford University and the University of Buffalo, made a study of DU. The Suzzallo Report made tough and wide-ranging recommendations based on careful observation. Its arguments in favor of closing the schools of dentistry and pharmacy were accepted and the schools were eliminated. Recommendations to drop two other programs, in electrical and chemical engineering, were not accepted at the time. The University adopted the proposal to add three important new departments—social work, librarianship, and fine arts.

The beginnings of the social work school in the thirties were, as Breck observed, only "in embryo," but the School of Librarianship was well-launched by 1932 and soon turned out well-trained graduates. Its "founding father," Malcolm Wyer, Denver's City Librarian, became Dean. An able director from Chicago was hired and, after a short stint in temporary quarters downtown, the new school moved into one half of the second floor space above Mapelli's Grocery and Meat Market at 15th Street and Cleveland Place in downtown Denver. The other half of the space housed the Law School.

Anne Evans, Art Education, and Denver University

Between the later 1890s and 1929, it appears that the Art Department of the University went into eclipse. The Suzzalo Report came up with the recommendation that it would be appropriate for the University to have a Department of Art—and that, lo and behold, an existing school being conducted at a venue called Chappell House just might be available for purchase.

It is difficult to imagine that this suggestion could have come effectively from anyone other than Anne Evans, so involved with the programs at Chappell House,[41] whose nephew was chairman of the Denver University Board of Trustees, and who had a lifelong interest in art education. Confirming this conviction that Anne Evans was the source of this new development is the curious fact that acquisition of the Chappell School somehow resulted in DU also taking over responsibility for the Santa Fe School of Art. Who else but Anne Evans at this time formed a strong connecting link between Denver University, Chappell House, and Santa Fe, New Mexico?

The Chappell School of Art was founded in 1924 by H. A. W. Manard. He retired from its management at the time of the sale to Denver University in December of 1928. The capable faculty, which included sculptor Arnold Ronnebeck and painter John Thompson, would continue under the University of Denver.

Chancellor Hunter and Suzzalo traveled to Chicago to interview a promising candidate to head up the new College of Fine and Applied Arts. This was Vance H. Kirkland, "a member of the faculty of the Cleveland School of Art and a painter of promising ability"[42]

Kirkland was destined to become a major figure in Denver's art world from the moment he arrived until his death in 1981. Indeed, as is true of so many artists, his reputation has only expanded since that date. Kirkland started immediately to build up a vigorous program, aiming at high standards for both faculty and students. The Art School offered the degrees of Bachelor of Fine Arts and Bachelor of Arts with a major or minor in art, as well as four-year and two-year diplomas. Very shortly, however, in 1932, Kirkland left the University of Denver due to a major disagreement over the degree of academic recognition granted to his programs. He believed that DU was reneging on promises made to him when he was first appointed. Kirkland first rented, then bought, the studio built

Vance Kirkland, Denver Public Library Western History Collection

by artist and civic activist Henry Read at 1311 Pearl Street. There he set up his own school, the Kirkland School of Art. Many of his DU students followed him, so he arranged to have his classes accredited by the University of Colorado.

The Art Department continued at Denver University. The Director of the Denver Art Museum, Cyril Kay-Scott, became the school's Dean in 1932. A three-member Advisory Committee was appointed, consisting of George Cranmer; Chairman, Anne Evans; and Thomas Dines. Anne Evans served on this committee until her death in 1941. Since there are no written records of her reactions, and few now alive who remember the controversy clearly, there is no way to know how Anne Evans viewed this damaging split in Denver's art education program. But her action in joining the Advisory Committee would argue that she supported Denver University's side in the matter.

There was no doubt that Kirkland's school presented serious competition to Denver University's Art Department. In 1946, then Chancellor Chester Alter "enticed Kirkland to return [to] ... the School of Art as its Director on the University campus. His several hundred students followed him there."[43] When Kirkland finally retired in 1969, his School of Art was the largest undergraduate department in the University, with some four hundred students.

Kirkland's retirement as teacher and administrator only accelerated his activity as an artist. All through his academic career, Kirkland continued to be a disciplined and prolific painter, almost to the day of his death in 1981. Since his wife, Anne, had died before him and they had no children, Vance Kirkland left his entire estate in the hands of family friend, Hugh Grant, who has imaginatively turned 1311 Pearl Street into the Kirkland Museum of Fine and Decorative Art.

Other suggestions in the Suzzallo Report for improving the University system academically were approved by the faculty. Sadly, the important recommendations about increasing faculty numbers and salaries, as well as hiring more highly qualified faculty members, ran into the realities of life during the Great Depression. By 1932, "college placement offices around the country were reporting that eighty percent of all their graduates were entering a world which did not want them."[44]

One new responsibility added to the roster for the University was ownership of the Central City Opera House. For that, Anne Evans and Denver University Professor Ida Kruse McFarlane were responsible. The unlikely and heartening Central City story—the last major accomplishment of Anne Evans' life—is told in the next chapter.

In spite of the best efforts of Chancellor Hunter and the Board of Trustees, the Depression was taking a heavy toll on a University that was dependent on student tuition for seventy-five percent of its income. The faculty had to take an annual pay cut and annual deficits could only be met by dipping into meager reserves. In the summer of 1935, Hunter resigned as Chancellor, feeling he had done what he could for Denver University.

An Iliff Graduate becomes Chancellor, 1935–41

Scottish-born David Shaw Duncan came to Denver University in 1906 as an Instructor in History and Political Science, becoming head of the department and then college Dean.

Duncan accepted the post of Chancellor reluctantly, fully aware of the University's serious economic problems. He focused on the single issue of improving the school's financial status. Beginning in the 1935–6 year, things began to turn around. As a result of a large gift from Mary Reed, the Alfred P. Sloan Foundation gave a grant to the School of Commerce to establish a department of government management. The Carnegie Corporation donated over half a million dollars to support the School of Librarianship. In 1940, in recognition of the improved academic status of the University, Phi Beta Kappa installed a chapter at DU, the third in the State, following Colorado College and Colorado University.

Perhaps the single most significant contribution during Chancellor David Shaw Duncan's term was the Mary Reed Library. Designed in "modified American Collegiate Gothic style,"[45] this building, with a 126 feet high tower, served as the iconic face of Denver University for the next fifty years. The new library had stack space for 400,000 books, reference room space for 400 readers, thirty-four study rooms for faculty research and a pleasant reading room on the second floor. Other encouraging developments were the achievement of accreditation by the University and the Law School, and the establishment of departments of International Relations and Journalism.

Duncan offered his resignation early in 1940. It was to take effect in the summer of 1941, so that he could return to his major interest, teaching. The Board chose a Princeton University administrator,

Caleb F. Gates Jr., to succeed Duncan in August of 1941, with the provision that he would come to Denver in January and function as Chancellor-elect. Duncan died suddenly in March of 1941, shortly after he had given the Founder's Day address.[46] This left Chancellor Gates in charge as the University moved into the demanding years of the Second World War and its aftermath.

The University Civic Theater and Helen Bonfils

Anne Evans served on another spirited body supporting the University of Denver's efforts in the arts, the Board of Directors of the University Civic Theatre. Operating in the 300-seat theater in the Margery Reed Mayo building, the Civic Theatre was "conducted under a membership plan by which those interested in production or audience participation subscribe to a membership for each season." In the 1941–2 season, the subscription fee, "entitling each member to one seat for each of the six productions" cost $6.00, and there were over 1500 members. Six plays were produced each year under the direction of Walter Sinclair, who also headed the University's Theater Department. Only subscribing members could try out for parts in the Civic Theatre productions. If chosen, they had to be prepared for a rigorous six weeks of intensive evening rehearsals.

The main impetus behind the creation of the Civic Theatre was Helen Bonfils, one of the major philanthropists and cultural pioneers of twentieth century Denver. Helen was the daughter of F. G. Bonfils, co-founder with Harry H. Tammen of the *Denver Post.*

Helen inherited from her father the management of the *Denver Post,* a large fortune, and a foundation. From 1936 to 1973, she gave almost eleven million dollars from the Bonfils Foundation to a wide variety of worthwhile causes in Denver, convincing each of the fundraisers that she was truly identified with their interests. "... a prominent fundraiser for the University of Denver recalled that 'Helen was tall, blonde and gaily energetic—and ... she was devoted to DU'."[47]

Bonfils joined with Mary Reed and Florence Martin to create the Civic Theatre, under the auspices of Denver University, for which the three of them underwrote most of the production costs. She herself played more than a hundred roles in the theatre's plays, most of them character parts.

Anne Evans and DU Professor Ida Kruse McFarlane sat on the Board of Directors of the University Civic Theater with Helen

Bonfils. These same two remarkable women, in 1932, persuaded the University of Denver to accept the gift of an aging Opera House in Central City, and then proceeded to create an annual summer Play Festival in that dying mining town. Bonfils became a generous benefactor of the Central City project during the remaining lifetimes of Anne Evans and Ida Kruse McFarlane, and she continued her liberal support of that project long after their deaths in 1940 and 1941.

Denver University Honors Anne Evans

Denver University valued Anne Evans, and she received several honors. In 1914, the University of Denver held an unusually festive Commencement Program celebrating the 50th anniversary of its foundation. Held in the recently completed City Auditorium, the ceremony included the conferring of fifty honorary degrees. Twelve of these were the degree Doctor of Letters (Litt.D.). No citations remain about the reasons for the degrees being awarded; recipients were simply described by their positions. Anne Evans was described as President, Denver Library Board. In that year, the same degree was awarded to Anne's friend, Ida Kruse McFarlane, Professor of English and Supervisor of the Courses in Efficiency, University of Denver, A.B. and A.M. Vassar College, and to Chalmers Hadley, Librarian Denver Public Library and President Denver Library Commission, with whom Anne Evans worked so closely to improve Denver's public library system and facilities.

In 1939, the University awarded just three honorary degrees, all to women. This was an unusual event. Anne Evans was in distinguished company—the other two honorees that year were Dr. Florence Sabin, who received a doctorate in Science, and Mary Reed, a Doctorate in Humanities for her philanthropic contributions. Evans was honored with a Doctorate of Fine Arts. The Denver City Librarian, Malcolm Wyer, read the citation about the accomplishments that justified presenting Anne Evans for the degree.[48]

> Anne Evans, distinguished daughter of Governor John Evans, founder of this institution seventy-five years ago, has upheld the family tradition through her leadership in cultural development in Denver, in Colorado, and in the Rocky Mountain region. Her vision and imagination coupled with a practical energy and an ability to translate dreams into accomplishments have been the

secret of her success in achieving results in the fields of her special interests. These interests have been community-wide in their scope, but among the many, special mention should be given to the Denver Art Museum, which under the direction of Anne Evans has acquired distinction among art institutions of the country for its services to the city; to the Denver Public Library which for many years has profited through her inspiration and wise counsel as a member of the Library Commission; to the Allied Arts, which has made possible advanced study to promising young artists and musicians; to the Central City Play Festival which has secured nation-wide acclaim, largely because of the vision, enthusiasm, and indomitable determination of Anne Evans. Throughout all of these activities, her interest has never been limited to any one institution, but her influence has ever been for a close integration of all cultural activities through cordial cooperation and coordination.

Denver University—Post Script

The Evans family continued the leadership tradition of the Governor and his son, William, for another two generations. William's son, John Evans Sr., served as a vigorous Chairman of the Board of Trustees and a generous benefactor from 1925 to 1943. His son, John Jr., served in his turn as Chairman from 1959 to 1969.

DU moved, after World War II, from being a regional institution to registering on the national scene. With a huge influx of students benefiting from the G.I. Bill, its student body soared to levels unprecedented before or since—around 15,000 at its peak. The tradition of opening new departments to meet current demands continued, as did the willingness to close programs when they could no longer be sustained. Successive chancellors, however, struggled with severe financial limitations—limitations that dogged the institution's efforts to adequately raise faculty salaries while building new facilities and offering scholarship help. Anne Evans would have been delighted to see the Penrose Library [1972] and the Schwayder Art Building [1977].

The financial situation changed dramatically in 1989 with the appointment of a Chancellor whose vision and resources, for his time, matched those of Governor Evans in his day. From 1989 to 2005, Daniel Ritchie served as the 16th Chancellor of Denver University, and then continued as Chairman of the Board of Trustees for an additional two years. In these years, the University Park campus was transformed by the addition of $500 million in new buildings, along with careful landscaping of the remaining open space and meticulous upkeep of the grounds. The spacious Ritchie Sports and Wellness Center and the $25 million Daniels College of Business were completed in 1999. Many of the University's Departments, which had been housed in buildings away from the main campus, gained handsome new premises. These included the $63.5 million Sturm School of Law and the $75 million Newman Center for the Performing Arts, the new home for the Lamont School of Music.

After Ritchie resigned his leadership role at Denver University, he took on major responsibilities at the Denver Center for the Performing Arts and at Anne Evans' legacy organization, the Central City Opera House Association. It is to Central City, the last chapter of the Anne Evans story, that we now turn.

23

Saving Central

The pioneers of 1859 who 'dreamed of yellow gold, who cut the conifers and ribbed the mines,' of the newly discovered Gregory Diggings, made the little Kingdom of Gilpin into the richest square mile on earth. Many millions of dollars of the precious metal came out of the mines of Central City, Black Hawk, Russell Gulch and Nevadaville; and part of it went back into the things that last when gold is gone. The miners wanted the riches of life, they wanted entertainment, and they wanted the best, for their daring and imagination was of the stuff that makes and demands good theater.[1]

—Anne Evans

Set in the midst of all this desolation—like a thing suddenly remembered with joy—is the most enchanting theatre in America, the old Central City Opera House ... What is more natural than that a group of public-spirited citizens of Denver should say: 'Why not make this lovely old theatre live again ... as a theatre of beauty and glamour, a theatre of dreams?' Is it any wonder that when this group invited me to produce a play in the opera house last summer I instantly accepted the invitation?[2]

—Robert Edmond Jones

It was July 16, 1932, in the City of Central[3] in the Little Kingdom of Gilpin, Colorado, and something miraculous was happening. On the stage of its Opera House, so recently the haunt of pack rats running freely over floors littered with fallen plaster, there appeared a brilliant new interpretation of an old play, Camille.[4] Outside, in this former mining community well on its way to becoming a ghost town,[5] animated crowds filled Eureka Street. Dressed in costumes of the 1870s, they eagerly watched the unfolding events of the first annual Central City Festival. It was a miracle that this festival happened at all in the middle of the Great Depression. Its overwhelming success involved the effort of hundreds, but it would never have happened without the courage and imagination of two remarkable women—Ida Kruse McFarlane and Anne Evans.

The Heyday of Central City

In the early days of Colorado Territory, Central City was wealthy and assertive, a rival to Denver. John Gregory, a prospector from Georgia, worked his way up into the hills west of Denver in the "Pike's Peak or Bust" gold rush. Early in 1859, he found a rich lode of gold some five miles north of Clear Creek. A historical marker notes the site today. Soon more than 2,500 gold seekers swarmed into the narrow

Central City, Colorado (c. 1878) The Central City Opera House is on Eureka Street across from St. James Methodist Church. Denver Public Library Western History Collection

valley, christened Gregory Gulch. A number of mining camps were established in the area; some were incorporated and of these, Central emerged as the main town, designated as the county seat of Gilpin County in 1861. Central City was one of the first places visited by Governor Evans after he arrived in 1862, and the first mountain community to which he introduced his wife, Margaret and their young son, Willie.[6] In its glory days, when gold poured out of its mines and smelters, and it could reasonably be described as "the richest square mile on earth," there was a strong drive on the part of Central City's residents to secure for their community more than the saloons, dance halls and brothels that were the inevitable out-croppings of a mining camp. They wanted all the facilities of a civilized town: churches, schools, banks, stores—and a theater.

A personal account of this aspect of the boom times in Gilpin County is to be found in *Yesterday Was Another Day*[7] by long-time Central City resident Louis J. Carter.[8] The author noted that after the first brief rush of placer miners, who were mostly itinerant, single males, the largest group of miners came from Britain. They brought their families with them, and were "law-abiding and God-fearing citizens." Between Central City, Black Hawk, and the other mining communities there were seven churches and thirty fraternal lodges. Even the thirty-eight saloons were primarily "people's clubs" where miners gathered after a hard day's work to drink, play cards and sometimes—particularly on Saturday nights—engage in "man-to-man" fights. There were two gambling establishments in Central City. Its citizens bet on everything, including baseball games, wrestling matches, prizefights, and the results of elections. There were also two houses of ill repute, known as Parlor Houses. Carter remarked on prevailing attitudes towards these. He reported that people "believed that if women were to be protected and safe in the community, the houses should be permitted to operate."

Central's First Theater

In 1874, the town's first theater, the Montana, burned to the ground in one of those periodic fires that were the scourge of every wooden settlement in Colorado's early days. A replacement, the Belvidere, was built a year later, but it proved small and unsatisfactory. In 1876, a hugely successful local production of a popular operetta, *The Bohemian Girl*, fueled a strong grassroots movement to build an Opera House in the town. Central City, like many mining towns whose operations demanded the services of experienced hard rock miners, had attracted large numbers of Welsh coal miners and Cornishmen, with skills developed by working in Cornwall's ancient tin mines. These men loved to sing, and they loved music. The Gilpin County Opera House Association was formed to solicit donations. By June of 1877, ground was broken for the ambitious project of building a real Opera House.

Architect Roeschlaub Designs an Opera House

The Association commissioned one of Denver's best young architects to design the Opera House. Robert Roeschlaub set some definite objectives in his design for the Opera House.[9] It had to be acoustically perfect and all seats had to have a good view of the stage. To this end, he provided for walls that were four feet thick and, according to one account, "he walked the scaffold throughout the theater, and had helpers strike the walls with tuning forks, so he could determine the best slope of the seating, to enable guests to hear well and see well wherever they sat."[10] To keep the building cool in summer, he provided vents in the roof. Also, underneath the building, "he used Eureka Creek as natural air conditioning by designing a flume through which the creek passes."[11] For cooler weather, there were two hot air furnaces. The stage was lit by 60 gaslights, "which could be dimmed or brightened in unison as the occasion demanded."[12] The theater seated 750 people, 500 in the parquette and dress circle and 250 in the balcony.[13]

Central City Opera House, (c. 1880) Denver Public Library Western History Collection

Roeschlaub chose San Francisco artist John C. Massman to paint "elaborate frescoes on the ceiling"[14] and on a dome in the center to give the illusion of an opening to the sky. A 32-jet chandelier hung from the center of the "dome." Further examples of trompe d'oeil art were the two winged horses, on either side of the proscenium, "painted in bold relief to give the illusion of being actual statuary."[15] Brothers Will and Peter McFarlane of Central

City were selected as contractors. The new Opera House—billed as the finest west of the Mississippi—was completed at a cost of $32,000. It held its first performance in March, 1878. For the first three years, the Opera House was a success, in terms of both attendance and finances. On its stage national and international stars performed in productions ranging from Shakespeare to grand opera, vaudeville to melodrama.

Competition from Denver Dooms the Opera House

In the fall of 1881, H. A. W. Tabor, the millionaire Silver King from Leadville, opened his Tabor Grand Opera House in Denver. It immediately eclipsed the one in Central City. Traveling companies could draw much bigger audiences in Denver and eliminate the tiresome travel into the mountains, so most of the first-class productions chose to bypass Central City.

The Central City Opera House began to lose more money each year. In 1882, it was sold to the County Commissioners for use as a courthouse. This did not sit well with the citizens, who had paid for a place of entertainment in their town. The Gilpin County Opera Association was reorganized as a stock-holding corporation, which bought back the building and engaged the biggest stockholder, Horace Hale, as theater manager. Hale struggled along for the next eight years, managing to put together a great variety of programs to keep the building open. Finally, he lost heart and moved to Denver. Central City's fortunes were on the decline, along with its gold production, and the little jewel of an Opera House fell into disrepair.

Custody of the building landed in the hands of Peter McFarlane, who, with his brother, had built it. Thanks to Peter McFarlane there remained, in 1930, an Opera House to be restored. McFarlane was born in Canada, the son of a Scottish farming family. He arrived in Central City in 1869 and, together with his brother, Will, "founded one of the most important mine and mill equipment companies in Colorado."[16] Although the company opened a branch in Denver, and Peter McFarlane even built a luxury home there at the insistence of his wife, his heart remained in Gilpin County where he preferred to spend most of his time.

According to his biographer, H. William Axford, "McFarlane was probably Gilpin County's most civic minded citizen, particularly during the long period of decline in the mining industry after the turn of the century." McFarlane slowly acquired all the outstanding shares of the Opera Association, patched up the many problems that had developed in the building due to flooding of the basement and general neglect, and attempted to operate the facility as a paying project. From the records that remain, it seems that he never made more than a few hundred dollars a year, and lost money in many years. He tried everything, including the new entertainment medium of film. Movies with Charlie Chaplin and Tom Mix were popular, but most of the ones booked into the theater were of poor quality. He finally gave up, and in 1927 closed the doors for the last time. Peter McFarlane died in 1929, leaving it up to his three grown children to decide the fate of the Opera House.

Peter and his wife, Marie, had one daughter, Yetta, and two sons, Frederick and George. Frederick McFarlane, with a partner, had acquired the Denver part of his father's business, while his brother, George, worked with the McFarlane interests in Central City and Black Hawk. Shortly after Peter McFarlane's death, the Opera House went up for public tax sale. The property taxes had not been paid for ten years. George had to pay the back taxes in order to secure the family's title to the building. The deal was not legally finalized until the end of 1931. While this was being arranged, the family debated what could be done with the property. The population of Central City was down to a few hundred people and real estate sales were slow. They considered selling the Opera House for use as a warehouse or a gymnasium, or even a garage space to repair cars and trucks. One family member, though, had a different and grander idea. Why not find a way to restore the Opera House to its former glory and, in the process, help to reinvigorate Central City as a cultural center?

Ida Kruse McFarlane

In 1906, Frederick McFarlane had married beautiful and talented Ida Kruse. The ceremony had been conducted by Denver University Chancellor Henry Buchtel and took place in the McFarlane home on Eureka Street in Central City.[17] Like Frederick, Ida was born in the Little Kingdom of Gilpin. Her father was a successful businessman in Black Hawk and a one-time Mayor. She attended St. Aloysius Catholic School, high up on Mt. St. Vincent on a site overlooking Central City. The site was fashioned into a memorial to her a few years after her death. She attended Vassar College, where she earned her B. A. and M. A. degrees. She then traveled extensively in

Europe, continuing her education at various universities there, and came home to Gilpin County to become Superintendent of Schools for a number of years. Later she joined the English Faculty of Denver University, where she worked her way up to a full professorship. She was appointed to the Mary Lowe Dickinson Professorship originally endowed by Governor Evans' wife, Margaret.

Ida McFarlane was an acknowledged authority on Shakespeare and a superb teacher. The 1915 issue of *Kynewisbok*, the D. U. student publication, was dedicated "To Mrs. Ida Kruse McFarlane ... whose ability and charming personality we shall always remember, and whose influence for culture and for efficient standards of work and life we shall not forget."

Ida Kruse McFarlane, 1916 Courtesy University of Denver Archives

Along with her insistence on high standards of scholarship, Ida was also a stickler for etiquette. In fact, "that delightful woman of rare charm and intellect"[18] gave a course in etiquette in conjunction with one of her English classes: no such indiscretion for young women as crossing their legs in Prof. McFarlane's class! Ida McFarlane was well known throughout the state for her enthusiastic patronage of all the arts and her support of organizations seeking to foster them.

When Peter McFarlane's first wife, Marie, died, she left no will. The mansion on 14th and Gilpin in Denver, which was in her name, was inherited half by her husband, with the other half divided among the three children, Frederick, George and Yetta. But sharing a mansion did not seem very practical; Frederick and Ida bought out the interests of the other siblings. Peter McFarlane gave them his half share of the building, and conscientiously took a number of years finding the money to compensate George and Yetta for their one-sixth shares. The McFarlane mansion became a venue for frequent, gracious, and stimulating entertaining.

Making the University of Denver Connection

Ida's idea of restoring the Central City Opera House, and thereby giving a new direction for the city itself, needed some kind of sponsoring organization to serve as incubator for the new venture. Her thoughts naturally turned to the University of Denver. She was fully aware that the University was perpetually short of funds for its own development and would not have money to contribute. It did, however, have community standing, permanence, and a large number of potential supporters for a novel cultural experiment. Ida broached the idea to her good friend, Anne Evans, a member of the family that for three generations had been closely identified with the University. Anne herself served with Ida on the Board of Directors of the Denver University Civic Theater and had been for many years a member of the University's Fine Arts Advisory Committee. In 1914, the University had conferred on Anne the honorary degree of Litt.D. for her services to the University and to the larger Denver community.

"When she mentioned her dream to Miss Anne Evans, that forthright lady is supposed to have said in her low, cultivated voice, 'How'll you get people up there, Ida—by balloon?'" wrote Ward Morehouse.[19] This was a reference to the fact that the only remaining direct transportation to Central City from Denver was by automobile, over the precarious shelf road through Virginia Canyon. This was known, for good reason, as the "Oh my God! Road." The railroad to Central City had long been discontinued and the one to Black Hawk was in its terminal stage and limited to freight.

Another source had Ida, who had been toying "with the notion through the Twenties" of a rebirth of the Opera House and Central City,

> finally appealing for aid and sympathy to her good friend, Anne Evans … Miss Evans … listened attentively, her eyes sparkling. At the end, she threw her arms around Mrs. McFarlane and said, 'A wonderful, wonderful plan, Ida. Let's go through with it.' 'We certainly will,' said Mrs. McFarlane. And they did.[20]

From the beginning, Anne Evans gave the entire Central City venture an additional emphasis—that it should serve as a memorial to Colorado's pioneers.

Though united in their interest in promoting the arts and preserving Colorado's pioneer heritage, in other ways Ida McFarlane and Anne Evans were total contrasts. Author Marshall Sprague described them as they sat together in the grimy seats of the Central City Opera House,

> Ida ... was a handsome, stylish woman and she complained of the gallery dust soiling her shoes. Plain Anne ... never seemed to ... care much how she looked.[21]

Helen Black and Walter Sinclair

Two other people are credited (though with variations on the stories in different accounts) with significant involvement in the beginning of the Opera House enterprise. One of these was another remarkable Denver woman, Helen Marie Black. A pioneer young reporter with the *Rocky Mountain News*, she gained a reputation for getting good, newsworthy interviews with interesting visitors to Denver. One summer, her assignment was to interview Walter Sinclair, then Director of the New Orleans Little Theater. He later became the head of the Theater Department at the University of Denver and Director of its University Civic Theater. During the interview, Sinclair "mentioned that he wanted to relax in the mountains." Helen recommended a chalet not too far from Central City "and tossed in the suggestion that Sinclair drive over to take a look at the Central City Opera House."[22] Sinclair followed her suggestion. Intrigued by the exterior of the Opera House, but disappointed to find it locked, he went next door to the Teller House to find out where he might find someone with a key. By chance, Ida McFarlane was lunching there. She did have a key and offered to show him around. In spite of its deplorable condition—rubbish-covered floors and moldy plaster falling off the walls and ceiling—Sinclair became wildly enthusiastic about the theater's potential. "This place has everything," he is said to have reported to Helen Black, "Charm, history, marvelous acoustics. It's too fine a theater to waste."[23] He was also quoted as imagining Central City as a "Salzburg of the Rockies" with a restored Opera House as its centerpiece.[24]

Birth of the Central City Opera House Association

With such a ringing endorsement from a knowledgeable theater professional, and at the urging of Ida McFarlane and Anne Evans— women both known for their record of seeing projects through to successful conclusions—Denver University agreed to accept the gift of the Opera House. They placed its development under the aegis of the Directors of the University Civic Theater. This venture, as noted in the previous Chapter, started in 1929, its purpose "to offer the theatre loving audiences of Denver the enjoyment of worthwhile plays well performed, thus filling a gap in the cultural life of the city."[25] The Board of Directors authorized the founding of the Central City Opera House Association in 1931. The Opera House was leased to the CCOHA for $1.00 a year for 99 years.

Allen True and the Cranmers

This action brought into the picture additional contacts invaluable to the hectic tasks to be accomplished in a few months in 1931–32, including restoring the Opera House, cleaning up the adjacent Teller House Hotel enough for it to offer a bar, dining facilities and party venues and securing a first-class theatrical production to inaugurate the new era in Central City's eventful history. Serving on the board of eleven directors of the Denver University Civic Theater, along with Ida McFarlane and Anne Evans, were Allen True and Jean Chappell Cranmer.

Anne Evans had been one of True's early patrons. In 1911,

> … at the Artists' Club of Denver spring exhibition, True presented what he considered to be his first mural, a canvas measuring sixteen by fifty-two inches titled *The Trappers*. It carried a price tag of $500 and sold within two weeks to Denver's most ambitious supporter of the arts, Anne Evans. Miss Evans intended the painting to decorate her new Burnham Hoyt-designed mountain cabin, sheltered in the alpine meadow below Mount Evans. It was embedded in the stonework above the living room fireplace.[26]

Allen True, one of the most creative and multi-talented Colorado artists of his day, was known primarily as a muralist. Anne Evans had worked closely with him on the development of the Denver Art Museum and had been involved in his selection as artist for several new Denver Public Schools and for structures at the Civic Center.

Born in Colorado Springs in 1881, True's family had moved to Denver by the time he was an adolescent. He graduated from Manual Training High School. True studied art for two years at The University of Denver before enrolling at the Corcoran Art School in Washington, D.C. Then for six years, along with N. C. Wyeth and other selected students from the best art schools in the nation, he honed his skills as a magazine illustrator in Howard Pyle's classes in Chadd's Ford, Pennsylvania.[27] His illustrations were published in the foremost magazines: *Scribner's, Saturday Evening Post, Colliers.* After a period of travel and study in Europe, and working with a well-known Welsh muralist, Sir Frank Brangwyn, True returned to Denver. From 1913-15, he continued to work with Brangwyn on the execution of murals for the Panama-Pacific Exposition in San Francisco and for the Missouri State Capitol. This helped to launch True on his own career as a painter of murals, most of them with themes from Western or Native American history.

Between 1915 and 1930, when he was drawn into the restoration of the art work in the Central City Opera House, True had been commissioned to paint an astonishing number of large, dramatic murals. These included murals for the State Capitol buildings of Utah and Wyoming, for many banks and other corporate buildings in Denver and other cities, for the Denver Public Library, and for a variety of schools and private residences. From 1934–45, True became a consultant to the U.S. Bureau of Reclamation in charge of all decoration and color schemes for the Boulder Dam power plant and the Grand Coulee and Shasta Dams. Allen True was a community activist as well as an artist, willing to take leadership positions in organizations that promoted the arts. For the first year, True served as the Chairman of the Central City project.

The second significant member of the Theatre Board was Jean Chappell Cranmer who, with her brother Delos Chappell, had given their parents' mansion to the Allied Arts organization and the Denver Art Museum. Chappell House, as we have seen, became the first permanent home of the arts in Denver. Delos was a successful Broadway producer who was apparently drawn into the Central City venture by his sister. He worked closely with his wife, Edna James Chappell, a talented actress.

The CCOHA gets to Work

Edna and Delos Chappell, Allen True, Ida Kruse McFarlane, and Anne Evans formed the first board of directors of the Central City Opera House Association (CCOHA). Each had special talents, experience and connections to bring to the almost impossible undertaking of staging a Festival in Central City in less than a year. When the five of them:

Mr. and Mrs. Delos Chappell (Miss Edna James), Denver Public Library Western History Collection

first opened the door to the Opera House in 1931, rats scurried through the darkened theatre, which was dank and decaying from years of neglect. Their flashlights swept the darkness and they could make out the classic lines of the proscenium stage. Shining their lights higher they saw the intricate ceiling murals. Blue sky peeked through holes in the roof, sections of the ceiling were lying in pieces on the floor, chairs and scenery were piled everywhere. The theatre was filled with grime, cobwebs, and dust blown in from the slag heaps of surrounding mines.[28]

To Allen True fell the major responsibility for the physical restoration of the building. It was in such a dire state of decay, rat infestation, and clutter that workers had to wear masks as they cleaned it out. The chandelier that had hung from the ceiling had disappeared, and backstage

everything was in a state of chaos. Bits of scenery, including some of the original drops, were scattered here and there. The stage floor needed shoring up with concrete. A leaky roof had damaged the ceiling.[29]

True enlisted the help of Denver architect Allen Fisher to help repair the most serious structural problems and to replace the missing railing on the musicians' balcony on the front of the building. He turned to a fellow artist—with the intriguing name of Paschal Quackenbush—for cooperation in restoring Massman's murals and painting the entire theater. Restoration of the Opera House was substantially completed by October of 1931, but one final piece was missing—replacement of the carpet. This was to be achieved by

Anne. Once again, her ingenuity came through. She was able to acquire the sumptuous Victorian red carpet from Denver's historic Windsor Hotel.[30]

Robert Edmond Jones

The Delos Chappells were responsible for persuading a brilliant Broadway Director, Robert Edmond Jones, to consider becoming involved with the Central City Opera House project. At the time, Jones was considered the foremost set designer on Broadway, having worked on *Green Pastures* and *Redemption,* and most recently with Eugene O'Neill on the premiere of his play, *Mourning Becomes Electra.* After visiting the Opera House, Jones' reaction was as lyrical and enthusiastic as Sinclair's had been before him. He wrote to the Opera House Association board "only death or world cataclysm would prevent me being present and producing the opening performance."[31] Jones took on the entire responsibility for the first performance. He selected the show and the cast and was producer, director and set designer, and designed a new red and gold curtain for the front of the stage, using themes from the ceiling frescoes, which was executed by Central City artist Frank (Pancho) Gates.

THE DENVER POST—F

Mountain Drama soon will be the menu again for theatergoers from far and near at the annual Central City Drama Festival, July 16 to 30. Preparations for the 1938 production, Victor Hugo's "Ruy Blas," will begin to "step up" immediately, for Robert Edmond Jones, the directing producer, arrived here Thursday to take personal charge. He is shown here being welcomed at the union station by Miss Anne Evans, chairman of the Central City Opera House association.

Robert Edmund Jones, director of Central City Drama Festival, is shown here being welcomed at Union Station by Anne Evans, chairman of the Central City Opera House association. Denver Post June 16, 1938. Denver Public Library Western History Collection

The Teller House

To prepare for the influx of visitors during the eight-day Festival it was necessary to do something about the decrepit Teller House next door to the Opera House. Its facilities were desperately needed to "house and dine the theatre-goers to the first festival."[32]

At the time of its original opening in 1872, the Teller House ranked as one of the premier hotels in Colorado Territory. No expense was spared in its construction. "One of its great bragging points was indoor water closets on every floor and baths in the basement!"[33] The four-story building boasted business spaces, including a bank, on the first floor; social rooms on the second floor; and two floors of rooms for hotel guests. An elegant atrium graced the first floor, with a granite fountain and glass-paned roof that made it possible to grow plants even in the coldest weather. The hotel was built by Henry Teller, "lawyer, gold mine owner … railroad president, militia-man, Masonic leader, pillar of the Republican party, family man, Secretary of the Interior, and a United States Senator."[34] Teller, as we have seen, was the successful rival to Governor Evans in the contest to become one of Colorado's first Senators, after the achievement of statehood. Teller had met Samuel Elbert at a Republican convention

The Teller House, (1930), Denver Public Library Western History Collection

in Illinois in 1860. Intrigued by Elbert's stories of gold strikes in Colorado, Teller came to Central City in 1861 and rapidly became a leader in the booming city. He served as Mayor and City Attorney before entering the arena of national politics.

Perhaps the most historic moment for the Teller House occurred when President Grant came to visit his old friend Henry Teller in 1873. A pathway of 30 silver bricks was laid for him to walk from his carriage to the hotel entrance. These were political bricks; the story is told that they were provided by silver barons who, in the middle of the congressional debate on whether to back United States coinage with gold or silver, were angry that Grant chose to only visit Gilpin County gold camps and not any of the silver mining towns. They wanted to do something to impress him. He is said to have ignored the ingots and used the boardwalk.[35] A Presidential suite was also prepared, with a rather magnificent bed. There seems to be general agreement, however, that Grant never slept in it, having left Central City after his dinner with Teller.

By 1932, the once-glorious Teller House was being run as a boarding house. The atrium was filled with old mattresses and garbage. Many of the upstairs rooms were dirty and had not been used for years.

Anne Evans decided that the Opera House Association should lease the first two floors of the hotel. With mostly volunteer labor, these were cleaned up. Workers started with the lobby and what used to be the billiard room on the main floor, which had been converted into a bar. The walls were covered with layers of peeling wallpaper. As these were scraped off, there unexpectedly appeared original paintings by artist Charles St. George Stanley of such classical figures as Leda, Mars, and Venus. Artist Paschal Quackenbush was brought in to salvage the paintings, which he did with great success. He found that the original artist had a sense of humor: each one of the figures had a visible flaw. One had a man's face on a woman's body, another had no left hand and a third sported two left feet. Mars fully armed, but lacked clothing, while Venus's left nipple had migrated to the apple. Quackenbush added one figure and gave it a flaw of his own invention.[36] In 1952, when called upon to do some further work on restoration, he added a second figure, with a second intentional defect.[37]

The "socializing" spaces on the second floor of the Teller House were cleaned and repainted, and some of the hotel rooms made presentable for guests. Anne Evans and Ida Kruse McFarlane "opened the restaurant and stocked the bar. A row of slot machines lined one full wall. Wide open gambling had come back to Central City in the effort to recreate days of the gold rush."[38] Throughout the thirties, gambling came and went in Central depending on the vigor of law enforcement, since gambling was technically illegal in Colorado. The slot machines sometimes disappeared into the Teller House basement, only to reappear when circumstances were more propitious.

Financing the "Theater of Dreams"

To secure support for the Central City venture, Evans and McFarlane activated their large network of friends and relatives, including many members of Denver's social elite, enlisting them as volunteers for the myriad tasks that needed to be done in preparation for the grand opening in July of 1932. Marshall Sprague characterized their efforts as "the 'polite extortion' ... of money from members of Denver society to refurbish the opera house and to stage the first performance of the Central City Festival ... Ida divided Denver society into infinite committees of infinite arrangements. Enough tea was drunk at countless teas to cause a flash flood in Gregory Gulch."[39] An astute observer, associated for many years with the Central City project, said, "Although she was a member of Denver's 'high society,' its pseudo-glamour did not interest Anne Evans. Her only use for 'society' as such was as an 'instrument' to accomplish what she wanted."[40]

Anne Evans' major role was to raise the funds for the project, as well as coaxing in-kind donations from any and all sources. It is said that even the staunchest supporters of her previous arts projects, like her nephew John Evans, feared that this time she was "dreaming the impossible dream." The Depression took a terrible toll on the economy and did not make it easy to raise money even for the best of causes. Anne Evans, though, proved indomitable when it came to finding donations for the Central City project—to which she committed herself wholeheartedly for the last ten years of her life. According to one observer,

> Anne Evans ignored the financial facts of festival life ... Cohorts like Thomas A. Dines, Frank Downer, Helen Black and Frank White, watched with terrified fascination as Anne spent money she didn't have to buy fantastically expensive shows and to try to keep

the Teller House from tumbling down. She became a marvelous fund-raiser.[41]

There were three main approaches that Anne used to finance the "Theatre of Dreams." She sought outright donations of cash or services from everyone she knew. Then from time to time, she had an inspired fund-raising idea. Finally, she relied on a combination of unique circumstances about the Central City Festival to persuade top-notch talents in the world of theater and opera to come west and work for ridiculously inadequate remuneration.

Seeking Individual Donors

One student of the early history of the Opera House Association said that at this time, when Anne Evans' friends and acquaintances saw her coming, they simply resigned themselves to the inevitable—and took out their checkbooks.[42] However, Anne Evans was not insensitive to the individual financial situations of donors. An interesting insight into this aspect, as well as into how she approached major donors, is contained in two 1936 hand-written drafts of letters to Alice Bemis Taylor of Colorado Springs. In the first letter, Anne Evans wrote:

> Our plans for the third Central City Festival are well under way ... Mr. Jones is full of enthusiasm ... He writes, 'This year we are going to give them not only delight but awe and majesty as well. To acknowledge that I am working in complete harmony with one of the greatest, if not the greatest, actor in America has seized my imagination in the completest possible way' ... All of his designs for the sets are marvelously beautiful ...[43]

The letter went on to explain that Anne Evans had requested a "guarantor" contribution from Taylor, noting that most of the money for a production had to be paid out before tickets went on sale. While the CCOHA would repay as much as possible of the guarantors' advances, she made it clear that no assurance could be given that this would be possible. "You were good enough to tell me that you would help us, and I am writing to find out what we may count upon—The contributions here in Denver range from 1,500 down to 500." "Someday," she noted, describing one of her fundamental beliefs about the value of individual donations, "we hope to accumulate a working capital, but I do believe the community and the state ought always to contribute part of the backing—it is really a healthier condition and keeps people interested." At the time, Alice Bemis Taylor was spearheading a visionary drive in Colorado Springs to build a Fine Arts Center, designed by New Mexico architect John Gaw Meem—the one-time protégé of Anne Evans.[44] Anne concluded her letter, "We hear grand things about your Art Center and rejoice that we are to have such a beautiful thing in Colorado."

Alice Taylor apparently responded with an offer of a loan of $500, with a plea that she needed it fully repaid. In a second letter, Anne Evans wrote, "the more I pondered the more I became convinced that it would be unwise for me to ask you for the five hundred dollars which you offered me as a loan." In spite of their very best efforts, she explained, the forthcoming production "will be expensive." The guarantors, Anne Evans wrote,

> expect to make up a deficit, and I just would not dare make an exception in one case by promising to return the amount in full. Please believe that I am most appreciative of your offer to help in this way, and that I quite understand that you must think first of the splendid thing you are doing for Colorado Springs—I do believe it will be one of the most beautiful buildings in the country.[45]

The best description of Anne Evans' ability to secure in-kind donations came from Dr. Benjamin Draper, Denver's Deputy City Clerk when the Central City revival began. He remembered, "the Central City Opera House Association opened its first office on the fourth floor of the newly-completed City and County Building." Mayor Begole "lent" Draper to Evans "to drive her back and forth to Central City during the first four seasons." When his secretary told the Manager of Parks and Improvements, Walter B. Lowry, that Miss Evans had called again, he replied, "Give her whatever she wants!" What she wanted that time was "flowers from the city greenhouses for opening night bouquets." She also persuaded State Highway Commissioner Vail to grade the Virginia Canyon road, normally a county responsibility. "She is often credited with later having persuaded State Highway officials to build the Clear Creek Canyon route."[46]

A Matter of Chairs

One of Anne Evans' inspired fund-raising ideas came to her during the preparations for the Festival's first year. It had to do with chairs. At some point in its early years, the original cheap seating in the Opera House had been replaced with solid, hand-carved hickory chairs, five hundred of which were still in good condition. Evans "located a furniture manufacturer in North Carolina to provide 250 more."[47] Then she announced that, for $100, anyone could have a chair inscribed with the name of a Colorado pioneer carved into the back of the chair, along with a single date—the date on which the pioneer had arrived in Colorado. From the outset, Anne Evans insisted that the whole Central City project should be a monument to Colorado pioneers.

Seventy chairs were "sold" the first year—enough to pay for the repair of the leaking roof. Many of the first names were those of early pioneers, connected with Central City; including John Gregory, Peter McFarlane, and Robert Roeschlaub. Anne Evans named a chair for her father, the Governor. Names of western heroes like Buffalo Bill Cody, Zebulon Pike, and Horace Greeley began to appear in the theater, as well as the major pioneers of Denver's early days; such as Bonfils, Boettcher, Tabor, Gilpin, and Elbert. Later, other categories of honorees were added: famous singers, actors and actresses who had played in the Opera House, directors and musicians who had made a particular contribution, and members of the Central City Opera House Association whose efforts enabled the annual festivals to continue to flourish through many financial crises.

The only problem with the hickory chairs was that, even when they were later furnished with cushions, they were excruciatingly uncomfortable. Though they no doubt performed a certain service, in that they made it almost impossible for members of the audience to fall asleep, they were mercifully replaced in 1999 with more conventional seating better suited to the contours of the human body. The names of those honored by the dedication of a hickory chair were transferred to the backs of the new seats. By no means all of the old chairs had been inscribed, so even though the Opera house lost 50 seats in the process of updating the seating, there are still plenty of chairs available for dedication, and the tradition, started in 1932, continues. The hickory chairs are stored in Williams

Stables on Eureka Street across from the Opera House, hanging from the ceiling. In exchange for a donation, the named chairs can be acquired by the original owners or family members, and unnamed chairs can also be obtained for a donation by anyone wanting a piece of Central City Opera history.

In 1932, donors of $100 for the privilege of dedicating a chair were entitled to a seat for the performance of *Camille*. A letter from the Ticket Committee urged such donors to attend the Grand Opening, "which will probably be as glamorous a production as the west has seen since the far off days when Modjeska played "*Camille*" in these parts, and was immortalized by Eugene Field's poem." The letter goes on to say that "Dinner is available in Central City, as well as comfortable rooms, at very moderate rates" and that additional tickets for the performance could be ordered for $2.50 each. Tickets for the Grand Ball at the Teller House following the performance were also $2.50 each, including refreshments.[48]

Paying Talent in Fulsome Appreciation

The third approach used quite effectively by Anne Evans to "get the show on the road" combined lavish appreciation for services rendered with very meager payment. To lure top performers, she relied on the quirky charm of Central City, its cool summer climate (New York theaters were not yet air-conditioned), and the spectacular mountain environment. In addition, there was always the warm western hospitality of the Festival's volunteers and supporters, many of whom were among the city's wealthy elite with beautiful homes. Top notch directors like Robert Edmond Jones and musical director Frank St. Leger became enthusiastic promoters of the Festival; their charisma proved invaluable in luring top acting and singing talents. There is a wonderful story from 1934, when Jones decided to stage a new production of Othello. He wanted to cast stage and film star Walter Huston and his actress wife, Nan Sutherland, as Othello and Desdemona. He wired Huston, "Dear Walter, I would like to invite you and Nan to come out to Central City, a little mining town in the mountains west of Denver, to do a production of Shakespeare's *Othello* for several weeks. I can offer you $1,000 for the season." At the time, as mentioned earlier, the couple was starring on Broadway in an extremely successful play. Huston wired back, "Dear Bobby, Your terms are entirely unsatisfactory. I accept."

About the same production, Anne Evans wrote,

Walter Huston is giving most tangible evidence of his faith in the production. He has made the great acting hit of the New York season in 'Dodsworth' ... tickets are selling 16 weeks in advance—the house takes in $23,000 a week—and he is closing it down the last of June for six weeks in order to come out here and play Othello in Central—for the munificent sum of $600!

The other $400 must have been for Huston's wife, Nan.[49]

Anne Evans herself played an important role in the welcoming of Festival participants. She met directors and stars at the train station, helped them with transportation to Central City, and saw that they had the best accommodations available. A 1938 newspaper photograph of Anne greeting Robert Edmond Jones at Union Station conveys her infectious enthusiasm better than any words.[50]

Anne Evans entertained some participants at her summer home on the Ranch. An affectionate and appreciative letter from Frank St. Leger, written just after his triumphant production of *The Gondoliers* in 1936, opened:

My dear, *dear* Anne. It seems ages and ages since we left Colorado, ... I can't tell you what a joy it has been to know you, and what a source of comfort you were to me when I most needed it. I really do not think I could have been ready for July 6 if you had not been so sweet and sympathetic, and most understanding. Bless you for that and for all the other grand things you do ... I do hope you feel satisfied with the season—it was *delightful*, and now when I feel a little blue I just think of the Chief and Evans[51] and those grand lofty peaks which have stood against all sorts of troubles for so long and become grander through the experience. We arrived during a heat wave and realized how lucky we had been to have escaped the summer this year ... Thank you a million times for all you did for us.[52]

It must be acknowledged that the habit of paying people as little as possible for services rendered, and preferably persuading them to work on a volunteer basis, was hard on professionals dependent on their earnings for a living. A poignant letter from the fine photographer, Laura Gilpin, illustrates this best. Gilpin had been commissioned to photograph the first two Festival productions in 1932 and 1933. Born in 1891 just outside Colorado Springs and educated at the Clarence White School of photography in New York, Gilpin had already made her mark as a photographer of note, especially of Southwestern themes.[53]

"My dear Anne," she wrote on April 10, 1934,

Laura Gilpin, Denver Public Library Western History Collection

... because of my own precarious financial situation I must tell you that I cannot consider photographing Othello this year unless I can be assured of cost plus a modest profit. I am sure you know how deeply interested I am in the Central City Festival, but in my present circumstances I cannot do so unless I can see how I am coming out ... the Association still owes me $60.00 on last year, and this in addition to the bad accounts I have still on my books from both years leaves me somewhat in the hole ... I have nothing but my own earnings for the support of my father and myself and I am sure that you will understand ...[54]

One participant reported,

Miss Evans just had a way of getting a lot for a little. She was very persuasive ... Chorus members were paid $28 a week, and they paid back $14 of it to the opera association for room and board.[55]

Helen Black, responsible for much of the extraordinarily creative and successful annual publicity for the Festival from 1931 until 1947, was a single woman dependent on her own earnings. In the second of two 1975 *Rocky Mountain News* articles on Helen's life and contributions, reporter Frances Melrose wrote the following:

What even some of her staunchest admirers don't know, however, is that during all the years Helen Black managed publicity for

Central City ... she worked entirely as an unpaid volunteer. The last two years she was allowed $75 a month for postage.[56]

Helen also volunteered her services for many years to the Denver Symphony, which she helped to organize. Eventually she became the first woman business manager of a major orchestra in the United States.

Another significant Colorado personality recruited to help in the publicity campaign was the able, eccentric and frankly snobbish Caroline Bancroft, who later developed into the most successful popular Colorado historian of her day. As the efforts to put on the first Festival accelerated, according to a recent book featuring the life of Bancroft,

Central City became the destination of every Brahmin in Denver, and to be on a CCOHA committee meant automatic membership in Denver society. Caroline, a charter member of the association, worked with scores of volunteers to clean the opera house. At the request of 'Aunt' Anne Evans, as Caroline called the daughter of former territorial governor John Evans ... she also served on the festival's publicity committee.[57]

A Memorable Opening Night—1932

No effort was spared to make the crucial opening night of the Festival in 1932 memorable and unique. In keeping with the original performance date of the chosen play, *Camille*—a time when Central City was flourishing—Robert Jones requested that the audience dress in 1870s costume. Helen Black found out that one of the grandest balls ever held in Central City was given in the early 1870s, in honor of the visit of the Grand Duke Alexis of Russia. Publicizing this information helped fuel the willingness of attendees to display appropriate finery. Jones is credited with selecting the date of opening night. It featured a full moon, which cast the entire event in a magical light.

Members of the Association "launched an intensive search for ancient carriages, buggies and victorias which would be used to transport theatre-goers up and down Central's steep streets."[58] These horse-drawn vehicles were used to bring passengers from the train

A crowd gathers in front of the Central City Opera House for opening night July 16, 1932. Denver Public Library Western History Collection

depot in Black Hawk to Central City. Passenger service to Black Hawk had been suspended by the Colorado and Southern Railroad in 1927 but they agreed to run a special train for this occasion. Most theatre-goers, however, had to brave the "Oh My God!" road by automobile, although the Rocky Mountain Transportation company "will run buses from Idaho Springs to Central City to accommodate those who do not wish to drive their own cars."[59] Ida McFarlane is credited with arranging with the Sheriff's Department that, during the Festival, Virginia Canyon would be turned into a one-way road going to Central for several hours before the performance, and a one-way road going down afterwards.

Authentic atmosphere was created by having "prospectors" lead pack trains of burros up the streets to the "diggings." For the first few festivals, revived gambling dens enlivened the streets; roulette and certain other games were officially permitted in the name of historical accuracy. Other nostalgic events were scheduled for a number of years during the days of the Festival including horse cart races, ore-drilling contests, and a Pony Express mule race to Idaho Springs.

The Association Board member charged with overall responsibility for publicity was Milton Bernet, a vice president of the Mountain Bell Telephone Company. He worked closely with Helen Black. The team generated excellent local and national coverage. Brochures were sent to all the railroads serving Denver and to the major hotels in the state. In addition to special sections or issues of Central City and Denver newspapers, the Festival received coverage in national magazines—*Time, Vanity Fair, Theatre Arts Monthly*—and in the *New York Times*.

The opening ceremonies outside the Opera House were broadcast on the NBC radio network. Delos Chappell interviewed Robert Edmond Jones, who "summed up the guiding mystique behind the festival":

> This opera house and this little mountain town can help America to understand its own past days of glory and romance. Central City today is a bit of Victorian America built out of mountain granite and therefore preserved for us ... I would like to feel that tonight we are placing a wreath on the altar of a beautiful memory.[60]

The play itself was a stunning success. The cast rehearsed for four weeks before the opening at the Delos Chappell estate west of Denver, apparently fulfilling Robert Jones' desire to create "harmonious intimacy and understanding between every individual and department". Many of the furnishings and props were lent by prominent Denver families.[61] Jones' offbeat casting of frail silent film star Lillian Gish in the role of Camille worked well in the romantic Victorian setting of the Central City Opera House. The *Denver Post* drama critic described the scene:

> Heretofore the Lady of the Camellias has been portrayed by women who have been part of the world, the flesh, and maybe the devil; the divine Sarah, Eleanora Duse, Modjeska ... At last, however, there has appeared a dainty, fragile, luminous creature wearing white, looking more like a spirit than a living, breathing woman ... At first it was difficult to take her role seriously. She was surrounded by gaily-dressed creatures in flaming scarlet ... Then

into the circle came Armand Duval ... and straightaway she began to be all those things that have ... set her apart as the genius of the silent films.[62]

Poor Lillian Gish herself had reason to turn white when she returned to her dressing room. Since she was playing the lady who

loved camellias, Robert Edmond Jones had sent her a large bowl of them, enough to last through the run of the play. After dying on stage the first night, she came into her dressing room in time to see a large pack rat sitting by the bowl, finishing off the last blossom. The restored Opera House still had a few problems.

The festivities continued after the play ended with a grand ball at the Teller House and celebratory toasts in the Teller House bar and other watering holes open late into the night. A *Rocky Mountain News* reporter summed up the general impression of that memorable first night, "This almost impossibly idealistic project so captivated the imagination of the press and the public of this state and the entire region that the play festival was a success from the start."[63] Financially, however, the Festival ended with the Association $5,000 in the red, and Delos Chappell wrote a check to cover the deficit.

Anne Evans dressed in Victorian costume for opening night, Denver Public Library Western History Collection

Flower Girls and Ushers

The tradition of naming Flower Girls, who on opening night each year distribute small bunches of flowers to the audience, started in 1932. There were two young girls, aged 13 and 14, who lived in homes near the Chappell estate, and they were fascinated watchers of the rehearsals taking place there. "It was probably Anne Evans who thought of including them in the festivities as debutantes. Robert Edmond Jones designed their gowns. At intermission on opening night they handed out nosegays to the ladies in the audience, explaining the flowers were to be tossed onstage during curtain calls."[64]

Time has elaborated on that simple beginning. These days, the group of around eighteen debutantes all dress alike on a theme decided each year: in 1941, when *The Bartered Bride* was featured, they were in peasant dresses; in 1950, in kimonos to fit in with *Madama Butterfly*. They are presented in an elaborate ceremony on opening night. Each Flower Girl is announced individually as she descends the attractive staircase in the Opera House garden, carrying a basket of traditional Central City yellow roses. It is said that some of the Cornish and Welsh miners brought with them cuttings of yellow rose bushes, which proved to be the roses that adapted best to Central City's altitude of 8,500 feet. Each year, they bloom luxuriously, and have become part of the symbolism of Central City and its Festival. The Flower Girls and their escorts move to the front of the Opera House to be welcomed by the officers of the Opera House Association.

> Then, according to tradition, the bells on St. James Church ring, there's a blast of dynamite from the hills above, and the doors of the Opera House are unlocked to officially open the season. The Flower Girls and their fathers dance to the Yellow Rose Waltz. Then everyone is invited to join in, dancing in the street on a summer night in June.[65]

Three of Anne Evans' grand nieces were Flower Girls in 1962. Today the names of the Flower Girls are announced from the Governor's mansion early in the year. In addition to their participation in opening night festivities, they are expected to be involved in significant community service projects.

The tradition of using festively attired young male ushers also started with the first performance in 1932. There were six of them that year, dressed in "frock coats, cravats and high-top boots ... with pants tucked into their boots so as not to get their cuffs muddy on the unpaved streets of Central City."[66] Today there is a core of fifteen male and female ushers each year who are also interns, during the Festival, in some aspect of theatrical production or administration.

Central City's Second Year

With the first hugely successful Festival over, work immediately started on planning for 1933. Robert Edmond Jones agreed to produce the second Central City offering, selecting the nostalgic Viennese operetta *The Merry Widow*. It was a show eminently suited to the Central City atmosphere, light-hearted, romantic, elegantly costumed—and in English. The original 1905 Viennese version in German had been translated for productions in London and on Broadway in 1907. Thanks to Robert Jones' powers of persuasion, the services of well-known opera stars Gladys Swarthout and Richard Bonelli and Broadway actress Natalie Hall were secured. Beyond these encouraging arrangements, an immense amount of work faced the Association board members, guided by the organizing skills of chairman Anne Evans.

The most pressing question was financial. Anne Evans had instituted a practice that was later, in 1936, officially incorporated into the Association's by-laws. This related to the contribution of "guarantors" described earlier in the correspondence between Anne and Alice Taylor. May 7, 1936, the Board of Directors of CCOHA unanimously approved the following amendment to the by-laws: "The membership of the Central City Opera House Association shall be limited to seventy-five persons who are divided into two classes, 'Guarantor Members' and 'Members at Large'."[67] Officially, this was a loan, to be repaid out of the season's receipts. In actuality, donors were fortunate in most years to receive even 50 percent of their "loan" back.

The need for accommodations in Central City for operagoers, as well as cast members and production staff, suggested to Anne Evans that the Association should rent the entire Teller House for the season in 1933. Volunteers were again recruited to help clean up and repaint rooms. Space was made on the second floor for a Night Club, which proved extremely popular. Enthusiastic Denver supporters of the Central City revival effort began to purchase houses in the town, old miners' cottages could be bought for $50, more elaborate Victorian homes for $150. Laura Gilpin, in the letter referred to above, tells Anne Evans,

I was quite in earnest the other day when I said we must sell our Central City House. It is a sad disappointment to the three of us who were undertaking it, but we are all in a position right now where it is utterly impossible for us even to think of spending anything on repairs, and the house should be repaired at once ... we will be glad to sell it for what we have put into it, which will be about $50.00 by the time the title is turned over to a purchaser.

Yetta McFarlane (who became first Mrs. Curt Schroeder and then Mrs. Ronald Demeter) became

the informal leader of Denverites who bought and restored summer homes in Central City. Names such as Bancroft, McFarlane, McGlone, Scott, Belford-Wayne, Wilson, McGrath, and a dozen others with Colorado antecedents appeared in the 1930's on gateposts of Central City homes as these third generation representatives reestablished roots and planted yellow roses.[68]

Since the demand for tickets for the first season had outrun the supply, *The Merry Widow* was scheduled to run for twelve nights. Again the opening night crowd came dressed in period costume—

the women in Floradora dresses, the men in early twentieth century costume ... When the Rhenish curtain slowly rose in the Opera House the audience ... saw a spangled, glittering period setting by Designer Jones. In the chorus they spotted socialite members of Denver singing and dancing schools who were working for fun. The professional cast, smoothly directed by Mr. Jones, ably unrolled the *Merry Widow's* famed plot. Last week, Denver socialites stomped, whistled and shouted their enthusiasm.[69]

The Teller House ballroom was decorated for a fancy dress ball following the performance, and again the streets around the Opera House were alive with gambling parlors, bars and nostalgic gift shops. Around this time, a cherished tradition started at the Teller House, and is still honored today. "After curtain calls, audience members crowd into the Little Kingdom Room, waiting for the cast to come in and sing some more."[70]

Cast party for "The Merry Widow", 1933. Denver Public Library Western History Collection, Samuel S. Newbury

Although there were "disastrous floods and terrible rains" during the first week of the Festival, which cut down on attendance, the second season was felt to be an unqualified success. And so, as in each of the following years until 1941, planning began immediately for the following season. It was not only top talent from New York that was drawn into the Central City project from the beginning, but also the finest that Denver had to offer. This included two women pioneers in the Denver performing arts world.

Florence Lamont and Lillian Cushing

Florence Lamont, born in 1884, spent her early years in Ontario, Canada, where she attended the London Conservatory of Music. At the age of seventeen, she made a pilgrimage to Denver to recover from tuberculosis. After regaining her health, she continued her music studies and had many successful performances as singer and accompanist in Denver and other cities in the U. S. In 1924, she married Leroy Hinman and together they founded the Lamont School of Music, which grew to be an important cultural fixture in Denver's art scene throughout the 1920s and 30s. It became part of the University of Denver in 1941. After functioning for years in a number of different buildings, it moved in 2002 into the handsome Newman Center on the University of Denver campus. Florence Lamont Hinman became a renowned voice teacher, lecturing and teaching widely in the United States and Europe. For a number of seasons, she served as choral director for the Central City Opera and supplied many of the singers for its productions.

Lillian Cushing, a pioneer on the Denver dance scene, headed up the choreography for many Central City productions, and supplied most of its dancers from the Festival's beginning to 1968. Born in Denver in 1901, she began dancing as a child and later graduated from North High School. In the summers of her teen-age years, she studied dance in Chicago and New York. In 1922, she opened her own dance school in Denver. It became a training ground for literally hundreds of dancers, many of whom went on to dance in major dance companies throughout the country or to found dance schools of their own. Cushing described the role of a ballet teacher: "The body can be molded into a thing of beauty under the hands of a sculptor," she said, "this is the real satisfaction in teaching—the results."[71]

For many years, she also choreographed the annual summer musicals presented in Cheesman Park under the sponsorship of the Denver Post. In 1950, ten years after the death of Ida Kruse McFarlane, Lillian Cushing married Frederick McFarlane. The couple continued as enthusiastic supporters of the Central City Festival, and Lillian continued as a nationally recognized ballet teacher.

> Calls ballet art of illusion ... says classic dancing, properly taught, is physically the producer of supple, strong body ... She has 300 students ... teaches four days a week ... with four assistants ... holds no classes whenever a professional troupe appears ... is often responsible for half the audience there.[72]
>
> Fred McFarlane lived until 1962, Lillian Cushing McFarlane until 1975.

The Seasons of 1934, 1935 and 1936—
Frank St. Leger Contributes His Talents

New supporters were drawn in each year, but there was one significant loss, that of Delos Chappell. This was due to a rift between Chappell and Robert Edmond Jones. Jones took his production of *Camille* from Central City to Broadway—where it was a total flop. Fragile Lillian Gish, without the otherworldly atmosphere of Central City and its Opera House, failed to convince either audiences or critics of the validity of her offbeat interpretation of Marguerite. Jones thereupon concluded that the Central City Festival was such a unique event that it could not function as a viable try-out locale for Broadway productions. For Broadway producer Chappell, who had been the main backer of *Camille* in Central City, this potential aspect of the summer season was apparently his primary interest. However, he advanced other reasons for his withdrawal. According to Anne Evans' report to the Board in August of 1933, Chappell considered Jones an "incompetent director," implying that either Jones' 5-year contract must be revoked or he—Chappell—would resign from the Board. "After a rather serious altercation over properties and lighting equipment he had lent the Association, Miss Evans accepted his departure."[73] Robert Jones also chose to resign from the Board, "because I feel that the Artistic Director of the project should not be a member of the board. I am sure that this step will make matters much simpler for us all in the future."[74]

1934 saw Jones' superb production of Shakespeare's *Othello*. For 1935, he devised a lavish, original entertainment called *Central City Nights*. This was an evocation of the Opera House's past: scenes from the great variety of plays and operas that had enchanted Central City audiences in the nineteenth century. "Because Central City was settled by Welsh and Cornish gold miners, the Revue will open with a scene at a mine shaft at night with songs by a male chorus of thirty Welsh voices."[75] The show should have been another hit. The sets and costumes were spectacular and the acting, dancing and music excellent. The *Rocky Mountain News* gave it a rave review, mingling appreciation for the musical extravaganza with a detailed description of the ladies' dress choices for the festive opening: "Mrs. Frederick McFarlane, a gold lace with a square cut décolleté. Miss Anne Evans, black lace combined with chiffon, with diamond clips distinguishing the neckline."[76] Overall, unfortunately, there were altogether too many people who felt that the show was better described as *Central City Frights* than *Central City Nights*.

Musical arrangements for the 1935 production were the work of Frank St. Leger, who had been brought into the project by Robert Jones and who became a vital member of the Central City Opera Association staff. Born in 1890 in India to British parents, St. Leger studied piano and conducting at the Royal Academy of Music in London, served in the Australian army for two years in the First World War, and then became pianist and conductor for opera star Dame Nellie Melba. This commission brought him to the United States in 1917, and led to positions with two American opera companies and with London's Covent Garden Opera. He first met Robert Jones while touring with Melba.

At the time of his first summer engagement in Central City, St. Leger served as music director of the Houston Symphony. In a letter to Anne Evans written after the end of the 1935 season, St. Leger wrote that he had not yet decided whether to return to Houston.[77] Eventually, he decided to resign. He focused on productions in Central City, and continued the affiliation even after accepting a position as assistant conductor for the Metropolitan Opera in New York. This direct association between the Central City Opera and the Met proved invaluable in future Central City productions, supplying "a steady stream of singers, directors and conductors." For the Central City productions, he fulfilled many roles over the years, "as artistic and musical director, conductor, arranger, stage director, and producer."[78]

In spite of the indifferent success of *Central City Nights*, the CCOHA Board decided to try another musical for 1936. Choosing Gilbert and Sullivan's popular operetta *The Gondoliers*, they engaged Frank St. Leger as Director, putting him in charge of the entire production. Robert Edmond Jones was not able to be involved that year because of new commitments in Hollywood.[79] As set designer, St. Leger chose the Central City artist Frank (Pancho) Gates, the same artist who, in 1932, had executed Robert Jones' design for the Opera House curtain. Qualifying Gates for his assignment in Central City were his many years of painting sets for a variety of Denver theaters, including Elitch's.

Some conditions had already changed in Central City between 1932 and 1936. Gambling was no longer permitted to flourish as it had done in the opening year. Ties between the Association and Denver University had loosened. The CCOHA no longer functioned as a department of the University. It had become an independent non-profit organization with Anne Evans, Ida Kruse McFarlane, Allen True and the Chappells as charter members. One of the reasons for separation was that the consumption of alcohol on premises owned by the Methodist-sponsored Colorado Seminary was distinctly unacceptable. Denver University properties, for tax reasons, were still legally under the ownership of The Colorado Seminary. Denver University, however, remained a steadfast supporter of the Central City Festivals.

CCOHA Buys the Teller House

Soon Anne Evans spearheaded another major change. Renting the Teller House seemed no longer satisfactory. In order to justify the expense of needed renovations, the Association needed to own it. To accomplish this, arrangements were made with Denver financiers to organize a bond issue. Divided in to small denominations, it quickly sold, for a total amount of $6,500. As with a substantial number of the annual payments of guarantor members, Anne

Evans managed to transmute many of the bond purchases into donations. Minutes of a 1940 CCOHA Board of Directors meeting held at her home at 1310 Bannock Street noted the following:

> Miss Evans said that the Association was now ready to retire all of the bonds which had been sold originally to purchase the Teller House. With the exception of four bondholders, all of the bonds were returned to the Central City treasury as donations, and the others will be paid off.[80]

Whose is the Face on the Barroom Floor?

It was while renovations were underway at the Teller House in 1936 that the famous "Face on the Barroom Floor" painting appeared. There are several versions of how this came about but general agreement that the artist was Herndon Davis. The website of the Denver Press Club, of which Herndon was a long time member, has this account.

> Herndon was commissioned to do a series of paintings for the Central City Opera Association ... While working on this project, Herndon became involved in an argument with project director Ann(sic) Evans about the manner in which the project should be executed. The result was either that he quit or was fired. On his last night in Central City he painted *The Face on the Barroom Floor*.

Herndon Davis worked for many years as an illustrator at both *The Denver Post* and *The Rocky Mountain News*. He painted murals all over Denver, "including the tearoom of the Denver Dry Goods store and one in the card room of the Denver Press Club showing Denver newspaper people of the 1940s ..."[81]

Mary Sawle Taitt, in her booklet, *Opera House Stories and Teller House Tales*, has a more colorful version of the face story, which she attributes to "one of the founders of the (Gilpin County) historical society." She wrote the following about what happened while Herndon Davis was working on the restoration of the Teller House bar:

> There were many times when he and the elegant Miss Evans differed. I doubt she liked the bar idea and the rowdy goings on disturbed her. Into this turmoil came an itinerant actor who would

recite *The Face on the Barroom Floor*[82], complete with gestures. He could earn enough money for drinks and made the rounds many times. There was another party who strongly objected to the pleasure (Herndon) Davis was getting from his job. His wife, Juanita, was a teetotaler and objected to the long hours he was working. A plot was worked out, and Herndon drew her picture on the floor, covered it with a drop cloth, and pulled it off just as the actor had reached the dying swan part of his act. The shock was so big that it took several shots of expensive whiskey to revive the poor fellow. The joke made news all over town and the actor was hired to do many return performances. Miss Evans was so angry she demanded the painting be removed, but local artist, Quackenbush, and others insisted it be kept. It is world famous today.[83]

In his paper *Central City Opera,* Grahame Macmillan has yet another perspective on the story:

> Anne had hired a painter, Herndon Davis, to restore the paintings in the Teller House Bar. Unfortunately, Herndon was a bit of a lush, and being able to paint in the bar took great advantage of that fact. He took so much advantage that very little, if any, painting was being done. Fed up with this situation, Anne told Herndon that she would fire him if he didn't stop his drinking ... Herndon ... decided he would get even with Anne. To this end, he painted the face of his wife on the floor of the bar. When Anne saw the face she was livid, but the bartender managed to calm her down and to get her to leave the face, as it was a beautiful painting.[84]

Ida Kruse McFarlane is credited with the following version:

> [Herndon] Davis, having heard the old ballad recited, awoke from sleep with this image in his mind. With the electricity temporarily turned off in the hotel, Mr. Davis lighted a candle, descended to the barroom, and painted the face on the floor.[85]

And then there is the story told by 90+ year-old Ethelind Austin. One summer, she said, when Anne Evans' guests, the Walker girls, were in the Teller House Bar, an artist approached Challis Walker and asked her if he could paint her portrait. Half-joking, she said she was willing, but only if he could do it right away. "I don't have a canvas with me," he responded—"but—what if I paint it right here, on the floor!" "I knew Challis well," Ethelind said, "and that is her likeness on the floor."[86]

Finally, there is the "Tale of a Face" told by Colorado Springs author Marshall Sprague, commissioned to write the story of Central City and its Opera Festival for a special issue of *Colorado Wonderland Magazine* in 1954. "If you can recite 'The Shooting of Dan McGrew,'" wrote Sprague, "you probably know Antoine D'Arcy's vintage ditty about the stew-bum who painted the visage of his faithless love on the barroom floor and then, 'with a fearful shriek … fell across the picture—dead.'"

> Well, very late one night in the Teller House bar … the well-known Denver artist and newspaper man Herndon Davis was reciting The Face to a convivial group—including bartender Louis Spies and the lovely young sculptress, Challis Walker, who was a friend of Anne Evans. When Davis finished the ballad, he stared a moment at Challis' haunting dark beauty and then he was on his knees painting her face on the barroom floor. It is still there and probably will be forever. In the cold light of next morning, Davis tried to remove his masterpiece, but Anne Evans would not hear of it. The world, Anne said, had been crying for a real Face ever since 'D'Arcy wrote the ballad, and the floor of the Teller House bar was just the floor for it.'[87]

The Teller House bar was renamed The Face Bar, and its fame spread far and wide. As Sprague noted, "Millions of Central City visitors have not seen the inside of the opera house, but most of them have seen The Face."

Much later, when the CCOHA had successfully entered the arena of commissioning new works, a crowd-pleasing one-act opera, *The Face on the Barroom Floor*, was first performed in the Teller House Bar in 1978. Composed by Henry Mollicone, with a libretto by John Bowman, and produced by Robert Darling, "The opera tells two tales, separated in time, but parallel in character and theme. Present day Isabel is a singer in the Central City chorus who dreams of singing Violetta in *La Traviata*. The beautiful Madeline is a saloon girl in a 19th-century gold camp. Both are loved by two men, and as the opera moves between two centuries, the parallel plots come to the same tragic end—a timeless tale of love and jealousy."[88]

The opera is now performed each year in the remodeled Williams Stables, across the street from the Opera House, by members of Central City's Bonfils-Stanton Artists' Training Program. This is one of the many fine programs that have been added to the basic Festival activities over the years.

The Seasons of 1936 to 1939

A number of cosmetic improvements were made to the Teller House in 1936. The lobby and some of the first and second floor rooms were furnished in Victorian splendor and arranged to display items celebrating Central City's pioneer past. Anne Evans apparently paid some of the bills herself.[89] She secured one room for her own use as headquarters for her endless CCOHA projects. Money was scarce but the efforts of volunteers and donors of services were gratefully accepted and used to the full.

Gondoliers was a success in 1936. Gilbert and Sullivan's creations were perfectly suited for Central City and the Thirties. A production of *The Yeoman of the Guard* in 1939 was also a hit. After the 1936 season was over, Anne Evans wrote her evaluation of the Central City project in a *Rocky Mountain News* article.

> This running and preserving of an authentic old mining camp with all the atmosphere and traditions brought vividly to life, grows each year in significance, for it is not only glorious fun, and a unique chance to see drama at its best, but it is carrying over the very spirit of the pioneers to new generations—the spirit that went forth to win all the good things of the world; gold first, which was here for the finding; and then all the good things which gold could buy. They wanted, and they got opera houses and drama, dance halls and music, libraries and churches, and hotels—all of the best and all lavishly supported and lustily enjoyed. It was a new phase of American life and here in Central City for a little time each year all this turbulent life can be relived and savoured and enjoyed.[90]

Between 1936 and 1939 there was one brave failure and one very dated play fashioned into a success only by "Robert Jones' genius."[91] The failure was Ibsen's *A Doll's House*. Produced by Richard Aldrich, in a brand new translation and with an outstanding cast including Ruth Gordon and Walter Slezak, the play should have been a triumph. However, in the words of a *Denver Post* reviewer, "It was a crowd in

search of gay entertainment and mountain music and celebration.
And it got three acts of Ibsen in which there were just three laughs
by the clock."[92] It probably did not help that actress Ruth Gordon
hated Central City and virtually refused to mingle with anyone.
"Anne Evans decided there and then that gloomy, esoteric plays
were out of key at Central."[93]

Evans was surprised and disappointed at the play's reception.
Earlier in the year, she had written enthusiastically about its
prospects to a young friend, Ann Matlack:

> We are 'all set' for Central, thank heavens, but there was a
> moment when we hung over the abyss. This seems to be part of
> the theatre game—I agree with you that Orson Wells is one of the
> most interesting people on the horizon, but some time ago we had
> an application from Richard Aldrich, and he is now in charge—we
> are going to give The Doll's House (interestingly adapted by an
> outstanding author whose name I must not reveal—[Thornton
> Wilder])—Ruth Gordon is going to play Nora—than whom there is
> none better—Jed Harris is going to direct—Aldrich is wonderful to
> work with and I think we are going to be on the theatrical map in
> great shape ... Aldrich was about to sail ... for Russia when we wired
> him—he cancelled his trip and had been working wonderfully on
> our behalf.[94]

For the 1938 season, a suggestion of Robert Edmond Jones was
accepted; the production would be another revival from the period
of the glory years of Central City. *Ruy Blas* by Victor Hugo had first
been produced in Europe exactly 100 years before, in 1838, but had
been revived in 1879 by Sarah Bernhardt and regularly performed
in the United States around the turn of the century. Although the
play was basically a romantic cloak-and-dagger melodrama, Jones'
artistic flair for set design and costuming, his skillful use of the Opera
House's distinctive atmosphere and acoustics, and the direction of
successful Broadway celebrity, Richard Aldrich, earned for *Ruy Blas*
the praise of local and national drama critics—and of the National
Broadcasting Company, which again covered the opening.

New York's Lucius Beebe Writes Up Central City

The liveliest commentary on this Festival came from New York
journalist Lucius Beebe. Bon vivant, author of books on railroad

history, connoisseur of travel, style, food and wine, Beebe is credited with inventing the term "café society"—in which he was both gleeful participant and shrewd observer. At the time, Beebe wrote a regular column, "This New York," for the *New York Herald Tribune* as well as articles for the *New Yorker* and other national magazines. In the Sunday *Denver Post* of July 24, 1938, under the heading MR. BEEBE COMES TO TOWN AND GOES TO TOWN FOR CENTRAL, he described how, a week before the Festival opening, "professional and social celebrities" began arriving in Denver, rolling in aboard the Union Pacific's City of Denver and the Burlington Zephyr—or the Pony Express, the Rocky Mountain Limited and the Grand Canyon. One "greatly daring" visitor "flew in." After a day or two spent sampling the offerings of Denver, including exotic cocktails at the bar of the Brown Palace Hotel and mint juleps at the Shirley Savoy, the "notables" found themselves

> taxied over the appalling chasms above Idaho Springs by the skilled Dick Crane, Anne Evans' chauffeur, who combines the functions of an airplane pilot with the potentialities of Charon. In places the drop is a sheer 1,000 feet and the only really safe way of going over the road would be on hands and knees and that very slowly.

Beebe then described Central City's beginnings, and the origin of the Festival:

> Six or seven years ago a group of engaging spirits conceived the notion of a summer theater season in the ghostly precincts of Central City's famed opera house. They opened amid magnificent tumult with 'Camille' and in the presence of everyone who was anyone in Colorado, and such a hilarious success was scored that ever since the Central City season has been one of the brightest and most important of the legitimate theater's non-Broadway events. Junketing and fancy flag-wavings have attended its progress. The Teller House bar, conveniently situated next door ... flourished wickedly. The livery stable across the way was the scene of dancehall merriment. A night club whose clientele was every inch as smart as that of Morocco was installed upstairs at the hotel. There were whispers of roulet and faro bank somewhere around the corner in Main Street.

By 8 o'clock, half an hour before Gov. Teller Ammons, Senator Ed C. Johnson and Mayor Benjamin F. Stapleton of Denver were scheduled to make addresses from the steps of the opera house, the photographers' flash bulbs were as fierce as heat lightning in Eureka Street. Anne Evans, who is the moving genius of the revivals, was able to announce that the entire house was sold out at $5 top with seats in the gallery at $2.25. Everyone was dressed to the teeth. There were dinner jackets of every imaginable shade, and here and there a tailcoat and white tie. The ushers wore frock coats, string ties and riding boots.

Beebe noted that there were reporters from both coasts, and many towns in between, filling fifty press seats, while *Life* magazine had two cameramen filming for a "Life Goes to a Party" assignment.

The ladies of the audience furnished reporters with an embarrassment of sartorial riches ... The arrival of Mrs. Delos Chappell, a notable dresser and celebrated beauty who was in a sort of Valentine rig of smoke gray with a trailing cape lined with white silk, caused a tremendous sensation. So did a gleaming town car with two footmen on the box.

When the play concluded, the audience stampeded over to the Teller House night club, where 500 people had reservations but

a good many more must have contrived to get into the premises ... Certainly it could not have been a more gala evening, and Miss Evans passed from table to table urging the guests to have themselves a time of it, a gesture both of hospitality and acumen, since the Opera Association owns the bar concession at the hotel ...

Opera Returns to Central City

By this time, Robert Edmond Jones was suffering from deteriorating health and Frank St. Leger had become the most important professional figure in Festival operations. He strongly favored starting to offer opera rather than plays in the Central City Opera House. "Anne voted to give it a whirl."[95] The season was expanded to three weeks for 1940 and the production was to be Smetana's *The Bartered Bride*.

For 1941 a daring undertaking was planned—the presentation of two operas, *The Barber of Seville* by Rossini and Gluck's *Orpheus*.

Anne and Ida Still Carrying the Load

The Board of the CCOHA was dedicated and hard-working, but the major responsibility for the continuing success and growth of the Central City Festival enterprise still rested with Ida Kruse McFarlane and Anne Evans. Ida, who had a working life as a full Professor of English at Denver University, took on organizing much of the volunteer committee work and the lively social entertainment which made such a contribution the appeal of the Central City project. She and her husband, Frederick, hosted lavish cocktail and dinner parties both in their Denver mansion at Colfax and Gilpin and in the ancestral McFarlane home on Eureka Street in Central City. In 1938, the McFarlanes moved into a new Denver home at 1200 Williams Street. Describing a hectic round of parties before the 1940 season of *The Bartered Bride*, columnist Ernie Pyle wrote about attending a cocktail party for "a few thousand people" at the McFarlane's home.[96] When, ten years after Ida McFarlane's death, Frederick married Lillian Cushing, the couple continued the tradition of lavish entertaining on behalf of the Central City Festival. Their Central City cocktail parties became a highlight of the Festival, with stars such as Julie Harris, Helen Hayes, and Shirley Booth among the many celebrities entertained by the hospitable McFarlanes.

Making the big decisions about forthcoming productions, organizing the myriad day-to-day tasks to pull off yet another successful season, and raising the money to pay for it all, were still largely Anne Evans' responsibility. The *Gilpin County Miner* reported that "To players, directors, musicians and audiences the annual Central City performance was known as 'Miss Evans' Show'"[97]

In 1937, the CCOHA Board agreed that the time had come to hire a new general manager for the Festival, replacing Frank White, who had served since 1931.

No one could have been more surprised than Justin M. Brierly one winter day in the middle of the Depression when he received a call from Anne Evans, one of the grande dames of Denver society. She asked him to come to a tea at the home of Ida Kruse McFarlane, another socialite. Since practically no one ever refused an invitation from Evans, Brierly rang the doorbell of the McFarlane mansion at the appointed time.[98]

Miss Evans, Brierly remembered, came to the point quickly. She said that she and the other board members had heard of Brierly's experience in the theater and had voted to offer him the job of general manager if he was interested. "Young Brierly gulped and said yes." Justin Brierly, though young, had an unusual background. With a partner, he had operated a talent agency in New York, had worked as a psychological counselor for child stars at the Hal Roach studios in Hollywood, and had recently graduated from Columbia University with a degree in education. He was back in his native city of Denver to pursue his love of teaching.

Reminiscing in 1975 about the eleven years he spent in the job—which he did in the summers while holding down a full-time assignment with the Denver Public Schools and still maintaining a law practice—Brierly remembered, "The Central City Opera Association had practically no money at the time. I worked for a small salary." First, he said, "Miss Evans chose the production and the cast—always a good one—then set out to raise the money to stage it." Brierly went on to say, "while everything about the productions may have been topnotch, everything about the opera house was not."

> The opera house is built over the creek, which accounts for its marvelous acoustics ... It also poses some problems, however. One night after the first act, someone reported to me that the floor was giving way under the audience, and they were in danger of being dumped in the creek ... Luckily, we found some heavy timbers nearby and were able to shore the place up, temporarily ... and the second act curtain was delayed only a few minutes.[99]

Of necessity, as the organization matured, the approach used by Anne had to change. The organization, Brierly said, "now works back from the allotted budget. With (Anne), the artistic came first."[100] With her passionate conviction that only the very best was good enough for Central City, Anne Evans set a general principle that is followed to this day.

An Unending "To Do" list for Anne Evans

Scanning newspaper clippings, the correspondence files of the early days of CCOHA in the Denver University Library's Archives Department, and the contents of the precious accordion file labeled "Anne

Evans, Her Folding File," yields an idea of the wide variety of matters that claimed Anne Evans' attention and time as President of the Association.

There are numerous invitations for her to speak about the Central City Festival. These included the Denver Lion's Club in 1934; a twenty minute talk on a Denver radio station with Ida Kruse McFarlane in 1935; and to secure Director Richard Aldrich to address the Cactus Club in 1937.

Robert Edmond Jones sent a cable in the spring of 1934, urging her to confirm "by telegram ... the earliest possible" the engagement of an actor for seven hundred and fifty dollars "because he has several other offers."[101]

A 1936 letter notes, on the recommendation of the Director, "Miss Evans ... has decided to make Friday, July 31, Colorado State College of Education Night."[102]

In the spring of 1935, Russell Lewis, director of the extensive dance numbers featured in *Central City Nights*, sent Anne Evans a long list of requirements for rehearsal facilities in Denver and Central City, including the services of an accompanist to be used for dance rehearsals exclusively and a studio available at all hours. "In Central City, the High School auditorium would be most satisfactory providing the floor be put into workable state, at present it is heavily oiled and extremely dirty."[103] Also in 1935, Mrs. Robert Bliss expressed concern over a box of costumes from the summer production that Anne Evans had sent, along with suggested prices for purchasing them. Apparently, the box never arrived.[104]

An article in the *Central City Weekly Register Call* in 1936 noted, "More remodeling and cleaning is being done this week at the historic Teller House ... Miss Anne Evans is up from Denver to spend the summer here and look after ... the remodeling." The same article announced, "The first contingent of operatic stars to travel on the new Union Pacific train "City of Denver" are the principals who will sing the stellar roles in *The Gondoliers* ... The seven famous singers will be met by Mr. Frank St. Leger ... and by Anne Evans, Mrs. Frederick McFarlane and members of the Central City Opera House Association."[105]

A letter from the Secretary-Treasurer of the Evans Investment Company informed a Black Hawk contractor that "Miss Anne Evans has directed us to forward you a check for $413.26 at this time to apply on your statement to her."[106] Further checks were to be sent in each of the following two months to pay off the balance. This letter is an indication that Anne Evans did indeed quietly contribute to CCOHA from her own funds.

Theatre Arts Monthly, a national magazine based in New York City, informed "My dear Miss Evans" that for the June, 1935 issue, "we are preparing a list of summer theatres: name, address, length of season ... and name of director. Will you send us this material for your little theatre by return of mail is possible."[107]

A delicate little note from Lillian Gish, written from Beekman Terrace in Manhattan, apparently accompanied a copy of a new biography of Gish. "Dear Anne Evans, You contributed so much to the last pages of this book. I am so grateful to you."[108] Central City only appears on the next to last page of the book, as *Camille* was apparently only in the planning stages when the book was written.

An assistant to Robert Jones sent Evans the sketch for six masks to be made by sculptor Ronnebeck. "Mr. Jones asks that just the *clay models* be ready when he arrives" so he could make changes in the models.[109]

As President of the CCOHA, Anne Evans wrote to the Colorado Secretary of State on April 30, 1940, about the need "to preserve the scenic value of the region known as the 'Alpine Basin.'" She noted that although a large part of the area was already protected as National Forests or the Denver Mountain parks, four State Highways and U. S. Highway 6 (all of which were approach roads to Central City) were, she wrote, "among the most beautiful in the state and most readily accessible ... These should be, to as great a degree as possible, excepted from the defacement of billboards, and I am petitioning you to take such steps as are needed with this object in view."[110]

In 1940, the Chairman of the Colorado Committee (a forerunner of the Opera House Association Guild) wrote to members bringing them up to date on 1940 Festival plans and enclosing press releases for them to take to their local papers. "Miss Anne Evans has asked me to tell you that your invitation to attend a tea to meet Mr. Frank St. Leger and the members of the cast will be mailed to you shortly."[111]

In the same archival box with the folding file is a black looseleaf notebook full of typed and handwritten entries. In it are names and addresses of many of the most famous musicians, singers, conductors, dance companies, opera companies and performers of the day, many along with the names of their agents. There was no limit when it came to Anne Evans' aspirations for Central City. There is also a section on "Persons to Interview while in New York."

How to Pay for It All

Always, there existed the need to raise money. By 1940, members helpful in this respect had been added to the Board, such as attorney Thomas Dines and the wealthy and generous Mrs. Spencer Penrose from Colorado Springs. Penrose had financed a complete overhaul of the ballroom in the Teller House in 1936, designed by architect Burnham Hoyt and interior designer Thornton Fuller. A Finance Committee had been formed, which included Dines and Anne's nephew, John Evans. Yet Anne Evans still played the major fund-raising role. Over her signature as President, a letter went out to former and potential "guarantor members, advancing each $250 or $500 annually." She wrote that the plans for the 1940 Festival were almost complete. "We believe there is no event of the year which gives greater pleasure, or has brought more publicity of the best type to Colorado."

She invited prospective donors to make a visit to her home, where it would give her great pleasure to show "our annual reports and our remarkable Central City publicity, which each year reaches every state in the Union and many foreign countries ... the clippings fill 90 volumes." For Frank St. Leger's production of *The Bartered Bride* the season was increased to three weeks "to avoid the serious over-crowding of last year and the necessity of refusing admittance to eager throngs who have driven long distances to attend the performance." She ended by assuring potential donors that "every effort will be made to administer the fund as economically as is possible while maintaining the high standard of former years."[112]

"I like work. I like people, I love Colorado." So goes a much-quoted statement made by Anne Evans.[113] "... Anne Evans got behind this project for an annual drama festival in Central City as tho she were planning a future for her beloved nieces and nephews. Energy, intelligence, imagination, and cash, she poured into the venture and admits she's had the time of her life doing it. I never went into anything in my life on a pass until, as a co-manager of the Central City project, I was given a pass to a New York theater. Did I feel important!"[114] It is interesting that, when she first began her efforts on behalf of Central City, she was already perceived as "elderly." Describing her role in August of 1933, *Time Magazine* noted, "To the rescue came Denver's able, elderly Art Patron Ann Evans." She was just 62.

Anne Evans' "work" was anything that contributed to the development of institutions and causes she valued. At the same time as she deeply involved herself in every aspect of the growing Central City enterprise, she still carried on her responsibilities to the Denver Art Museum, functioning as its Executive Secretary; to the Denver Public Library, as a member of the Library Commission; and to the Denver Art Commission until 1937 and her very public disagreement with Mayor Stapleton. How she could cope with this extraordinary, self-imposed work load was due, in part, to another of her gifts—she knew how to play. She applied to her own life the advice she gave to guests at her summer home on the Evans Ranch, "You Must Have Fun!"

Anne Evans also apparently took time to be alone with the spacious beauty of the mountain environment and be refreshed by its grandeur. A poem, believed by family members to have been written by her at this time, is titled *Central City Nights*:

> I stand alone in silent wonder—dreaming—
> Amid the far-flung gray-green hills a-teeming
> I try to find an answer to this complex life—out there
> Beneath the clouds—the sky—the stars—the fair
> Soft night—with all its jeweled glories overhead—
> In mute communion I stand there—where the great feast
> Is spread.
> I stand alone—yet not alone—for—in my dreaming
> I hear great hymns amid those gray-green hills a-teeming
> Hymns that I know within my time I cannot write
> That's why I stand alone way out there in the night—
> And when alone—God's lamp in silv'ry radiance spreads
> Its soft—cool—liquid light upon my fevered head.
>
> Out there—alone—far from the ebb and flow of life's mad teeming
> I find a something as I stand just waiting—dreaming—
> For human flesh—its greed—its lusts—it stifles me
> I hurry out into the quiet moon-drenched night to see
> If I can wash away the grime and filthy dust of life a-seeming
> To come back fresh—and new—and clean from those
> Great gray-green hills a-teeming.

I love to stand out there—alone—in silent wonder—dreaming—
I love to stand out there—alone—amid those far-flung
Gray-green hills a-teeming
For—as I stand alone—Lo—something happens, I
am not alone

The End of the McFarlane-Evans Era

1940 would be the closing year of the McFarlane-Evans era of the Central City renaissance. The attraction of Czech composer Smetana's gay comic opera, *The Bartered Bride,* was somehow enhanced by the somber events in Europe, and especially by the tragic fate of Czechoslovakia which had been occupied by Hitler's troops in 1938. Anne Evans was apparently the one who insisted that operas be performed in English—a custom which persisted long after her death. The brilliant production by St. Leger made the new three-week season memorable. Ida Kruse McFarlane, however, did not live long enough to see it; she died on June 18, 1940. A serious heart condition forced Anne Evans to remain in Denver on opening night, rather than taking the risk of travel to Central City's higher altitude. An ingenious rigged-up radio connection enabled her to listen to the opening night festivities from her room at 1310 Bannock Street.

Central City Memorial to Ida Kruse McFarlane

Anne and Ida had always talked about creating "an inspiration point built above Central City where visitors might view the town below and the beautiful mountains beyond."[115] They settled on the old site of St. Aloysius Catholic School, which Ida Kruse had attended as a girl. Opened in 1873 on the top of a hill named Mount Vincent, the school was in operation for forty-four years. It closed for lack of students and financial support in 1917 and was finally razed in 1936. Ida McFarlane bought the land from the sisters who owned it. She managed to salvage a few relics of the old building: the large iron cross which had crowned the school building, two smaller crosses, part of an iron railing and some dusty tiles from window sills. Anne Evans, with a committee of Ida's friends and admirers, carried the plans forward after Ida's death. Architect Burnham Hoyt was commissioned to design the space as a peaceful viewing platform and as a memorial to Ida Kruse McFarlane. But Anne Evans, too, died before the project could be completed.

Ida's memorial was finally dedicated on July 7, 1946. It consisted of a simple fifty-feet-square, paved rectangle, following the lines of the school foundation, surrounded by a native stone parapet. An entry gate was fashioned from the salvaged piece of iron railing, the tiles from the window sills were used to form part of an aisle that followed the old school hallway. The three crosses were mounted high on a platform so as to be seen from most streets in the city. A simple bronze plaque on the wall under the crosses is inscribed "Ida Kruse McFarlane, 1940," along with a quotation from the twentieth-century Spanish poet, Antonio Machado, "He who leaves work well done is with us still." The memorial, still there though sadly neglected, is easily reached by a path that starts in the Opera House garden. The 1946 dedication ceremony was conducted jointly by the University of Denver and the Central City Opera House Association, with ownership of the memorial jointly accepted by the two organizations. Chancellor Caleb Gates presided. Thomas Dines read a moving tribute in which he celebrated Ida's love of her mining camp background.

Ida Kruse McFarlane Memorial in disrepair, 2009

In her mind's eye she could see the booted miners and their gay and courageous women, she could hear the Cornishmen as they sang their songs of home, she could see the groups of excited men as some new rich strike was discussed, she could attend the performances in the Central City Opera House.

Dines recalled Ida's "long and rich education at Vassar and in Europe," her "really prodigious knowledge of the world's literature" which, he said, "was so varied, so wide and so accurate that she was both the admiration and despair of those who were her friends." Finally, Dines talked about the Central City Festival which, he called "the consuming interest of Ida Kruse McFarlane during her last years."

> Except for Ida Kruse McFarlane there would be no Central City Festival. With her originated the first germ of the idea which has grown to the great proportions we all know. With the love for the drama which was hers, with the sentimental attachment to the old Opera House with its poignant memories which were hers, and in cooperation with Anne Evans along both the artistic and practical financial lines, this renowned and lovely Festival has become a monument to these two great women far surpassing even this dignified monument which we dedicate this July evening.[116]

Death of Anne Evans

In 1940, Anne Evans knew that her time was running out. As far as the Central City Festival was concerned, she felt secure in the knowledge that plans were well under way for a successful 1941 season, featuring two ambitious opera productions under the experienced baton of Frank St. Leger. She had also made perhaps her greatest contribution to the future of the Festival—she had brought Frank Ricketson Jr. onto the Association Board.

> John Evans, the nephew of Association cofounder Anne Evans ... recalled a conversation with his aunt just before her death in January 1941 ... At this tenuous time for the Association, and for the world at large, others might have despaired for the future of the still-fledgling summer festival. Not iron-willed Anne. According

to John, his aunt told him she knew the one person 'who has the vision, the intelligence, the ability to carry the project on'—board member and Fox Intermountain Theaters' manager Frank Ricketson. As usual, Anne Evans proved a shrewd judge of character.[117]

Anne Evans died early in the morning of January 6, 1941.

Anne Evans and Ida McFarlane Eulogized in State Memorial

The passing of Ida Kruse McFarlane and Anne Evans was marked in the State Legislature by a memorial eulogizing their services to Colorado:

> During recent months the citizens of the state of Colorado have been bereaved by the loss of two of the outstanding women of the state in the death of Anne Evans, daughter of John Evans, second territorial governor of Colorado, and Ida Kruse McFarlane, noted educator.
>
> Anne Evans gave her personal effort in behalf of every good cause and more recently was the chairman of the Central City Opera House Association, which made the name of Colorado known throughout the nation as a center of culture and art.
>
> Ida Kruse McFarlane, in addition to her co-operation and assistance in the management of the Central City Opera House Association, was held in high regard and esteem throughout the nation as a teacher and educator.
>
> It is fitting that the members of the general assembly give recognition to the outstanding ability and faithful and useful endeavors of these women and express their regret upon their deaths. Now, therefore be it resolved by the house of representatives of the thirty-third general assembly:
>
> That in the deaths of Anne Evans and Ida Kruse McFarlane the people of Colorado have lost citizens of the highest ability and usefulness; that this body recognizes the value of the services rendered to the state by these citizens, and that the members hereof express their sincere regret and sorrow upon their passage from us.

Central City Memorials to Anne Evans

Two memorials to Anne Evans' involvement in the Central City Festival eventually materialized. One is a simple bronze plaque on the outside wall of the Teller House designed by her friend, architect Burnham Hoyt. It still hangs there, unobtrusive, but with a message easily read by interested visitors, "This historic building has been restored as a memorial to Anne Evans whose spirit is an inseparable part of Central City and its festivals." Costs of that round of Teller House restoration—improvements to floors, rest rooms and kitchen— were contributed by John Evans, Julie Penrose, and Helen Bonfils.

Anne Evans Memorial on the Teller House, 2009—The Anne Evans Memorial Observation Point above Central City has vanished.

The second memorial; the Anne Evans Observation Point "near Bald Mountain cemetery," faced Mount Evans. The proposal to name this point in honor of Anne Evans was made by the Mayor of Central City and the Gilpin County Commissioners. A *Denver Post* article of June 21, 1950, described the ceremonies that were to take place on July 4, after the matinee performance of *Madame Butterfly*. Some of the opera stars were to sing; Frank St. Leger would make the dedicatory address; and the Dean of Denver University's Law School oversaw the arrangements. "A large ornamental gateway is being installed now ... With parking space for a large number of cars, the observation point is expected to be one of the most popular in the area. It is a short drive from the Teller House and the opera."

The ceremonies took place and the Observation Point was created. I know, because I was part of a Denver University group of opera goers who picnicked there early in the 1950s. However, it has disappeared. The Director of the Gilpin County Historical Society, on being asked about it in 2003, had never heard of it,[118] neither had the volunteer manning the town's Visitor's Bureau. A drive round the area found no trace of this Anne Evans memorial. Not that the loss of it would have disturbed Miss Evans. As one observer, who played a part in the early days of the Central City revival, commented,

> Anne and Ida were in the forefront when it came to shouldering the load. Yet they kept nearer the background in the more public aspects. They neither sought nor took credit. They were ever quick

to give accolades to the many patrons and backers. Central City committee members numbered in the hundreds.[119]

After Ida and Anne—The Festival Continues

The 1941 Festival season went ahead as planned and was accounted a success. John Evans assumed the interim leadership, and together with Helen Black had the honor of welcoming the Director of the New York Metropolitan Opera at the Denver City airport. They took him straight to Central City, where he stayed at the Teller House and attended the performances of *The Barber of Seville* and *Orpheus* produced by his colleague, Frank St. Leger.[120]

With the bombing of Pearl Harbor and the entry of the United States into World War II, the doors of the Opera House closed on entertainment until the war ended. However, great interest had been generated in Central City by the annual festivals:

> Literally thousands of people, soldiers and civilians, crowded its streets during the war summers. The Opera House was opened for a number of war bond drives. In the summer of 1942, the Teller House was open and guided tours were conducted through both the Opera House and the Teller House.[121]

There were pessimists who doubted that the Central City Opera House could continue, with finances so strained and without the two dynamos who had initiated the whole Festival and sustained it by their singular effort and dedication through its first ten years. Yet when the war ended in 1945, "enthusiastic plans were immediately made for the eleventh, or Victory Festival." Frank Ricketson had assumed the leadership role in 1943. He was the undoubted choice of Anne Evans to succeed her. A *Denver Post* columnist wrote that he had been, "'volunteered' to the cause by Helen Black."[122] Milton Bernet became Chairman of the Board of Directors, an influential and dedicated group that included Ida's husband, Frederick McFarlane; Anne's nephew, John Evans; Helen Bonfils; (Mrs. Spencer) Julie Penrose; Malcolm Wyer, head of the Denver Public Library; and energetic Polly Grimes, who assumed many of the essential social responsibilities formerly borne by Ida McFarlane. Justin Brierly continued as Executive Manager and Helen Black as Publicity Director.

Both were still part-time workers, and were replaced in the late 1940s by full-time staff.

The years from 1950 to the present have been filled with creative new developments, expansion of programs and a few grave financial challenges. CCOHA has acquired some 30 vintage properties in Central City, including houses to accommodate artists and staff and the handsomely rebuilt McFarlane Foundry, which provides large and small rehearsal rooms, offices and storage space. New operas have been commissioned and staged, including the ever-popular *Ballad of Baby Doe*. Initiation of the Bonfils-Stanton Foundation Artists' Training Program would have pleased Anne Evans immensely, dedicated as she was all her life to encouraging young and talented artists.

For ambitious young singers, the Central City Program is considered one of the top summer programs in the country. Touring groups of the Central City Opera Ensemble, whose members are local singers and musicians, travel out to schools, community centers, senior centers and libraries throughout Colorado and neighboring states. They especially aim at cultivating the next generation of opera goers, according to Daniel Ritchie, one of the most effective Chancellors in the history of Denver University, who was Chairman of the CCOHA Board of Trustees from 1994–2005, when he was named Chairman Emeritus.

The invaluable CCOHA Guild was started in 1974 with the mission of consolidating the efforts of many different volunteer groups. Today it has more than 600 members, and their services are legion. Following closely in the tradition set by Ida McFarlane and Anne Evans, "Guild members dedicate a lot of time and a lot of hard work, and in return, they have a lot of fun … Like most things with the Central City Opera house Association, it's a labor of love."

24

Epilogue: Something So Solid and Substantial

You have reached the pinnacle of success as soon as you become uninterested in money, compliments, or publicity.
—Thomas Wolfe

But, someway, she filled such a special place in the many and varied activities of the city's cultural life, that it was difficult to think of Denver without her. For fifty years she had lived in the Evans home at thirteenth and Bannock streets ... There was something so solid and substantial about Miss Evans. Perhaps it was living so many years in the same house.
—The Denver Taxpayers' Review

Preparing for Death

By 1940, Anne Evans knew that her days were numbered. She "had suffered a heart attack and had been warned by attending physicians to temper her activities to her strength. During a long period of enforced idleness when she found herself improving, she again would assume responsibility for numerous projects, suffer a relapse, 'take her medicine' like a soldier, and then rest to await another chance to be up and doing."[1] Her friend, poet and essayist Thomas Hornsby Ferril, noted, "Death was one of the routine disagreeable things Anne Evans had to put up with and that's about the way she felt about it if you talked with her over the past year or so."[2] In one of the many letters of condolence sent to John Evans after the death of his aunt, Mrs. Walker Van Riper said, "I have never seen such gallantry as hers in facing death."[3] In the most practical way, Anne Evans made preparations for her death.

On August 29, 1940, she signed her will, giving "all of my Indian collection, consisting of blankets, potteries and baskets, to The Denver Art Museum." She left her mountain cabin to her nephew John Evans and another piece of her Evans Ranch property to her niece, Margaret Evans Davis. The rest of her modest estate, she left to John Evans as Trustee to manage so as to pay her "dear friend, Mary Kent Wallace" a monthly income of $75 for life and her "dear friend, Josephine Hurlburt," $25 per month. The remaining income from her estate was to be paid annually to her nieces, Josephine and Katharine Evans.

In June of 1940, Anne Evans wrote a letter of resignation from her position as executive secretary of the Denver Art Museum, a position in which she had served for many years "without remuneration."[4] The board of trustees promptly responded by naming her an honorary vice-president for life.

The Denver Library Commission, after receiving notice of her resignation on grounds of illness in April of 1940, passed a resolution:

> Whereas, Miss Anne Evans has been a member of the Library Commission of the City And County of Denver since 1907; has served as President for many years; was largely responsible for introducing progressive library administration and policies; has ever devoted her energy, her enthusiasm, and her imagination to the welfare of the Public Library; has freely given of her time, her knowledge of the community, and her personal interest to the Library.
>
> Whereas, We, her fellow members, have profited as well as the Library, through our association with her in fulfilling the duties of our office.
>
> Therefore be it resolved, That we record and pay this tribute to the faithfulness, the inspiration, and wise counsel she has brought to her work for the Library; that we express our admiration and affection for Anne Evans as a colleague and a friend; that we strongly regret the necessity for a limitation of activities calling for her resignation; and that we extend to her our heartiest best wishes for health and happiness in the future.

The feelings of Chalmers Hadley in reaction to her resignation were expressed in a letter from Cincinnati dated May 14, 1940.

> Today's mail brought me a copy of the 'Staff Look-out,' sent out by the Denver Public Library staff, which announced your resignation

as a member of the Board of Library Trustees. It gave me a real shock, for somehow I cannot think of the library functioning without you as a Trustee. Through these many years, even before I appeared in Denver in 1911, you gave your fine judgment and influence to the library's support and no one can realize what this meant more than I.

The resignation was announced at the first annual Denver Public Library breakfast honoring the staff, held at the Denver Country Club. It was an occasion for the staff to meet Board members and the Mayor. To celebrate the occasion, Anne Evans sent a "beautiful basket of glorious spring flowers" and a personal note.[5] Long-time staff member, Helen Ingersoll wrote a moving letter to Anne, including the paragraph quoted as the lead-in to Chapter 14.

When it came to doing what she could to secure the future of the Central City Opera Association, we have seen that Anne's greatest contribution was to make sure that a worthy successor in leadership, Frank Ricketson, was willing to take on the challenge. Anne Evans and Ida Kruse McFarlane, according to Ferril, used to talk about death a great deal and plan how "their own deaths were to be merely incidents in a schedule that must not be interrupted."

Both had literally given their hearts to Central City. They had been warned by their physicians. Both began to lead what, to the outer world, were cloistered lives. But by telephone and letter they were making practical plans for the future of Central.[6]

In November of 1940, Anne Evans made a gift from her personal library—almost one hundred books—to Denver University. This was an eclectic mix. There were fourteen books in German and seventeen in French. A considerable number of the works in English were on religious and spiritual topics, such as *The Aquarian Gospel of Jesus Christ*; *Natural Law in the Spiritual World*; *How Count Tolstoy Lives and Works*; Dean Martyn Hart's examination of Christian Science; works on political and cultural topics, including W.E.B. Du Bois, *The Souls of Black Folks*; *Up from Slavery,* Booker T. Washington's autobiography; and Emerson's *Letters and Social Aims*. She donated books about cities in the United States and abroad and studies of other cultures, some literary studies and a few books on scientific topics.

Death, and A Life Reflected in Obituaries

On Sunday evening, January 5, 1941, Anne Evans felt better than she had in many weeks. She celebrated what she believed to be an improvement in her health by dining with her sister-in-law, Cornelia, and her two nieces, Josephine and Katharine, in the home they shared with her at 1310 Bannock Street. "She talked cheerfully of present and future plans."[7] The "improvement" was illusory, a final flare of that eternal optimism that had characterized her life. At 1:30 a.m. on Monday, January 6, 1941, Anne Evans died of a heart attack. Simple services were held at the family home at 1310 Bannock Street the following Wednesday afternoon. Attended by family and friends, they were conducted by Chancellor D. Shaw Duncan of Denver University. Anne Evans was buried at Fairmount cemetery.

All of the Denver newspapers and many others in the Rocky Mountain region carried obituary articles. Condolences poured in to the Evans family from organizations and individuals, many of which can be read in Evans family collections of the Denver Public Library Western History Department and the Colorado Historical Society. The following excerpts are quoted because they highlight a particular contribution, or express an interesting opinion about her approach to art or to life.

The *New York Times* (January 7, 1941) noted that since the early 1890s Anne Evans had been active in the Denver Artists Club,

> and ever since then she had been aiding young painters and sculptors, often with her own checkbook, so that, even before her restoration of life to the ghost mining town of Central City, she was often called the patron saint of Colorado artists. Her method of raising funds for Central City was described as 'Visits here and there—no hurrah campaigns, but quiet talks across tea tables or desks ...' The article paid tribute to her insistence on the highest standards for the Festival offerings. 'The standards have been maintained and the ghosts have shown no signs of returning to Central City.'

The *Denver Taxpayers' Review* (undated clipping) reported,

> All Denver was shocked with the word that Anne Evans was gone. Not but that it was to be expected that one of these days that very

thing would happen. There is no need for a monument for Miss Evans. Her personality is so stamped upon the Denver Art Museum and the Central City Opera House that one never thinks of either without the sweet, firm directing features of Anne Evans with her empire-building strength, rising like the sun, always at the right time and ever in the right place to quietly dominate the picture.

Writing the regular column "At the Art Museum"[8] Fred S. Bartlett tried to explain what there was about Anne Evans' influence that made the Denver Art Museum different from similar museums in other cities.

> First of all, the artist is the person most concerned. Next comes the public, and then the drawing together of these two for mutual benefit. This idea was Miss Evans' guiding principle in all her years of faithful work in building up the museum. Kind, full of wisdom, and, above all, with the gift to make others see her vision, Anne Evans was the friend and mentor of each member of our staff. We mourn her loss as a friend, for it has been given to few people to be what she was to her friends.

The *Fine Arts Committee of the City Club of Denver* on January 22, 1941, wrote a letter to the members of the Evans family expressing "their appreciation of all Miss Anne Evans has meant to this community."

> We recalled the many young and talented artists she had assisted by the purchase of their work and then presenting it to the Denver Art Museum, invariably as a gift from 'an anonymous donor.' We express appreciation for the advice and encouragement she had given the Fine Arts Committee of the City Club in its compiling and issuance of five different publications as guides to art and cultural activities in Denver.

A paragraph in the *Biennial Report of the Denver Public Library* for 1939–1940, noting Anne Evans' death, reads:

> During the construction of the present library building she studied public libraries in various cities of the country, discussed library policies with library leaders, and became familiar with progressive library services for which American libraries had become famous.

To the librarian she was a warm and sympathetic friend, a wise counselor, constructive in her criticism and encouraging in her interest and enthusiasm for high standards in library development.

A long obituary in the *Denver Post*, referred to earlier, explained the reasons for her choice of winter and summer places to live.

The apartment in 1310 Bannock Street fulfilled an important element in her life, 'I want to be near the children' she said, referring to her brother's children and their friends ... For her country home she elected to build on a high crag across the valley from Mt. Evans and there, in a charming setting of polished logs and wide windows, deep fireplaces and cheery rooms, she presided like a matriarch over an estate which included the homes of those nearest and dearest to her.[9]

Perhaps the most moving tribute was the one by Thomas Hornsby Ferril in his *Rocky Mountain Herald* editorial of January 11, 1941:

Death and Anne Evans are disparates. She was one of those people who always gave you the feeling that all that she was and all that she stood for would continue indefinitely.

He noted that her age never seemed important.

Anne Evans could go into any atelier of kid artists and be greeted with 'Hello, Anne,' or maybe old Billy Hamilton, custodian of the Opera House in Central City, would say 'Miss Anne'—but 'Miss Evans' happened only with strangers or with directors' meetings where Anne would be pushing one of her favorite projects—usually some whim made of solid steel.

Ferril made an interesting observation about the attitude Anne thought young artists should take to the heritage of western history. "Anne Evans was proud of the records of the Evans family in western history ... yet historic honor for its own sake was meaningless to her ... She was forever urging young artists to know the past, but to digest history only as food to give them strength for starting from scratch in their own generation. If you were sentimental about the past, then your art museums might just as well be laid away in mothballs."

The article ended with Ferril's evaluation of Evans' legacy:

> Continuation of Anne Evans' attitude in matters of regional culture would be a memorial in itself, for few people, in the field in which she found herself, could work and love and fight with such integrity. Practical memorials are her own accomplishments and will be the fulfillment, with revision by others (which she would understand) of some of her long dreams for our city and our state.

Of the many personal letters written to John Evans, the one from Helen Bonfils most simply and elegantly conveys the seemingly universal sentiments about the death of Anne Evans:

> I simply cannot express my sorrow over our blessed Anne's passing. Denver and all of us have lost something so precious and so fine that we can never replace it, and I want to add my words of sympathy to countless others who mourn with you.[10]

At Home with Anne Evans—
A Visit to the Byers Evans House Museum

The flavor of Anne Evans' life in Denver can be experienced through a simple visit to the Byers-Evans House Museum at 13th and Bannock. There her quarters have been painstakingly reconstructed, making it possible to see her in the setting in which so much of her effective action on behalf of Denver's developing cultural organizations took place. This was her winter home. Her unique mountain house on the Evans Ranch has also, as we have seen, been sensitively restored and updated—but it is still a private residence.

Of course, stepping into a house that has become a museum can never be the same as knocking at its door in the days when it was a home occupied by a family, animated by the pulse of daily life. Time has to be frozen at a particular point, in a house museum. So today this dark remnant of Victorian days cannot possibly convey to us what it was like when it was new. Built in 1883 for *Rocky Mountain News* founder William Byers and his family, it was on the fashionable outer fringes of the growing city of Denver, in the Evans Addition. In the 1880s, Capitol Hill and the Evans Addition were the newest "in" locations to which families of means were moving, away from a downtown that was becoming increasingly noisy, busy, and commercialized.

A tranquil set piece, with every decorative object neatly in place, cannot create for us the original atmosphere of that household. It was alive with the voices of four healthy children, the weighty business and political discussions taking place in William Evans' domain, or the cheerful planning in Anne Evans' quarters for yet another advance in the cultural life of her beloved Colorado. Nor can this well-kept house museum give us the true flavor of the home's later, quiet years as a private dwelling for three adult sisters, after the deaths of their Aunt Anne in 1941 and mother, Cornelia, in 1955.

1955–1981—Quiet Years for the Byers-Evans House

Roblin Davis, the husband of Margaret Evans Davis, the oldest of William Evans three daughters, passed away unexpectedly in 1945. After a few years, Margaret moved back into 1310 Bannock to live with her mother, Cornelia, and sisters, Katharine and Josephine. Family memory has it that Cornelia, before she died, made Margaret promise to continue living in the house to look after the well-being of her two sisters. And so, while 1310 Bannock was becoming a last residential remnant in an area increasingly given over to public and commercial uses, it remained the home of the three aging women.

The Evans family had learned, through painful experience, to avoid publicity. When a rare invitation was given to *Denver Post* reporter Olga Curtis to come inside the home and interview the three residents, the resulting article was titled *The House That Time Forgot*.[11] Curtis described the lives of the three sisters. Margaret was the most active. She was "a small pixieish woman with white hair and a fondness for sporty clothing, like red socks and plaid skirts ... She is the only one who married ... Her life centers around her three children and seven grandchildren, and she spends much of her time in her stone eyrie mountain house on the Evans ranch above Evergreen."

> Miss Jo has been in poor health since she served as a nurse during World War I. Now her eyesight is failing, her blue eyes are filmed by thick glasses, and her hair is snow-white. A frail woman in a cotton wash dress, she spends most of her days reading mystery stories ... or laying out solitaire with an over-sized deck of cards.

Kay, reported Curtis, was the one who ran things, answering the telephone and the doorbell and doing the cooking. Described as "a small, plump, gray-haired woman with a quick smile and a brisk step" it was she who gave *Empire Magazine* a rare tour of the house. The wing built for Anne Evans and her mother was kept almost as a family museum, preserving especially the furnishings that belonged to Governor and Mrs. Evans. Very little had been added to the rest of the house since the 1950s except necessities like a gas stove, refrigerator and large television set.

The three sisters remembered their Aunt Anne fondly, not as a cultural or civic leader but as "an exciting woman who introduced them to real live Indians and read them scary stories." Margaret Evans Davis described her most vivid memory of her Aunt. It was when she was "whipping up" a costume to wear at a ball. Anne Evans was going as the Goddess of Plenty and had smeared herself and her costume "all over in gold radiator paint."[12]

After the deaths of Josephine in 1969 and Katharine in 1977, ownership of the house went to Margaret and her brother, John Evans Sr. When he died, just one year after Katharine, his heirs—in cooperation with Margaret and her heirs—made the decision to donate 1310 Bannock and most of its furnishings to the Colorado Historical Society, with the provision that Margaret would retain a lifetime interest. Margaret Evans Davis, the last surviving grandchild of Governor John and Margaret Evans, was born in the house in 1889 and its only resident when she died in December of 1981.

Gift House Poses Challenges for the Colorado Historical Society

Inheriting this historic Victorian home confronted the Historical Society with major tasks, including commissioning comprehensive architectural, engineering, and historical studies of its development and current condition; deciding at what point in its long history to set its restoration; and raising the funds to do the work necessary before the house could be opened to the public as a museum.

There is a wealth of written material about 1310 Bannock Street. Edith Eudora Kohl included it in her 1957 book on *Denver's Historic Mansions*.[13] About the house, Kohl noted:

> The outstanding features of this place were its spaciousness and its simplicity. The Evanses never were strong for show and Will Evans

often said as he entered the front door that it was the nicest place on earth: there was nothing grandiose about it.[14]

Victoria of Civic Center is a well-researched booklet about the house, its occupants, and the adjacent Civic Center, written in 1984. It is amply illustrated with black and white photographs of the Byers and Evans families and of the buildings and sculptures of the Civic Center area.[15] Another narrative about the house was written by Frank Jewell in December of 1984. It told of its various additions and alterations over the years, and the furniture, art and other contents of the building at the time of its acquisition by the Historical Society.[16] For the official opening of the house as a museum, historian David Fritjof Halaas wrote a long, lyrical article, *The House in the Heart of a City,* published in *Colorado Heritage*, the magazine of the Colorado Historical Society.[17] After the opening in January 1990, additional materials were developed for the use of volunteer tour guides and for the public.

The original main entrance of the home on Bannock Street (originally called S. 14th Street) is still preserved, although entry today is from 13th Avenue. The consensus of the historical studies is that the house had no architect but was adapted by the builder, Halleck and Howard, from a Victorian "pattern" book. It was built for William Byers in 1883, after he had retired as editor of the *Rocky Mountain News* and was serving his second, highly efficient, term as Denver Postmaster. When William Evans bought the house in 1889, he had some minor alterations made. Then, as we have seen, they built a major addition to the house, after the death of Governor Evans in 1897, to accommodate William's mother and sister, Anne. The Museum's Director, Kevin Gramer, learned to his surprise from a visitor to the Museum that during the three years of this construction the house was apparently occupied, and possibly rented, by another family[18]. For this time, the William Evans family presumably lived with Mrs. Evans in the old Evans home at 14th and Arapahoe.

The two-story addition created bedrooms and a sitting room upstairs for Mrs. Evans and Anne, a small room for their maid, Bridget, and spacious main floor areas where many of the furnishings and books from the Evans home were installed. The new configuration meant that an additional entrance to the house was created on 13th Avenue though, as noted, the other entrance remains to this day, and the postal address for both family units continued to be 1310 Bannock.

Deciding on the Restoration Period

There were several more additions and alterations as the years went by. The last construction which altered the footprint of the house occurred in 1912. After considering all the information contained in the comprehensive Historical Structures Report by Long Hoeft Architects, as well as from other sources, the Historical Society chose the period. They decided to restore the house to the period between 1912, the year of the last major addition, and 1924, the year of William Evans' death. The roof was replaced, the overgrown garden re-planned and a careful restoration undertaken, room by room, based on the most meticulous period research about wall and ceiling designs, floor finishes and lighting fixtures. One small room, a parlor, was restored to the earlier time of the Byers occupancy, between 1883 and 1889. When the Historical Society received the house, it had already been listed on the National Register of Historic Places—on August 25, 1970—and became a Denver Historic Landmark property on April 23, 1976.

The restoration was costly, amounting to over a million dollars, and time-consuming. The house was opened to the public as a museum in two stages, the main floor spaces in January of 1990 and the second floor rooms a year later. The building is larger than it looks from the outside, containing almost 9,000 square feet on two levels with additional space in the basement. Because the public entry to the museum is by way of the driveway on 13th Avenue, it became necessary to redesign this in such a way as to steer visitors naturally in the right direction. In 2007 the driveway surface was changed into a welcoming flagstone pathway, incorporating a staircase and ramp. This entry area is attractively landscaped, with large potted plants and espaliered apple trees against the brick wall marking the eastern boundary of the property. A striking metal arch signals the entrance.

Anne Evans' Quarters

From the point of view of Anne Evans' biographer, interest centers first on her sitting room and bedroom, and then more generally on the art displayed throughout the house. Since Anne Evans left most of her Native American artifacts to the Denver Art Museum, the Indian furnishings of her sitting room and bedroom have been carefully selected from the collections of the Historical Society to mirror her taste. The sitting room is particularly warm and welcoming in southwestern colors, with the fireplace stuccoed to resemble the stoves so common in New Mexico homes. The room has comfortable furniture which includes the reclining chair (this was known at the time as an "invalid chair") in which her father spent much of his last months of life. It was this chair in which he was sitting when painted by both Emma Cherry and Anne Evans.

The art displayed throughout the house is a good representation of the work of the early artists of Colorado and has been described earlier.[19] Much of it was commissioned or acquired by Governor John Evans and his wife, Margaret. In 2008, the Byers-Evans House museum presented an art exhibit titled *The Anne Evans Connection*. This spotlighted the art in the Byers-Evans House collection belonging to this period, especially the portraits of Governor Evans by Emma Richardson Cherry and Anne Evans herself, Cherry's delightful portrait of Anne Evans as a young woman in party finery, Elsie Ward's bas reliefs of Anne's mother, Margaret Evans, and Anne's young nephew, John Evans. There were a few other works on loan for the event.

To grasp the full range of places that influenced Anne Evans' concepts of what made a desirable city, what was beautiful in sculpture, art and furnishings, and under what conditions artists could flourish, it would be necessary to journey far and wide. One would need to visit the civilized settlement of Evanston, Illinois where she learned a great deal from Cousin Nina about how to create a joyful and productive life. Then it would be necessary to travel to the old cities of Europe, especially Paris and Berlin, where Anne spent the impressionable years of her late teens. Another destination would be the Art Students' League in New York, where she studied, and that city's wonderful array of museums and art galleries which she visited periodically throughout her life. One would have to travel to Santa Fe, the Navajo Reservation, and the unique Pueblo settlements and mission churches of New Mexico; and to Mesa Verde National Park, which Anne Evans felt was one of Colorado's most precious tourist experiences. And then to Colorado Springs, where she was from early days familiar with an art colony as old as Denver's, and for which she delighted, at the end of her life, in knowing that one of her many former protégés was designing a unique Fine Arts Center. Time would be spent in the beautiful Evans Ranch area, once so remote and now hardly more than an hour's travel from Denver, and in the old gold mining town of Central City. That visit would have to be in the middle of summer to take part in the Festival, started by Ida Kruse McFarlane and Anne Evans at the height of the Great Depression, which still flourishes in the miraculously preserved and restored little jewel of an Opera House. Such a travel itinerary is possible only for a few. However, anyone can spend an hour visiting the Byers-Evans House and get an authentic feel for the place that was home to one of Colorado's significant women pioneers for more than forty years.

Anne Evans, photograph by Samuel S. Newbury, Courtesy Margaret E. Hayden

Appendices:

Ancestors and Family of Anne Evans

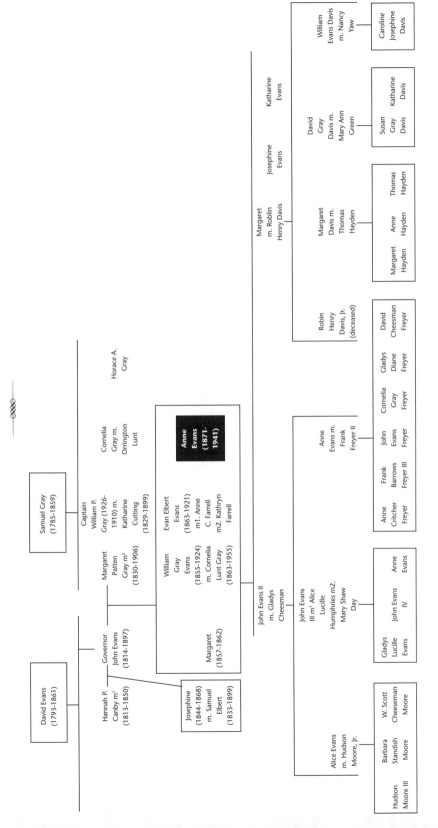

Chronology

1814   Anne Evans' father, Governor John Evans, born in Waynesville, Ohio

1830   Anne Evans' mother, Margaret Patten Gray, born in Bowdoinham, Maine

1838   John Evans earned M. D. from Lynn Medical College in Cincinnati. Married Hannah Canby.

1841   John and Hannah Evans converted to Methodism by Bishop Matthew Simpson

1842   Cornelia Gray, older sister of Margaret Gray, married Orrington Lunt.

1843   Anne's cousin Nina (Cornelia Gray Lunt) born in Chicago.

1844   Josephine, only child (out of four born) to survive infancy, born to John and Hannah Evans.

1845   John Evans appointed Superintendent in charge of construction of Indiana State Asylum for the Insane.

1848   John Evans appointed Professor of Obstetrics and Gynecology at Rush Medical College, moved with family to Chicago. Population of the city was approximately 20,000.

1850   Hannah Evans died of tuberculosis. John Evans, Orrington Lunt, and seven others, developed plan to found Methodist Northwestern University.

1852   John Evans met Margaret Patten Gray, a sister of Orrington Lunt's wife Cornelia, at the Lunt home.

1853   John and Margaret married in Bowdoinham, Maine.

1855   William Evans, Anne's older brother, born. John Evans closed his medical practice, moved to a new home he built in Evanston, where Northwestern University ready to open its doors.

1857   Birth of Margaret (Little Maggie) Evans.

1858   Gold discovered at junction of Cherry Creek and South Platte River. Auraria town site established on west bank of creek, Denver town site laid out on east bank. Colorado still part of Kansas territory.

1859   Auraria and Denver merge to create one town. William Byers distributed first issue of *Rocky Mountain News*. Prospector John Gregory found rich lode of gold five miles north of Clear Creek. Soon thousands of gold seekers swarmed up to Gregory Gulch. Central City emerged as leading settlement in the area.

1860   Creation of Denver City celebrated at a midnight moonlight party on newly completed bridge over Cherry Creek. John Evans elected as delegate to the 1860 Illinois State Republican Convention, which nominated Abraham Lincoln for President.

1861   Lincoln took office as President. Outbreak of American Civil War. Colorado Territory separated from Kansas Territory. William Gilpin appointed by President Lincoln as Colorado Territory first Governor.

1862   In March, the First Regiment of Colorado Volunteer defeated Texan attempt to seize Colorado gold fields at Glorieta Pass, making hero of Col. John Chivington. In April, Gilpin relieved of his position as Governor. John Evans, appointed to replace him. His friend, Samuel Hitt Elbert, appointed as Territorial Secretary. Evans arrived in Denver to face serious economic, governmental and security problems. Death of "Little Maggie" in Evanston. Gov. Evans brought remainder of family to Denver in November.

1863   In April, a major fire destroyed most buildings on east side of Cherry Creek. Evan Elbert, Anne Evans second brother, born in June. Evans family moved into new home at 14th and Arapahoe. In July, Gov. Evans headed drive to erect first Methodist Church building in Denver. Margaret Evans helped organize Soldiers' Aid Society to care for needs of wounded soldiers at Camp Weld Hospital.

1864   In May devastating flood swept away all the structures built in bed of Cherry Creek, including that of *Rocky Mountain News*, and drowned thousands of farm animals. In summer a massive plague of grasshoppers decimated crops. The Colorado Seminary opened, with William Evans as one of the students. In August, Gov. Evans issued proclamation authorizing citizens to kill hostile Indians and inviting friendly Indians to put themselves under military protection. Permission granted from Washington to raise a Third Colorado Regiment for 100 days to fight the Indian threat. On November 29 Col. Chivington's men fired without warning on sleeping camp of Indians who had put themselves under military protection. Indiscriminately slaughtered and mutilated bodies of men, women and children. Sand Creek Massacre became a national scandal.

1865   Marriage of Josephine Evans to Samuel Hitt Elbert in Evanston. First services held in new St. Lawrence Street Methodist Church in Denver. End of Civil War. Assassination of President Lincoln. Congressional report on Sand Creek highly critical of Gov. Evans. President Johnson asked for, and received, Evans' resignation. Evans continued to work for statehood for Colorado. Named one of two Colorado Senators-elect by Territorial Legislature. Successive Colorado Statehood bills vetoed by President Johnson. Work on Transcontinental Railroad, interrupted by Civil War, resumed. Decision made to route it through Cheyenne, Wyoming, rather that over mountains via Denver. Hard times for Denver: city losing population, gold mining stalled by lack of technical ability to process gold ore mined from deep underground.

1867   Colorado Seminary closed. Drive begun to build a railroad to connect Denver with Cheyenne and the transcontinental railroad, spearheaded by John Evans, David Moffat and William Byers.

1868   Baby son of Samuel and Josephine Elbert died in infancy. Josephine died in October. Wolfe Hall, Episcopal School of Girls, opened at Champa and 17th Streets. Gov. Evans and Samuel Elbert bought nucleus of Evans/Elbert Ranch in Clear Creek County.

1870   Census reported Denver's population 4,759, Colorado's 39,864

1870   Connection to national rail network completed, first train arrived in Denver. Family summer home—called The Cottage or The Cottage Yard—built on Evans/Elbert Ranch.

1871   Anne Evans born in London on January 23. John Evans sold major Chicago properties one month before the Great Chicago Fire.

1872   John Evans built the Evans Block on corner of 15th and Lincoln. Started remodeling his one-story home at 14th and Arapahoe into "three-story mansion."

1873   Samuel Hitt Elbert appointed Governor of Colorado. Financial
        "Panic of 1873" started difficult days economically for Denver. Birth
        of Ida Kruse MacFarlane in Central City.

1874   Elbert removed as Governor.

1875   Gov. Evans accompanied Margaret Evans and children to London
        for a two-year stay in Europe.

1876   Colorado achieved statehood. Elbert elected to new Colorado
        Supreme Court.

1877   Gov. Evans to Europe to try to raise funds for his railroad project.
        Margaret and family came back with him to Denver.

1878   Opening of Central City Opera House, designed by architect
        Roeschlaub. Evans Memorial Chapel, built by Gov. Evans in
        memory of his daughter, Josephine, opened at West 13th Avenue
        and Bannock.

1880   Population of Denver, 35,369; of Colorado, 194,327.

1880   University of Denver incorporated as degree-granting body with tax-
        exempt Colorado Seminary holding all property in its name.
        University opened in November.

1881   H. A. W. Tabor, silver millionaire from Leadville, opened Tabor
        Grand Opera House in Denver, eventually dooming the Central
        City institution. Arapahoe County Courthouse built at Fourteenth
        and Larimer Streets. Sunie Lowell married to Howard Evans, nephew
        of Gov. Evans, in Evans home in Denver. Organization of Denver
        Fortnightly Club with Margaret Evans as President.

1882   Colorado Mining and Industrial Exposition featured first major art
        show in state's history.

1883   William Gray Evans, older son of Gov. and Margaret Evans, married
        in Evans Chapel to his cousin, Cornelia Lunt Gray. William Byers
        built what is now the Byers-Evans House Museum.

1884   Son John Evans (who came to be known as either John Evans Senior
        or Banker John Evans) born to William and Cornelia Evans.

1885   William Evans began his long and successful career in leadership of
        Denver Tramway Company.

1886   Denver Chamber of Commerce established subscription Mercantile Library. Anne Evans spent her "civilizing year" with Cousin Nina in Evanston. University of Denver started to acquire new University Park campus.

1887   Josephine Evans, daughter of William and Cornelia Evans, born.

1887–91 Anne Evans studying in Paris at Misses Ferris School and in Berlin at the Willard School.

1888   Trinity Methodist Church completed.

1889   Birth of Margaret, daughter of William and Cornelia Evans. William Evans bought 1310 Bannock house from William Byers. Denver Public Library opened in West Wing of new East Denver High School.

1890   Population: Denver, 106,713; Colorado, 413,249.

1890   Cornerstone laid for first University Park campus building, University Hall (now called Old Main). Cornerstone laid for State Capitol.

1891–2   Anne Evans enrolled in art classes at University of Denver.

1892   Debut of Brown Palace Hotel. Iliff School of Theology building completed on University Park campus.

1893   Colorado second state to give vote to women. Repeal of Sherman Silver Act resulted in major economic depression. Emma Richardson Cherry organized Denver Artists' Club (which eventually evolved into Denver Art Museum.) Margaret Evans and daughter, Anne, among earliest associate members. Beginning of long and crushing depression, which dealt heavy blow to Evans family fortunes.

1894   Denver Artists' Club put on its first exhibition in Denver University's Fine Arts Building. Third daughter, Katharine, born to William and Cornelia Evans.

1895   Anne Evans became a professional member of the Denver Artists' Club.

1895–9   Anne Evans engaged in intermittent studies at Art Students' League in New York.

1896   Anne Evans elected to governing Council of Denver Artists' Club.

1897   Gov. John Evans died September 7 in his home at 14th and Arapahoe.

1898   Mercantile Library and Denver Public Library merged.

1899   Samuel Elbert died in Galveston, Texas. Newly consolidated Denver Public Library opened in new building constructed by Prudential Insurance Co. at 15th Street and Court Place.

1900   Population: Denver, 133,859; Colorado, 539,700.

1900   Old home of Evans family at 14th and Arapahoe slated to be razed to make room for Denver Tramway Company building. William Evans added new wing to Byers-Evans house to accommodate his mother and sister, Anne.

1902   Denver Public Library bought rundown La Veta Place as site for new Library.

1903   Denver Public Library received $200,000 from Andrew Carnegie towards cost of new building. Half of La Veta property retained as temporary quarters for Library. Evans Investment Company organized, on recommendation of Evan Evans, to manage properties salvaged from Gov. John Evans estate. Anne Evans became one of its four directors.

1904   Robert W. Speer elected Mayor of Denver. Began his transformation of Denver into a City Beautiful. Anne Evans appointed to the new Municipal Art Commission.

1905   Denver Art Commission recommended to Mayor Speer that a consultant be hired to develop a city plan for Denver. William Evans became President of the Board of Trustees of Denver University.

1906   Death of Anne Evans' mother, Margaret Patten Gray Evans, on September 7. Anne Evans now had a large share in the Evans/Elbert Ranch property covering more than 4,000 acres. Charles Mulford Robinson made his recommendations to the Art Commission about a plan for Denver, including first schematic proposal for the creation of a civic center. Henry Buchtel ran successfully for 2-year term as Governor of Colorado.

1907   Anne Evans appointed member of Denver Public Library Commission. Helped to secure agreement for gallery space for the Denver Artists' Club in proposed new Carnegie Library. Sculptor

Frederick MacMonnies, who had been commissioned to create a monument honoring Colorado's pioneers, proposed more feasible design for proposed civic center. Art Commission recommended his plan to Mayor Speer.

1909   Marriage of John Evans Sr. to Gladys Cheesman at Cheesman home (now Governor's mansion) in Denver. Acquisition of land for Civic Center under way. The Cottage on the Evans/Elbert Ranch burned down.

1910   Population: Denver, 213,381; Colorado, 799,204.

1910   Gala opening of Denver Artists' Club Galleries in new Carnegie Library on what was to become Denver's Civic Center. Anne Evans voted to a four-year term as President of Denver Public Library Commission. Anne Evans began exploring the settlements, arts and culture of the Native Americans of New Mexico. Made many trips, sometimes in the company of Canon Winfred Douglas and his son, Eric (Frederic), sometimes with Mary Kent Wallace and others. Started her own Native Arts collection. Also began collecting New Mexican Santos. Anne Evans' mountain home, designed by her, built on her 40-acre site on Evans Ranch. In 1924, 1931 and 1936, several major additions and alterations were designed by her friend, architect Burnham Hoyt.

1911   Anne Evans one of a two-person team who recruited Chalmers Hadley as Denver City Librarian. David Moffat died in New York, still unsuccessful in quest to raise money to complete his dream of a railroad tunnel under Continental Divide.

1912   In March, Anne Evans presented recommendations to the Library Commission for four library branches, with suggested locations, budgets and architects. Denver voted to approve establishment of a series of mountain parks and roads to service them.

1913   Denver citizens voted to try a Commission form of government instead of the strong mayor system. William Evans suffered breakdown, resigned from all his business leadership positions. First documentation of Anne Evans' being an active member of the Denver Branch of the Theosophical Society in America.

1914   World War I began in Europe. Anne Evans resigned from Denver Art Commission. Anne Evans awarded an honorary Doctor of Letters (Litt. D.) degree by the University of Denver.

1915   John Evans Jr., son of John Evans Sr. and Gladys Cheesman Evans, born in Denver. Anne Evans re-elected as President of Denver Public Library Commission.

1916   Denver citizens voted for a charter amendment restoring strong mayor form of city government and electing Speer again to that office. Work on Civic Center began in earnest. Chicago landscape architect, E. H. Bennett, commissioned to draw up final plan. Soon work underway on the Colonnade of Civic Benefactors and the stone balustrades. Anne Evans incorporated Evans Ranch property as the Kuhlborne Ranch Company, in cooperation with her brother, Evan Evans and nephew, John Evans. Carnegie gave additional grant to DPL for four more branch libraries. Anne Evans worked on various committees to complete the new libraries.

1917   U.S. entered World War I. Denver Artists' Club changed name to Denver Art Association.

1918   Fitzsimons Army Hospital, for which William Evans lobbied earnestly, established in Aurora. Mayor Robert Speer died unexpectedly in office.

1919   20 million worldwide died in influenza pandemic. Eighteenth Amendment inaugurated era of Prohibition. First paid Director of Denver Art Association started on his duties. Anne Evans became a member of the Denver Fortnightly Club.

1920   Population: Denver, 256,491; Colorado, 939,629.

1920   Beginning of period of Ku Klux Klan dominance in Denver, with election of Benjamin Stapleton as mayor, and in Colorado, with election of Clarence Morley as Governor. Nineteenth Amendment to U. S. Constitution gave women the right to vote. Anne Evans read her paper, *The Art Impulse of the Hopi Indians* to a meeting of the Denver Fortnightly Club. Buchtel suffered major stroke, resigned as Denver University's Chancellor.

1921   Death of Evan Elbert Evans, second son of Gov. and Margaret Evans and brother of Anne Evans, in Denver.

1922   Chappell House donated to Denver Artists' Association by Delos Chappell Jr. and Jean Chappell Cranmer. Chappell House became the first home owned by the Denver Art Museum. Anne Evans a major factor in formation of informal Committee for the Preservation of New Mexico Mission Churches. Anne headed

fund-raising effort, securing support of Denver businessman
William McPhee. Involved Denver architect, Burnham Hoyt, in the
project. Helped young New Mexico sanatorium patient, John Gaw
Meem, who later took leadership role in preservation efforts, get
training as an architect in Denver.

1923   Denver Art Association became the Denver Art Museum. Anne Evans
became President of Denver Branch of Theosophical Society in
America, with Mary Kent Wallace as Secretary. First restoration project
of the Preservation Committee started at Zia Mission.

1924   William Gray Evans, oldest son of the Governor and brother of Anne
Evans, died at 1310 Bannock. Henry Buchtel died one day later.

1925   First DAM exhibit of Native American Art at Chappell House. Anne
Evans started her long history of donating art objects from her own
collection to the Museum.

1927   Anne Evans read paper on *Primitive Ceremonials* to a January
meeting of the Denver Fortnightly Club. This paper, later renamed *A
Christmas Pilgrimage to the Southwest*, was the most widely read of all
Anne's writings. Edgar C. McMechen appointed first (part-time)
Curator of Native Arts at Denver Art Museum.

1928   Completion of Moffat Tunnel under Continental Divide, providing
direct railroad link between Denver and Pacific coast and bringing
west slope water to supplement Denver's water supply.

1929   Opening of Denver's Stapleton Airport. Great Depression began
with Wall Street crash. Anne Evans involved in negotiations to
secure gallery space for the Denver Art Museum in the new City and
County Building. Anne Evans acts briefly as Interim Director of
Denver Art Museum.

1928–9 Though she had not been a practicing artist for many years,
Anne Evans joined as one of the founders of the 52-member
Denver Artists' Guild.—She also became a member of the Board of
Directors of the University Civic Theater, a group headed by Helen
Bonfils.

1930   Population: Denver, 287,861; Colorado, 1,035,791.

1930   Eric Douglas appointed full-time Curator of Native Arts
Department of Denver Art Museum.

1931   Ida Kruse MacFarlane and Anne Evans persuaded the University of
        Denver to accept ownership of the run-down Central City Opera
        House. The University authorized the formation of the Central City
        Opera House Association (CCOHA) and leased the Opera House to
        it for $1.00 a year for 99 years.

1931–2 Intensive work to restore Opera House and lower floors of Teller
        House and plan first-class theatrical production under direction of
        Broadway Director Robert Edmond Jones.

1932   Opening in the new Denver City and County Building of the fourth
        floor Denver Art Museum galleries. Debut of Central City Summer
        Festival with production of *Camille* starring Lillian Gish. Five-year
        drought began on eastern plains; dust storms suffocated crops and
        darkened daytime skies in Rocky Mountain region. Anne Evans
        appointed one of three-member Advisory Committee to the Denver
        University Art Department: continued this service until her death.

1933   Second Central City Festival production, *The Merry Widow*. Entire
        Teller House rented and cleaned up. Prohibition ended.

1934   Summer Festival in Central City featured a production of
        Shakespeare's *Othello*. Formation of Denver Symphony Orchestra.
        Death of Anne Evans' "Cousin Nina" (Cornelia Gray Lunt) in
        Evanston, Illinois.

1935   *Central City Nights* at Central City Festival.

1936   Anne Evans donated her collection of Santos to the Denver Art Museum. As
        member of Denver Art Commission, Anne Evans and Mayor Ben
        Stapleton had very public disagreement over Ronnebeck design for
        Speer Memorial to be installed at Civic Center. CCOHA became
        independent non-profit organization. Anne Evans financed purchase
        of Teller House with a bond issue totaling $6,500. Herndon Davis
        painted the *Face on the Barroom Floor* in the Teller House. *The
        Gondoliers* a success in Central City Summer Festival.

1937   Ibsen's *A Doll's House* bombed in Central City.

1938   Colorado College conferred a Doctor of Laws Degree on Anne Evans.
        Ruy Blas favorably received at Central City's Festival.

1939   Anne Evans awarded an honorary Doctorate in Fine Arts by the
        University of Denver. *The Yoemen of the Guard* a big success in
        Central City. Anne Evans suffering from heart trouble.

1940   Population: Denver, 322,412; Colorado, 1,123,296.

1940   Ida Kruse MacFarlane died on June 18. Anne Evans resigned from
        the Denver Library Commission and from her position as voluntary
        executive secretary of the Denver Art Museum on grounds of ill
        health. Unable to get up to Central City for the summer production
        of *The Bartered Bride*, she listened to it on a radio hook-up in her
        bedroom.

1941   Death of Anne Evans on January 6 in Byers-Evans House. Pearl
        Harbor bombing brought U. S. into World War II.

1945   Death of Roblin Henry Davis, husband of Anne Evans' niece,
        Margaret Evans Davis.

1955   Death of Cornelia Lunt Evans, Anne Evans sister-in-law.

1969   Death of Josephine Evans, Anne Evans' oldest niece.

1977   Death of Anne's youngest niece, Katharine Evans.

1978   Death of Anne's nephew, John Evans Sr. 1310 Bannock donated to
        Colorado Historical Society.

1981   Death of last surviving occupant of 1310 Bannock St., Anne's niece,
        Margaret Evans Davis.

Anne Evans' Accomplishments and Honors

In her lifetime, Anne Evans compiled an impressive record of achievements which earned for her a mass of unsought honors, awards and tributes. Others were added after her death. Because these reflect different aspects of her contributions, it is worthwhile to summarize them.

Official honors bestowed upon her included:

- **Honorary D. Litt. Degree** in 1914 and **Honorary Doctorate in Fine Arts** in 1939 both from the University of Denver.
- A **Medal** honoring Anne Evans for "a lifetime devoted to honoring and fostering art interests in Denver" was awarded at a **Denver City Club** luncheon in June of 1930.
- Anne Evans was proclaimed **"Honor Woman of the Year"** by the **Denver Professional and Business Women's Club** in March of 1933. The Club's practice was to honor one outstanding Denver woman each year.
- In a ceremony in May of 1933, dedicating the newly opened galleries of the Denver Art Museum in the City and County Building, a **bronze bust of Anne Evans by sculptor Arnold Ronnebeck was presented to the Museum.** This was paid for entirely by friends and was in recognition of Evans' forty years of service to the Denver Art Museum and her extraordinary and long-time dedication to the advancement of art in Denver.
- In March of 1937, when Anne Evans was the **"honor guest"** at a luncheon given by the **Robert W. Speer Club** to celebrate the birthday of her father, John Evans. It was proclaimed "… she has worked, without thought of financial reward, to create beauty for Denver, especially to guard the development of the civic center along lines that will prevent acceptance of anything but the best for placement within its borders. If Denver has an outstanding art museum, it is due to the unflagging efforts of Anne Evans. If the Denver Public Library stands second to none in the west, it is in no small degree to her enthusiastic service and influence … she has been eager to advance the welfare of Denver University and its various schools."

- In 1938, **Colorado College conferred a Doctorate of Laws degree** on Anne Evans.[1]
- In the July 23, 1938 issue of the *Denver Post,* one of the **New Faces in the Denver Post Gallery of Fame** was Anne Evans "who, as impresario, is making the seventh annual Central City Drama Festival and its presentation of "Ruy Blas" the stellar event of them all, reviving the high color and life of the one-time Gilpin County mining empire and again attracting world attention to this midsummer drama venture."
- In the **1941 Session of the Colorado State Legislature**, the Colorado House of Representatives approved **Memorial No. 5** noting "the loss of two of the outstanding women of the State, in the death of Anne Evans … and Ida Kruse McFarlane, noted educator." The Memorial said that "Anne Evans, during her lifetime gave her personal effort in behalf of every good cause and more recently was the Chairman of the Central City Opera House Association, which made the name of Colorado known throughout the nation as a center of culture and art …" Of Ida McFarlane, the Memorial noted that "in addition to her cooperation and assistance in the management of the Central City Opera House Association, was held in high regard and esteem throughout the nation as a teacher and educator."
- In 1947, after a complete restoration and remodeling of the **Teller House** in Central City, **a bronze plaque, designed by Burnham Hoyt, was placed on the cornerstone**. It states, "This historic building has been restored as a memorial to Anne Evans whose spirit is an inseparable part of Central City and its festivals."
- In 1950, the **Anne Evans Observation Point** outside Central City was dedicated in memory of her many contributions to the creation of the Central City Festival. It seems to have disappeared.[2]
- In 1958 **Regis College inaugurated its Civis Princeps (Leading Citizen) Awards.** 17 citizens some living, some dead were awarded this honor in different categories. **Anne Evans'** citation was for the area of Fine Arts. "The citation acknowledged her work "as a founder and builder." The text pointed out that she had been instrumental in bringing the Denver Public Library collection from old East High School to the Civic Center. Thereafter "she personally traveled the country over to select the right librarian and brought Chalmers Hadley to Denver for the Post."[3] The 17 also included Burnham Hoyt, Charles Boettcher, Otto Mears, Palmer Hoyt, Moses Hallett, David May and Frederick Bonfils. The number of awards after 1958 was limited to three to five each year. Anne Evans' nephew, John Evans, received the honor in 1962.
- Service on official bodies was something Anne Evans took in stride. In 1917 she was appointed a member of the "**Women's Council of Defense**," which was part of the Colorado Governor's quite effective

organization to meet needs arising from the entry of the United States into the first World War.

- In the late 1930s, Anne Evans was appointed as one of three Coloradans to **represent the state "on the general and advisory committees of the World's Fair to be held in New York City in 1939.**[4] The other two members were Mrs. Ralph Burgess and Ira K. Young of Pueblo. "The appointment of Miss Evans is a national recognition of her abilities as an organizer and of her unselfish devotion over a long period to the development of art and education in her city and state." According to the newspaper article, the three representatives had no small assignment: to "organize a program which will bring Colorado to the front in what is claimed will be the greatest world's fair in the history of such enterprises."

Achievements Wrongly Attributed to Anne Evans

Because the achievements of Anne Evans were so numerous, it seems unnecessary to credit her with contributions with which she had little or nothing to do. Here we do our small part to remove them from future biographical summaries:

- In several brief biographies the assertion is made that she, "was a moving spirit in the founding of the anti-tuberculosis society" in Denver. There are some records of the activities of that society[5] in which we found only one mention of Anne Evans' name. This was in connection with an intensive lobbying campaign to have the city of Denver build a municipal tuberculosis sanatorium ("Miss Evans gave generous and valuable assistance in editing the leaflet and circular letters ...") There is no indication that she was an important factor in the operations of the society.
- An article titled "Adjustment and the Dispossessed" in the *Journal of Adult Education*[6] is indeed by an author named Anne Evans, but the profile in the magazine makes it clear that she was a member of the staff of the Adjustment Service of New York.
- In some biographies, it is stated that Anne Evans was a member of the Denver City Planning Commission. This assertion may have arisen from confusion about the roles of the Art Commission, of which she was a member, and the Planning Commission, on which she never served.
- The statement is made in several biographical sketches that Anne Evans was an important factor in founding the Western History Department of the Denver Public Library. As discussed in Chapter 14 on the Denver Public Library,[7] there seems to be no documented basis for this claim.
- Anne Evans was never a member of the Board of Trustees of the University of Denver. As described in the Chapter on Denver University, her father, mother, brother William, and nephew John all

served as Trustees. Anne was on committees related to the Art Department and the University Civic Theater.

Contributions Rarely Mentioned or Poorly Documented

On the other hand, research turned up references to activities and contributions made by Anne Evans that are either not mentioned in brief biographies or are generally asserted but poorly documented.

- A charming little invitation invites women of the Denver University faculty to a gathering to hear a talk by Miss Evans. The invitation is undated, but its content indicates that it was around 1914.

  Miss Evans is the daughter of the founder of the University of Denver. Like her father, she has interested herself in the public welfare and public culture. She holds the following official positions: President of the Denver Library Board; Member of the Council of the Denver Artists' Club; Member of the Municipal Art Commission; *President of the Out-Door Art League.* Miss Evans will speak 'On the Enjoyment of Pictures.'

Research failed to reveal much about the Out-Door Art League in Denver, but if Anne Evans chose to put her energies into it, it must have served some worthy purposes.

- There is little evidence of exactly what projects Anne Evans undertook over the many years she acted as Executive Secretary of the Denver Art Museum. One undated little newspaper clipping in the Anne Evans clipping file in the Western History Department of the Denver Public Library provides a clue that she was probably characteristically creative in developing activities to entice people into the Art Museum. Headed *Miss Anne Evans is Prime Mover in New Project*, the article described a new cause for women to espouse "that of stimulating interest of children in exploring the museums." Children of public schools, as well as Kent and Graland, were to bring to school "the toys which appeal most to them, particularly those of historical or artistic interest." The toys were to be judged by volunteers, who would make a choice as to which would be exhibited at Chappell House during Museum Week. What was interesting about this brief account was not only the objective of the project, but the number of people Miss Evans who "has been evolving the project for several months" had enlisted to help. Thirty-two names were mentioned.
- There are many references in tributes and obituaries to Anne Evans' role in encouraging and financially aiding artists, especially young artists, typified by a much-quoted assertion that she "grub-staked young artists the way her father grub-staked miners."[8] Because there are so few personal records, we could find only two or three specific

examples of how she went about giving this kind of support. Quietly helping New Mexico's **John Gaw Meem** to become an architect and develop a practice[9] was one example, and supporting artist **Margaret Van Waganan** to obtain her art education in Chicago and New York[10] was another. **Lucille Du Pre** was a violinist. No record was found of just what Anne Evans' contribution to her training or life was, but Du Pre obviously felt close to her; she made Anne the Executor of her Will. A typed paragraph under *Horses at Night,* a large mural by artist **Frank Mechau** which hangs in the Denver Public Library Western History Department, notes:

> It is fitting that the Denver Public Library exhibits the artwork of Frank Mechau. In 1934, the Mechaus were living in Denver when the federal government established the Public Works of Art project, whereby artists would be commissioned to create art work for public buildings. **At the recommendation of Anne Evans, daughter of the second territorial governor and a founder of the Denver Art Museum, Mechau was selected to paint a mural for the Denver Public Library.** *Horses at Night* was enthusiastically received by the government, art critics, and the citizens of Denver. The mural was exhibited at the Corcoran Gallery in Washington and the Whitney Museum in New York City before returning to Denver to be displayed in the Fine Arts Department of the library. **For Mechau, this was the beginning of the several more commissions under the aegis of the WPA.** (emphasis added)

A special protégé and young friend was **Ann Matlack**, who apparently worked or volunteered for a time at Chappell House, taught at Kent School, helped out at Central City, and undertook various other responsibilities connected with Anne Evans' projects. Some letters and cards written to Matlack by Anne Evans are in the archives of the Colorado Historical Society. They reveal an affectionate and caring concern on Evans' part and a genuine enjoyment of Anne Matlack's company in these endeavors. There was a vogue for staging elaborate costumed pageants in the 1920s. Anne Evans was involved in helping to produce several of these. On April 22, 1927, she wrote a note to Ann Matlack, who had obviously put a lot of effort into an outdoor pageant staged in the garden of W. W. Grant. It read: "My dear Ann Matlack, Yesterday afternoon was beautiful a very great triumph and I am sending you this little book of poems to mark the date and tell you of my appreciation." In 1938, after the death of Matlack's father, Evans wrote,

> It is hard to find words when one really needs them—and sometimes it seems to me that sympathy and understanding are best when silent—but I want you to know how sorry I am—I know what wrenching experience it is—and how it changes the shape of one's world—Soon I hope you will be where I can come to you.

In two 1937 letters relating to the coming Central City season,[11] Anne Evans wrote that the selection of staff that year is entirely up to Richard Aldrich, "the play is to be rehearsed in New York up to July 9 and then go direct to Central City." But, she really wanted Matlack "attached in some capacity" and she enclosed a note "about you and your value to this project" for Matlack to take to Aldrich.[12] On the occasion of Ann Matlack's marriage in 1939, Anne Evans sent a note,

> If I could personally choose just exactly the right wedding gift for you, I would enjoy doing it—but next to that I enjoy thinking of you jingling the prosaic cash in your pocket while you travel, until you see something you do very specially want—and then that you will think 'there is Anne Evans' wedding present!' I know you and Don will have a wonderful time, for you carry it with you—and 'the song is to the singer'—I send all the good wishes that I know.

The last communication with Matlack in the collection is a one cent postcard postmarked July 4, 1940, during the Central City season, that Anne Evans could not attend because of her heart condition. She had obviously arranged for Anne Matlack to have dinner at the Teller House: "Louise, my cousin (Mrs. Leonard Everett) will be waiting in the Teller House dining room about 6:30 Saturday night; just ask for Miss Evans table." (Postcard, same collection)

- Thomas Hornsby Ferril mentioned another instance of Anne Evans' quiet aid to a talent in distress:

> Nobody loved Denver, Colorado or New Mexico more than Anne Evans. But her fine influences went far beyond. One of America's most distinguished contemporary novelists, for example, was very ill a few years ago and in financial distress. At that time this novelist was practically unknown. It was Anne Evans, working at long range, who did the trick; and such a story belongs in a context with scores of others to give some sense of her passion to give a lift to people who could do good work if they got a few breaks.[13]

Image Credits

Grateful acknowledgement is made for permission to reproduce the images on the following pages:

Color Insert

Anne Evans, *Untitled (Portrait of Territorial Governor John Evans)*, ca. 1890
Oil on board, 22.6 x 26.6, (Courtesy History Colorado)

Anne Evans, *Margaret,* n.d. Watercolor 27.25 x 17.5, (Courtesy History
Colorado)

Anne Evans, *Winter Scene*, n.d. Oil on board, (Denver Public Library Western
History Collection)

Alfonso Roybal, *Harvest Dance*, (Denver Art Museum, 1932.207)

Abel Sanchez, *Man and Buffalo*, (Denver Art Museum, 1932.232)

Guadaloupe Montoya, *Corn Dance*, (Denver Art Museum, 1932.235)

Edmund Tracey, *Father Sky and Mother Earth*, (Denver Art Museum, 1932.156)

Elisabeth Spalding, *Anne Evans Living Room,* (Courtesy Ethelind Elbert Austin)

Elisabeth Spalding, *Anne's Cabin*, (Courtesy Jan Mayer)

Vance Kirkland (1904–1981, American), *Moonlight in Central City*, 1935 Oil
on linen, 29 X 36, (Collection of Kirkland Museum of Fine & Decorative
Arts, Denver. VK1935.12)

Vance Kirkland (1904–1981, American), *Central City Opera House*, 1933
Watercolor on paper, 25 X 19, (Collection of Kirkland Museum of Fine &
Decorative Arts, Denver. VK1933.01)

Bibliography

Books

Arps, Louisa. *Cemetery to Conservatory: A Jubilee History of Denver Botanic Gardens 1951–1976*. Denver: Denver Botanic Gardens, 1980. Maps drawn by Julia Andrews-Jones.

Baker, Frank. *Methodism and the Love Feast*. London: Epworth Press, 1957.

Breck, Allen duPont. *William Gray Evans 1855–1924: Portrait of a Western Executive*. Denver: The University of Denver Department of History, 1964.

_____ . *John Evans of Denver: Portrait of a Twentieth Century Banker*. Boulder: The Pruett Publishing Company, 1972.

_____ . Alton Templin and Martin Rist. *The Methodist, Evangelical, and United Brethren Churches in the Rockies, 1850–1876*. Denver: Rocky Mountain Conference of the United Methodist Church, 1977.

Catalogue of Denver University, 1886–7.

Goodstein, Phil. *Denver From the Bottom Up, Vol.1 from Sand Creek to Ludlow*. Denver: New Social Publications, May 2003.

Hafen, Le Roy R. *Men and Women of Colorado: Past and Present*. Phoenix, Tucson, Denver: Pioneer Publishing Co., 1944.

Harris, Neil, Marlene Chambers and Lewis Wingfield Story. *The Denver Art Museum, The First Hundred Years*. Denver: The Denver Art Museum, 1996.

History of the City of Denver, Arapahoe County, and Colorado. Chicago: W. B. Vickers, Baskin and Company, 1880.

James, Edward T. and Janet Wilson James. *Notable American Women. 1607–1950: A Biographical Dictionary*. Cambridge, Mass: Belknap Press of Harvard University Press, 1971.

Johnson, Charles A. *Denver's Mayor Speer: The Forgotten Story of Robert W. Speer*. Denver: Bighorn Books, Green Mountain Press, 1969.

_____ . *Opera in the Rockies: The History of the Central City Opera Association 1932–1992*. Central City: Central City Opera Association, 1992.

Jung, CG. *Psychological Reflections*. Bollingen Series xxxi New Jersey: Princeton University Press, 1978.

Kelsey, Harry E. Jr. *Frontier Capitalist: The Life of John Evans*. Denver: State Historical Society of Colorado and the Pruett Publishing Company, 1969.

Kirby, Linda K. *Heritage of Heroes: Trinity United Methodist Church 1859–1988*. Denver: Trinity United Methodist Church, 1988.

Kohl, Edith Eudora. *Denver's Historic Mansions: Citadels to the Empire Builders.* Denver: Sage Books (Alan Swallow), 1957.

Landgren, Marchal E. *Years of Art: The Story of the Art Students' League of New York.* New York: Robert M. McBride and Company, 1940.

Limerick, Patricia Nelson. *Something In The Soil: Legacies and Reckonings in the New West.* New York and London: W. W. Norton and Company, 2000.

Lindsey, Judge Ben Barr and Harvey J. O'Higgins. *The Beast.* Garden City, New York: Doubleday, Page and Company, 1910.

Lotito, Robert F., ed. *Enchanted Central City.* Denver: A. B. Hirschfeld Press, undated.

Lunt, Cornelia Gray. *Sketches of Childhood and Girlhood Chicago, 1847–1864.* Evanston, Ill.: Cornelia Gray Lunt, 1925.

McMechen, Edgar Carlisle. *The Life of Governor Evans: Second Territorial Governor of Colorado.* Denver: Wahlgreen Publishing Co., 1924.

_____ . *Robert W. Speer: A City Builder.* Denver: The City and County of Denver, 1919. Copyright by the Robert W. Speer Memorial Association.

Noel, Thomas, editor. *The Glory That Was Gold: The Central City Opera House.* Central City: Central City Opera House Association Guild, 1992.

Noel, Thomas J. and Barbara S. Norgren. Denver: *The City Beautiful.* Denver: Historic Denver, 1987.

Perkin, Robert L. *The First Hundred Years, An Informal History of Denver and the Rocky Mountain News 1859–1959.* Garden City, Kansas: Doubleday, 1959.

Prieto, Laura R. *At Home in the Studio.* Cambridge, Mass.: Harvard University Press, 2001.

Reese, Rena. *History of the Denver Public Library, 1860–1928.* Denver: The Library, 1928.

Smith, Duane A. *Henry M. Teller: Colorado's Grand Old Man.* Boulder: University Press of Colorado, 2002.

Sprague, Marshal. *Colorado: A History.* New York and London: W. W. Norton and Company, 1984.

Student, Annette. *Riverside Cemetery Tour Book.* San Diego: CSN Books, 2006.

Swinth, Kirsten. *Painting Professionals: Women Artists and the Development of Modern American Art, 1870–1930.* Chapel Hill and London: University of North Carolina Press, 2001.

Trenton, Patricia and Peter H. Hassrick. *The Rocky Mountains: A Vision for Artists in the Nineteenth Century.* Norman, OK: University of Oklahoma Press, 1983.

Wyer, Malcolm. "Western History Collection, Its Beginning and Growth." Denver Public Library Publication.

Yonce, Frederick J. *Our 100th Anniversary: Denver Public Library.* Denver Public Library Centennial Celebration Committee, Gail M. Dow, Chairman; Project coordinated by Eleanor M. Gehres; produced by Denver Public Library Publications/Design Office, 1989.

Young, Allen. *The Allied Arts Inc. 1920–1995.* Denver: Spectrographics, Inc., 1995.

Journal Articles

Cannon, Helen. "First Ladies of Colorado—Margaret Gray Evans. (Governor John Evans—1862–1865)." *Colorado Magazine* XXXIX (October 1962): 18-28.

Evans, Alfred. "John Evans, M.D. (1814–1897). His Contributions to Medicine and Other Fields." *The Journal of the American Medical Association* 176 (1961): 930-934.

Evans, Anne. Executive Secretary of the Board of Trustees of the Denver Art Museum. "The Genesis of the Denver Art Museum." *Art Register.* 2, #2: November 1931.

Halaas, David Fridtjof. "The House In the Heart of a City." *Colorado Heritage Magazine*: Issue 4, 1989.

Kay-Scott, Cyril. "The Art Museum as a Civic Force." *Municipal Facts.* Vol. 14, nos. 1-2: Jan.-Feb. 1931.

McMechen, Edgar C. "Brinton Terrace." *The Colorado Magazine.* XXIV, No. 3: May 1947.

Sprague, Marshall. "The Renaissance of the Gregory Gulch." *Colorado Wonderland Magazine.* Special Extra Edition, 1954: 14.

Whicker, Wesley J. "Dr. John Evans." *Indiana Magazine of History.* XIX (September 1923): 226-240.

Newspaper Articles

Barnes-Gelt, Susan. "The Long Road for a Landmark." *Denver Post.* June 3, 2004.

Barrett, Marjorie. "An Empire Builder in the Arts." *Rocky Mountain News.* 21 June 1964.

Curtis, Olga. "The Evans Dynasty: Part two, The House That Time Forgot." *Denver Post Empire Magazine.* 2 March 1969.

The Denver Post. "Anne Evans to Continue Valiant Fight for Good Art." 6 June 1937.

Denver Post. "Empire Builder John Evans Sr. Dies at 93." April 26, 1978.

The Denver Post. "Anne Evans is Dead From Heart Attack." 6 Jan. 1941.

Rocky Mountain News. First issue. 29 April 1859.

Kelly, Guy. "Colorado Millennium 2000, a year-long project by The Rocky Mountain News, NEWS 4, and the Colorado Historical Society." © Copyright, Denver *Rocky Mountain News.* 8 June 1999.

Rocky Mountain News, "Obituary Margaret Gray Evans." September 8, 1906.

Swagerty, John. "John Evans: Dreamer Behind State Empire." Quoting Hubert Howe Bancroft. Article second in a series: "Some of Colorado's Notable Families." "Shrine Arouses Curiosity." *Rocky Mountain News.* 30 Sept. 1984.

Rocky Mountain News. 1 Jan. 1930.

Wilson, William H. "A Diadem for the City Beautiful: The Development of Denver's Civic Center." *Journal of the West.* 16 May 1983.

Academic Papers

Breck, A. Ph.D. "William Gray Evans, 1855–1924." Ph.D. Dissertation, University of Denver, 1964.

Davis, K. "Anne Evans: A Preliminary Biographical Sketch." Lake Forest College, Independent Study, 1976.

Dorward, R. "The Evans Family and Their Historic Ranch, Clear Creek County, Colorado." Masters Thesis, University of Colorado at Denver, 1998.

Kelsey, Harry E. Jr. "John Evans." Research paper. University of Denver, Penrose Library, Special Collections, John Evans Collection: 1960.
Knittel, Bernard J. "John Evans, Speaker and Empire Builder." Thesis, University of Denver, 1950.
Marturano, Mary Lou. "Artists and Art Organizations in Colorado." Master's Thesis, University of Denver, 1962.

Web Sites

http://www.colorado.gov/dpa/doit/archives/govs/elbert.html (accessed February 20, 2010)
Colorado Historical Society Website: http://www.coloradohistory.org (accessed February 20, 2010)
Whitten, David and Douglas Steeples. "Democracy in Desperation: The Depression of 1983." http://eh.net/encyclopedia/article/panic/1893.
"The Silver Crash of 1893." website: jellenc@ionet.net (accessed February 23, 2010).
http://www.askart.com/AskART/artists/biography.aspx?searchtype=BIO&artist =9579. *www.gov/DenverCityGovernment.* History of the charter amendments from the City of Denver.

Archive Collections

Austin, Ethelind Elbert Collection.
Bancroft, Hubert Howe. Boulder: Archives of the University of Colorado at Boulder Libraries, Box 1, John Evans Collection. MS, P-L23, Fol. II.
Central City Opera House Association Archives. University of Denver Penrose Library.
Denver Fortnightly Club Collection. Denver Public Library, Western History Collection.
Denver Post Archives. Denver Public Library, Western History Collection.
Denver Public Library Commission Minutes. Denver Public Library, Western History Collection.
Evans Family Archives. University of Denver Penrose Library.
Evans, John Collection. Colorado State Historical Society.
Evans, Margaret. Personal Diaries. Evanston and Denver: Colorado Historical Society, 1 January 1861 through 9 October 1861, and 1 January 1863 through 19 May 1863.
Evans, Margaret Gray Collection: Denver Public Library, Western History Department.
Ingersoll, Helen F. "I Remember: The Reminiscences of my years in the Denver Public Library," 1947. Ingersoll's own stories in her own words as told to the editor, May Wood Wiggington. Denver Public Library, Western History Department, 1947. Typescript.
Lunt, Cornelia Gray. Cornelia Gray Papers (1843–1934), 1866–1964, Series 1/11, Box 1. Northwestern University Archives. Biography, 3.
Municipal Facts Archives. Denver Public Library, Western History Collection.
Rocky Mountain News Archives. Denver Public Library, Western History Collection.

Interviews

Austin, Ethelind Elbert, Mary Ann Davis, Mag Hayden. Interview with Barbara Sternberg and Megan Boone. July 16, 2002 and August 5, 2002. At Austin's home on the Evans Ranch, Evergreen, Colorado.

Gramer, Kevin, Director Byers-Evans House Museum. Interview with Barbara Sternberg and Francesca Starr.

Lincoln, Frederica. Interview with Barbara Sternberg. 2 April 2002. At Lincoln's Upper Bear Creek home in Evergreen.

Hayden, Mag (Margaret). Many phone conversations and meetings with Barbara Sternberg starting April 6, 2002.

Rumsey, Barbara. Interview with Barbara Sternberg and Megan Boone February 12, 2003. Follow-up interview May 12, 2003.

Sweeney, Anne Freyer. Interview with Barbara Sternberg March 12, 2003.

Other Sources

U.S. Congress, Senate. "The Chivington Massacre. Condition of the Indian Tribes: Report of the Joint Special Committee Appointed under Joint Resolution of March 3, 1865." 39th Cong., 2nd Sess.: 1867. Doc. No. 156: 26-98.

National Register of Historic Places, Inventory: September 27, 1979.

Wadsworth, Deborah A. and Jennings, Cynthia A. *Denver Artists Guild Founders: Fifty Two Originals.* Denver: Denver Public Library, 2009.

Walker, Mary. Personal Diaries. 3 August to 2 September 1927 and 1 August to 29 August, 1930. Typescript provided by Ethelind Elbert Austin.

Notes

Acknowledgments

1. Davis, Katharine. "Anne Evans: A Preliminary Biographical Sketch." Unpublished Independent Study Paper. Chicago: Lake Forest College, July 11, 1976.

2. Dorward, Rebecca C. "The Evans Family and Their Historic Ranch, Clear Creek County, Colorado." Masters Thesis, University of Colorado at Denver. Auraria Campus: 1998.

Chapter 1. Who Was Anne Evans?

1. Gene and Barbara Sternberg, *Evergreen: Our Mountain Community* (Boulder, CO: Johnson Publishing Company, 1987, 1993, 1994).

2. We were also interested because, in the 1980s, a family development had forced the sale of the major portion of the Evans Ranch. An innovative planning process was underway to conserve most of the land as open space. This was the first project of a new conservation organization, Colorado Open Lands.

3. Karen Jagelle, letter to the author, 15 May 2004.

4. Marilyn Griggs Riley, *High Altitude Attitudes: Six Savvy Colorado Women* (Boulder, CO: Johnson Publishing Company, 2006).

5. Thomas Noel, "Dr. Colorado," is Professor of History and Director of Colorado Studies at the University of Colorado Denver. He writes a bi-weekly column for the Sunday *Denver Post* and has published 38 books on Colorado History.

Chapter 2. Patriarch John Evans: Doctor, Governor, Methodist, Capitalist, Philanthropist

1. Susan Barnes-Gelt, "The Long Road for a Landmark," *Denver Post,* June 3, 2004. This building is a Denver Historic Landmark that has been owned since 1974 by developers who have been unable, to date, to remodel it for any current use. Designed by Denver architect David W. Dryden and built in 1904.

2. Harry E. Kelsey, Jr., *Frontier Capitalist: The Life of John Evans* (Denver: State Historical Society of Colorado and the Pruett Publishing Company, 1969), 13.

3. Kelsey, 23.

4. Alfred Evans, "John Evans, M.D. (1814–1897). His Contributions to Medicine and Other Fields," *The Journal of the American Medical Association*, Vol. 176 (1961): 930-934.

5. John Evans, Letter to Hannah Canby Evans, 28 May 1842. John Evans Collection: Colorado State Historical Society.

6. Kelsey, 32.

7. Bernard J. Knittel, "John Evans, Speaker and Empire Builder," Thesis, University of Denver: 1950: 20.

8. Wesley J. Whicker, "Dr. John Evans," *Indiana Magazine of History*, Vol. XIX (September 1923): 226-240.

9. Evans, 930-934.

10. Kelsey, 59.

11. Outbreaks of yellow fever prompted Congress to pass the first federal quarantine legislation in 1878; the Chicago cholera outbreak traced to ships arriving from Europe spurred reinterpretation of the law in 1892. *http://www.cdc.gov* (accessed 10/6/2009).

12. Kelsey, 69.

13. Kelsey, 69.

14. Kelsey, 75.

15. Kelsey, 81.

16. Edgar Carlisle McMechen, *The Life of Governor Evans* (Denver: Wahlgreen Publishing Company, 1924), 69.

17. Kelsey, 88.

18. John Evans, Letter to Margaret Patten Gray, August 1853. John Evans Collection: Colorado State Historical Society.

19. Kelsey, 95.

20. Kelsey, 96.

21. In our research on the Evans and Lunt families, my granddaughter, Megan Boone Witucki, and I had difficulty sorting out the identities of Cornelias, Katherines, Josephines, Margarets, Annes, Johns, Horaces and Williams: the same names lovingly recycled generation after generation. Consult the family tree in Appendix.

22. Cornelia Gray Lunt, *Sketches of Childhood and Girlhood: Chicago, 1847–1864* (Evanston, Ill.: Cornelia Gray Lunt, 1925).

23. John Evans, Letter to Cousin Benjamin in 1834. John Evans Collection: Colorado State Historical Society.

Chapter 3. New England Mother: Cultural Pioneer

1. Mary Lyon founded Mount Holyoke College in 1837. The motto carved on Lyon's gravestone could well have served as Margaret's own.

2. Cornelia Gray Lunt, *Sketches of Childhood and Girlhood: Chicago, 1847–1864* (Evanston, Ill.: Cornelia Gray Lunt, 1925)

3. Lunt, 22.

4. Lunt, 22.

5. Helen Cannon, "First Ladies of Colorado—Margaret Gray Evans. (Governor John Evans—1862–1865)," *Colorado Magazine* XXXIX (October 1962): 18-28.

6. These diaries were preserved in the Evans family and given to the Colorado Historical Society in December 2002.

7. Margaret Evans, *Personal Diaries* (Evanston and Denver: Colorado Historical Society, 1 January 1861 through 9 October 1861, and 1 January 1863 through 19 May 1863).

8. M. Evans, 10 January 1861.

9. M. Evans, 1 May 1861.

10. M. Evans, 30 April 1861.

11. M. Evans, 4 September 1861.

12. John Evans, Letter to Margaret Evans, 8 June 1862. John Evans Collection: Colorado State Historical Society.

Chapter 4. Life in Colorado Territory

1. Marshal Sprague, *Colorado: A History* (New York and London: W. W. Norton and Company, 1984), 31.

2. Harry E. Kelsey, Jr., *Frontier Capitalist: The Life of John Evans* (Denver: State Historical Society of Colorado and the Pruett Publishing Company, 1969), 118.

3. Robert L. Perkins, *The First Hundred Years, 1859–1959* (Garden City, Kansas: unknown publisher, 1959), 233.

4. *Rocky Mountain News*, First issue, 29 April 1859.

5. Kelsey, 119.

6. Kelsey, 120.

7. Le Roy R. Hafen, *Men and Women of Colorado: Past and Present* (Phoenix, Tucson, Denver: Pioneer Publishing Co., 1944), 4.

8. Phil Goodstein, *Denver From the Bottom Up* (Denver: New Social Publications, May 2003), 17.

9. Goodstein, 25.

10. Helen Cannon, "First Ladies of Colorado—Margaret Gray Evans. (Governor John Evans—1862–1865)," *Colorado Magazine* (January, 1962): 21.

11. Allen Breck, J. Alton Templin and Martin Rist, *The Methodist, Evangelical, and United Brethren Churches in the Rockies, 1850–1876* (Denver: Rocky Mountain Conference of the United Methodist Church, 1977), 80.

12. Kelsey, 127.

13. Colorado Historical Society Website: http://www.coloradohistory.org (accessed February 20, 2010).

14. Margaret Evans, *Personal Diaries*. Evanston and Denver: Colorado Historical Society, 1 January 1861 through 9 October 1861, and 1 January 1863 through 19 May 1863.

15. Margaret Evans, *Personal Diaries*.

16. Margaret Evans, *Personal Diaries*.

17. Margaret Evans, *Personal Diaries*.

18. Margaret Evans, *Personal Diaries*.

19. Linda K. Kirby, Heritage of Heroes: Trinity United Methodist Church 1859–1988, (Denver: Trinity United Methodist Church, 1988), 24.

20. Kirby, 26.

21. Kirby, 7.

22. Kirby, 11.

23. Kirby, 14.

24. Kirby, 16.

25. Kirby, 42.

26. Margaret Evans, *Personal Diaries*.

27. Frank Baker, *Methodism and the Love Feast* (London: Epworth Press, 1957).

28. Camp Weld, named for Governor Gilpin's territorial secretary, later sometimes known as Camp Elbert. It was on a thirty-acre site south of Denver's city limits, the in area around 10th and Tejon (*Denver Post*, 8/20/06).

29. Margaret Evans, *Personal Diaries*.

30. Kirby, 42.

31. The addition included the area from West Colfax south to the alley between 11th and 10th Avenue and from Broadway to the alley behind Cherokee, originally Evans Street.

32. Kirby, 91.

33. Kirby, 75.

34. Kelsey, 214.

35. Edith Eudora Kohl, *Denver's Historic Mansions: Citadels to the Empire Builders*, (Denver: Sage Books (Alan Swallow), 1957).

36. Ibid.

37. Cannon, 23.

38. Margaret Evans, *Personal Diaries*.

39. Allen duPont Breck, Ph.D., *William Gray Evans, 1855–1924* (Denver: The University of Denver Department of History, 1964), 47.

40. Cannon, 265.

41. Cannon, 265.

42. Cannon, 268.

43. Cornelia Gray Lunt, *Sketches of Childhood and Girlhood: Chicago, 1847–1864* (Evanston, Ill.: Cornelia Gray Lunt, 1925), 69.

44. Cornelia Gray Lunt, 211.

45. Cornelia Gray Lunt, 211.

46. Cornelia Gray Lunt, 215.

47. Cannon, 265.

48. Edgar McMechen, *The Life of Governor Evans, Second Territorial Governor of Colorado* (Denver: Wahlgreen Publishing Co., 1924), 107.

49. Cannon, 265.

50. Cannon, 268.

51. Breck, 105.

52. Barbara Moore Rumsey, "Evans Memorial Chapel," 3 January 1994.

53. See chapter 8, "Life Lessons From Cousin Nina."

54. Kelsey, 212.

55. *Denver Times*, 27 November 1899.

56. *http://www.colorado.gov/dpa/doit/archives/govs/elbert.html* (accessed February 20, 2010).

57. Kelsey, 214.

58. Annette Student, *Riverside Cemetery Tour Book* (San Diego: CSN Books, 2006), 131.

Chapter 5. Sand Creek and After

1. Patricia Nelson Limerick, *Something In The Soil: Legacies and Reckonings in the New West* (New York and London: W. W. Norton and Company, 2000), 34.

2. Hubert Howe Bancroft, Boulder: Archives of the University of Colorado at Boulder Libraries, Box 1, John Evans Collection. MS, P-L23, Fol. II: 11.

3. MS. Bancroft, P-L329, Fol II, 19.

4. Allen Breck and J. Alton Templin and Martin Rist, *The Methodist, Evangelical, and United Brethren Churches in the Rockies, 1850–1876* (Denver: Rocky Mountain Conference of the United Methodist Church, 1977), Section 1, 84.

5. Ibid.

6. A Second Regiment had been raised and called to duty outside Colorado Territory.

7. Phil Goodstein, *Denver From the Bottom Up, Volume One: From Sand Creek to Ludlow* (Denver: New Social Publications, 2003), 67.

8. Harry E. Kelsey, Jr., *Frontier Capitalist: The Life of John Evans* (Denver: State Historical Society of Colorado and the Pruett Publishing Company, 1969), 152.

9. Robert L. Perkins, "1865 Report of the House of Representatives on the Sand Creek Engagement," *The First Hundred Years, 1859–1959* (Garden City, Kansas: unknown publisher, 1959).

10. U.S. Congress, Senate, "The Chivington Massacre. Condition of the Indian Tribes: Report of the Joint Special Committee Appointed under Joint Resolution of March 3, 1865," 39th Cong., 2nd Sess.: 1867. Doc. No. 156: 26-98.

11. Kelsey, 153.

12. Goodstein, 73.

13. In spite of the fact that brave souls like the 26-year-old Captain Soule and Major Wynkoop denounced the action immediately after it occurred, full official acknowledgment of the truth about the Sand Creek massacre has taken many years. A Civil War monument erected at the west entrance to the Colorado State Capitol in 1909 to "honor all soldiers who had fought in battles of the Civil War in Colorado and elsewhere" designated Sand Creek as a battle. The controversy this provoked was not settled until 2002, when a bronze plaque was installed in front of the monument, authorized by Senate Joint Resolution 99-017 as a token of "Coloradans' struggle to understand and take responsibility for our past." The wording on the plaque reads, "By designating Sand Creek a battle, the monument's designers mischaracterized the actual events. Protests by some Sand Creek descendants and others throughout the twentieth century have since led to the widespread recognition of the tragedy as the Sand Creek Massacre."

For a national monument at the site of the event, it took Senator Ben Nighthorse Campbell, the first Native American Senator from Colorado, working with many others, almost 25 years to have the Sand Creek Massacre location recognized as a National Historic Site: it was dedicated on April 28, 2007. The 12,300 acres site includes the actual area of the massacre, the site of the encampment there, and a wide area where Indians trying to escape were hunted down by the attacking volunteers. As of January, 2008, only 3,000 acres had actually been acquired. The Northern Cheyenne tribe was trying to raise money for further purchases from the private landowners who own the majority of the land.

14. Denver was part of Arapahoe County until the Home Rule Amendment of 1902 created the City and County of Denver. In the following year, Denver annexed all the adjacent suburbs resulting in a City and County that covered almost 60 square miles. All of the existing school districts were merged into Denver School District No. 1.

15. In the early years of the twentieth century, Anne Evans developed a profound interest in the culture of the Pueblo Indians of New Mexico. She admired their way of life. As a collector of their art, she became an advocate for its acceptance as a value equal to that of any civilization. It has been speculated that in this she may have been motivated by guilt over her father's role in the Sand Creek Massacre. No evidence came to light in the research for this book to support such speculation. All her writings about the long-settled Pueblo Indians indicate that becoming familiar with them and their ancient ways was a new and deeply meaningful experience for her.

16. Duane A. Smith, *Henry M. Teller: Colorado's Grand Old Man* (Boulder: University Press of Colorado, 2002).

17. Goodstein, 94.

18. Guy Kelly, Colorado Millennium 2000, a year-long project by The Rocky Mountain News, NEWS4, and the Colorado Historical Society, June 1999. © Copyright, Denver *Rocky Mountain News*.

19. Kelsey, 179.

20. Marshall Sprague, *Colorado: A History* (New York and London: W. W. Norton and Company, 1984), 51.

21. Sprague, 52.

Chapter 6. A Birth in London and an Uncommon Childhood

1. Harry E. Kelsey, Jr., *Frontier Capitalist: The Life of John Evans* (Denver: State Historical Society of Colorado and the Pruett Publishing Company, 1969), 212.

2. McMechen, 108.

3. McMechen, 108.

4. Allen duPont Breck, *William Gray Evans 1855–1924: Portrait of a Western Executive* (Denver: The University of Denver Department of History, 1964), 37.

5. John Evans, Letter to Margaret: 3 August 1876. John Evans Collection: Colorado State Historical Society.

6. *Rocky Mountain News*, September 8, 1906. Obituary Margaret Gray Evans.

7. Kelsey, 183.

8. John Evans, Letter to Margaret, 3 August 1876.

9. John Evans, Letter to Margaret, 6 December 1875.

10. Margaret Evans, Letter to John Evans, 8 March 1876.
11. Ibid.
12. Ibid.
13. John Evans, Letter to Margaret, 10 June 1876.
14. John Evans, Letter to Margaret, 16 June 1876.
15. John Evans, Letter to Margaret, 31 July 1876.
16. John Evans, Letter to Margaret, 24 Sept. 1876.
17. John Evans, Letter to Margaret, 3 Nov. 1876.
18. John Evans, Letter to Margaret, 27 February 1876.
19. Margaret Evans, Letter to John, 8 March 1876.
20. John Evans, Letter to Margaret, 7 November 1875.
21. John Evans, Letter to Margaret Evans, March 13, 1870.
22. Margaret Evans, Letter to John, 8 March 1876.
23. Margaret Evans, Letter to John, 8 March 1876.
24. John Evans, Letter to Margaret, 13 March 1876.
25. John Evans, Letters to Margaret, 23 and 29 April 1876.
26. Margaret Evans, Letter to John, 7 May 1876.
27. John Evans, Letter to Margaret, 10 June 1876.
28. John Evans, Letter to Margaret, 2 July 1876.
29. John Evans, Letter to Margaret, 2 July 1876.
30. John Evans, Letter to Margaret, 31 July 1876.
31. John Evans, Letter to Margaret, 12 August 1876.
32. John Evans, Letter to Margaret, 3 Nov. 1876.
33. Ibid.
34. Kelsey, 218.

Chapter 7. Denver School Days, "Wild, Free" Mountain Summers

1. Allen duPont Breck, *John Evans of Denver: Portrait of a Twentieth Century Banker* (Boulder: The Pruett Publishing Company, 1972), 26-7.

2. Cannon, Helen, "First Ladies of Colorado—Margaret Gray Evans. (Governor John Evans—1862–1865)," *Colorado Magazine* (January, 1962): 25.

3. Mrs. Howard Evans is Sunie Lowell. They were married in the Evans home on December 12, 1881.

4. Samuel Elbert, Interview with Margaret Hayden. 31 May 1983: typescript: 1. Quoted in Rebecca Dorward. "The Evans Family and Their Historic Ranch, Clear Creek County, Colorado," Master's Thesis, University of Colorado at Denver, Auraria Campus: 1998.

5. Information from National Register of Historic Places, Inventory: September 27, 1979.

6. Ethelind Elbert Austin, Interview with Barbara Sternberg and Megan Boone, 16 July 2002 and 5 August 2002, at Austin's home on the Evans Ranch, Evergreen, Colorado.

7. According to Mag Hayden, the "Trumpet" part of the name came from the shape of the meadow viewed from above, and the "Silver" from a

"sage-y" kind of plant that grew there in abundance and looked silver at dusk and in the moonlight. It was thought to be undesirable and was later eradicated.

8. For which historic fact, Evergreenites are truly grateful: acres of barren mine tailings, like the ones around many nearby mining towns, would have ruined the scenic beauty they prize so highly.

9. Horace Fletcher Lunt, Letter to Phelps Dodge, 29 July 1935: 7.

10. Horace Fletcher Lunt, Letter to Phelps Dodge, 29 July 1935: 7.

11. Horace Fletcher Lunt, Letter to Phelps Dodge, 29 July 1935: 8.

12. Horace Fletcher Lunt, Letter to Phelps Dodge, 29 July 1935: 9.

13. Louise Everett, Unpublished manuscript. Quoted in Dorward Thesis: 45.

14. Dorward, 46.

15. Horace Fletcher Lunt, Letter to Phelps Dodge, 29 July 1935: 11.

16. Ibid.

17. Horace Fletcher Lunt, Letter to Phelps Dodge, 29 July 1935: 11.

18. Horace Fletcher Lunt, Letter to Phelps Dodge, 29 July 1935: 11.

19. John Fiske, 1842–1901, was an American philosopher and historian. What Margaret Evans was reading to her young audience was probably not from his early books, which attempted to reconcile Spenserian theories of evolution with religious beliefs, but from his later historical writings. These were "popular accounts...noted for an easy, lucid and dramatic style." Information from Columbia Encyclopedia, Sixth Edition, 2007.

20. Everett 4. Quoted in Dorward: 51.

21. Everett 4. Quoted in Dorward: 51.

22. Breck, 26.

23. Katharine Davis, "Anne Evans: A Preliminary Biographical Sketch," Chicago: Lake Forest College, Independent Study," 11 July 1976: 11.

24. Allen duPont Breck, *The Episcopal Church in Colorado, 1860–1963* (Denver, Big Mountain Press: 1963), Quoted in Michael Churchman. The Kent School 1922–1972.

25. We were unable to find anything in the available archives to document with certainty that Anne Evans attended this school, but those archives are far from complete, and it is unlikely that Katharine Evans would be mistaken about this recollection. Undoubtedly, many of Anne's friends and contemporaries in Denver were students at Wolfe Hall.

26. Davis, 11.

27. Ibid.

Chapter 8. Life Lessons from Cousin Nina

1. Cornelia Gray Lunt, *Sketches of Childhood and Girlhood: Chicago, 1847–1864* (Evanston, Ill.: Cornelia Gray Lunt, 1925).

2. His efforts to have Anne reproduce her mother's elegant, copperplate handwriting were in vain. His daughter was preparing for life in a different age, for which her bold, free writing style was eminently suitable.

3. This was written at the request of her niece, Regina Lunt Dodge, the daughter of her brother, Horace.

4. C. Lunt, 6.

5. C. Lunt, 101.

6. Marshall Sprague, "The Renaissance of the Gregory Gulch," *Colorado Wonderland Magazine*. Special, Extra Edition, 1954: 14.

7. Frederica Lincoln, Interview with Barbara Sternberg. 2 April 2002. At Lincoln's Upper Bear Creek home in Evergreen.

8. C. Lunt, 24-5.

9. C. Lunt, 72.

10. Lincoln interview.

11. C. Lunt, 30.

12. C. Lunt, 212.

13. C. Lunt, 214.

14. C. Lunt, 25.

15. *The Denver Post*, "Anne Evans to Continue Valiant Fight for Good Art," 6 June 1937.

16. Katharine Davis, "Anne Evans: A Preliminary Biographical Sketch," Unpublished Independent Study Paper. Chicago: Lake Forest College, 11 July 1976: 11.

17. Anne Freyer Sweeney, interview with the author.

18. Picture of Cornelia Gray Lunt with the Evans family at the Evans Ranch. *Colorado Magazine*, Vol. XXXIX, Jan. 1962: 26.

Chapter 9. Paris, Berlin, Denver, New York: the Artist Years

1. Kirsten Swinth, *Painting Professionals: Women Artists and the Development of Modern American Art, 1870–1930* (Chapel Hill and London: University of North Carolina Press, 2001), 40 and 43.

2. Catalogue of Denver University, 1886–7.

3. Swinth, 2.

4. Swinth, 17.

5. Swinth, 1.

6. Swinth, 2 to 3.

7. Swinth, 3.

8. Swinth, 4.

9. Laura R. Prieto, *At Home in the Studio* (Cambridge, Mass.: Harvard University Press, 2001).

10. Swinth, 82.

11. Swinth, 82.

12. Swinth, 93.

13. Allen duPont Breck, *William Gray Evans, 1855–1924* (Denver: The University of Denver Department of History, 1964), 69.

14. Helen Arndt, (Mrs. Karl), Arndt's paper was one of four presented to the Club prior to a re-reading of Anne Evans' "Christmas Pilgrimage to the Southwest." Minutes of the Club are in the Fortnightly Club Archives in the Western History Department of the Denver Public Library.

15. Robert L. Perkin, *The First Hundred Years: An Informal History of Denver and the Rocky Mountain News 1859–1959* (New York: Doubleday, 1959), 358.

16. "The Silver Crash of 1893," website: *www.ellensplace.net/hcg_fac8.html* (accessed February 23, 2010).

17. Perkin, 358.

18. Nathanial C. Meeker (1817–1879) was a journalist who, with the backing of his editor, Horace Greeley, organized the successful agricultural Union Colony in 1869 near present-day Greeley. In 1878, with no experience of dealing with Native Americans, he was appointed Indian Agent on the White River Ute Reservation. He tried to convert the Utes from their traditional way of life to farming and succeeded in rousing them to fury with his high-handed methods. On September 29, 1879 they rebelled, killing Meeker and the other white males at the Indian Agency and capturing Meeker's wife and daughter. The Utes won a short-term victory, but ultimately the "Meeker Massacre" led to their forced withdrawal from nearly all their lands in western Colorado.

19. David Whitten and Douglas Steeples, Article excerpted from *Democracy in Desperation: The Depression of 1983*. The article was posted on the internet: *http://eh.net/encyclopedia/article/panic.1893*.

20. Ibid.

21. Harry E. Kelsey, Jr., *Frontier Capitalist: The Life of John Evans* (Denver: State Historical Society of Colorado and the Pruett Publishing Company, 1969), 226.

22. Ibid.

23. See Chapter 5.

24. Kelsey, 228.

25. Mary Walker, Personal Diaries. 3 August to 2 September 1927 and 1 August to 29 August 1930. Typescript provided by Ethelind Austin.

26. Marchal E. Landgren, *Years of Art: The Story of the Art Students' League of New York* (New York: Robert M. McBride and Company, 1940), 63.

27. Mary Walker, Personal Diaries, 3 August to 2 September 1927 and 1 August to 29 August 1930. Typescript provided by Ethelind Austin.

28. Miriam Washburn Adams (Mrs. Frederick Atherton Adams), "Artless, Mostly Less," Read 6 March 1973 to the members of the Denver Fortnightly Club, as one of the four introductions to the re-reading of Anne Evan's "A Christmas Pilgrimage to the South West": 7.

29. Washburn Adams, 5.

Chapter 10. Entering Denver's Art World

1. Elizabeth Spalding, "Something of Art In Denver As I Think of It." The Denver Fortnightly Society, December 1924: 8 and 9.

2. *History of the City of Denver, Arapahoe County, and Colorado* (Chicago: W. B. Vickers, Baskin and Company, 1880), 482.

3. Patricia Trenton, "Something of Art In Denver As I Think of It," The Denver Fortnightly Society, Patricia Trenton and Peter H. Hassrick, *The Rocky Mountains: A Vision for Artists in the Nineteenth Century* (Norman, OK: University of Oklahoma Press, 1983).

4. Mary Lou Marturano, "Artists and Art Organizations in Colorado," Thesis (M.A.) University of Denver, 1962: 36.

5. *Denver Daily Tribune*. 30 January 1879. Quoted in Marturano, 37.

6. John Harrison Mills, Letter: 1916. Denver: Denver Public Library Western History Collection. Quoted in Marturano.

7. Marturano, 39.

8. Dawson Scrapbook, Vol. I, 5. Quoted in Marturano, 39.

9. Henry McCarter, Letter to Elisabeth Spalding, 8 January 1942. Elisabeth Spalding papers, Denver Public Library Western History Department, WH 14, Box 1.

10. Barbara Moore Rumsey, "Elizabeth Spalding (1868–1954)," with Photographs (Copies) of Spalding's Art Work). Paper presented to the Denver Fortnightly Club. Denver Public Library Western History Department, Box 11: 7.

11. Rumsey, 2.

12. Elizabeth Spalding, "Something of Art In Denver As I Think of It." The Denver Fortnightly Society. December 1924: 6.

13. Marturano, 43.

14. Marturano, 43.

15. Marturano, 40.

16. While it was still a Territory, Colorado had an active Board of Immigration whose publications "were designed to extol the virtues of the Territory as a health-inducing area." An 1874 Report of the Board attempted to balance the area's very real potential for curing consumption with the reality that not everyone who came was cured, and that some varieties and stages of the disease made a recovery unlikely. Information from Ubbeholde, Carl, A Colorado Reader, Pruett Publishing Co., Boulder, CO, 1962.

17. Spalding, 12.

18. Spalding, 17.

19. Marjorie Barrett, "An Empire Builder in the Arts." *Rocky Mountain News*, 21 June 1964.

20. Spalding, 18.

21. Spalding, 19-20.

22. http://www.askart.com/AskART/artists/biography.aspx?searchtype=BIO&artist=9579.

Chapter 11. John Evans Dies, William Evans' Star Rises

1. Allen duPont Breck, *William Gray Evans 1855–1924: Portrait of a Western Executive* (Denver: The University of Denver Department of History, 1964), Foreword.

2. Breck, 74.

3. Breck, 48.

4. Olga Curtis, "The Evans Dynasty: Part Two, The House That Time Forgot." *Denver Post Empire Magazine*, 2 March 1969.

5. Harry E. Kelsey, Jr., *Frontier Capitalist: The Life of John Evans* (Denver: State Historical Society of Colorado and the Pruett Publishing Company, 1969), 228.

6. John Swagerty, "John Evans: Dreamer Behind State Empire," Quoting Hubert Howe Bancroft. Article second in a series: "Some of Colorado's Notable Families," *Rocky Mountain News*, 1 July 1979.

7. Hubert Howe Bancroft, Boulder: Archives of the University of Colorado at Boulder Libraries, Box 1, John Evans Collection. MS, P-L23, Fol. II.

8. Kelsey, 228.

9. Harry E. Kelsey, Jr., "John Evans." Term Paper. University of Denver, Penrose Library, Special Collections, John Evans Collection, 1960.

10. Kelsey Preface, xi.

11. *Rocky Mountain News,* 4 July 1890.

12. Marjorie Barrett, *Rocky Mountain News,* 21 June 1964.

Chapter 12. The Legacy of Margaret Evans

1. Allen duPont Breck, *John Evans of Denver* (Boulder: The Pruett Publishing Company, 1972), 13.

2. Robert F. Lotito, ed. *Enchanted Central City* (Denver: A. B. Hirschfeld Press, undated), 42.

3. Anne E. F. Sweeney, Interview with Barbara Sternberg 12 March 2003.

4. *Central City Opera House Association, The Glory That Was Gold* (Denver: Opera House Association: 1936), with supplements. Quoted in Breck: 47.

5. Harry E. Kelsey, Jr., *Frontier Capitalist: The Life of John Evans* (Denver: State Historical Society of Colorado and the Pruett Publishing Company, 1969), 216.

6. Helen Cannon, "First Ladies of Colorado—Margaret Gray Evans," Colorado Magazine XXXIX, October, 1962, 28.

7. Denver Fortnightly Yearbook. 1930–31. "History of the Club" in the 1930–1. Denver Public Library Western History Department.

8. Unnamed paper. Hand-written history of the Fortnightly Club. Box 10, Fortnightly Club Collection: Denver Public Library Western History Department, 1891.

9. Denver Fortnightly Yearbook, 1930–1931. In collection of Denver Western History Department.

10. Unnamed paper. Hand-written, 1891: 10.

11. See chapter "New Mexico: Advocate for Native American Art and the Preservation of Mission Churches."

12. Allen duPont Breck, *William Gray Evans 1855–1924: Portrait of a Western Executive* (Denver: The University of Denver Department of History, 1964), 82.

13. General Frank Hall, Article, no date. Denver Public Library, Western History Department. George Fredrick Watrous Scrapbook, M833: 79.

14. Undated clipping. Margaret Gray Evans Collection: Denver Public Library, Western History Department.

15. See chapter "You Must have a Good Time!"

Chapter 13. Tribulations and Resurgence of William Evans

1. CG Jung, *Psychological Reflections* (Bollingen Series xxxi New Jersey: Princeton University Press, 1978), 147.

2. Olga Curtis, "The Evans Dynasty: Part Two, The House That Time Forgot." *Denver Post Empire Magazine.* 2 March 1969: 14-23.

3. Curtis, 21.

4. Phil Goodstein, *Denver from the Bottom Up: From Sand Creek to Ludlow* (Denver: New Social Publications, 2003), 272-3.

5. Allen duPont Breck, *William Gray Evans 1855–1924: Portrait of a Western Executive* (Denver: The University of Denver Department of History, 1964), 218.

6. Goodstein, 273.

7. Allen duPont Breck, *John Evans of Denver* (Boulder: The Pruett Publishing Company, 1972), 76.

8. Breck, *John Evans of Denver*, 78.

9. Louisa Arps, *Cemetery to Conservatory: A Jubilee History of Denver Botanic Gardens 1951–1976* (Denver: Denver Botanic Gardens, 1980). Maps drawn by Julia Andrews-Jones.

10. Breck, *John Evans of Denver*, 79.

11. Colorado State History of Colorado's Executive Residence http//www.colorado.gov/dpa/doit/archives/residenc.html.

12. Breck, *John Evans of Denver*, 85.

13. This home is of more than passing interest to Coloradans. It is now the official residence of the state's Governor. After the death of Mrs. Cheesman, the house was sold to Claude Boettcher, a prominent businessman, who is said to have presented it to his wife, Edna, as a Valentine's Day present in 1924. The Boettchers traveled extensively and brought back many pieces of furniture and decorative items with which they embellished their home. Claude Boettcher died in 1957 and his wife a year later. She left the house to the Boettcher Foundation, "requesting that his beautiful house be offered to the State of Colorado, to be used as the Governor's residence." Several state agencies originally objected to the gift, and after two years of trying and failing to give the house to the State, the foundation hired someone to catalog the contents in preparation for an auction. The house itself was scheduled to be razed, because the property's main value was now the land. Governor Stephen McNichols stepped in almost at the last minute, late in 1959, and gratefully accepted the mansion on behalf of the State of Colorado.

14. Judge Ben B. Lindsey, and Harvey J. O'Higgins, *The Beast* (Garden City, New York: Doubleday, Page and Company, 1910).

15. Lindsey, 104-5.

16. Lindsey, 23.

17. John Swagerty, "John Evans: Dreamer Behind State Empire," Quoting Hubert Howe Bancroft, Article second in a series: "Some of Colorado's Notable Families." *Rocky Mountain News*, Sec. "Denver Times," 1 July 1979.

18. Allen duPont Breck, *William Gray Evans 1855–1924: Portrait of a Western Executive.* (Denver: The University of Denver Department of History, 1964), 105.

19. Ibid., 105.

20. *Denver Post*, November 11, 1914.

21. Among the stimulants William Evans used was Antikamnia. The Antikamnia Chemical Company made its appearance around 1890 in Saint

Louis, Missouri. The trademark was registered that year, but the medicine was never patented. It was described as a coal-tar derivative, but it was half or more acetanilid, a somewhat dangerous and habit-forming compound. The company also offered it mixed with codeine—which is addictive—quinine, and several other items either singly or in combination. A typical recommended dosage for Antikamnia with codeine for treating "Worry (nervousness: 'the Blues')" was one or two every three hours.

22. Evan E. Evans to Anne Evans, October 14, 1913, Martha Evans Collection, Colorado Historical Society, Denver, CO.

23. Evan E. Evans to W. A. Dyche, October 11, 1913, Martha Evans Collection, Colorado Historical Society, Denver, CO.

24. Ibid.

25. Ibid.

26. Ibid.

27. Evan E. Evans to Anne Evans, October 14, 1913.

28. Evans E. Evans to W. A. Dyche, October 11, 1913.

29. Ibid.

30. John Evans to William G. Evans, November 9, 1913, Martha Evans Collection, Colorado Historical Society, Denver, CO.

31. Cornelia Evans to Katharine Evans, December 19, 1913, Margaret (Peg) Hayden Collection.

32. Margaret Evans to Katharine Evans, no date, Margaret (Peg) Hayden Collection.

33. Ibid.

34. Forbes Parkhill, Newspaper Article, Friday 17 June 1921. No newspaper named. Denver Public Library, Western History Department. George Fredrick Watrous Scrapbook, M833.

35. David Fridtjof Halaas, "The House In the Heart of a City." *Colorado Heritage Magazine*: 4, 1989: 29.

36. "Shrine Arouses Curiosity," *Rocky Mountain News,* 30 Sept. 30 1984.

37. Breck, *William Gray Evans,* 69.

38. Tom Noel, *Rocky Mountain News* column.

Chapter 14. Anne Evans and the Denver Art Museum

1. *Rocky Mountain News,* 1 Jan. 1930.

2. Neil Harris, Marlene Chambers and Lewis Wingfield Story. *The Denver Art Museum, The First Hundred Years* (Denver: The Denver Art Museum, 1996), 85.

3. Paul Schofield, Letter to Anne Downs, 8 August 1940, Chicago, Ill., and Letter from assistant to Anne Downs to Paul Schofield, 14 August 1940.

4. Elizabeth Spalding, "Something of Art in Denver as I Think Of It." Denver Public Library, Western History Department, Denver Fortnightly Society Collection, Dec 1924: 14-15.

5. Artists Club Bulletin 1897, Denver Public Library.

6. *Denver Republican,* 22 April 1900.

7. Chambers, "First Steps toward an Art Museum; The Artists' Club," 64.

8. Chambers, 66.

9. *DAM The First Hundred Years*, Note 56: 286.

10. *The Open Door*. Denver: Saint John's Cathedral, 4 February 1968.

11. Ibid.

12. Edgar C. McMechen, "Brinton Terrace." *The Colorado Magazine*, Vol. XXIV, No. 3: May 1947.

13. McMechen, 273.

14. McMechen, 97.

15. "Anne Evans is Dead From Heart Attack." *The Denver Post*, 6 Jan. 1941.

16. A collaborative exhibition of Allen True's work was mounted by the Denver Art Museum, the Denver Public Library and History Colorado in 2009.

17. McMechen, 108.

18. Spalding, 15.

19. Chambers, *DAM The First Hundred Years*, 65.

20. Chambers, *DAM The First Hundred Years*, 65.

21. See Chapter 11.

22. Spalding, 23.

23. Story, *DAM The First Hundred Years*, 72.

24. Ibid.

25. Spalding, 24.

26. Ref. Note attached to a photograph in the Denver Western History Department, "Residence of Mr. H. W. Bennett, Denver."

27. Allen Young, *The Allied Arts Inc. 1920–1995*. (Denver: Spectrographics, Inc.,1995.)

28. Young, 1.

29. Ibid.

30. Anne Evans, as Executive Secretary of the Board of Trustees of the Denver Art Museum. "The Genesis of the Denver Art Museum," *Art Register*. Vol. 2, #2: November 1931.

31. Story, *DAM The First Hundred Years*, 85.

32. Story, *DAM The First Hundred Years*, 85. Also Henrietta Bromwell Scrapbook, Colorado Historical Society.

33. Deborah A. Wadsworth and Cynthia A. Jennings, *Denver Artists Guild Founders: Fifty Two Originals* (Denver: Denver Public Library, 2009).

34. Deborah, a DPL Volunteer par excellence, is working on a book about Colorado artist John Thompson. She and her husband are long-time Colorado Art collectors. Cynthia Jennings is the daughter of Guild founder and leader, artist Clarence A. Durham; she is working on a book about the Guild.

35. Wadsworth.

36. For her volunteer services, Deborah Wadsworth received the Western History/Genealogy Department's prestigious Eleanor Gehres Award on August 26, 2009.

37. Story, *DAM The First Hundred Years*, 86.

38. Kay-Scott, Cyril. "The Art Museum as a Civic Force." *Municipal Facts*. Vol. 14, nos. 1-2: Jan.-Feb. 1931.

Chapter 15. A Center of Public Happiness: The DenverPublic Library

1. Helen F. Ingersoll, (Long-time DPL staff member), Letter to Anne Evans, 23 April 1940.

2. Helen F. Ingersoll, "I Remember: The Reminiscences of my years in the Denver Public Library," 1947. Ingersoll's own stories in her own words as told to the editor, May Wood Wiggington. Denver Public Library, Western History Department, 1947. Typescript.

3. *Rocky Mountain News*, column, 17 April 2004.

4. Frederick J. Yonce, *Our 100th Anniversary: Denver Public Library*, Denver Public Library Centennial Celebration Committee, Gail M. Dow, Chairman; Project coordinated by Eleanor M. Gehres; produced by Denver Public Library Publications/Design Office, 1989.

5. Yonce. Quoting RMN, 1885: 2.

6. Ingersoll, 3.

7. Ingersoll, 5.

8. Ingersoll, 4.

9. Ingersoll, 16.

10. Ingersoll, 36.

11. Ingersoll, 20.

12. Ingersoll, 19.

13. Ingersoll, 17.

14. Yonce, 6.

15. Ingersoll, 17.

16. Ingersoll, 24.

17. Yonce, 7.

18. Ingersoll, 25.

19. Yonce, 9.

20. Denver Public Library Commission Minutes, 11 March 1907.

21. Rena Reese, *History of the Denver Public Library, 1860–1928*, Denver: The Library, 1928, 39.

22. Reese, 39.

23. Ingersoll, 29.

24. Denver Public Library Commission Minutes, 7 March 1910.

25. Ingersoll, 38.

26. Ingersoll, 27.

27. Yonce, 6.

28. Ingersoll, 30.

29. Ingersoll, 31.

30. Yonce, 10.

31. Ingersoll, 31.

32. *Rocky Mountain News*, September 12, 1912.

33. Yonce, 23.

34. Yonce, 14.

35. Yonce, 18.

36. Malcolm Wyer, "Western History Collection, Its Beginning and Growth," Denver Public Library Publication: June 1950.

Chapter 16. The Dream of a Civic Center

1. William H. Wilson, "A Diadem for the City Beautiful: The Development of Denver's Civic Center," *Journal of the West.* 16 May 1983.

2. Helen F. Ingersoll, "I Remember: The Reminiscences of my years in the Denver Public Library." 1947. Ingersoll's own stories in her own words as told to the editor, May Wood Wiggington. Denver Public Library, Western History Department, 1947. Typescript.

3. Edgar C. McMechen, *Robert W. Speer: A City Builder.* Denver: The City and County of Denver, 1919. Copyright by the Robert W. Speer Memorial Association.

4. Charles A. Johnson, *Denver's Mayor Speer: The Forgotten Story of Robert W. Speer* (Denver: Bighorn Books, Green Mountain Press, 1969).

5. Johnson, xx.

6. Denver Art Commission, *A Short History of the Civic Center: Denver, Colorado* (Denver: Denver Art Commission, 1911).

7. Charles Mulford Robinson, *Proposed Plans for the Improvement of the City of Denver,* Art Commission, City and County of Denver, 1906.

8. *Denver Times* 29 March 1902: 6. c. 3.

9. According to Noel and Norgren, MIZPAH "was the Hebrew parting salutation found in Genesis 31:49, "The Lord watches between thee and me, when we are absent one from another." *Denver: The City Beautiful,* Noel and Norgren, Historic Denver, Inc, 1987.

10. Denver Art Commission. *A Short History of the Civic Center: Denver, Colorado,* Denver: Denver Art Commission, 1911: 2.

11. Ibid, 2-3.

12. McMechen.

13. McMechen.

14. McMechen.

15. McMechen, 20.

16. Frederick Law Olmsted, Jr., Architect, "Plan of Developing Civic Center in The City of Denver." *Municipal Facts,* Vol. 1, No. 13, 13 April 1913.

17. Neil Harris, Marlene Chambers and Lewis Wingfield Story, *The Denver Art Museum, The First Hundred Years* (Denver: The Denver Art Museum, 1996), Story 85.

18. History of the charter amendments from the City of Denver web site: Denver City Government.

19. McMechen.

20. McMechen, 48.

21. "Completion of Civic Center by Voters" Municipal Facts. Vol. 6, #5, May 1923: 4.

22. Minutes of the Art Commission, 14 January 1919.

23. Members of the Fine Arts Committee of the Denver City Club. Letter to members of the Evans family after the death of Anne Evans, Colorado Historical Society, Evans Family Collection, 22 Jan. 1941.

24. Elizabeth Spalding, "Something of Art in Denver as I Think Of It," Denver Public Library, Western History Department, Denver Fortnightly Society Collection, Dec 1924: 22.

25. *DAM First Hundred Years*, note 61: 286.

26. *DAM First Hundred Years*, note 79: 297.

27. *DAM First Hundred Years*, 89.

28. *DAM First Hundred Years*, 88.

29. *DAM First Hundred Years*, note 62: 291.

30. *Rocky Mountain News*, 18 May 1933.

31. Johnson, 246.

32. *Rocky Mountain News*, 2 May 1935: 1.

33. Edward T. James and Janet Wilson James, *Notable American Women. 1607–1950: A Biographical Dictionary* (Cambridge, Mass: Belknap Press of Harvard University Press, 1971), 587.

34. Katherine Davis, "Anne Evans: A Preliminary Biographical Sketch." Unpublished Independent Study Paper. Chicago: Lake Forest College, 11 July 1976: 13.

35. Johnson, 248.

36. *Denver Post*, 6 June 1937.

37. *Denver Post*, 6 June 1937.

38. *The Denver Post*, 1937.

Chapter 17. Anne Evans and the Theosophical Movement

1. Caleb Gates, Letter from Gates at Princeton University to John Evans: 15 Jan. 1941. Colorado Historical Society, Evans Family Collection.

2. This statement appeared on the front page of every issue of the *Theosophical Quarterly,* which was published from 1903 to 1938. The text of most of the volumes of proceedings at the *Society's* annual conventions and of the articles printed in each issue is available on line and in research libraries.

3. Helena Blavatsky, *Collected Works*, Volume XI, 129.

4. Kevin Gramer searched Google for information about Mary Kent Wallace for an education program at the Byers-Evans House.

5. Janet Kerschner, e-mail message to author, January 4, 2010.

6. Ibid.

7. Cornelia Gray Lunt, *Sketches of Childhood and Girlhood: Chicago, 1847–1864* (Evanston, Il. 1925), 212.

8. Ibid.

9. Bernard Knittel, "John Evans, Speaker and Empire Builder," (Thesis, University of Denver, 1950), 277.

10. Allen du Pont Breck, *William Gray Evans 1855–1924: Portrait of a Western Executive* (Denver: The University of Denver Department of History, 1964), 187.

11. Anne Evans, "Hopi Paper" (1920), Fortnightly Club Collection, Denver Public Library, Denver.

12. Anne Freyer Sweeney, interviewed by author, March 3, 2003.

13. Helena Blavatsky, *Collected Works*, Volume XI, 129.

14. Ibid.

15. Ibid.

16. *Theosophical Quarterly*, Vol. XIII, July (1925): 79.

17. *Theosophical Quarterly*, Vol. XXII, July 1924.

18. *Theosophical Quarterly*, Vol. XXIII, July 1925.

19. www.teosofia/mumbai/7409/vivetachudamani.html (accessed Dec. 2009).

20. Ibid.

21. Ibid.

22. Ibid.

23. Ibid.

24. Ibid.

25. Anne Evans, "Norse Mythology," *Theosophical Quarterly*, Vol. XXII, (1913–1914): 127-135.

26. Ibid.

27. Ibid.

28. Ibid.

29. Ibid.

30. Ibid.

31. A Nordic version of Armageddon, after which a newer and better world would emerge. *Theosophical Quarterly,* Vol XII, (1913–1914): 127.

32. Ibid, 129.

33. Ibid.

34. Ibid.

35. Anne Evans, "The Eastern Church, I, II, III," *Theosophical Quarterly*, (1913–1914): 102-305.

36. Ibid.

37. Ibid.

38. Ibid

39. Ibid.

40. Ibid.

41. Ibid.

42. Ibid.

43. Ibid.

44. Ibid.

45. Ibid.

46. Ibid.

47. Ibid.

48. Ibid.

49. Ibid.

50. Anne Evans, "The Renaissance," *Theosophical Quarterly* (1915): 45-52.

51. Ibid.

52. Ibid.

53. Ibid

54. Ibid.

55. Ibid.

56. Ibid.

57. Ibid.

58. Ibid.

59. Anne Evans, "Foundations of the Moravian Church," *Theosophical Quarterly*, (1917–1918): 267-273.

60. Ibid.

61. Ibid.

62. Ibid.

63. Ibid.

64. Ibid.

65. Ibid.

66. Ibid.

67. Anne Evans, "The Bhagavad-Gita," *Theosophical Quarterly* (1923–1924): 321-329.

68. Ibid.

69. Ibid.

70. Ibid.

71. Ibid.

72. Ibid.

73. Ibid.

74. Ibid.

75. Ibid.

76. Ibid.

77. Ibid.

78. Ibid.

79. Ibid.

80. Ibid.

81. Ibid.

82. Ibid.

83. Ibid.

84. Ibid.

85. Ibid.

86. Ibid.

87. Helena Blavatsky, *Collected Works*, Vol. XI.

88. Anne Freyer Sweeney, interviewed by author, March 3, 2003.

87. Helena Blavatsky, *Collected Works*, Vol. XI, 129.

Chapter 18. Anne Evans, Mary Kent Wallace and the Kent School

1. Michael Churchman, assisted by Aileen Pearson Nelson, *The Kent School 1922–1972*. 933 Sherman St., Denver (home of Kent School 1922–1951): 16.

2. See chapter "Denver School Days, 'Wild, Free' Summers on the Mountain Ranch."

3. Churchman, 7.

4. Churchman, 7.

5. Quoted in Churchman from a memoir by Miss Wilma Wallace, at one time secretary to her older sister. Unfortunately, this memoir has disappeared from the school archives.

6. Anne Evans, Letter to Ann Matlack 1937. Colorado Historical Society, Anne Evans Collection.

7. Churchman, 24.

8. Churchman, 25.

9. Churchman, 29.

10. Prue Grant, interviewed by Lewis Story, Denver Art Museum archives, July, 1991.

11. Mary Rathvon, From tapes made by Miss Rathvon. Quoted by Churchman: 36.

12. Ibid.

13. Mary Bogue, Notes. Quoted in Churchman: 36.

14. Churchman, 40.

15. Churchman, 39.

Chapter 19. New Mexico: Advocate for the Art of Native Americans and the Preservation of Mission Churches

1. Anne Evans, "The Art Impulse of the Hopi Indians," Denver Public Library, Western History Department, Denver Fortnightly Society Collection. 1920. 7.

2. Anne Evans, "The Art Impulse of the Hopi Indians." 1920. "Primitive Ceremonials," later called "A Christmas Pilgrimage to the South West," 18 January 1927. "The Franciscan Missions of New Mexico," 11 November 1924. "Social customs and Government of the Zuni Indians," 19 March 1929.

3. The archives of the Fortnightly Club have been placed in the Western History Department of the Denver Public Library. Fortnightly Club member and Evans family descendant, Barbara Rumsey, notes that according to her research, Anne Evans presented a total of 8 papers to the Club, in 1921, 22, 24, 27, 29, 34, 36, and 38.

4. Beatrice Chauvenet, *John Gaw Meem: Pioneer in Historic Preservation*. Historic Santa Fe Foundation/Museum of New Mexico Press: 1985. Bainbridge Bunting. *John Gaw Meem: Southwestern Architect. A School of American Research Book* (Albuquerque: University of New Mexico Press, 1983).

5. This is Anne Evans' spelling of what today we would call Kachina.

6. Anne Evans, "The Franciscan Missions of New Mexico." Denver Public Library, Western History Department, Denver Fortnightly Society Collection. 1924.

7. Ibid.

8. Caroline Bancroft, "She Created an Indian Cult," *Independent Woman*, Vol. XIV, No. 11: Nov. 1935: 371.

9. Bancroft, 372.

10. Mary Kent Wallace, Typescript about her travels with Anne Evans, 1925, 1926 and 1927.

11. Nolie Mumey, "Saints and Santos." Quoted in Maurice Frink and Francis B. Rizzari. *The Denver Westerners Brand Book*: IX (Boulder: The Johnson Publishing Company, 1954), 207.

12. Chauvenet, 18.

13. Chauvenet, 16.

14. Bunting, 15.

15. Chauvenet, 19.

16. Bunting, 15.

17. Katharine Davis, "Anne Evans: A Preliminary Biographical Sketch." Unpublished Independent Study Paper. Chicago: Lake Forest College, 11 July 1976: 20. Citing an interview with Katharine Evans, 21 April 1976.

18. Chauvenet, 19.

19. Bunting, 9.

20. Chauvenet, 12.

21. Chauvenet, 13.

22. Chauvenet, 29.

23. Chauvenet, 36.

24. Chauvenet, 36.

25. Chauvenet, 37.

26. Chauvenet, end note 37.

27. Ibid, 37.

28. Chauvenet, 41.

29. Chauvenet, 41.

30. Chauvenet, Foreword vii.

31. Anne Evans, Hopi paper, 1920.

32. Anne Evans, Hand-written notes. Denver Public Library, Western History Department, Evans Family Collection—Box 1, files marked Anne Evans, no date.

33. Anne Evans, Hopi paper, end note: 7.

34. Fine Arts Committee of the City Club, *Art in Denver*, Publication Number 14, January 1928.

Chapter 20. Introducing Native Arts at the Denver Art Museum

1. Caroline Bancroft, "She Created an Indian Cult," *Independent Woman*, Vol XIV, No. 11: Nov. 1935.

2. Robert Frost, "The Road Not Taken," *www.batleby.com* (accessed February 18, 2010).

3. Richard Conn, *Introduction to Native American Art in the Denver Art Museum* (Seattle and London: The Denver Art Museum. Distributed by the University of Washington Press), 1979.

4. Ibid., 81.

5. Neil Harris, Marlene Chambers and Lewis Wingfield Story, *The Denver Art Museum, The First Hundred Years* (Denver: The Denver Art Museum, 1996), note 23: 289.

6. *DAM First Hundred Years,* 81.

7. Ibid.

8. *DAM First Hundred Years,* note 25: 289.

9. Edgar C. McMechen, *Life of Governor Evans, Second Territorial Governor of Colorado* (Denver: Wahlgreen Publishing Company, 1924).

10. *DAM First Hundred Years,* note 34: 289.

11. Denver Public Library. Biographical Data accompanying portrait of Mr. Frederic H. Douglas in the Portrait Collection, undated: c. 1932.

12. Helen Bromfield, Oral history tape, interview of Helen Bromfield for Hiwan Homestead Museum. Evergreen, Colorado.

13. Frederica Lincoln, Interview with Barbara Sternberg, 2 April 2002. At Lincoln's Upper Bear Creek home in Evergreen.

14. *DAM First Hundred Years,* 81.

15. *DAM First Hundred Years,* note 27: 289.

16. *DAM First Hundred Years,* note 28: 289.

17. *DAM First Hundred Years,* note 29: 289.

18. Frances Melrose, *Rocky Mountain News,* 21 June 1949.

19. Ibid.

20. Ibid.

21. Lingo the Drifter. *KFML Program Guide.* Date illegible.

22. Frances Melrose, *Rocky Mountain News,* 21 June 1949.

23. *First Hundred Years,* 82.

24. Ibid.

25. *Rocky Mountain News,* 22 April 1934.

26. *DAM First Hundred Years,* 81.

27. Michael Churchman, assisted by Aileen Pearson Nelson. *The Kent School 1922–1972.* 933 Sherman St., Denver (home of Kent School 1922–1951): 29.

28. Frederic (Eric) Douglas, *Rocky Mountain News,* 3 July 1932.

29. DAM *First Hundred Years,* 82.

30. Otto Karl Bach, no newspaper name, July 1954.

31. Frederic Douglas and Rene d'Harnoncourt, Foreword by Eleanor Roosevelt. *Indian Art of the United States Museum of Modern Art* (New York: Simon and Schuster, 1941.)

32. DAM *First Hundred Years,* 83.

33. Larry Frank, Forward, Thomas J. Steele. *A Land So Remote. Religious Art of New Mexico, 1780–1907* (Santa Fe: Red Crane Books, 2001), Foreword, vii-viii.

34. Ibid.

35. Ibid.

36. Frank, xii.

37. *DAM First Hundred Years,* 97.

38. Ibid.

39. Ibid.

Chapter 21. You *Must* Have a Good Time!
Summer Life on the Evans Ranch

1. Marion Hendrie, Letter to Hendrie's sisters, approx. 1899. Contained in a report by Prue (Mrs. William) Grant regarding a visit to the Hendrie sisters in Cincinnati. Denver Art Museum Library archives, 15 February 1966: 8.

2. Mary Walker, diary August 3, 1927. Ethelind Elbert Austin Collection.

3. John M. Rosborough, Letter to Anne Evans, 28 August, no year. University of Denver, Penrose Library, Special Collections, Anne Evans Collection: 1960.

4. Anne Reynolds Garrey, As one of four introductions to the re-reading of Anne Evans' "A Christmas Pilgrimage to the South West" to the Members of the Denver Fortnightly Club, 6 March 1973. The original was read to the Denver Fortnightly Club January 18, 1927.

5. See chapter "Denver School Days, 'Wild, Free' Summers on the Mountain Ranch."

6. "'Anne Evans' Draft" (for a biography of Anne Evans), Jan and Frederic Mayer Collection.

7. Kay Klepetko, Tales of the Bar PD. A History of the Jefferson County Outdoor Education Laboratory School Mt. Evans. Evergreen, Colorado. Lakewood, CO: Jefferson County Public Schools R-1. 1978: 10.

8. Horace Fletcher Lunt, Letter to Phelps Dodge, 29 July 1955. Margaret (Peg) Hayden Collection.

9. Lunt, 13.

10. Klepetko, 11.

11. http://www.outdoorlabfoundation.org/evans.html.

12. Rebecca Dorward, "The Evans Family and Their Historic Ranch, Clear Creek County, Colorado," Master's Thesis, University of Colorado at Denver. Auraria Campus: 1998: 107.

13. Interview with Ethelind Austin, July 16, 2002.

14. Margaret Davis Hayden, "Evans Ranch", in, History of Clear Creek County: Tailings, Tracks, & Tommyknockers. Denver: Specialty Publishing, Inc., Historical Society of Idaho Springs, 1986: 87-91.

15. Holcombe and Ethelind Austin, Nomination Form to place the house on the National Register of Historic Places, 27 September 1979.

16. Austin, Description page of Nomination Form.

17. Austin, Significance page of Nomination Form.

18. Dorward, 108.

19. Dorward, 109.

20. Dorward. Interview with Professor Tom Noel, 20 August 1998, 214.

21. Mag Hayden, Interview with Barbara Sternberg, 12 July 2007.

22. Lunt, 16.

23. Theodore Fisher, "Forty Miles West of Denver." American Home Magazine, v. 21, Feb. 1939. Republished in The Architectural Record, no date.

24. Christine Bradley and Gary Long. National Register of Historic Places Registration Form for the Anne Evans house, 30 May 30 1991.

25. Bradley, 6.

26. Bradley, Sec. 7: 2.

27. Fisher.

28. Miriam Washburn Adams, "Artless, Mostly Less." Excerpts read to the members of the Denver Fortnightly Club, 6 March 1973 by her sister, Mrs. Charles Emery as one of the four introductions to the re-reading of Anne Evan's

"A Christmas Pilgrimage to the South West." Originally read to the Denver Fortnightly Club, 18 January 1927.

29. Adams, 9.

30. Bryan Schwartz, Tape 10 of interview by Margaret Hayden: 14-15. Quoted in Dorward: 160.

31. Schwartz interview, 14.

32. See chapter "The Dream of a Civic Center."

33. *House Beautiful* June 1917, Denver, CO; *Denver Municipal Facts*, March 1919, May-July 1926; *The American Home Magazine* vol. 21, Feb. 1939; *The Open Door* June 1939; and articles in the *Rocky Mountain News*, 23 Sept. 1934, Society Section: 1 and 9 August 1936, Society Section: 1.

34. "Town and Mountain Homes Reflect Taste of Owners. *Rocky Mountain News*, 23 Sept. 1934.

35. From The Will of Anne Evans. Filed in County Court, Denver, CO, 22 January 1941.

36. Austin, Ethelind Elbert, Interview with Barbara Sternberg and Megan Boone, 16 July 2002 and 5 August 2002. At Austin's home on the Evans Ranch, Evergreen, Colorado.

37. "COL's History Reflects Colorado Diversity." *Colorado Open Landscape.* Vol. 3, No. 2, Fall 2002: 1. A publication of Colorado Open Lands.

38. Frederick R. Mayer, Typescript, undated. Mayer Collection.

39. Ibid.

40. *Magazine of Historic Preservation.* Jan./Feb. 1996: 78.

41. Allen duPont Breck, *John Evans of Denver* (Boulder: The Pruett Publishing Company, 1972), 36.

42. Mary Walker, Personal Diaries. 3 August to 2 September 1927 and 1 August to 29 August 1930. Typescript provided by Ethelind Austin.

43. Ethelind Austin, "Some Early Recollections of the Ranch." Ethelind Austin Collection, 22 Dec. 1955.

44. Mary Walker mentions that Louise Everett, who went to school in the East, was "one of Mona's old gang", 1927 diary, p. 2, and also indicates that her mother knew Elisabeth Spalding well, "We had dinner at Miss Spalding's, the famous "Sapphira" that Mona has always talked about." p. 15.

45. Walker, 2.

46. Walker, 6.

47. Walker, 13.

48. Walker, 6.

49. Walker, 9.

50. Austin, "Some Early Recollections of the Ranch."

51. See chapter "The Dream of a Civic Center."

52. Walker, 5.

53. See chapter "Introducing Native Arts at the Denver Art Museum."

54. Walker, 2.

55. Helen N. Brush and Catherine P. Dittman, *Indian Hills: The Place, The Times, The People.* Denver: Graphic Impressions Inc., 1976: 50.

56. Brush/Dittman, 51.

57. Brush/Dittman, 6.

58. Brush/Dittman, 6.

59. Walker, 7.

60. Walker, 8.

61. Walker, 1.

62. Walker, 2.

63. Walker, 2.

64. Walker, 3.

65. Walker, 4.

66. Walker, 4.

67. Walker, 11.

68. Walker, 6-7.

69. Walker, 15.

70. Letter from John M. Rosborough to Anne Evans, dated August 28, no year: Penrose Library Archives, Denver University.

71. *Denver Post*, 11 April 1936: 4.

Chapter 22. The Evans/Denver University Connections

1. Allen duPont Breck, *From the Rockies to the World: A Companion to the History of the University of Denver, 1864–1989* (Denver: University of Denver, 1989), 10.

2. Breck, 10.

3. Harry E. Kelsey, Jr., *Frontier Capitalist: The Life of John Evans* (Denver: State Historical Society of Colorado and the Pruett Publishing Company, 1969), 221.

4. Mike Patty, "Evans Planted Seeds of Education," *Rocky Mountain News*, 22 April 1984.

5. Breck, 24.

6. Allen duPont Breck. *William Gray Evans, 1855–1924* (Denver: The University of Denver Department of History, 1964), quoted from notes in the W. G. Evans Papers, University of Denver Archives.

7. Breck, *From the Rockies to the World* 50.

8. Breck, 48.

9. Kelsey, 222.

10. Kelsey, 224.

11. David Shaw Duncan, "Seventy-Five Years of Growth: A Brief History of the University," *University of Denver Pioneer Magazine*, March 1964.

12. Breck, 100.

13. Duncan.

14. Helen Cannon, "First Ladies of Colorado—Margaret Gray Evans," *Colorado Magazine* XXXIX October 1962.

15. James H. Baker and LeRoy R. Hafen, *History of Colorado*, Vol. 3 (Denver: Linderman Co., Inc., 1927).

16. Elizabeth Spalding, "Something of Art in Denver as I Think Of It." Denver Public Library, Western History Department, Denver Fortnightly Society Collection, Dec 1924: 8.